EFFECTIVENESS

Diction

50 Standard Usage	51 National Usage	52 Idiom	53 Nonstandard Expressions	54 Improprieties	55 Appropriate Diction
56 Slang	57 Connotation	58 Exact Diction	59 Emphatic Diction	60 Triteness	61 Fine Writing
62 Wordiness	63 Euphony	64 Enlarging Vocabulary	65 Using a Dictionary	66 Glossary	

Unity

67 Sentence Unity	68 Coördination	69 Sub-ordination	70 Choppy Sentences	71 Incomplete Thought	72 Incomplete Constructions
73 Incomplete Comparisons	74 Miscellaneous Omissions				

Emphasis

75 Suspense	76 Climax	77 Balance	78 Repetition for Emphasis	79 Subordination for Emphasis	80 Separation for Emphasis
81 Variety	82 Word Order	83 Faulty Repetition	84 Weak Passive	85 Absolute Phrases	

Clearness

86 Parallelism	87 "And which"	88 Correlatives	89 Transi	[illegible]	[illegible]
92 Dangling Modifiers	93 Reference of Pronouns	94 Mixed Constructions	95 Spli Constructions	Figur	[illegible]
98 Point of View	99 Logical Thinking	100 Letter Writing	101 Précis Writing		

A Handbook of

WRITING AND

HOUGHTON MIFFLIN COMPANY

Composition and Revision · FIFTH EDITION

THINKING

BY Norman Foerster AND J. M. Steadman, Jr.

Revised by

James B. McMillan, UNIVERSITY OF ALABAMA

The Riverside Press Cambridge

The Riverside Press
CAMBRIDGE, MASSACHUSETTS
PRINTED IN THE U.S.A.

PREFACE

THIS REVISION of *Writing and Thinking* follows the time-tested plan of the 1931 and 1941 editions, but within that framework the book has been largely rewritten.

Two fundamental principles have controlled the revision. First, the book is designed to help the college student, under the guidance of an instructor, improve his ability to communicate in writing. Such improvement involves the student's mental processes as well as his use of the resources of the English language. Throughout the book the student is encouraged to seek knowledge, to think carefully and maturely, and to write honestly and lucidly. We believe that the nonstandard elements in the language of the normal college freshman are usually limited to a few matters which can be corrected by intensive drill, but that most freshmen need some training in adapting their language to the more formal expression expected in college writing. We also believe that most freshmen need extensive training in thinking soundly and writing with precision, clarity, and grace. Having something to communicate and learning how to communicate are considered of first importance; mechanical correctness is regarded as necessary but instrumental.

The second principle has been to present such facts of current English usage as are usually needed in a composition course, accepting the methods of modern linguistic science for determining and interpreting the facts, and accepting the findings of modern investigators on the facts themselves.[1] Style and correctness are assumed to be essentially different, although for simplicity in presentation the same nomenclature is frequently applied to both. Correctness is regarded as appropriateness of language to cultural levels and to such functional varieties as formal, informal, and colloquial. If liberal, in respect to language, means "tolerant of change," this book is liberal. If it means "not strict," the book is not liberal, or at least not intentionally so. The rules, which are phrased as statements of advice to students of composition, are intended to be as strict as the usage they describe. Where usage is categorical, the rules are simple. Where it is complex, divided, or nicely discriminating, the rules make fine distinctions in order to describe the usage strictly. However, some divided usage cannot be labeled precisely. For example, the textbook writer who dislikes *different than* or *cannot help but* is tempted to say that "educated people" or "careful writers" object to the locutions. But such judgments are not justified by the evidence. When formerly substandard expressions are now used by people of obvious cultural attainments, it is circular reasoning to call these people "uneducated" or "careless" merely because they use such expressions. It therefore seems best to be content with a warning that "some people" or "many people" object, and to let the student and his instructor evaluate the construction in specific contexts.

Many of the statements about rhetoric — unity, coherence, clearness, and emphasis — are essentially unchanged from the earlier editions, because we believe them to be still sound, both substantively and pedagogically. Some statements about correctness have been revised to bring them up to date, and these may be

[1] See the works listed on p. 333, the bibliography in A. G. Kennedy, *Current English* (Boston, 1935), and the bibliography section in the journal *American Speech*. The occasional citations of special studies in footnotes in this book are illustrative and suggestive.

expected to require further revision as the language continues to change. The student should get from the handbook of revision not a set of absolute dicta, but an objective attitude toward language, some sense of its complexity and variety, and a useful technique for evaluating disputed usage.

Fitting acknowledgment of indebtedness in a book of this kind is impossible. The influence of the late Leonard Bloomfield, too fundamental and pervasive to be footnoted, is obvious. The bibliography on p. 333 lists some of the standard sources used, and these in turn are indebted to numerous other works in which our knowledge of modern English is recorded and organized. This revision has been greatly improved by criticisms and suggestions from Professors Henry W. Adams, Eliot D. Allen, Laird Bell, F. E. Bowman, Karl W. Dykema, A. C. Edwards, Archibald A. Hill, Francis Hulme, Bryson L. Jaynes, Walter MacKellar, H. Prentice Miller, A. Lawrence Muir, Ernest Samuels, Martin Steinmann, Jr., Walter Powell Stewart, George D. Stout, and John Weimer.

JAMES B. MCMILLAN

CONTENTS

Book One
A Handbook of Composition

SENTENCES AND THINKING 3

THOUGHT AND EXPRESSION 3
PREDICATION 4
SUBORDINATION 7
PARALLELISM 17
EMPHASIS 24
DIRECTNESS 34
VARIETY 39

PARAGRAPHS AND THINKING 43

TOPIC SENTENCE 43
SUBSTANCE 46
METHODS OF DEVELOPMENT 50
ORDER 57
TRANSITION 64

THEMES AND THINKING 72

SUBSTANCE — GATHERING MATERIAL 73
ORDER 77
PROPORTION 82
BEGINNING AND ENDING 84

Book Two

A Handbook of Revision

CORRECTNESS 89

Grammar 89

1. SENTENCE DEFINED 95
2. PERIOD FAULT, OR SENTENCE FRAGMENT 100
3. COMMA FAULT 104
4. "FUSED" SENTENCE 107
5. AGREEMENT OF SUBJECT AND VERB 108
6. AGREEMENT OF PRONOUN AND ANTECEDENT 115
7. CASE 117
8. SUBJUNCTIVE MOOD 122
9. TENSE 124
10. SEQUENCE OF TENSES 132
11. ADJECTIVES AND ADVERBS 134
12. CONJUNCTIONS 137
13. PRONOUNS 139
14. CONFUSION OF CLAUSES 144
15. DOUBLE NEGATIVE 147
16. GRAMMATICAL TERMS 152

Punctuation 167

17. THE COMMA 168

18. UNNECESSARY COMMAS 177
19. THE SEMICOLON 185
20. THE COLON 188
21. THE PERIOD 190
22. THE EXCLAMATION POINT 191
23. THE QUESTION MARK 192
24. THE DASH 194
25. THE APOSTROPHE 196
26. PARENTHESES AND BRACKETS 199
27. QUOTATION MARKS 201
28. DIALOGUE AND QUOTED MATTER 204

Mechanics 208

29. ITALICS 208
30. REPRESENTATION OF NUMBERS 211
31. SYLLABICATION 213
32. CAPITALS 214
33. ABBREVIATIONS AND CONTRACTIONS 220
34. GENERAL MANUSCRIPT FORM 221

Composition 224

35. CHOOSING A SUBJECT 224
36. OUTLINING 226
37. THE PARAGRAPH 229
38. USING THE LIBRARY: FINDING MATERIAL 237
39. PREPARING THE RESEARCH PAPER 248
40. STYLE AND MECHANICS IN RESEARCH WRITING 259

Spelling 272

41. CONFUSION OF SIMILAR FORMS OR SOUNDS 274
42. ETYMOLOGICAL KINSHIP 276
43. EI AND IE 277
44. DOUBLING A FINAL CONSONANT 278
45. DROPPING FINAL –E 279
46. FINAL –Y 280
47. PLURALS 281
48. COMPOUND WORDS 284
49. SPELLING LIST 286

EFFECTIVENESS 293

Diction 293

50. STANDARD USAGE 295
51. NATIONAL USE 295
52. IDIOM 296
53. NONSTANDARD EXPRESSIONS 299
54. IMPROPRIETIES 299
55. APPROPRIATE DICTION 301
56. SLANG 302
57. CONNOTATION AND DENOTATION 304
58. EXACT DICTION 307
59. EMPHATIC DICTION 309
60. TRITENESS 310
61. FINE WRITING AND PRETENTIOUS WRITING 312
62. WORDINESS 313
63. EUPHONY 316
64. ENLARGING THE VOCABULARY 317

65. USING A DICTIONARY 318
66. GLOSSARY OF DICTION 332

Unity 349

67. SENTENCE UNITY 349
68. COÖRDINATION 351
69. SUBORDINATION 354
70. CHOPPY SENTENCES 356
71. INCOMPLETE THOUGHT 357
72. INCOMPLETE CONSTRUCTION 359
73. INCOMPLETE OR ILLOGICAL COMPARISONS 360
74. MISCELLANEOUS OMISSIONS 362

Emphasis 365

75. SUSPENSE — THE PERIODIC SENTENCE 365
76. CLIMAX 366
77. BALANCE 368
78. REPETITION FOR EMPHASIS 369
79. SUBORDINATION FOR EMPHASIS 370
80. SEPARATION FOR EMPHASIS 372
81. VARIETY IN SENTENCE STRUCTURE 374
82. SMOOTH AND EMPHATIC WORD ORDER 376
83. FAULTY REPETITION 380
84. WEAK PASSIVE VOICE 382
85. ABSOLUTE PHRASES 383

Clearness 385

86. PARALLELISM 385
87. "AND WHICH," "AND WHO" 387
88. CORRELATIVES 388
89. TRANSITION 389
90. SEQUENCE 391
91. POSITION OF MODIFIERS 392
92. DANGLING MODIFIERS 394
93. REFERENCE OF PRONOUNS 397
94. MIXED CONSTRUCTIONS 401
95. SPLIT CONSTRUCTIONS 403
96. MIXED OR INAPPROPRIATE FIGURES 406
97. REPETITION FOR CLEARNESS 408
98. POINT OF VIEW 409
99. LOGICAL THINKING 412

LETTER WRITING 417

100. LETTER WRITING 417

PRÉCIS WRITING 429

101. PRÉCIS WRITING 429

INDEX 433

Book One

A HANDBOOK OF COMPOSITION

SENTENCES AND THINKING

PARAGRAPHS AND THINKING

THEMES AND THINKING

Sentences and Thinking

In the activity of thinking itself, speech reaches the highest and most typical of its autonomous functions. — De Laguna

Thought and speech are inseparable from each other. Matter and expression are parts of one. — Newman

THOUGHT AND EXPRESSION

All of us think all of the time. From infancy to old age, awake or asleep, we keep up a continuous covert activity, much of it too hazy and fleeting to report, some of it pleasant daydreaming or unpleasant worrying, and some of it a conscious "talking to ourselves" while trying to make decisions or reach conclusions or solve problems. Occasionally thinking produces robberies, murders, and wars, and thinking commonly produces new houses, daily newspapers, and legislation. On rare occasions a gifted thinker like Charles Darwin writes a seminal book, or like Albert Einstein reduces matter itself to an elemental formula. But in spite of the fact that all people think and always have thought, in spite of the fact that all our literature, science, and technology are products of thought, we know little about what goes on inside a person when he thinks.

Not many years ago thinking was assumed to be an activity of the mind with little or no relation to language. According to this theory, people could be successful thinkers or could improve their thinking by training without being able to "express" their ideas to other people in words. Language was assumed to be as different from thought as a freight car is different from the goods it carries. Today psychologists are more inclined to believe that thinking (at least the kind of thinking we are concerned with in a college) is silent talking, that deliberate thinking is making up meaningful sentences in a language. According to this later theory, a person cannot have a useful thought that he cannot state in words.

Without going into this knotty and complex problem, we can agree that *for all practical purposes* thinking is no better or more useful than the thinker's ability to use words to communicate. A scientist who said he knew the cause of cancer but couldn't explain it to doctors would be of little comfort to cancer patients, and of no use to the medical profession. A college student who says he knows the answer to a question but can't express it gets just as low a grade as the student who frankly says he doesn't know it. Lawyers' reputations are not based on the law in their heads, but the law in their briefs and pleadings, just as college students are not graded on the thoughts in their heads but the answers they give on tests and examinations. Thus we assume in this book that learning to use language effectively is learning to think effectively.

PREDICATION

The first chapter of this book is on sentences and thinking because the sentence is the primary unit of every known language. All languages are spoken in sentences, words come later than sentences in language history, and children all over the world learn sentences (frequently one-word sentences) before they learn words as combining units.[1]

At this point we must note a fundamental fact: language is speech, not writing. Writing, which we will study in this book, is derivative and secondary; it always represents speech. All people talk more than they write, and all people who learn to write do so after they have learned to talk. Since writing is a relatively recent invention, and since writing and reading have never been learned by all the speakers of any language, whereas

[1] Grace Andrus de Laguna, *Speech, Its Function and Development* (New Haven, 1927), pp. 86–93.

speech has evidently been universal among normal human beings from the beginning of mankind, we look first to speech to define the sentence, the basic unit of language.

If we become grammarians (linguistic scientists) for a while and observe the language of English-speaking people, we will immediately notice that some elements of speech can be spoken alone while others have to be included in longer utterances. For example, we do not hear the combinations *whenever she, on which they, too old for,* and *as soon as* spoken alone with meaning; they must be parts of longer utterances, such as the following:

Whenever she sang, he groaned.
The train on which they left was late!
Isn't that dog too old for hunting?
As soon as you finish, come home.

Linguistic science makes use of this difference between isolated and included utterance and defines the sentence as *a relatively complete segment of speech.* If we examine English utterances more carefully, we find that these complete segments occur in a few fixed patterns. For example, we can pronounce the words *helps, crops, rain* without making a sentence. But if we change the order to *rain helps crops* and let the voice drop at the end (signaled by a period in writing) we have an English sentence. Or we can pitch and stress these words in two other ways, making two other sentences, which we represent in writing as *Rain helps crops?* and *Rain helps crops!* We can even make a brief sentence by saying *Crops?* as a question, *Rain* as the answer to a question, or *Help!* as a call of distress. These utterances are relatively complete because they can be understood in relation to particular situations. We cannot, however, meaningfully pronounce the *-s* in *helps* or *crops* or the *-ing* in *helping* alone; they must be included in larger segments of speech.

If we classify the English word-patterns that occur as sentences, we find immediately that there are two main types of English sentences. One, more common in conversation than in writing, is called the *minor* sentence type. Examples are:

"Hello, Fain speaking."
"Going, Joe?"

"Sure."
"Tonight?"
"No. Tomorrow."
"Early?"
"About eight."

We call these brief utterances sentences because each stands alone, does not have to be included in a longer expression in order to be understood. Words like *yes, why, what, please,* and *don't* frequently occur in speech as relatively complete utterances (minor sentences).

The *major* type of sentence, on the other hand, always contains a verb which predicates (says or asks) something about a subject and is not grammatically dependent on anything outside the sentence; it is always complete and independent. There are three sub-types of major sentences, each of which makes an independent predication about a subject: (1) statement, like *Poe died in 1849,* in which the verb *died* makes a predication about the subject *Poe;* (2) question, like *When was Poe born?* in which the verb *was born* makes a predication about the subject *Poe,* and (3) request or command, like *Please look up Poe's birth date,* in which the verb *look up* makes a predication about the subject (the person addressed). Statements and questions in major sentence form must include a subject but requests and commands have no expressed grammatical subject because the writer or speaker is directly addressing someone who is the subject of the predication.

Going further with our analysis of the major type of English sentence, we can distinguish several kinds of independent predication:

SUB-TYPE OF SENTENCE	KIND OF VERB [1]	EXAMPLE
Statement (report)	Transitive	*Dogs eat meat.*
	Intransitive	*Dogs bark.*
	Passive	*The meat was eaten.*
	Linking	*Dogs are useful.*
Question	Transitive	*Do dogs eat meat?*
	Intransitive	*Can all dogs bark?*
	Passive	*Are dogs hunted?*
	Linking	*Are dogs mammals?*

[1] See § 16 for definitions of transitive, intransitive, passive, and linking.

Request (command)	Transitive	*Open the door.*
	Intransitive	*Come in!*
	Passive	*Please be seated.*
	Linking	*Be yourself.*

Every major sentence must include at least one independent predication. A minor sentence may have an incomplete predication (depending on the situation for completeness) or no predication.

It is not hard to see why minor sentence types, which are generally successful in spoken communication, are used much less in writing than major types. In conversation much of the meaning is conveyed by the immediate circumstances of the talking, by the tone of voice used, and by gestures and facial expressions. Writing is intended to be read by people who are not present, who may not know the circumstances, and who cannot see the gestures or hear the tones of voice. Readers need grammatical completeness to compensate for the missing context, expressions, and tones.

Any student who has reached the freshman year in college speaks in sentences and has spoken in sentences for most of his life. But many students are not used to *writing* sentences, particularly the fuller major sentence types which college-level writing demands. In order to benefit from instruction in writing and thinking, every student must learn to recognize the principal sentence types, which are discussed in more detail in § 1.

SUBORDINATION

Once we have learned to distinguish between major and minor sentences, between statements, questions, and commands, and between the kinds of predication made by transitive, intransitive, passive, and linking verbs, we can make a useful distinction between *simple, compound,* and *complex* sentences. To do so we must learn the difference between *subordinate* and *independent* predications. The words *if the river rises* include a subject (*river*) and a verb (*rises*), and the verb predicates something about the subject. But the word *if* makes the predication grammatically subordinate to something else. When the question *Will the levee break?* is answered by the words *If the river rises,* the answer is completely meaningful in the situation, and is therefore a sentence (minor type). By omitting the word *if* we make the utterance *The river rises* a major sentence, independent of the situation, hence an independent predication. (We also, of course, change its meaning, so that it is no longer an answer to the question above, though it might easily fit into another context.) Other words which, like *if*, make a predication subordinate are listed on pages 13–14.

A major sentence which contains only one predication — one independent subject-verb combination — is called a *simple* sentence. A major sentence which contains two or more independent predications is called a *compound* sentence: for example, *The river rose and the levee broke.* A major sentence which contains at least one independent predication and one dependent (subordinate) predication — for example *The levee will break if the river rises* — is called a *complex* sentence.

While a simple sentence has only one subject-verb combination, it can have two or more subjects; for example:

> Oak and walnut are called hardwoods.
> Harding, Coolidge, and Hoover were Republican presidents.

Or, a simple sentence can have two or more verbs; for example:

> Some politicians enjoy attacks and even provoke them.
> We have conferred, negotiated, and bargained long enough.

Or, a simple sentence can have two or more subjects and two or more verbs.

People apparently do most of their thinking in simple sentences. The following is a typical example of a train of thought:

> That girl coming in looks like Ann Evans. She is wearing a plaid suit like Ann's. She could be Doris. Ann's sister. Ann's sister isn't supposed to be here. Not this semester.

Although this series of major and minor sentences may accurately represent a person's train of thought, and even the way he reports it in speech, when he decides to describe the incident in writing he will not be satisfied with such a monotonous and ineffective series of simple and minor sentences. An obvious way to improve the report would be to tie the related statements together with connectives. So he might write:

That girl coming in looks like Ann Evans, and she is wearing a plaid suit like Ann's. She could be Doris, Ann's sister, but Doris isn't supposed to be here this semester.

The improvement is made by eliminating the minor sentences and tying the simple sentences together in pairs, joined in each case by a coördinating conjunction, *and* to indicate addition, *but* to indicate disagreement. The result is two compound sentences, each of which unites two thoughts of equal importance in one complete unit of speech. This is better and less childish than the series of simple sentences, but a series of compound sentences would become just as monotonous as a series of simple sentences. Furthermore, a string of compound sentences usually cannot tell the whole story, because they make all predications of equal importance and do not indicate a good many relationships which are necessary parts of the thinking of mature people. A child might make the following report:

Aunt Elsie is coming to see us, and Father is going on a trip.

By using a subordinating conjunction we could make a complex sentence such as

Because Aunt Elsie is coming to see us, Father is going on a trip.
Or Although Aunt Elsie is coming to see us, Father is going on a trip.
Or Aunt Elsie is coming to see us because Father is going on a trip.
Or Aunt Elsie is coming to see us even if Father is going on a trip.

Each of these four interpretations is much more informative than the original sentence, and the four sentences differ in meaning. Choosing the proper sentence is a matter of telling the truth; choosing the proper connective is thus of basic importance in writing and thinking.

To visualize the difference between simple sentences, compound sentences, and complex sentences, it is useful to think of a sentence as being like a tree. The main thought is the trunk, which divides into subordinate thoughts (large branches), which themselves divide into further subordinate thoughts (small branches), as il-

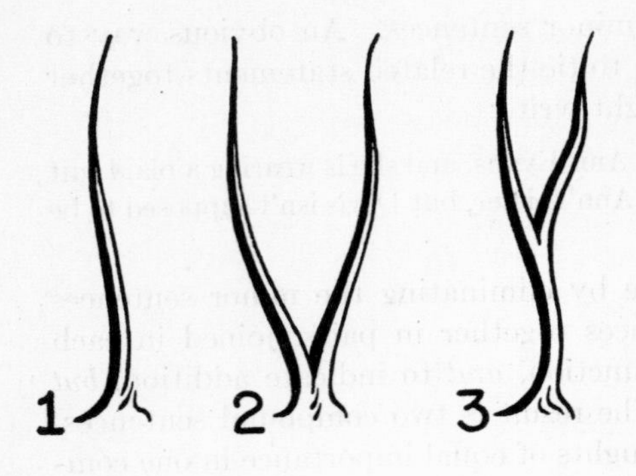

1. *The simple sentence, rudimentary form.*
2. *The compound sentence, rudimentary form.*
3. *The complex sentence, rudimentary form.*
4. *The simple sentence highly developed.*
5. *The compound sentence highly developed.*
6. *The complex sentence highly developed.*

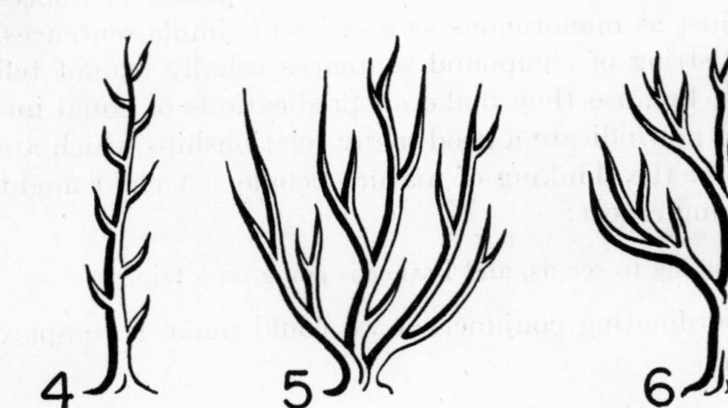

lustrated in the accompanying drawings. To make this analogy still clearer, suppose we consider the following sequence of eleven simple sentences:

The people suffered from hunger. They were desperate for leadership. There were great numbers of them. They voted for Martin. He was a newcomer to politics. They believed his campaign promises. He was apparently sincere. He promised to obtain unemployment insurance. He also promised tax relief. Both were badly needed. Martin failed them.

We could string these simple sentences together in two or three compound sentences, linking the predications with *and* or *but*; however, the passage would still be monotonous and childish, since it would not reflect the many refinements in the relationship of the parts of the total thought. The proper solution is to find a few main ideas, make them the independent clauses (trunks), and put the less important ideas in subordinate clauses and phrases (branches). The following is one possible revision:

Suffering from hunger and desperate for leadership, *the people* in great numbers *voted for Martin*, who was a newcomer to politics, and *they believed his* apparently sincere *campaign promises* to obtain unemployment insurance and tax relief, which were badly needed, but *Martin failed them.* (The principal clauses are italicized.)

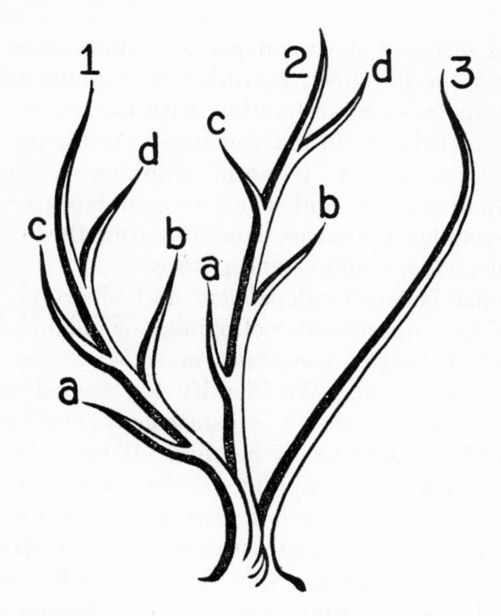

The structure of the sentence above.

The drawing indicates the structure of this revised sentence, which we can analyze as follows:

Three main clauses (instead of eleven):

1. The people voted for Martin.
2. They believed his campaign promises.
3. But Martin failed them.

All the other ideas are subordinate:

to 1: *a.* Suffering from hunger.
b. Desperate for leadership.
c. In great numbers.
d. Who was a newcomer to politics.

to 2: *a.* Apparently sincere.
b. To obtain unemployment insurance.
c. And tax relief.
d. Which were badly needed.

to 3: None.

Although a series of short independent statements is occasionally used for a special effect, maturity in thinking normally produces an abundance of subordination, with the important elements standing out forthrightly in main clauses. As the immature child becomes adult he learns to refine his thinking and to express relationships more exactly, and hence to combine his simple statements into complex sentences, subordinating the less important elements in dependent clauses and phrases.

The difference between independent and subordinate structures is a matter of fact, not a matter of opinion or judgment. Consider this sentence: *Although communism must be defeated, freedom of speech must be preserved.* We identify the second clause as the independent element because it is a statement containing a subject and a verb and a complete predication. It could be pronounced alone or written alone, beginning *freedom* with a capital letter. The first clause, *although communism must be defeated,* must be dependent (subordinate) because it does not make an independent predication. In pronouncing this clause we tell the listener by the voice pitch that the word *defeated* is not the end of the utterance; something else is to come. The word *although* provides the cue; it is a subordinating conjunction.

But the choice of *communism must be defeated* or *freedom of speech must be preserved* as the main clause cannot be settled by formal rule. This is a matter to be decided by the writer. If he is conceding the importance of preserving freedom of speech but emphasizing the need to defeat communism, he will write *Although freedom of speech must be preserved, communism must be defeated.* If he is conceding the need to defeat communism but emphasizing the importance of preserving freedom of speech he will write *Although communism must be defeated, freedom of speech must be preserved.* If he is unwilling, at least for the moment, to emphasize either idea at the expense of the other, he will use a compound sentence, joining the elements with *and* or *but,* depending on the relationship he wishes to express. Your textbook and instructor can help you put statements in independent and dependent form; you must decide for yourself the relative importance of the sentence elements.

The English words that mark subordination indicate the logical relationships between clauses and phrases within sentences. If, for example, you have to combine the statements *his mother is ill* and *he lives at home,* it is likely that the first will be subordinated. If the relationship is time, you may write *When his mother is ill, he lives at home.* If the relationship is cause, you will probably write *Because his mother is ill, he lives at home.* Concession would be indicated by *Although his mother is ill, he lives at home.* Choosing the most exact connective, like selecting the important clause, is a crucial part of thinking and of using language. Fortunately, the English language is rich in connectives that make the various logical relationships. When there are a half dozen connectives for us to choose from, we ought to be able to recall one immediately, and to recall the most suitable one after a little reflection. Following is a table that includes some of the most useful connectives:

CONDITION

if	provided that
in case that	unless

TIME

when	until
before	as
after	whenever
while	as long as
since	as often as
till	as soon as

PLACE

where	whence
wherever	whither

CONCESSION

though	in spite of
although	notwithstanding
even if	no matter how

CAUSE

since	inasmuch as
as	in that
because	now that

PURPOSE

that	for the purpose of
so that	with a view to
in order that	lest

RESULT

that	so..........that
so that	such..........that

COMPARISON

as	as..........so
than	so..........as
as..........as	such..........as

MANNER

as	as though
as if	like

RELATION

as	that
who	whoever
which	whichever
what	whatever

EXERCISES

A. Combine the statements in each of the following groups into a single sentence. Make the statement you consider most important an independent clause and put the minor elements in subordinate clauses and phrases.

1. Political science is a fairly new department in American colleges. It is an offspring of the department of history.
2. The chairman is a tall, heavy-set man. He is a native of South Carolina. He is famous for his conferences on park benches. He has been asked for advice by five presidents.
3. The Senate majority leader voted against rolling back the price of beef. He came from a cattle-growing state. He had been expected to lead the fight to impose the rollback.
4. Some people profit more than they lose during inflation. They do not live on fixed incomes. These people frequently oppose price controls.
5. Other people object to price controls. They suffer from monetary inflation. They still dislike any kind of government control of business.
6. Rationing was not popular. It was expensive to administer. It is generally conceded to have been necessary during World War II. There was an acute shortage of goods. War production cut down the supply of many kinds of goods.
7. Manufacture of civilian goods was resumed in 1945. The war ended that year. Price controls were removed. Rationing was ended.
8. Many people opposed price controls in 1944. They obeyed the regulations. There was a war on. These people violently opposed price controls in 1951. The country was not at war.
9. Economists are hopelessly divided on the question of price and wage controls. They are professional students of such matters.
10. Some economists favor other methods of counteracting and resisting inflation. They oppose governmental controls. They do not favor unrestricted inflation.

B. Directions given under Exercise A.

1. Arizona is a southwestern state. It was admitted to the Union in 1912. It lies between New Mexico and California. Arizona was the forty-eighth state to be admitted.
2. The Bahama Islands lie southeast of Florida. They belong to Great Britain. There are several good harbors and they are convenient to several Southern ports. For this reason they were the headquarters of blockade runners during the Civil War.
3. Silver is a soft metal. Coins made of pure silver would wear out in a short time. Silver coins are really made of alloys containing silver. The alloys make the coins hard.

4. The earth passes between the sun and the moon. This causes an eclipse. The earth throws a shadow on the moon.
5. A vehicle with four-wheel drive is more powerful than one with two-wheel drive. The jeep has front and rear wheel drive. The army finds the jeep very useful in rough country.
6. Franklin Roosevelt became president of the United States in 1933. There had not been a Democratic president since 1921. Roosevelt was nominated by the Democratic party. He succeeded Herbert Hoover.
7. A general police order went out to pick up the car. It was a cream and tan Buick convertible. The right front fender was badly crumpled.
8. The damaged fender was quite noticeable. The color scheme was unusual. Someone should have seen the car near the outer drive.
9. A new dormitory may be built on that corner. If so, the old observatory will have to be moved. It occupies more than half the corner lot.
10. This new plastic paint is waterproof. There is not a very wide variety of colors. It can be sprayed on. One coat is sufficient.

C. Revise each of the sentences below in three different ways to make the italicized clause show (1) time, (2) concession, and (3) cause.

1. *The antique table has been refinished*, and we can sell it for a profit.
2. *The stake has been moved;* we can locate the property line.
3. *It is raining*, and the children enjoy playing in the old barn.
4. *The sheriff was notified;* Clarice left town on the milk train.
5. The acoustics in the hall are good; *the loudspeaker is mounted in a corner*.
6. She is a beautiful woman, and *she is wearing stage makeup*.

D. In a selection assigned by the instructor, make a list of the subordinate phrases and clauses that indicate (1) time, (2) relation, (3) cause, (4) place, (5) comparison, (6) condition, (7) concession, (8) purpose, (9) result, and (10) manner. Underline the subordinating connectives in the phrases and clauses.

E. Write a description of the high school you attended, using only simple and compound sentences. Rewrite the description, subordinating all subordinate elements.

F. Either of the clauses in the sentence below can be subordinated. Make a list (1) of the subordinating words that you could use to subordinate the first clause, and (2) of the subordinating words that you could use to subordinate the second clause.

His style is much more formal in this book; it is likely to receive better reviews than his first one did.

G. Directions given under Exercise F.

Miss Stein is studying with Serge Dala; she doesn't spend much time on keyboard technique.

PARALLELISM

Let us follow out our principle that the structure of the sentence depends on the nature of the thought, and observe how it applies to one or two other important matters of sentence construction. We have seen that when any parts of a sentence (thought) are *different* in rank — when some are chief and others are subordinate — we must, in order to be strictly truthful, express this logical difference through a structural difference. It naturally follows that when any parts of our sentence-thought are of the *same* rank, are logically coördinate, we must express this logical sameness through a structural sameness. For example, let us suppose that we desire to express a complete thought composed of two parts logically coördinate. We then write a compound sentence containing two clauses:

The chairman was Mr. Simpson, and the secretary was Mr. Holt.

If our thought has three parts, we write:

He stopped, he turned, he stared.

In these cases, subordination would positively distort the thought; it would not be quite the truth to say:

The chairman was Mr. Simpson, the secretary being Mr. Holt.
Having stopped, he turned and stared.

If we wish to construct a sentence composed of three constituent thoughts, one of which is a main thought and two of which are subordinate thoughts, we shall of course make the main thought the principal clause, and the subordinate thoughts parallel subordinate clauses:

72-81

If the rain stops and if the roads are good enough, the hunters will drive on to Stockton in the morning.

The first two thoughts have been put into conditional clauses introduced by *if*, because they are related to the third and main thought in precisely the same way: the hunters' driving on to Stockton is dependent on two contingencies. Since the subordinate ideas are parallel, they are put into parallel constructions. It would not do to write

Should the rain stop and if the roads are good enough, the hunters will drive on to Stockton in the morning.

Should is a verb; *if* is a conjunction. The use of the two different parts of speech falsely implies to the reader that different kinds of statement are being made; actually the two clauses are of the same kind and should have the same structure.

Two practical suggestions, if borne in mind, will help in the detection and correction of faulty parallelism. First, remember that parallelism is *grammatical* — there should be two or more participles, infinitives, pronouns, prepositions, verbs, or what not. If the principle of parallelism gives trouble, we may be reasonably certain that the cause of the trouble is an imperfect acquaintance with grammatical forms. In this event, the obvious remedy is to study carefully, among other things, the parts of speech. Before we can master parallel construction, we must be able to state the part of speech of every word in any sentence.

Second, fix your attention on the first word or phrase. This is usually the sign of parallelism. Provided that we have two clauses introduced by *if*, or two clauses introduced by *should*, we may be sure that they are parallel even if the latter parts of the clauses differ. For example, in the sentence already given —

If the rain stops and if the roads are good enough, the hunters will drive on to Stockton in the morning.

— the phrase *good enough* follows the *are* of the second clause, whereas the verb *stops* of the first clause stands alone; and yet the two clauses are regarded as parallel in construction, just as two lines may be parallel without being of the same length or thickness.

In many instances of parallelism, the similarity in grammatical forms affects only a word or two, as in this sentence:

> He said *that it* ought not to be done and *that he*, for his part, had no interest in it.

Sometimes, however, the two constructions are parallel throughout, as in this sentence of Matthew Arnold's:

> To know Italian *belles lettres* is not to know Italy, and to know English *belles lettres* is not to know England.

Here the two members, being equivalent, form a balanced as well as a parallel construction. The principle of balance is simply an extension or intensification of the principle of parallelism. Neither parallelism nor balance is restricted to a single sentence; either, indeed, may affect any number of successive sentences. Here is a familiar illustration from *Julius Cæsar*:

> Who is here so base that would be a bondman? If any, speak; for him have I offended. Who is here so rude that would not be a Roman? If any, speak; for him have I offended. Who is here so vile that will not love his country? If any, speak; for him have I offended.

One of the most useful types of balanced construction is that in which the balance rests on correlative conjunctions[1] — conjunctions used in pairs to connect sentence-elements of equal rank. For example:

> Sincerity is of the utmost importance, not only in the choice of subject, but also in the execution of every detail.
>
> Both the choice of subject and the execution of every detail should be entirely sincere.

Note that the grammatical forms following the correlatives in these sentences are the same: "not only *in* . . . but also *in*"; "Both *the choice* . . . and *the execution.*"

And now a word of warning. After we have become familiar with the parallel construction, and have observed how often the use of it immediately clarifies a murky thought, we may be inclined to resort to it on occasions when the thought does not lend

[1] The most common correlatives are *both — and, not only — but also, either — or, neither — nor, so — as, as — as*, and *whether — or*.

itself to this construction. Thus the following sentence contains constructions which are undoubtedly parallel but have no right to be.

When he reached the city and when we remember how unaccustomed he was to its noise and turmoil, he naturally began to question his decision.

The two thoughts in the two *when*-clauses are not parallel thoughts. The difficulty is not a *faulty* parallel construction (one which fails to mirror parallelism of thought), but a *false* parallel construction (one in which the thought does not justify parallelism). So long as we remember the possibility of committing this blunder, we may employ parallelism as freely as we like. (See also §§ 86–88.)

EXERCISES

A. Study the value of parallelism in Lincoln's Gettysburg Address, reprinted below:

Fourscore and seven years ago our fathers brought forth on this continent a new nation, conceived in liberty, and dedicated to the proposition that all men are created equal. Now, we are engaged in a great civil war, testing whether that nation, or any nation so conceived and so dedicated, can long endure. We are met on a great battle field of that war. We have come to dedicate a portion of that field as a final resting-place for those who here gave their lives that that nation might live. It is altogether fitting and proper that we should do this. But, in a larger sense, we cannot dedicate, we cannot consecrate, we cannot hallow this ground. The brave men, living and dead, who struggled here, have consecrated it, far above our poor power to add or to detract. The world will little note nor long remember what we say here, but it can never forget what they did here. It is for us, the living, rather, to be dedicated here to the unfinished work which they who fought here have thus far so nobly advanced. It is rather for us to be here dedicated to the great task remaining before us; that from these honored dead we take increased devotion to that cause for which they gave the last full measure of devotion; that we here highly resolve that these dead shall not have died in vain; that this nation, under God, shall have a new birth of freedom; and that government of the people, by the people, for the people, shall not perish from the earth.

B. Complete each of the sentences below by adding three phrases or clauses in parallel form.

Example: Even at home with their families some men dress formally, speak formally, and behave formally.

1. Movies are a form of entertainment which . . .
2. The nation is kept informed of what goes on in Congress by . . .
3. Examples of blue laws are those which forbid people to . . .
4. Students find it hard to study when . . .
5. Most Americans reject Communism because . . .
6. Citizens should vote in elections in order to . . .
7. Some pleasant and healthful recreations are . . .
8. Many modern homes now have . . .
9. There are many kinds of licenses, licenses for . . .
10. Radio programs would be more entertaining if . . .

C. Directions given under Exercise B.

1. College students earn money by . . .
2. A repairman should be called whenever . . .
3. The best vacation is one which . . .
4. My parents taught me to . . .
5. Haines is a successful athlete, although . . .
6. It was impossible to . . . because of the flood.
7. Students who . . . usually make the best grades.
8. Even if politicians are . . . they are still necessary.
9. Students spend too much time . . . when they should be studying.
10. Habits like . . . are hard to break.

D. Convert each of the following sets of rough notes into a sentence containing parallel structure:

1. Automobile and truck collision this morning at 6th and Broad. Two men killed. Injuries to two women.
2. Cellini often in trouble. Frequently in danger losing own life. Suffered long imprisonment.
3. Dana's purpose was to give information on sailors' conditions. Calling attention their welfare needs. Promote their betterment.
4. Stello whitens teeth. Hardened gums result. Leaves pleasant taste in mouth.
5. Rockwell spent year in Mexico. Became acquainted Mexican culture.

Learned many habits and customs Mexican people. Now knows Spanish.

6. Woman protested arrest. Said driving only forty. Kept to right. Horn blown and car stopped at intersection. Angry.
7. Library small for college this size. Many books fiction and biography. Science collection very small. Foreign languages fair number.
8. League of Nations disbanded after World War II. Called failure. Several international disputes settled peacefully. Made many useful studies social and political conditions. Couldn't stop Second World War.
9. Indians treated badly in early days. Lands taken away. Unscrupulous whites cheated Indians. No education provided. Most people indifferent, regarding Indians as animals.
10. This air conditioner on new principle. No water connection. Cleans air. Humidity is lowered. Smoke and dust strained out. Cools air to desired temperature.

E. Write a one-sentence summary of two short stories or narrative poems assigned by your instructor, using parallel structure. Let each sentence contain only one main subject and one main predicate; that is, do not write a compound sentence.

F. Write a one-sentence description, using parallel structure, of a painting, a statue, or a piece of music.

G. Point out the parallel constructions in the following sentences and passages, stating in each case whether the constructions begin with infinitives, or participles, or gerund phrases, or conjunctions, etc. See § 16 for a list of grammatical terms.

Example (*Participle 1*) Smiling quizzically, and (*Participle 2*) lowering his voice, the speaker observed that our decision might have strange consequences.

1. Academic progress is certain to follow the person who is successful in budgeting his time, concentrating on the subject at hand, being meticulous in writing details, reading assignments carefully, taking notes both on outside reading and in class, paying careful attention in class, and having the will and the desire to learn.
2. In winter she appears to be warm and comfortable while everyone else is shivering; but in summer she can look cool and unruffled even after a strenuous game of tennis.

3. Folk customs play a great part in *The Return of the Native*: it was at the annual raffle that Christian won the woman's dress; it was at a gipsying, a village picnic, that Wildeve met Eustacia after her marriage; it was at the yearly Maypole dance that Venn found Thomasin's glove.
4. The long imprisonment, the fetid dungeon, the weary suspense, the tyrannous trial, the barbarous sentence, the savage execution, the rack, the gibbet, the knife, the cauldron, the numberless tortures of those holy victims, O my God, are they to have no reward? (CARDINAL NEWMAN)
5. He [a gentleman] is patient, forbearing, and resigned, on philosophical principles; he submits to pain, because it is inevitable, to bereavement, because it is irreparable, and to death, because it is his destiny. (CARDINAL NEWMAN)
6. There is one fable that touches very near the quick of life; the fable of the monk who passed into the woods, heard a bird break into song, hearkened for a trill or two, and found himself on his return a stranger at his convent gates; for he had been absent fifty years. . . . (R. L. STEVENSON)
7. Upon retirement my father hopes to enjoy his hobbies, to continue his research in biology, and to travel in the tropics.
8. Mr. Elliot Paul in this story tells of noon on the island with its siestas, of fishermen selling their wares at the market place, of sleepy dogs roaming the streets, and of colorfully clad women in the doorways.
9. I saw people of every description: old men with crutches, sportsmen with cameras, boys whose eyes were wild with excitement, and girls whose high voices rang out everywhere.
10. Meanwhile our rotatory island loaded with predatory life, and more drenched with blood, both animal and vegetable, than ever mutinied ship, scuds through space with unimaginable speed, and turns alternate cheeks to the reverberation of a blazing world, ninety million miles away. (R. L. STEVENSON)
11. Then came those days, never to be recalled without a blush, the days of servitude without loyalty and sensuality without love, of dwarfish talents and gigantic vices, the paradise of cold hearts and narrow minds, the golden age of the coward, the bigot, and the slave. (THOMAS BABINGTON MACAULAY)
12. What is it to be free from King George and continue the slaves of King Prejudice? (HENRY THOREAU)

EMPHASIS

The public speaker who gives two thirds of his time to introductory remarks, and only one third to the body of his speech, is not telling the whole truth because he is not giving the parts of his thought proper emphasis. The writer whose paragraph is top-heavy, or who brings it to a conclusion suddenly because it is becoming alarmingly long, is not writing a truthful paragraph. The writer whose sentence does not throw into relief what is important and leave in the background what is relatively unimportant has not yet learned to write even an approximately truthful sentence. Coördination, subordination, and parallelism are ways of increasing the truthfulness of our language. There are still other ways of doing so by giving thoughts conspicuousness or emphasis.

ITALICS. Putting important words and phrases in italic type (equivalent to underlining) is a mechanical device like the use of capital letters and boldfaced type for emphasis. If we carefully observe the practice of professional writers, for example in the paragraphs on pages 51–62, we find that italics are sparingly used for emphasis. Schoolgirls commonly underline (italicize) too many words in their letters, weakening the reader's response to phrases which are genuinely important and deserve italics. The occasional use of italics for emphasis is effective; over-use of this device is like crying "Fire!" when there is no danger: the reader gets used to italicized words and they no longer strike him forcibly.

CLIMAX. Assuming that the words chosen are strong enough to bear our meaning,[1] we have also to consider the emphatic ordering of them. When our thoughts are parallel but different in value — in intensity, in importance, in definiteness, in interest — we may indicate the gradations by the use of a climactic arrangement, an ascending series. The English word "climax" comes from a Greek word meaning "a ladder." In a ladder the rungs are, of course, placed one above the other, so that the climber progresses toward the top; similarly, in a sentence involving parallel members of differing values, the parallel members should be so placed that there is progress from those of lesser value to those of greater. "Your

[1] The choice of words is discussed on pages 40–41. (See also §§ 57–59.)

son is very ill — seriously ill — desperately ill" has emphasis because the order is climactic. We should have an anticlimax if we wrote, instead, "Your son is desperately ill — seriously ill — very ill." This would violate the rising intensity of the thoughts. Again, "The wind had ceased, the color faded out of the western sky, and a dozen mocking birds began calling insistently, till our ears throbbed with the sound," has emphasis through climax. Instead of a rising intensity, we have an increase in both definiteness and interest. To have produced our mocking bird concert first and then gone back to the bare fact of the wind's ceasing would have been to overshadow one thought through the greater interest of another. As Herbert Spencer remarks, you cannot see the light of a fire after looking at the sun, but if you look at the fire first you can see both.

Departure from the Normal Word Order. Any deviation from the norm, whether in manners or in rhetoric, attracts attention. Everyone who has learned to read has become so accustomed to a certain word order — subject, verb, and complement — that he notices, or feels unconsciously, every clear case of departure from this standard. For this reason these sentences —

The leading man never did show any sign of nervousness.
The legislature frittered away a month quarreling and filibustering.
They asked Aaron Vincent at our suggestion.

— are less emphatic than these:

Never did the leading man show any sign of nervousness.
Quarreling and filibustering, the legislature frittered away a month.
At our suggestion, they asked Aaron Vincent.

In speech, words and phrases can be made important, regardless of their position in the sentence, by stress (pitch and loudness); in writing word order is the normal means of indicating importance.

Placing Important Matter at the End of the Sentence. An excellent means of securing emphasis — one that can be used in nearly every sentence, and that can be applied with ease — consists in placing important matter at the end of the sentence. The beginning of the sentence is also a conspicuous place, but since the end is much more conspicuous, we shall concentrate our attention on the end. It is not hard to see why the end is emphatic: upon reaching the period, the reader stops for a moment to reflect, to get his mental wind, before going on to the next thought, and while he is pausing he notices most vividly what is nearest him — the last words of the sentence. In all sentences there are what we might term "pivotal words," on which the central meaning rests — the substantial words, as distinguished from the merely functional words. In the sentence "I think, however, that his attitude is wrong," there are words that simply indicate relation, such as "that" and "is," and there are also words that contain the substance, such as "attitude" and "wrong," the latter being the most important and likewise the last word in the sentence. The sentence has emphasis. But place another word at the end, and observe how the sentence loses its ring:

> I think that his attitude is wrong, however.
>
> However, his attitude is wrong, I think.

The difference in arrangement is slight; the difference in effect is highly important. Again, when Woodrow Wilson wrote:

> A steadfast concert for peace can never be maintained except by a partnership of democratic nations.

— he chose to place at the end the pivotal words, *democratic nations*. Tuck away these words in the interior of the sentence, and you change the effect:

> A steadfast concert for peace can never be maintained except by the democratic nations in partnership.

— which makes *partnership* the pivotal word.

When we have acquired the habit of reserving our important words for the close of the sentence, we are ready to extend this practice to the rest of the sentence. If the reader pauses at the end of a sentence, it is also true that he pauses, more briefly, wherever there is punctuation within the sentence. Generally speaking, the punctuation indicates what can be called constituent thoughts. A sentence in which the logical divisions are not thus indicated is ordinarily not so easy to understand as one in which the divisions are indicated by punctuation. The following sentence from Theodore Roosevelt's "Charter of Democracy" speech is an example:

> Let us remember, also, that Conservation does not stop with the natural resources, but that the principle of making the best use of all we have requires with equal or greater insistence that we shall stop the waste of human life in industry and prevent the waste of human welfare which flows from the unfair use of concentrated power and wealth in the hands of men whose eagerness for profits blinds them to the cost of what they do.

Here and there such a sentence, if emphatically phrased, is effective; ordinarily, however, it lacks emphasis because no words in it, save the last, are stressed, and the total effect is more or less a blur. Not content, then, with placing the pivotal words just before the period, we should make some effort to place other important words just before the commas and semicolons, as Roosevelt does in this sentence:

> We stand for applying the Constitution to the issues of to-day as Lincoln applied it to the issues of his day; Lincoln, mind you, and not Buchanan, was the real upholder and preserver of the Constitution, for the true progressive, the progressive of the Lincoln stamp, is the only true constitutionalist, the only real conservative.

SUSPENSE. Another principle, allied to that just discussed, serves the end of emphasis. The close of the sentence, we have found, is the most emphatic part of it; we can add still more to the emphasis at the close if we suspend the thought, keep the secret of the sentence, until we reach the last word. Compare the following sentences:

> The impulse of the English race toward moral development and self-conquest has manifested itself in Puritanism, and more powerfully than anywhere else.

> The impulse of the English race toward moral development and self-conquest has nowhere so powerfully manifested itself as in Puritanism.

The second sentence is stronger, not only because the pivotal word *Puritanism* is placed at the end, but also because grammatical completeness is not satisfied until we reach the concluding word. The meaning is suspended — the reader retains the thought expectantly — till illumination comes suddenly and brilliantly with the word *Puritanism.* A sentence in which grammatical completeness is thus reserved to the end is termed a *periodic sentence*; a sentence in which the thought is completed piecemeal is termed a *loose sentence.* In nearly all good writing, the loose sentence predominates; but no modern style is likely to be effective in which periodic sentences, or virtually periodic sentences,[1] are not frequent. Since a loose sentence may be composed as the writer proceeds, without much concern for what is coming, it is only too good a medium for the expression of flaccid thought — firm when composed by a skillful writer, it often sprawls at the touch of an inexperienced hand. Though a style that is constantly periodic makes tiresome reading, a writer who is still serving his apprenticeship would not go far astray if he tried to employ the principle of suspense whenever an opportunity presented itself. When the meaning is suspended to the last words of the sentence, the writer is obliged to see his goal, however dimly, before he begins to write his sentence. That makes for well-knit sentences. A practical hint to remember when one is trying to cast a sentence in a periodic mould is this: reserve the subject of the sentence for a position as near the end as possible, or, what often amounts to the same thing, put the subordinate clauses and phrases first and the principal clause last. (See also § 82.)

BALANCE. Emphasis is also secured by the use of balance. We have already considered, in our study of parallelism, the need of expressing similar thoughts through similar constructions. We have now to consider the same need viewed as a matter of emphasis.

When our thoughts correspond to each other, we can best emphasize their correspondence by stating them in the form of a balanced sentence — a sentence, that is, in which the similarity of the constituent thoughts is pointed up by the similarity of the syntax. Oftenest two ideas, or two sets of ideas, are placed side by side, as if the thoughts were being weighed in scales. These ideas, or sets of ideas, may agree with each other in either of two ways:

[1] A sentence in which the predication is completed within a very few words of the end. (See also § 82b.)

(1) They may agree through resemblance, as in the following sentence:

> Just as an intern learns much about medicine by observing and assisting the staff physicians in a hospital, so an apprentice teacher learns much about teaching by observing and assisting the regular teachers in a school.

In the above sentence the object is to emphasize an analogy — a resemblance between things that are different.

But (2) the ideas may agree through unlikeness, by matching each other in their differences, as in this sentence:

> One critic argued that the realism of *Main Street* makes it a work of art; another argued that its realism prevents its being a work of art.

Here the object is to emphasize a contrast, a sharply defined difference. Though the two thoughts may perhaps be regarded as of the same weight, the object is not to emphasize the identity of weight but the contrast between two equally weighty substances, as if one were a pound of iron and the other a pound of copper, or a pound of iron and a pound of feathers. Since this is the commoner and more emphatic type of balanced sentence, it will be well to inspect several other examples:

> Talent is that which is in a man's power; genius is that in whose power a man is. (LOWELL)
>
> The memory of other authors is kept alive by their works; but the memory of Johnson keeps many of his works alive. (MACAULAY)
>
> Art must not aim at morality, else it is not art; but it must not violate morality, else it is not human.

In each of these sentences two ideas are set in sharp contrast by the use of balance, as if the writer said, "This may look like that, but do not be deceived, for in their very likeness lurks a profound difference. It is true, they correspond part for part — but only as black to white or night to day." Accordingly, to make emphatic this difference between kindred things, the writer reveals their antithetical correspondence by a correspondence in sentence structure. (See § 77.)

REPETITION. A teacher once summed up the art of teaching by saying, "First tell them you're going to tell them; then tell them, and then tell them that you've told them." Although the art of teaching certainly comprehends more than that, it would be hard to exaggerate the value of repetition in education or in any other activity in which knowledge or opinion is transmitted. What we have heard but once, we are prone to forget. What we have heard often, we are likely to remember — and even to believe, whether it is plausible or not, as demagogues understand only too well. In a political speech, in a sermon, in an editorial, in a college lecture, we encounter again and again the same ideas, or facts, or emotions — sometimes repeated without variation, more often repeated with an interesting difference, with additions, that is, or with illustrations, or with comparisons, or with applications — until the ideas, facts, emotions have been driven home. In the composition of an effective paragraph, again, the same principle holds: the idea is nakedly stated, and then it is represented with detail, illustration, and the like, until the reader has received a clear and lasting impression. Even within the limit of a single sentence, there is room for emphasis through repetition.

One of the most valuable kinds of repetition is the repeated use of important words, of what we have termed "pivotal words." Observe the repetition in this paragraph written by Maurice Hindus:

> And what shall one say of Russia's capitulation to the smile? Whether you are Stalin or a milkmaid, if you have your picture taken for a publication you must smile. If you are decorated you smile, if you are the mother of twelve children you smile, if you don't believe in abortions you smile; you may even smile when you pronounce a curse on Fascists! From the window of my hotel in Moscow I see over the children's theater a huge portrait of Stalin with a little girl in his arms, and both are smiling. "See the picture of our leaders," said a factory director as he was pointing to the portraits of Lenin and Stalin in the auditorium of a newly opened engineers' clubhouse; "They are smiling. That's the way we want them to look. Life has become better and more cheerful and people should smile." Hail, therefore, to the Soviet smile! [1]

Repeating a pivotal word is an effective way to show emphasis. But this does not excuse the kind of repetition which results from

[1] Maurice Hindus, "Russia Grows Up," *Harper's Magazine*, May, 1937. Reprinted by permission of the publisher.

a writer's ignorance of synonyms, from a poverty of vocabulary, nor does it excuse the kind of repetition which results from the writer's being too lazy to find synonyms. Repetition is good when it has a purpose.

EXERCISES

A. Point out the pivotal words (defined on page 26) in the following sentences:

1. There were barriers still, it is true, but barriers that could in time be swept away. (HELEN KELLER)
2. To conclude, this whole mystery of genera and species, which make such a noise in the schools, and are with justice so little regarded out of them, is nothing else but abstract ideas with names annexed to them. (JOHN LOCKE)
3. I have said that the words in plays written in poetry are more lively than the same words written by the same poet in other kinds of poetry. (GERTRUDE STEIN)
4. In mathematics then, as in the other sciences, it is inevitable that the conceptions used should grow. (F. S. C. SCHILLER)
5. Our pleasure at finding that a chaos of facts is the expression of a single underlying fact is like the relief of a musician at resolving a confused mass of sound into melodic or harmonic order. (WILLIAM JAMES)
6. We ourselves, if we had been living then, should most of us have by no means seen things as Plato saw them. (MATTHEW ARNOLD)
7. I have been surprised to consider that the only obvious employment, except wood-chopping, ice-cutting, or the like business, which ever to my knowledge detained at Walden Pond for a whole half day any of my fellow-citizens, whether fathers or children of the town, with just one exception, was fishing. (HENRY THOREAU)
8. Forming an opinion of our people and their manners by what is seen among the inhabitants of the seaports is judging from an improper sample. (BENJAMIN FRANKLIN)
9. Few people take the trouble of trying to find out what democracy really is. (JAMES R. LOWELL)
10. For all the pleasures of my visit, I beg you to accept my thanks. (SIR WALTER RALEIGH)

B. Classify the sentences in Exercise A as loose, virtually periodic, and periodic. Which of these sentences do not have the usual subject-verb-complement order?

C. Change the following sentences from loose to periodic or virtually periodic structure:

1. Traveling by air has become commonplace since the war.
2. Many people disagree with the equal rights principle in the Constitution, not all of them Southerners.
3. Cotton-growing is becoming more important in California, although it still is trifling compared to the citrus fruit industry.
4. Mr. Roosevelt was Assistant Secretary of the Navy during World War I.
5. Who can tell an ambitious young writer that he has nothing to say without hurting his feelings?
6. The TVA pattern will be repeated all over the country in time.
7. Well do I remember Mr. Adams, my first interesting professor.
8. The room was stuffed with nothing but junk, old furniture, broken toys, dog-eared magazines, empty cans, and old tools.
9. It is hard to tell which countries we can trust in these times.
10. Secretary Acheson had done an excellent job, in my opinion.

D. Compare the placement of pivotal words in a serious magazine article and in conversational sentences in a story.

E. Write ten sentences in which pivotal words are put at the end.

F. Write ten sentences in which emphasis is gained by departures from the normal subject-verb-object word order.

G. Rewrite the periodic sentences in Exercise A as loose sentences, and the loose sentences as periodic sentences. Compare the revised sentences with the originals in emphasis.

H. Complete the following sentences by using balance:

1. The manager's intentions are always good; nevertheless . . .
2. Transatlantic passage is cheaper on freight boats, but . . .
3. Intercollegiate sports are . . .; intramural sports are . . .
4. A shingle roof looks better, but it will develop leaks; a galvanized iron roof . . .

5. Even if you don't have an accident, the insurance policy will cost you very little; if you do . . .
6. A portrait photographer . . ., but a news photographer . . .
7. The State Department needs people who speak many foreign languages, because it deals with foreign countries; the Interior Department . . .
8. Linen is . . ., but wool is . . .
9. Students prefer desk dictionaries because . . .; teachers prefer unabridged dictionaries because . . .
10. Men like football but not necessarily football players; women . . .

I. Copy from books or magazines ten examples of sentences with balanced structure.

J. Examine the passages used for Exercise I to determine whether the writers use two or more balanced sentences in sequence.

K. Revise any of the following sentences which can be improved by repeating a word or phrase for emphasis:

1. There should be no Democrats in this cabinet; the election was not won by them.
2. The campus echoed all night the refrain, Beat Notre Dame!
3. Loyalty oaths are not popular among teachers; they don't like to be subjected to blanket suspicion of disloyalty.
4. There are medals for war heroism, for hazardous lifesaving, for winning sports events, but none for umpiring baseball games.
5. These starving people need food, need it desperately, but we send them propaganda; let's win their support by sending them things to eat.
6. Health departments all over the country are urging people to take advantage of the free chest X-ray examinations.
7. Not one of his poems is sentimental; none of them are trite or silly.
8. How to make furniture, to feed babies, to set type, to ventilate school buildings — this is what colleges are teaching!
9. Whether newspapers honestly report and interpret the news, or whether they seek sensationalism and pander to advertisers is too general a question to be answered yes or no.
10. Books can inform and enlighten a man, but they can't follow him around and force him to use his information and enlightenment.

DIRECTNESS

Most serious writing has a purpose. If the purpose of a piece of writing is to persuade someone to contribute to a charity, to arouse voters to oppose an office-seeker, to explain why a new play is likely to be a success, to convince an instructor that the writer has mastered a subject, to give directions for designing a stage setting, to win approval of a public proposal — or in any way to accomplish something — the writer should use language which is direct and effective. Not only should he keep out dead wood — words which do not forward the communication — but he should also avoid words and constructions which distract the reader. Purposeful language should not call attention to itself, should not mislead the reader; it should be clear, simple, exact, and appropriate, omitting nothing of importance, wasting no words whatsoever. Offensive misspellings, misleading punctuation, uncalled-for cleverness, inappropriate diction, monotony of construction, harsh combinations of sounds, and unnecessary words are distractions which lower the efficiency of a communication. Once more we return to the fundamental principle: the truth, the whole truth, and nothing but the truth. There are several common faults which slow up direct and effective communication.

TANGLED CONSTRUCTIONS. When the structure of your sentence is confused, you are unconsciously asking the reader to untangle it, to recast it mentally — to repair your machinery — before he can quite grasp the meaning.

Tangled constructions arise from two chief causes:

1. MIXED CONSTRUCTIONS. A sentence is tangled whenever the writer fails to complete a construction that ought to be completed, shifting without reason from one construction to another. For example:

> It was a rule in the classes of this pedantic professor that whenever a student used a slang expression in recitation for him to get a failing grade on the theme handed in that day.

The blunder, in such a sentence, can be readily revealed by looking for the main line of the sentence, or, what amounts to the same thing, eliminating for the moment all the branch lines. Thus:

It was a rule (in the classes of this pedantic professor) that (whenever a student used a slang expression in recitation) for him to get a failing grade.

By setting aside the branch lines we get "It was a rule that for him to get a failing grade," which doesn't make sense. The writer has confused two different constructions, "for him to get" and "that he would get." Revising the main clause to read "It was a rule that he would get a failing grade" clears up the trouble.

2. Misplaced Modifiers. A sentence is tangled, again, whenever the writer fails to place together matter that is logically, and therefore structurally, closely related. For example:

The papers he then placed in her hand without a tremor for which he had so long struggled and so hopelessly until the hour before.

The sense does not shine forth luminously, to say the least; in particular, we are uncertain whether that "for which he had struggled" was a tremor, or her hand, or the papers. Placing modifiers close to the members modified, we secure, instead, this result:

Without a tremor he then placed in her hand the papers for which he had struggled so long and, until the hour before, so hopelessly. (See also § 91.)

Mixed Figures. Akin to the tangled construction is the mixed figure of speech, except that here it is not the construction that is at fault; it is the thought itself, which begins with one comparison and then confuses the reader by unexpectedly shifting to a different one. A newspaper editor once wrote:

If the government does not stop shearing the wool from the sheep that lays the golden egg, it will soon pump it dry.

It is well enough to compare the citizen with a sheep, a goose, or a tank, but not with all three at the same time. (See also § 96.)

Unnecessary Words. When you use an unnecessary word or phrase, you are putting an obstacle, however slight, before the reader. Words should be adequate, neither too few nor too many. The danger of using too few words is not serious, since to say a thing briefly is harder than to say it verbosely. But it is always easy to use too many words. Sometimes the number of words can be reduced by mere omission, as in this sentence:

In the case of this room, modern type furniture is best. (11 words)
In this room, modern furniture is best. (7 words)

Often one can condense by changing the construction, using a subordinate clause or even a phrase or a word instead of an independent clause:

Jones studied the old manuscript a long time and finally decided that it was written in Tocharian; this is a language that was once used in central Asia. (28 words)

After studying the manuscript a long time, Jones decided that it was written in Tocharian, a dead language of central Asia. (21 words)

At other times it can be done by altering words:

The roller that the paper goes round needs cleaning. (9 words)
The platen needs cleaning. (4 words)

But the briefest is not always the best; brevity in the interest of economy is one thing, and brevity as a result of impatience is quite another. Do not use words unnecessarily, but use enough words to enable the reader to grasp the meaning and remember it. The trees must be free of dead wood, but they must also be fully developed. (See also §§ 62, 78, and 83.)

UNPLEASANT SOUNDS. Again, when a writer uses combinations of words that are disagreeable to the ear, he is not communicating his meaning directly. As we have said, any form of expression that calls attention to itself violates the principle of directness. Cacophony, or "bad sound," grates on the ear even when the reader does not audibly pronounce the words, and thus distracts his attention from the sense. When the poet Browning wished to ask whether the animal that has fed to repletion suffers from care and doubt, he wrote a vigorous but obtrusively harsh line:

Irks care the crop-full bird? Frets doubt the maw-crammed beast?

Euphony is perhaps most frequently violated by the use of unpleasant *repetitions* of sound — by the use of such chance combinations as "the present president," "the visitor admired the vista," "a shrill trill," "he pitched hay all that day," and by the excessive use of the same consonant, as in this sentence:

The *p*artner *p*erceived a *p*er*p*lexed ex*p*ression in the face of the *p*rinci*p*al s*p*eaker. (See also § 63.)

EXERCISES

A. Revise the following sentences so that the reader will not have to search for the meaning:

1. The reason he was discharged was because of he could not learn to write his news stories in brief, clear sentences.
2. As we tried to return over the highway by which we had come was a harder job than we had thought.
3. The fact that the *Oxford Dictionary* is in so many volumes, I decided to use the big *Webster's* in the reading room.
4. In regard to social security payments, if these people get unemployment compensation who have refused to take suitable jobs offered to them should be prosecuted for fraud.
5. We left the beach because it was so hot and drove to a resort in the mountains that could be reached in an hour.
6. There was only one game warden, knowing what he did it was not hard to dynamite a stream and get a mess of fish without getting caught because the warden couldn't watch all the streams.
7. Why doesn't the government dam up the outbursts of radicals?
8. Cullen could get medical services because he has hospital and medical insurance when he was injured in a train wreck.
9. Then it was very hard to find engineers because of the industrial boom for jobs of this kind.
10. A car, when a person has to start and stop frequently on city streets, it should be adjusted to use not so much gasoline.

B. Condense the following sentences without losing any of the significant meaning:

1. Outstanding for the year is the volume of building construction that took place, particularly and especially in home building.
2. The most disappointing phase of the picture of the year was the huge quantity of cotton that was destroyed by the boll weevil.
3. New passenger car sales approximated one new car for every 35 persons in the state, or one for approximately every seven families of citizens.
4. There was a definite upturn in business activity even before the Korean War occurred.

5. The scare buying of things reached its highest peak in the month of August and then tapered off after that time.
6. Coal mining in mines in the state was restricted somewhat in the early months of the year by strikes of miners.
7. During the last three months of the year, October, November, and December, the outlook in the line of retail business improved.
8. Electric energy sales to industries for industrial purposes in 1950 increased 15 per cent over sales in 1949.
9. Cement consumption by people who buy and use cement was the highest on record in the history of the industry in 1951.
10. During the last quarter of the year, nonresidential building of structures, especially manufacturing building, claimed the highest percentage of total construction by builders.

C. Comment on the repetition of ideas, words, and sounds in the following sentences, stating whether you think the repetition is accidental or deliberate, undesirable or effective. All the sentences are enclosed in quotation marks in order to furnish no clue as to the standing of the writer quoted.

1. "Richard Dana, a student at Harvard College, wanted to see the world and went to sea in a small merchant brig named the *Pilgrim.*"
2. "The audience is soon given a complete insight into the characteristics of the characters."
3. "When his stove began to sell well, he decided to patent his invention."
4. "The elaborately tinted interchangeable lights change rapidly and present scenes that never seem to be repeated."
5. "In proportion as man simplifies his life, the laws of the universe will appear less complex, and solitude will not be solitude, nor poverty poverty, nor weakness weakness."
6. "In spite of his embarrassment, he tried to handle the situation with a jest and a gesture."
7. "We were all comfortably seated in comfortable chairs."
8. "One fact that nearly caused the trip to be a failure was the fact that Parkman was in poor health most of the time."
9. "The summer soldier and the sunshine patriot will, in this crisis, shrink from the service of their country."
10. "Gentlemen may cry peace, peace — but there is no peace."

11. "The first advice that I would give to a high school senior is that he should learn to study, for study is absolutely necessary in college."
12. "I knew that unless I acted quickly the bear would tear me limb from limb."
13. "College life, with its new experiences, new adventures, new acquaintances, and new friends, is not conducive to steady study."
14. "These people were the first settlers to settle in the Sudeten territory."
15. "Of all the seasons in the year, the Christmas season is the one which brings forth the most gaiety everywhere all over the world."

D. Write a paragraph of 150 to 250 words explaining why you prefer some particular magazine, sport, restaurant, poet, short-story writer, or musician. Then try to condense the paragraph by eliminating and rephrasing wherever possible. If you cannot condense without sacrificing meaning, your writing is economical and direct.

VARIETY

If a writer pays careful attention to the need for subordination, parallelism, and emphasis, subordinating what is logically subordinate, making parallel what is logically parallel, and emphasizing his important thoughts, he will automatically write with considerable variety of sentence structure. Inevitably he will have short sentences and long sentences; simple, compound, and complex sentences; loose, periodic, and balanced sentences; and occasional interrogative or exclamatory sentences or departures from the normal word order. However, even professional writers tend to repeat some types of sentences too frequently, unconsciously using favorite sentence patterns when the thought is more important than the kind of sentence. The monotony in sentence structure which results is best corrected in revision, when the writer can look back at what he has already written and make occasional changes to give his writing variety.

A deliberate effort to secure variety in the first draft may divert the writer from his meaning and may produce artificial constructions. The student should concern himself first with writing what he means, paying little attention to repetition of sentence structure, then choose occasional sentences which can be revised to avoid monotony without distorting the meaning.

Monotony in words is not simply the repetition of any word. We hear our names spoken many times a day without getting tired of them; we hear and say words like *doctor, breakfast, teeth, water, head, book, time, bed,* and *door* day after day and year after year without feeling that such words are over-worked. Evidently no variety is necessary in large segments of the common vocabulary. Think of the hundreds and thousands of times that you have used *I, who, was, if, and, why, the, am, this, when,* and *to* without getting tired of them. Yet we all know people who over-use pet expressions like *so what, swell, okay, fine,* and *nice* to the point of making themselves tiresome and unpopular. Some people seem unable to speak more than a few minutes without using *kid,* or *goodness,* or *sweet,* or *I said,* or some other favorite expression.

How can we distinguish the words that can be used time and again without monotony from those which are likely to be boring and ineffective? Apparently a common standard word like *head* can be used an indefinite number of times without monotony. The humorous or figurative substitutes for *head,* however, such as *bean, block, dome, noggin, noodle, nut,* do not wear well, especially when one of them occurs with high frequency in the speech of one person or group. Of course such synonyms do arise to provide variety for people who wish to avoid saying *head,* but the origin is not so much in boredom with *head* as it is in a search for novel effects. So long as we have the common standard word, the picturesque substitutes wear out fast, and stale slang is a symptom of stale mental processes.

Another kind of word which can become very monotonous is the very general adjective. People whose vocabulary of praise is limited to *fine,* or *swell,* or *nice,* or *okay,* and whose vocabulary of disapproval stops with *sorry,* or *poor,* or *no good,* are not making distinctions in degree of approval or disapproval; they seem unable to go beyond a simple judgment of good or bad. Since we all make judgments very frequently, the person who uses only a few judgment words tends to over-use those few. Variety can be achieved here by cultivating the use of more precise synonyms. (See §§ 58 and 60.)

A third kind of monotony in diction arises when the subject of the discourse demands that a particular notion be repeated frequently. In a story with much conversation, a writer can easily overwork *said*. In a review of a play, the reviewer runs the danger of over-using *play*. If you are describing a hike, you can bore your reader by using *walk* too often. Seeking variety in situations of this kind, sports writers and announcers desperately coin synonyms for *bat, ball, hit, score, basket,* and other words that would occur dozens of times in one broadcast or news story. Not having the freedom of the sports writer, the student must turn to his dictionary or thesaurus of synonyms [1] to vary his diction when the nature of the subject seems to demand the tiresome repetition of a word or phrase. And a word of warning is necessary here. In serious writing do not use over-clever or inappropriate words merely to avoid repeating a common word. Readers of comic strips expect their characters to avoid the word *policeman* and to use instead *bull, flatfoot, copper, John Law, flattie, cop,* and similar synonyms; readers of a newspaper editorial on policemen's pensions would not object to frequent use of the word *policeman* or *police officer* or *member of the police force.*

Remember, finally, that there is no short cut to effective diction; that "fine writing" (flowery language) is always cheap and ugly; that affected mannerisms of style only obscure the thought and annoy the reader; that strained, contorted language is not an indication of strength; that deliberate smartness suggests only the spoiled child. You are not to toy with words; you are to think honestly and write honestly. (See also §§ 54–61, 64, 65, and 81.)

EXERCISES

A. Compare the two paragraphs on page 60 for variety of sentence structure, noting (1) loose and periodic sentences, (2) simple, compound, and complex sentences, (3) unusual word order, (4) sentence length, and (5) ways of beginning sentences. (It is useful to make comparative tables of these features to bring out the differences between the passages.)

[1] For example, see *Webster's Dictionary of Synonyms,* Springfield: G. & C. Merriam Co., 1942; *American College Dictionary* (abbreviated *ACD*), New York: Random House, 1947, Harper & Brothers, 1948; *Webster's New Collegiate Dictionary* (abbreviated *NCD*), Springfield: G. & C. Merriam Co., 1949.

B. Repeat Exercise A, using the paragraphs on page 61.

C. Repeat Exercise A, using passages assigned by your instructor.

D. Substitute a synonym for each italicized word in the sentences below.

1. A *red-faced* man jumped angrily from the red fire truck.
2. The detective watchfully *circled* the circle of people around the barker's stand.
3. Women teachers always chaperon the *women* at Hill College when they go in to the city.
4. The physics *teacher* was unable to teach because of illness.
5. Only a few *books* of poetry were on his bookshelves.
6. The boys at Brookwood prefer the Star Amusement Park for *amusement* on Saturday nights.
7. Judge Jackson is a *true* man of the people, no aristocrat.
8. The labor unions *labor* very hard for civic improvements in some towns.
9. When the beef-control bill came up, the senator from the leading cow state said he was not *cowed* by lobbyists.
10. She returned from China with a set of handpainted *china*.

E. Supply at least four substitutes for each italicized word or phrase in the following sentences:

Example The plane *landed* at seven fifteen. Substitutes: came down, touched earth, hit the runway, settled to the ground, left the air.

1. Marion *went* across the street to the hospital entrance.
2. A noisy *group of people* had suddenly collected in the park.
3. Girls' mothers usually prefer boys with *nice* manners.
4. Davis *led* the organization through a ticklish campaign.
5. Joe is *attending* the university this winter.
6. Edson had a *scrap* with a clerk over a mistake in his bill.
7. "Guys and Dolls" was said by critics to be a *choice show.*
8. Dr. Best was last seen driving a big green *car* on Front Street.
9. In the modern home many electrical *gadgets* are considered necessary.
10. "Blabbermouth" is a *fine* example of expressive word coinage.

F. For what more common word can each of the following be substituted? *bemused, carmine, cogent, delineate, depict, enhance, fulsome, Gallic, imbroglio, innate, specious, venal.*

Paragraphs and Thinking

The paragraph is a plastic mass, and it takes its shape from the thought it has to express: its shape IS *the thought.* — HERBERT READ

paragraph, n. *A distinct section or subdivision of a discourse, chapter, or writing, whether of one or many sentences, that forms a rhetorical unit as dealing with a particular point of the subject, or as comprising the words of a distinct speaker, etc.* — WEBSTER'S NEW INTERNATIONAL DICTIONARY, SECOND EDITION.

A good paragraph is an *ordered* series of sentences — or sometimes a single sentence — making a complete unit of communication. A good paragraph has unity, coherence, and emphasis; its parts are organized and closely inter-related. Although paragraphs by professional writers usually cannot be analyzed into a few simple patterns, it may help the inexperienced writer to imagine that an ideal structure exists and that good paragraphs are variations of its architecture. This ideal pattern can be described in terms of (*a*) topic sentence, (*b*) arrangement of content, and (*c*) transitions. In this section we describe paragraph writing, exhibit models of paragraphs, and provide exercises for practice.

TOPIC SENTENCE

It is customary to indicate the unity of the paragraph, the special nature of the thought it contains, by means of a topic sentence. Although it may occupy any position in the paragraph, and indeed is sometimes omitted altogether, in most paragraphs the topic sentence is placed at the beginning, because this is ordinarily its logical place. Something is to be explained: what is that something? As the reader passes from paragraph to paragraph, the topic sentences inform him promptly of the changes in subject-matter. It is not their function, of course, to state everything that the paragraph contains, nor even, in most cases, to summarize the contents of the paragraph; their object is simply to point out the thought to be developed — to state the topic. For example, a paragraph might begin with the topic sentence: "Students should acquire the habit of thinking for themselves." All the rest of the paragraph would deal with various aspects of this one statement: the number of students who have or have not this habit, the precise nature of the habit itself, the obstacles to the formation of the habit, and especially the reasons why the habit is desirable. Subtopics like these should be implied by the topic sentence, but they need not be stated in that sentence. In general it is unnecessary for the sentence to include more than the main topic.

EXERCISES

A. Find the topic sentences of ten paragraphs on pages 51–62, or other paragraphs assigned by your instructor.

B. Supply the missing topic sentences in the paragraphs below:

1

His impatience with foolish questions is illustrated by his answer to a student who asked one day, "Professor Mauldin, how would you spell *to* in the sentence 'There are three *to's* in the English language, *to*, *too*, and *two*'?" The old man glared at the freshman and answered, "That statement is either nonsense or a lie. You are not in this class to learn how to write either nonsense or lies. There are not three *to's*, three *too's*, or three *two's*. If you are serious about this, you can learn phonetic symbols and write 'There are three homophones pronounced [tū] in English.' If you are not serious you are wasting our time." His patience with mere ignorance is evident in his spending a whole class hour one day explaining to us why *could of* is a misspelling of *could've*, a contraction of *could have*, and not an error in grammar. He had to show us what is meant by "unstressed syllable" and how people in conversation correctly pronounce *of* and *have* identically, but never say *could of*. Professor Mauldin had us pronounce such expressions as *give them up*, *used to do it*, and *that will do* in different ways to explain how some words have both stressed and unstressed forms. These are not rare examples; many more could be cited.

2

It is quite true that many people drive their automobiles only within their own towns. Some people never take business trips or go on vacations by car. Others use delivery trucks, tractors, bulldozers, and such gasoline-engine machines within city limits, never driving them on state highways. Then there are many, many people who use the highways only occasionally, perhaps for a vacation trip once a year, or shopping trips to a city a few times a year, or a visit to relatives at Christmas. They make very little use of state highways. But everybody is benefited by having good state highways. Good transportation makes goods flow faster and cheaper, and salesmen can spread industrial improvements all over the state if they have good roads to drive on. Doctors, lawyers, preachers, lecturers, experts of all kinds can reach more people where the state keeps up a good highway system. The gasoline taxes that people in towns pay for state roads do benefit them, even if they drive little or not at all on the highways. Furthermore, it would be practically impossible to tax gasoline used on highways at one rate and gasoline used only within towns at another rate. How would service station men know what tax to collect when anybody buys gas?

C. Write five topic sentences that might be developed into paragraphs on the subject of taxes. (HINTS: income taxes, sales taxes, tobacco taxes, exemptions, collectors, evasions, uses, effects.)

D. Using one of the sentences below as the topic sentence, write a paragraph of five to eight sentences. Be very careful to keep the paragraph on the subject announced by the topic sentence.

1. Most students are in college for more than one reason.
2. The President of the United States has many duties.
3. Some women's handbags are like junk shops.
4. Indoor and outdoor sports are (are not) equally popular.
5. College is different from high school.

E. Using one of the phrases below as the subject of the topic sentence, write a paragraph of five to eight sentences. Be very careful to keep the paragraph on the topic selected.

1. Labor unions
2. T. S. Eliot
3. Singing commercials
4. Comic strips
5. Taking notes
6. Hospitals
7. Window shopping
8. College expenses
9. Recent movies
10. War novels

SUBSTANCE

The substance of a paragraph is its content — the facts and ideas that are to be communicated to the reader. Sometimes the writer begins a composition with the substance already in his head, as when you write a description of your own preferences in food or movie stars, or when you describe something you have seen on a trip. At other times the writer has to search for substance, as when you are assigned a report in a college course on a subject you know little about. Sometimes the writer has the necessary facts in his head but has never thought about them in a certain way or organized them coherently, as when you are asked to describe exactly what you do when you worry.

For certain kinds of writing problems the writer knows from the beginning what his main topics are, and proceeds to draw on his memory, his reasoning ability, or outside sources for substance, finally formulating the topic sentences around the set topics and developing each into a paragraph by putting the substance into sentences. For example, in planning a letter recommending someone for a position, the writer would ordinarily know that such letters have such topics as education, experience, and general ability. After exploring his memory and knowledge of the applicant and thinking about his qualifications, the writer might formulate three topic sentences as follows:

> Mr. Becker's formal education equips him for the job.
> His experience in this work has been extensive.
> In temperament and habits he is ideally qualified.

The substance of the first paragraph would be a recital of the schools Becker attended, the curricula he studied, the grades he made, and the degrees he earned. The writer might supply some of this substance from memory, and might have to consult records or ask for some of it. The second topic sentence would be made into a paragraph by reciting the jobs Becker has held. Again, the substance could come from the writer's memory or from outside sources. The third paragraph would be provided with substance from the writer's knowledge of Becker and thinking about his habits and temperament. Frequently the new substance turned up by reading and inquiry will modify the original tentative topic sentences. For instance, our letter writer might discover, after collecting specific details, that his second topic sentence should read "His experience is extensive, but not in this particular work." In the third paragraph the substance would include the writer's judgments about Becker, his evaluation of Becker's personal qualifications. These judgments would be reached by thinking — by the writer's asking himself questions about Becker's honesty, dependability, intelligence, adaptability, and behavior under stress, and phrasing the answers to these questions as informative statements.

In other types of writing the writer may know little or nothing about his subject when he begins, not even what his paragraph topics are likely to be. Such writing occurs when a student is assigned a report on some aspect of a subject he is studying. To obtain substance he will read, or collect specimens, or perform experiments, storing his notebook and his memory with facts, and classifying the facts into categories, separating things that are unlike and relating things that are alike, eventually deciding on the topics and making topic sentences to unify the related bits of substance into paragraphs. But the substance of a paragraph does not normally consist of a mere catalogue of similar facts. The relationships between them, the statements of cause and effect, of major and minor importance, of time, concession, contrast, and consequence, and the writer's evaluations are likewise part of the substance. What the writer has to communicate in each paragraph — the substance of the paragraph — is not determined by inanimate facts alone. The substance is a product of complex interactions between a nervous system with a history and the sensations received by the nervous system from the outside, the whole moulded by the habits, beliefs, and standards of the individual writer-thinker.

Every paragraph should have sufficient substance to support, explain, clarify, or exemplify its topic sentence (whether the topic sentence is expressed or implied). After the writer becomes familiar with his data and begins writing, he is likely to find that some topic sentences are mistakes, that he does not have enough substance to develop them fully; or that some topic sentences are too inclusive, that he has more substance than some topic sentences will bear. When this happens, he reëxamines his material, discarding or rephrasing some topic sentences, searching for additional material, or discarding unrelated material, making new divisions, and rephrasing his communication. If there is not sufficient substance to support a topic sentence, either new material must be added or the topic sentence must be altered. If a paragraph contains too much substance or substance too diverse to be stated in a topic sentence, the paragraph must be divided or revised.

For example, suppose your English instructor notices that you use a good many contractions in your writing and asks you to justify them. Not having thought much about the subject you might say something like this:

> Contractions are all right and I use them because they are easier to write and they are just as clear as any other words. All good writers, at least all that I know about, use plenty of contractions, even if high school English teachers don't like them, and good writers are above the rules in the books anyway. What is wrong with contractions anyway? It's easier for me to write if I use contractions, and as far as that is concerned I'm not trying to be a writer anyhow. Even if I intended to be a writer of editorials or advertising copy, I would still think contractions are all right.

This paragraph — rather, series of sentences — has no substance; it gets nowhere, gives no information about contractions, repeats itself, and contains not one statement that can be verified objectively. All the reader knows is that the writer uses contractions and is annoyed because his usage has been criticized.

On the other hand, suppose that you had gone to a reputable publication and made a study of the actual occurrence of contractions, tabulating the occurrences and comparing the writers and writings which do and do not employ contractions. You might write a paragraph report like this:

> To study the use of contractions in a literary magazine, I read the fifteen principal book reviews in the November 17 issue of the *Saturday Review of Literature*, written by fifteen different reviewers. Nine of the reviews contain no contractions, and one contains an occurrence of *don't* and two occurrences of *it's* quoted from the novel being reviewed. Thus ten of the reviewers, two-thirds of the total, used no contractions, and

eight of the ten used constructions like *is not, has not,* and *does not,* which could have been contracted. In the five remaining reviews I found two occurrences of *doesn't,* and one each of *can't, don't, won't, isn't,* and *you'd.* One review of a volume of political reminiscences contains *doesn't* and *can't,* and one review of a picture-book contains *isn't* and *won't;* both these reviews are by nationally known university professors. Three of the reviews contain one contraction each. To sum up, in these fifteen reviews contractions are not favored, and contractions of *not* are by far the most common of those used.

This paragraph has substance. It contains verifiable statements and provides information and a conclusion for the reader. A series of such paragraphs, each on a different magazine, would constitute a report on current practice in periodicals, and would probably call for one or more paragraphs of interpretation, comparison, analysis, and conclusion.

EXERCISES

A. Write a paragraph describing a person that you know well. Make the description as accurate as you can, so accurate that your reader could recognize the person in a group. Include such details as height, weight, and build; coloring; posture, walk, gestures, mannerisms; head, hair, ears, eyes, eyebrows, lashes, nose, mouth, lips, teeth, complexion, facial expression; quality of voice, pitch of voice, typical laugh; shoulders, arms, wrists, hands, fingers, fingernails; usual clothing and shoes.

B. After gathering some facts that you did not know before, write an explanatory paragraph that would inform a reader. To find new information, consult one of the following sources or one suggested by your instructor:

1. A telephone directory. (Note which names occur most frequently, the rank of the most common names, rare names, unusual trade names.)
2. A train, bus, or airline schedule. (Note the number of arrivals and departures, how the trips are spaced through the day and night, relative number of local and express schedules, special details.)
3. One page or one issue of a daily newspaper. (Note the proportion of news to advertising to features; proportions of local, state, national, and international news; of crime, disaster, and good news; prominence given particular kinds of news.)

4. One section of classified ads in a newspaper, such as positions wanted, help wanted, rentals. (Note shortages and surpluses, types and locations.)
5. A college time schedule. (Note the favored and the little-used hours for classes, uses of afternoon hours, unusual time schedules.)

C. Write a paragraph reporting something you observe carefully, such as how motorists obey a particular traffic light; the gestures used by an instructor; the efficiency of a particular clerk in a café, store, or library; the kinds of shrubbery on the campus; the sideline behavior of a football coach; the display in a show window; the notices on a bulletin board; a groundskeeper at work; how some person parks a car; or the mannerisms of a speaker. Notice as many details as possible, no matter how minute or how inconsistent. Fifteen or twenty minutes observation should provide you with nore than enough substance for a paragraph.

D. Write a paragraph reporting information that you get from a conversation with one or more people. Bring up a controversial topic, such as subsidized athletics, segregation in schools, a tax on bachelors, military aid to foreign countries, the closed shop, compulsory medical insurance, required class attendance, student honor systems, allowing communists to teach in colleges, or dormitory curfews, and listen particularly for new points of view, surprising attitudes, arguments that you had not heard before, and arguments that seem weak or biased.

E. Write a paragraph in which you reveal your own thinking about one of the topics listed in Exercise D. Try to avoid mere repetition of notions that you have heard or read; put yourself in a position where the issue affects you personally, and consider your interests thoughtfully and honestly.

METHODS OF DEVELOPMENT

Since a unified, coherent paragraph is an elaboration of a topic sentence, which may be written or implied, the nature of the topic sentence will normally determine how the remainder of the paragraph is developed. If the topic sentence is argumentative, the paragraph may consist of instances or examples which support the argument, or it may consist of a recital of evidence. If the topic sentence is a definition, the paragraph may refine and explain the definition. A paragraph which describes an event or a process is usually developed by taking up separate steps, one after another. Several methods or types are illustrated below.

1. *Examples and instances*

PARAGRAPH 1

It is pitifully easy to prove our rules of grammar arbitrary, unintelligent, inconsistent. One mistake or change gets by, another gets stopped. The adjective *like* may become a preposition freely, the adjective *near* is admitted with some reluctance to the same class, but the adjective *worth* must remain an adjective, though its use is plainly prepositional. The phrase *already* may be written as one word, but not the phrase *all right.* Scores of verbs, such as *write, incline, begin, end* — the list is endless — may be either transitive or intransitive, but not *lay* or *set.* We may *lay a floor* but not *lay down, set the table* but not *just set.* We may use what was originally a past tense as a past participle when we say "I have fought," but we must not say "I have fell." Why not?[1]

PARAGRAPH 2

In every domain, men, a little queer to their neighbors, have hurled strange ideas at the rock of ages: Vesalius daring to lay profane hands on the human corpse, lately the dwelling place of the soul, to prove that Galen was wrong in his anatomy. Copernicus deposing the Earth and installing the Sun in its place as the center of the universe. Newton daring to assert that the very force which caused the apple to fall held the heavenly bodies to their celestial courses. Intellectual adventurers contriving instruments with which to explore a micro-realm which lies beyond the reach of human eye and ear — and employing infra-sensory fact to create a new physical universe. Curious spirits restoring to life the old theory of the four humors in the marvelously intricate system of hormones with which of late the human organism has been fitted out. Here great men have emancipated the human race — or a lucky fraction thereof — from an assortment of bondages. But great men could not have become great discoverers had not a multitude of lesser men, defying reputable belief, allowed their minds to be bold.[2]

[1] Janet Rankin Aiken, "Good and Bad Grammar," *The American Mercury*, November, 1932. Reprinted by permission of the publisher.

[2] J. Bentham Mill, "Gospel for the Crossroads," *The American Scholar*, Autumn, 1950. Reprinted by permission of the publisher.

2. *Causes and effects*

PARAGRAPH 3

As year followed year of prosperity, the new diffusion of wealth brought marked results. There had been a great boom in higher education after the war, and the boom continued, although at a somewhat slackened pace, until college trustees were beside themselves wondering how to find room for the swarming applicants. There was an epidemic of outlines of knowledge and books of etiquette for those who had got rich quick and wanted to get cultured quick and become socially at ease. Wells's *Outline of History*, the best-selling non-fiction book of 1921 and 1922, was followed by Van Loon's *Story of Mankind*, J. Arthur Thomson's *Outline of Science* (both of them best sellers in 1922), the Doubleday mail-order *Book of Etiquette* and Emily Post's *Book of Etiquette* (which led the non-fiction list in 1923), *Why We Behave Like Human Beings* (a big success of 1926), and *The Story of Philosophy*, which ran away from all other books in the non-fiction list of 1927.[1]

3. *Logical divisions (classes, reasons, steps in a process, etc.)*

PARAGRAPH 4

We may say, in briefest summary, that the method of science consists in (*a*) asking clear answerable questions in order to direct one's (*b*) observations, which are made in a calm and unprejudiced manner, and which are then (*c*) reported as accurately as possible and in such a way as to answer the questions that were asked to begin with, after which (*d*) any pertinent beliefs or assumptions that were held before the observations were made are revised in light of the observations made and the answers obtained. Then more questions are asked in accordance with the newly revised notions, further observations are made, new answers are arrived at, beliefs and assumptions are again revised, after which the whole process starts over again. In fact, it never stops. Science as method is continuous. All its conclusions are held subject to the further revision that new observations may require. It is a method of keeping one's information, beliefs, and theories up to date. It is, above all, a method of "changing one's mind" — sufficiently often.[2]

[1] Frederick Lewis Allen, *Only Yesterday* (New York: Harper and Brothers, 1931). Reprinted by permission of the publisher.

[2] Wendell Johnson, *People in Quandaries* (New York: Harper and Brothers, 1946). Reprinted by permission of the publisher.

PARAGRAPH 5

The motion picture began as a silent photograph of stage action. Photography soon acquired a nuance and idiom of its own that took the photoplay the farthest possible distance from its point of origin, the stage play. There was a brief return to the footlights formula at the beginning of talking pictures when microphones had to be hidden in flower pots and behind chandeliers and sofas. Not a year elapsed before the camera had its free range again, this time with a soundtrack. There was an immediate return to the screen's expressionism and its employment of plot as a string on which to hang its wares.[1]

4. *Comparison and contrast*

PARAGRAPH 6

He differs in this respect from Miss Katherine Mansfield, another writer who takes the traveler's-eye view of human beings. For Miss Mansfield has a lively fancy. Like Conrad, she sees her characters from a distance, as though at another table in a café; she overhears snatches of their conversations, — about their aunts in Battersea, their stamp collections, their souls, — and she finds them extraordinary, charming beyond all real and knowable people, odd, immensely exciting. She finds that they are Life itself, — lovely, fantastic Life. Very rarely does she go beyond this long-range café acquaintanceship with her personages, rarely makes herself at home in their flat everyday lives. But where Conrad bewilderedly speculates, Miss Mansfield uses her imagination. She invents suitable lives for the fabulous creatures glimpsed at the café. And how thrilling those fancied lives always are! Thrilling, but just for that reason not very convincing. Miss Mansfield's studies of interiors are like those brilliant paleontological reconstructions one sees in books of popular science, — the ichthyosaurus in its native waters, pterodactyls fluttering and swooping in the tepid tertiary sky, — too excitingly romantic, in spite of their air of realism, to be quite genuine. Her characters are seen with an extraordinary brilliance and precision, as one sees a party of people in a lighted drawing-room at night, through an uncurtained window, — one of those mysteriously significant Parties in Parlors of which we read in *Peter Bell*:

> Some sipping punch, some sipping tea,
> And all as silent as could be,
> All silent, and all damned.

[1] John Rosenfield, "The Real Story in the Motion Picture," *Southwest Review*, Summer, 1950. Reprinted by permission of the publisher.

One sees them for a moment, haloed with significance. They seem fabulous (though, of course, in point of actual fact and to those sitting in the room with them, they are nothing of the kind). Then one passes. They disappear. Each of Miss Mansfield's stories is a window into a lighted room. The glimpse of the inhabitants sipping their tea and punch is enormously exciting. But one knows nothing, when one has passed, of what they are really like. That is why, however thrilling at a first reading, her stories do not wear.[1]

PARAGRAPH 7

Perhaps the first requisite to getting a clear notion of the Spaniard is to realize in what respects he is *not* like the Frenchman. We should not allow ourselves to be misled by any supposed solidarity of the Latin races. In certain essential traits the Spanish differ from the French almost as much as the Hindus from the Chinese, and in somewhat the same manner. The chief thing that strikes one in French literature is the absence of what the Germans call *Innigkeit*, of inwardness, — the subordination of everything in man to his social qualities; among the Spaniards, on the other hand, there is vastly greater capacity for solitude and isolation. In France, reason, insufficiently quickened by the imagination, easily degenerates into dry rationalism; whereas in the land of Don Quixote the imagination tends to break away from the control of the senses and understanding, and is unwilling to accept the limitations of the real, and then follows the inevitable disenchantment when the world turns out to be different in fact from what it had been painted in fancy. *Engaño* and *desengaño*, illusion and disillusion, eternal themes of Spanish poetry![2]

5. *Analogy*

PARAGRAPH 8

Heat is always being transferred in one way or another, whenever there is any difference in temperature. Just as water will run down hill, always flowing to the lowest possible level, so heat, if left to itself, flows down the temperature hill, always warming the cold objects at the expense of the warmer ones. The rate at which heat flows depends on the steepness of the temperature hill as well as on the properties of the materials through which it has to flow. The difference of temperature per unit distance is called the

[1] Aldous Huxley, *Essays New and Old* (New York, 1927). Reprinted by permission of Harper and Brothers, copyright owners.

[2] Irving Babbitt, "Lights and Shades of Spanish Character," *The Atlantic Monthly*, August, 1898. Reprinted by permission of the publisher.

temperature gradient in analogy to the idea of steepness of grade, which determines the rate of flow of water.[1]

6. *Definition*

Paragraph 9

In the previous essay I described "modernism as a tendency of poets to keep the values of their poems to themselves — or offer them to the reader incidentally to be enjoyed as a kind of colored puzzle." If all literature may be described as a verbal communication of values, the modernists may be described as absorbed in the values to the neglect of the act of communicating them. They are unsociable poets, unfriendly, and in extreme cases their language approaches that of the insane or idiotic. Indeed, the word *idiot* means in its origin nothing more slanderous of the character of much of their writing than "private."[2]

Paragraph 10

What, then, is my concept of liberalism? In answering this, it is first necessary to brush aside the misleading and erroneous analogy of the spectrum, with communism on the left, conservatism on the right, and liberalism in the middle. Liberalism is freedom from orthodoxy — independence of mind. It is radical on some questions and conservative on others. While it may at times go down the middle of the road, it may at others range far to either side. It has no kinship with doctrinaire positions at any extreme. The essential characteristics of free thinking, and hence of liberalism, are the recognition of, and tolerance for, natural facts. The perfect liberal would be tolerant of both reactionaries and radicals, of good and evil, of everything that is in nature. Notice that tolerance does not mean approval. Webster defines tolerance as "endurance," and I would add as a prefix "understanding." Because he understands it, a tolerant person can endure such evil as he must. He will disapprove of it and take advantage of reasonable opportunities to correct it, but he knows that it cannot be abolished through a great flurry of committee meetings. A liberal, then, is a tolerant person in this sense. He must retain freedom for his own thought, he must be free to reverse his position on any question if dispassionate judgment convinces him of an error. If he is to be free to

[1] Marsh W. White and others, *Practical Physics* (New York: McGraw-Hill Book Company, Inc., 1943). Reprinted by permission of the publisher.
[2] Max Eastman, *The Literary Mind* (New York: Charles Scribner's Sons, 1931). Reprinted by permission of the publisher.

do this, he will find few if any "action groups" which he can join with equanimity. On the contrary, he will find himself quite alone in a crowd.[1]

7. *A combination of two or more methods*

PARAGRAPH 11

What, then, is this Statism? (1). The political organization of society is based on either one of two systems: a system of compulsory co-operation or a system of voluntary co-operation (2). A perfect example of the first system's typical structure is seen in a band of convicts working under a sentence of forced labor, or in a company of conscript soldiers taking part in a battle (3). Their co-operation is involuntary; it is enforced upon them by the State. If they do not co-operate as they are ordered, the State punishes them (4). Statism is the policy of indefinitely extending the system of compulsory co-operation into all departments of human activity (5). When this policy is worked out to the full, the individual's power of self-direction is completely confiscated; he plants, sows, reaps, under orders; conducts his business under orders; even his amusements and the conduct of his domestic life, his education and cultural processes, are prescribed and supervised by the State; even his personal relations with others, his friendships and sentimental attachments, all are subject to State control (6).[2]

1. Note that the topic sentence is a question which the paragraph is planned to answer. 2. This sentence announces the two divisions of a larger topic, the first part of which is developed in this paragraph; the second part, in the following paragraph, which begins: "As to the second system, the system of voluntary co-operation, an example of its typical structure is seen. . . ." 3 and 4. Examples for illustration. 5. Definition. 6. Examples of the effects of Statism upon the lives of the individuals who live under this system of social organization. Notice the climactic order of the examples.

EXERCISES

See page 50 for suggested subjects on which the following paragraphs might be written.

[1] William S. Hopkins, "An Affirmation of Liberalism," *Bulletin of the American Association of University Professors*, Autumn, 1950. Reprinted by permission of the publisher.

[2] Albert Jay Nock, "The State of the Nation," *The American Mercury*, May, 1939. Reprinted by permission of the publisher.

A. Write a paragraph in which most of the substance is composed of the *causes* which produced the effect or effects stated in your topic sentence. First study Paragraph 3 on page 52.

B. Write a paragraph in which the substance consists of one *example*, or several examples, illustrating the thought of the topic sentence. First study the paragraphs on page 51.

C. Write a paragraph involving a *logical division* of the substance — based, that is, on a list of classes, or reasons, or causes, or results, etc. First study the paragraphs on pages 52–53.

D. Write a paragraph involving a *comparison* or *contrast*. First study the paragraphs on pages 53–54.

E. Write a paragraph developed by means of *definition* and *examples*. First study the paragraphs on pages 51 and 55.

F. Write a paragraph involving a *combination* of at least two methods of development. First study the paragraph on page 56.

G. What methods of development are used by the writers of Paragraphs 20–24, pages 69–71?

H. Examine an editorial in a current newspaper to determine whether the writer uses only one or several methods of paragraph development.

ORDER

The third problem in the writing of a paragraph is the orderly arrangement of the sentences making up the paragraph. Good substance badly arranged loses most of its value. Suppose we write in this fashion:

Students should acquire the habit of thinking for themselves. I have never understood why women so meekly adopt the fashions of Paris. To be human, one must use his power of reason. To think for oneself does not mean to have thoughts different from everybody else's. As early as the sophomore year, students all tend to think alike. But thinking for oneself means to consider the possible ways of viewing a particular question and finally to make an independent choice. . . .

Here the order of the thoughts is simply a disorder; the thinking is confused, and consequently the writing is confused and the reader will be confused. The paragraph lacks order.

If the substance of the paragraph is an incident exemplifying a student's failure to think independently, or if it is the process of acquiring the habit of independent thought, it will obviously follow a chronological order. If it contains a number of reasons why students should think for themselves, it will become a series of arguments, some more, some less important, and the more important ones will belong together, usually at the end. If the substance is made up of instances of imitative opinions, the natural order will be one giving first the familiar instances (those that doubtless occurred first to the writer, because they were obvious) and afterward the more unfamiliar instances. Wherever the substance is not homogeneous but is of several kinds, the several kinds should not be indiscriminately jumbled but classified; for example, the instances might be presented first, and the arguments afterward, or *vice versa*, or instances might be offered in support of each argument. In any case, remember that order of any sort is better than disorder.

Whatever the principle of order chosen, the thought must progress *from* somewhere *to* somewhere else. It must follow a definite direction, not ramble aimlessly. In the entire paragraph, ideally, each sentence should have a place of its own, and a place so plainly its own that it could not be shifted to another place without losing coherence. When the substance of a paragraph is not in place, we have what may be termed a *jumbled* paragraph, as in the example given on page 57. Such a paragraph is the result of disorderly thinking, and is most likely to occur when the substance is complex. The remedy is to divide complex material into parts, into the several *stages* in the onward march of the thought. Thus if we are amplifying a list of reasons, we may regard the discussion of each reason as a stage in the progress of the thought, and make sure that we are saying all we have to say about each stage before passing on to the next. There must be no confusion in the stages, no returning to sub-topics previously dealt with, no happy or unhappy afterthoughts, or belated efforts to emphasize matter already dismissed. If new matter occurs to us, we must insert it in its place when rewriting the paragraph. In sum, order requires a steady forward movement.

The only exception to what has just been said is the case of summary sentences, retrospective sentences that gather up the thought of the paragraph; for example, the last sentence of the paragraph just above: "In sum, order requires a steady forward movement." Although such sentences are rather infrequent at the ends of paragraphs, they are occasionally valuable when a paragraph is long or complex.

The most widely used kinds of order are given here. For expository or argumentative writing the most common orders are (1) from less to greater value, the order of climax; (2) from the familiar to the unfamiliar; (3) from the general to the particular (the deductive method); (4) from the particular to the general (inductive). For narrative writing the usual order is chronological, that is, from an earlier to a later time; for descriptive writing, from place to place or from one part to another part.

Below are some specimen paragraphs illustrating various kinds of order used in paragraph development.

1. *From less to greater value: order of climax — increasing importance of interest*

Paragraph 12

The cultural laggards are noisy; but tangible events since the impasse was reached show net gains for dynamo behavior and losses for stagecoach behavior; not only in the United States, but all over the world. Vendibility is definitely in retreat. Nation after nation has left the gold standard, to embark on managed currency policies in which the bankers correctly find no hope for maintaining a private monopoly of credit. The State has been forced to support millions of citizens without requiring the traditional *quid pro quo* of work, because there was no work for them to do. Autarchy has all but destroyed the world free market. Dictatorships, one after another, supersede voting, parliaments, checks, and balances. Centralization and government control of industry proceed at a violent pace. The end no man can foresee, but the general direction is clear enough. All industrial nations are in the turmoil of a transition period, seeking more or less blindly for stabilities which accord with technological imperatives. History is at one of its most momentous passages.[1]

[1] Stuart Chase, *The Economy of Abundance* (New York: The Macmillan Company, 1934). Reprinted by permission of the publisher.

2. *From the familiar to the unfamiliar*

PARAGRAPH 13

Early in life I cultivated the habit of watching the human body and trying to interpret its movements, which are very expressive. One winter day I noticed a crowd of people hurrying along a cold, windy city street. Their faces were taut, their arms were rigidly clamped to their sides, and their coat collars were turned up. What a contrast to a group of children playing in the snow! Most children take particular delight in exposing themselves to cold, in rolling about in the snow. Head-up, they face an icy wind with relazed muscles and carefree minds. Adults, by tensing their minds and their muscles defensively, deny their bodies the freedom of natural self-regulation, they resist homeostatic balance, and thereby prepare the way for different kinds of pathologically heightened sensitivity, and invite colds and respiratory infections. Children, however, when they are not fettered by too many civilized restraints, will make free spontaneous use of the body's self-regulating, air-conditioning unit, and thereby lessen their susceptibility to infection. A relaxed organism preserves its homeostatic balance more easily and naturally than an organism subject to continuing tension.[1]

3. *From the general to the particular*

PARAGRAPH 14

Let no man deceive himself. The great American office is much more completely a female bailiwick than the great American home. It has, it is true, its necessary male. But so has the ant hive, which is essentially neuter, its necessary queen. The male is the name on the door, the hat on the coat rack, and the smoke in the corner room. But the male is not the office. The office is the competent woman at the other end of his buzzer, the two young ladies chanting his name monotonously into the mouthpieces of a kind of gutta-percha halter, the four girls in the glass coop pecking out his initials with pink fingernails, on the keyboards of four voluble machines, the half dozen assorted skirts whisking through the filing cases of his correspondence, and the elegant miss in the reception room recognizing his friends and disposing of his antipathies with the pleased voice and the impersonal eye of a presidential consort.[2]

[1] Max Jacobson, "Functional Disorders in Our Civilization," *Tomorrow*, April, 1951. Reprinted by permission of the author.

[2] "Women in Business," *Fortune*, August, 1935. Reprinted by permission of the publisher.

4. *From the particular to the general*

Paragraph 15

Nineteen forty-eight saw the beginning of the systematic suppression of the Greek guerrillas — a rather baffling police operation executed by indigenous forces, with the United States supplying only material aid and technical advice. Nineteen forty-nine was the year that turned the tide in Berlin — through a massive logistic effort carried out primarily by the Americans themselves. The current year has seen United Nations intervention in Korea, again an operation in which American forces have played the leading role. These examples suggest that the number of *active* danger spots at any one time is limited, and that it is possible to shift the emphasis and to divert resources from one place to another nearly as rapidly as the Soviet Union can itself shift its point of attack. The resources, the technique, perhaps some of the same planes that won the struggle for Berlin went into the air movements of troops and supplies that contributed so decisively to the American advance in Korea. In sum, the containment policy rests on the idea of a strategic reserve — a flexible concept as opposed to the static and impossible notion of simply manning a wall.[1]

5. *Narration*

Paragraph 16

Kafka, Franz (1883–1924, German novelist and essayist), was born in Prague of a well-to-do middle-class Jewish family, in an atmosphere overshadowed by his father's dominant personality (see "Brief an den Vater," 1919) and reminiscent of the early days of Proust. After rigid schooling he took, in 1906, his law degree at the German University of Prague and eventually obtained a position in the workmen's compensation division of the Austrian government. Devotion to literature was nevertheless his real concern, and it was only the slowness and conscientiousness of his writing that made it impossible for him to gain a livelihood by it. Several attacks of tuberculosis compelled him to spend several years in sanatoriums. On two occasions, hopes for a marriage that might have steadied his life failed because of his own sense of inadequacy.[2]

[1] James P. Warburg, "Plea for a Positive Policy," *The Nation*, December 16, 1950. Reprinted by permission of the publisher.

[2] Horatio Smith, editor, *Columbia Dictionary of Modern European Literature* (New York: Columbia University Press, 1947). Reprinted by permission of the publisher.

6. *Description*

Paragraph 17

Time had made Mr. Belcher different from Mr. Gibson in other ways. He was a sleeker type, polished to a nice bourgeois gloss. There was nothing whatsoever in his appearance to indicate that he belonged to the revolutionary party. He was tall, slender, sallow, and very dapper, as if perpetually prepared for inspection by someone whom he accepted as having the right to pass judgment on him. He was growing bald, and on his shining, yellowish pate a little tuft of hair was combed out to a shadowy ace of clubs. At the back of his head, which bulged in a conformation often considered a sign of unusual brain-power, the blue-black hair was still thick and was carefully cut and brushed sleek. During the twenty-five days the Tribunal sat, his face seemed always ajar with apprehensive geniality. He never seemed to close the door of himself against the world and tell it to go hang. This was perhaps because from his youth he had lived a very public life.[1]

7. *Combination of narration and description*

Paragraph 18

From the mound, Mr. Tanimoto saw an astonishing panorama. Not just a patch of Koi, as he had expected, but as much of Hiroshima as he could see through the clouded air was giving off a thick, dreadful miasma. Clumps of smoke, near and far, had begun to push up through the general dust. He wondered how such extensive damage could have been dealt out of a silent sky; even a few planes, far up, would have been audible. Houses nearby were burning, and when huge drops of water the size of marbles began to fall, he half thought they must be coming from the hoses of firemen fighting the blazes. (They were actually drops of condensed moisture falling from the turbulent tower of dust, heat, and fission fragments that had already risen miles into the sky above Hiroshima.) [2]

Many other combinations of methods are possible and are frequently used. In fact, most good paragraphs employ more than one plan of development, since these orders are not mutually exclusive. Part of a paragraph can be from general to particular and part from particular to general; description usually involves

[1] Rebecca West, "The Tribunal That Stirred England," *Harper's Magazine*, June, 1949. Reprinted by permission of the publisher.

[2] John Hersey, *Hiroshima* (New York: Alfred A. Knopf, 1946). Reprinted by permission of the publisher.

both particulars and generalities; and any one of the kinds of order may include narration of events in chronological order.

EXERCISES

A. Write a paragraph in which the thought progresses from the *less important or interesting* to the *more important or interesting* (order of climax). First study the paragraph on page 59.

B. Write a paragraph in which the thought progresses from the *familiar* to the *unfamiliar*. Choose a topic about which you know more than most people do. First study the paragraph on page 60.

C. Write a paragraph in which the thought progresses from the *general* to the *particular* (deductive order). First study the paragraph on page 60.

D. Write a paragraph in which the thought progresses from the *particular* to the *general* (inductive order). First study the paragraph on page 61.

E. Write a narrative paragraph in which the progress of the thought is as strictly chronological as possible, moving from *earlier* to constantly *later* time.

F. Write a descriptive paragraph in which the progress of the thought shifts attention from *one place to another*, beginning with the nearest and ending with the farthest, or beginning with the most prominent and passing to the less prominent, or employing any other scheme that is definite and suits the substance. First study the paragraph on page 62.

G. The paragraphs below are jumbled. Rewrite them by reordering the sentences.

1

The body was clean and smooth, with no dents, crumpled spots, or cracks, and the paint, though somewhat faded, was glossy and well polished. The greasing points were all dry, and the engine sounded as if it had water instead of oil in the crankcase. The upholstery and floor mats were unspotted, suggesting that they had been used to regular treatment with a vacuum cleaner. Under the hood everything was dirty and run-down: wires were frayed, hose connections were cracked, nuts were missing from bolts, electric connections were loose, and caked mud and grease covered everything. It looked like a good car from the outside, but a mechanic could tell instantly that it had been neglected underneath. The chromium trim shone, but the tires were unevenly worn, indicating wheels out of line. The fan belt was ragged, and the oil filter clogged. (STUDENT THEME)

2

I have had three years experience as a proofreader and copy editor on a daily newspaper. My education was interrupted by the war, as I was drafted at the end of my junior year in college. It has long been my ambition to be an editor in a publishing firm, and I am willing to start from the bottom. For a short time I was a court reporter, and in this job I became proficient at shorthand. In both high school and college I worked on student publications, having edited my high school year book my senior year, and having been news editor of my college paper. My work for the newspaper was entirely satisfactory to the managing editor, and he has said he would write me a letter of recommendation at any time. After I was demobilized, I could not afford to go back to college, so I have spent the past five years in various jobs. (FROM A LETTER OF APPLICATION)

3

The most loathsome and at the same time the most pitiful politicians on any campus are those who wait too long to get on the winning side. One leading "harmony boy" in the current campaign is a perfect example of me-tooism too late. Now he proposes a coalition of fraternity members and independents "to work together for the best interests of the student body." Two years ago he campaigned with a bunch that wanted the trustees to abolish fraternities. Last year he ran for a campus office as an independent, saying the independents could whip the fraternities in an election if they would just get out and vote. It has long been obvious that the fraternities, although including a minority of the eligible students, are so well organized and interested that they cannot easily be beaten, and the fraternity machine is not likely to fall for a coalition candidate whose sympathy with them is questionable. (FROM A STUDENT NEWSPAPER)

TRANSITION

In discussing sentences we said that one mark of maturity is the ability to sense and express the relationships between thoughts or parts of a thought. As the writer moves on from thought to thought, transitional words or phrases must reflect the relationships that exist in his mental processes if he is to be understood readily and clearly. Suppose we have two thoughts to express:

> I am glad to see the President powerful. He has too much power.

Though these sentences may accurately represent our two thoughts, they do not accurately represent the *relation* of our two thoughts. What we have in mind, and what we should accordingly write, is:

> I am glad to see the President powerful. But he has too much power.
>
> I am glad to see the President powerful, but I think he has too much power.

The first statement may be called positive, the second negative, subtracting something from the first, somewhat as $4 - 1 = 3$. The omission of a mere *but* may cause a whole passage to be obscure.

We have at our disposal three means of transition used within the paragraph. First, we may repeat a word or phrase used in a preceding sentence:

> The result was a conflict between the *Senate* and the President. A majority in the *Senate* believed that . . .

Secondly, we may use a reference word — a pronoun or demonstrative adjective:

> The result was a conflict between the Senate and the President. *Such* a situation is always fraught with . . .

Thirdly, we may use a transitional expression:

> The result was a conflict between the Senate and the President. *Thus* it happened that . . .
>
> The result was a conflict between the Senate and the President. *On the one hand*, the Senate held that . . .; *on the other hand*, the President held that . . .

Among the many transitional expressions are:

Addition: *moreover, further, furthermore, again, in addition, first, secondly* (etc.), *finally, lastly.*

Subtraction and Contrast: *but, yet, nevertheless, still, however, on the*

other hand, on the one hand . . . on the other hand, it is true, on the contrary, after all.
Comparison: *likewise, similarly.*
Coincidence: *equally important, meanwhile, in the meantime, at the same time, at the same place.*
Purpose: *for this purpose, to this end, with this object.*
Result: *hence, accordingly, consequently, thus.*
Emphasis: *indeed, in fact, in any event.*
Exemplification: *for example, for instance, thus.*
Summary: *in sum, to sum up, on the whole, in brief.*
Time: *at length, meanwhile, in the meantime, immediately.*
Place: *near by, beyond, adjacent to, opposite to.*

A good writer may be recognized by the skill with which he uses these several means of revealing relationships in thought — repetition of a key word or phrase, reference words, and transitional expressions.[1] Note the use of these means in the following passage, in which the links between sentences have been printed in capital letters; the links between parts of sentences, in italic type:

Actually, there was nothing particularly new about the principles of the ball-point pen. During the war, American fliers who had occasion to stop off in Argentina found BALL-POINT PENS in the shops there *and* brought back numbers of *them* to pass around as novelties among *their* friends. THESE PENS were the handiwork of Lászlo Jozsef Biro, a Hungarian *who* had been, at one time or another, a medical student, a painter, a sculptor, a hypnotist, a journalist, and a proofreader. BIRO, *who* felt the need of a BALL-POINT PEN after splaying innumerable fountain-pen points on newspaper proofs, made *one* in Paris and took out a patent on *it there* in 1939. Shortly AFTERWARD, HE moved to Buenos Aires, *and*, in 1943, *he* interested an English financier named Henry G. Martin, *who* had *also* moved to Buenos Aires, in backing the manufacture of the PEN on a modest scale. For THIS purpose, a company known as Eterpen S.A. was set up, with MARTIN at *its* head. The BIRO PEN differed from conventional fountain PENS in three important respects: *first*, instead of a nib *it* had a miniature socket *that* held a ball bearing one millimetre in diameter; *second*, instead of using ordinary ink *it* contained a gelatinous dye with an oil base *that*, rolled onto a writing surface by the ball bearing *it* at the same time lubricated,

[1] For a table of subordinating conjunctions used in linking parts of sentences, see pages 13–14.

dried almost instantly; *and, third, it* held enough of *this* unconventional INK to perform for several months without refilling. The special nature of the INK used in the PEN *also* enabled one to write with *it* at high altitudes without the risk of leakage that ordinary fountain PENS, because of the effect a change in atmospheric pressure has on liquid, have always been subject to. THIS particular advantage appealed to the Royal Air Force, *whose* bomber crews had been constantly plagued by leaky fountain PENS. BEFORE LONG, MARTIN *and* BIRO farmed out the British rights to a British aircraft company.[1]

Besides transition within the paragraph a writer must also clearly reveal the transition of his thought from one paragraph to another. He may use a *transitional sentence* linking one paragraph to the preceding paragraph or he may use a *transitional paragraph* linking one distinct division of his composition to another. In some cases a summarizing or outlining paragraph may reveal the relationship among the paragraphs that precede or follow. Study the following examples.

Transitional sentences

Having analyzed the benefits of the proposed plan, we will now study the disadvantages.

It is obvious, on the other hand, that our enemies are going to do their best to break through the economic blockade.

Transitional paragraph

Nevertheless, I want to point out to you certain strange characters in this goddess of yours. She differs from the great Greek and Medieval deities essentially in two things — first, as to the continuance of her presumed power; secondly, as to the extent of it. (RUSKIN)

Summarizing paragraph

In this division, then, three general periods have been touched upon: (1) that from the beginning to the dawn of civilization; (2) that from the fall of the Roman Empire to the flowering of the Renaissance; and (3) that from the rise of modern Europe to the present.

EXERCISES

A. List all the transitional expressions that occur in a theme or

[1] Thomas Whiteside in *The New Yorker*, February 17, 1951. Reprinted by permission. Copyright 1951, The New Yorker Magazine, Inc.

two that you have written, and compare them with the list on page 65.

B. Choose from the list on page 65 six transitional expressions that you rarely or never use, and write a passage, or several passages, in which you use them discriminately.

C. Copy two of the specimen paragraphs given on pages 51–62, and reveal the means of connection by underlining once the words and phrases that connect parts of sentences and twice those that connect sentences.

D. Clip from a newspaper an editorial in which connectives are used with skill. Underline as in Exercise C.

E. Write an editorial opinion (200 to 300 words), attacking or defending the present emphasis on "college activities," in which each sentence is linked with the preceding sentence or sentences. Underline twice the connecting words or phrases.

F. Write an editorial opinion on an assigned subject. Then underline once the words and phrases that connect parts of sentences and twice those that connect sentences.

G. Find and copy two examples of a transitional sentence used to link two paragraphs.

H. Find and copy one example of a purely transitional paragraph.

I. In order to review your knowledge of paragraph construction, analyze the following paragraphs by pointing out (1) the topic sentence, (2) the ampleness of substance used, (3) the methods of paragraph development used, (4) the kinds of order used, and (5) the means of transition between the sentences and paragraphs. For further practice in analyzing paragraphs, see the paragraphs in § 37e.

PARAGRAPH 19

From afar, outlanders regard southern politics as a comic opera staged on a grand scale for the amusement of the nation. They roared when Texans elected "Ma" Ferguson as their governor to serve as proxy for her husband, barred from office by earlier impeachment and conviction. They shuddered when Louisiana was ruled by Huey Long, a flamboyant advocate of the subversive doctrine of "Every Man A King." Yet he put on a good show. The connoisseurs of rabble-rousing relished the performances of Gene Talmadge, he of the "red galluses" and the persuasive way with the wool-hat boys. Bilbo's artistry in demagoguery excited, if not admiration, attention from beyond the hills of Mississippi. Alabama's "Big Jim" Folsom, the "kissing governor," Texas' W. Lee O'Daniel, flour salesman and hillbilly bandsman, South Carolina's "Cotton Ed" Smith, eloquent exponent of the virtues of southern womanhood, and other fabulous characters have trod the southern political stage to the accompaniment of hilarity — often derisive — from the other side of the Mason and Dixon line.[1]

Paragraph 20

Between chapters and appointments, on days when Miss Kellems is in New York and isn't lunching or dining with one of her numerous gentlemen admirers, she usually takes her meals alone in the coeducational dining room on the roof of the Yale Club, where she is a great favorite. One recent afternoon there, the headwaiter and three assistants hurried up to congratulate her on the outcome of her war with the United States, only to look suitably sympathetic when she explained a few minutes later that the trouble was, those grasping Washington characters were probably going to appeal. "But don't you worry about me, Alfred," she said, patting the headwaiter affectionately on the arm. "I'll take this case to the Supreme Court, if I have to. And, you know, even if I lose my case there, I'll win. Since I made all those speeches, the whole country's been fermenting like yeast on the subject of taxes, so if in the end I lose my case" — here her voice ascended effortlessly in the fervid crescendo of the practiced evangelist — "it will be a sign to the people. They will see the terrible truth for what it is and rise up against their tyrants. How's that famous black-bean soup today, Alfred?" She picked up a menu and, holding it at arm's length from her farsighted eyes, went on, "Of course, if they don't, if the people of this country, even the *women* of this country, don't have that much covered-wagon spirit left after all these years of claptrap paternalism — why, I'll just have to work out some other way to bring them to their senses. Don't you worry your head about it, Alfred," she said, baring her pearl-like teeth in a bright smile. "I'll think of *something*."[2]

[1] V. O. Key, *Southern Politics* (New York: Alfred A. Knopf, 1949). Reprinted by permission of the publisher.

[2] Andy Logan in *The New Yorker*, February 10, 1951. Reprinted by permission. Copyright 1951, The New Yorker Magazine, Inc.

PARAGRAPH 21

Behold the gem-strung towns and cities of the good, green East, flung like star-dust through the field of night. That spreading constellation to the north is called Chicago and that giant wink that blazes in the moon is the pendant lake that it is built upon. Beyond, close-set and dense as a clenched fist, are all the jeweled cities of the eastern seaboard. There's Boston, ringed with the bracelet of its shining little towns, and all the lights that sparkle on the rocky indentations of New England. Here, southward and a little to the west, and yet still coasted to the sea, is our intensest ray, the splintered firmament of the towered island of Manhattan. Round about her, sown thick as grain, is the glitter of a hundred towns and cities. The long chain of lights there is the necklace of Long Island and the Jersey shore. Southward and inland, by a foot or two, behold the duller glare of Philadelphia. Southward further still, the twin constellations — Baltimore and Washington. Westward, but still within the borders of the good, green East, that night-time glow and smolder of hell-fire is Pittsburgh. Here, St. Louis, hot and humid in the cornfield belly of the land, and bedded on the mid-length coil and fringes of the snake. There at the snake's mouth, southward six hundred miles or so, you see the jeweled crescent of old New Orleans. Here, west and south again, you see the gemmy glitter of the cities on the Texas border.[1]

PARAGRAPH 22

Everybody has several vocabularies. Which is merely saying in other words that each of us belongs to a number of communities. We talk in the bosom of our family in a way different from that in which we discourse on state occasions. I permit myself, in speaking to a body of students with whom I have come to stand in fairly close relations, a freedom in the use of colloquialisms which I should not indulge in, were I reading a formal paper before a learned society. The diction of a sermon is not quite that of an after-dinner speech. Nor do people write for the *British Quarterly* exactly as they write for *Punch*. We shift our vocabularies, as we pass from clothes to clothes, and for the same reason. The character of the occasion determines each. Moreover, there is an extensive tract common to all the vocabularies that we possess. We don't talk like a book at one time, and at another discard every word that might adorn the printed page. But we do, on grave or more formal occasions, draw largely on one element of our vocabulary; whereas, in the freedom of intimate circles, when the touch is light, our drafts are on an entirely different fund. Given the same subject-matter, and there are words which we are apt to use on

[1] Thomas Wolfe, *You Can't Go Home Again* (New York: Harper and Brothers, 1940). Reprinted by permission of the publisher.

this occasion, others on that; but there is a far larger residuum which we use on all. This is common experience, and needs no argument.[1]

PARAGRAPH 23

The situation in Greece was indeed an ugly one. There had been serious fighting in the streets of Athens involving British forces and members of the resistance groups which bore the initials E.A.M. and E.L.A.S. It was reported that some of the rebels had marched through the streets shouting, "Long Live Roosevelt!" American public opinion was not too well informed as to the merits of this complicated situation or the extent to which the resistance groups might be under Communist domination; all that was apparent on the surface was that British troops, engaged in the task of "liberation," were killing Greek patriots who had been fighting the Germans, and it was even possible that the British were using American Lend-Lease weapons for this purpose.[2]

PARAGRAPH 24

Yet it ought to be plain that no one would wish to censure Lowell merely because of his unionist sympathies. Supporting that faction was natural enough to New England residents of his day. But Lowell was a public figure, the voice of a large segment of his region, and his blindness to the underlying causes of the sectional struggle, his refusal to face the issue at all except in terms of a glib morality, would seem to suggest a fundamental limitation in his nature which every responsible student of his career is bound to notice. He never understood history, in any important way, despite his many references to it. He never comprehended politics, although the most instructive commentary upon the nature of political action ever available to an American had been enacted before his eyes in the published utterances of Webster, Clay, Calhoun, Cushing, Davis, Choate, and a host of other contemporary figures. Moreover, Harvard scholar though he was, he never made any effort worth mentioning to understand the civilization of the South. He proved himself, from his undergraduate days, a dupe of the most irresponsible propaganda his age afforded. He even became, as we have seen, an ardent and continuous manufacturer of it. In somewhat more technical terms, one feels compelled to term him, in simple honesty, the most completely didactic major author in American literature.[3]

[1] John Livingston Lowes, *Convention and Revolt in Poetry* (Boston: Houghton Mifflin Company, 1919). Reprinted by permission of the publisher.

[2] Robert E. Sherwood, *Roosevelt and Hopkins* (New York: Harper and Brothers, 1948). Reprinted by permission of the publisher.

[3] Richmond Croom Beatty, *James Russell Lowell* (Nashville: Vanderbilt University Press, 1942). Reprinted by permission of the publisher.

Themes and Thinking

A whole is that which has beginning, middle, and end. — ARISTOTLE

In the whole composition there should be no word written of which the tendency, direct or indirect, is not to the one pre-established design. — POE

The word *theme* has two common meanings: (1) the subject of a speech, a piece of writing, or a musical composition, and (2) a short piece of writing, an essay. To many students a theme is a composition written solely to be graded by an instructor, an artificial piece of writing which will never reach its natural readers. Although it is true that most "themes" written in composition classes never get into books or magazines, they should be regarded as genuine efforts to inform, persuade, or impress particular readers. Every theme should be written as if it were a letter with a definite purpose, or an editorial trying to impress a specific audience, or an explanation which will make something clear to certain readers. In this book a *theme* is considered to be any kind of short written composition with a definite object. It includes arguments such as you might present to a student council or a state legislature; expositions like those you must write in such courses as history, political science, sociology, and biology; letters applying for jobs or asking for information; reports of events such as newspaper stories or records of meetings; directions such as military briefings written to guide other people accurately and fully; and even fiction written to hold the attention of discriminating readers. Ideally, every theme should be an effort to accomplish something of immediate importance to the writer; in practice, however, it is usually necessary to regard each assignment *as if* it were a real-life problem to be solved by writing, by communicating with others. When you write in a composition course, try to approach each assignment as you would a writing problem away from the college classroom, just as a musician goes through a dress rehearsal as if the audience were seated before him. Remember that students of engineering have to work out problems of design, student lawyers have to prepare cases for mock courts, medical students have to dissect animal bodies, business students have to prepare classroom profit and loss statements, just as football players have to scrimmage in preparation for official games. Learning to write by writing themes is no more artificial than the exercises which train you in other courses in college.

SUBSTANCE — GATHERING MATERIAL

Composing a piece of writing is not the same problem for a person who writes because he has something to say as it is for a person who writes because he has to write something. If you have a body of facts or a set of arguments and a purpose for communicating them to someone else, your problem is presentation — organization, sentence and paragraph structure, and diction. You are not faced with having to find something to say, except that you may need to find additional facts to fill out a general statement. For example, if you have witnessed a traffic accident at an intersection where there is no stop sign, or inspected a slum district, or noticed neglect of the animals in a zoo, or discovered favoritism in local law enforcement, you may be impelled to write a letter to a newspaper or to a public official. You would have most or all of your substance — the meat of your communication — although you might have to look up a law or ask for some information to make your protest more effective.

On the other hand, we all have to write on occasions when we have to look for something to write. If a high school friend asks you to write him about a particular curriculum at your college which you know nothing about, if an employer sends you to inspect a store or a construction job and write a report on it, if an instructor assigns you a book to read and report on, if you are appointed to rewrite a student organization's constitution, you would not have the substance of your writing already at hand. You would have to seek substance before you could write. Listening to lectures, studying textbooks, working laboratory problems, reading collateral assignments, asking questions and discussing moot points in class, and thinking about the subject matter of a college course are all methods of gathering substance. When you come to write answers to examination questions, you put this substance to use in a practical writing exercise.

The substance of a paper, as of a paragraph, may come to you in various ways: you may start with a general notion and dig up details to fill it out; or you may amass details first and then reach a generalization; or you may start with a generalization and change it after you have collected factual information.

For example, suppose that you are preparing to write a letter to your parents or your dean explaining why you are not making progress in certain courses. It may occur to you that these courses are the ones which meet on Saturdays, and, since Saturday classes have more holidays than other classes, you might decide that your lack of progress is due to the smaller number of class meetings. Before writing the letter, you might examine the college calendar and count the actual number of holidays in the term, comparing the number that fall on Saturday with those on other days. This is acquiring substance — facts, evidence. Or, suppose that you wonder whether your favorite newspaper is presenting both sides of a vital issue: a bond election, a labor dispute, or a political campaign. You might make a systematic study of the fairness of presentation, or compare your newspaper with another in the region, trying to discover whether or not the paper is unbiased. This is seeking facts — substance for a report or a letter to the editor. Again, suppose you know that the women in your college make higher average grades than the men and assume that women are inherently brighter in school than men. But before writing this conclusion you make an actual study of the situation and find that the women average fewer hours in athletics and school activities and that the women's dormitories have more rigid study hours than the men's dormitories, and as a result conclude that the women make higher grades because they put in more hours studying than the men do. This is acquiring substance, both facts and a new conclusion.

No one way of finding substance is best for all writers or all subjects. Some people are more observant than others, some have better memories than others, some are more curious than others, some reflect more than others on what they see and hear, asking such questions as Why? How long? What is the cause? What is the effect? How does that differ from this? Would it be true elsewhere? Is this general? Has it always been thus? Is it important? Who is affected? In what way? Is it an end or a means? If a means, is it efficient? How does one judge it? Can it be verified? By what test? Some people think best by beginning with tentative conclusions and modifying or discarding them as the facts are gathered and relations observed. Others think best by first gathering all the available facts and then trying various conclusions to fit the facts. Since thinking, and hence writing, is the product of interactions between human nervous systems and the impressions received from the outside world, and since every human being is unique, it is impossible to expect everybody to see the same things or to reflect in the same way about anything. It is a common experience to compare the reports of two people on trips they have made or incidents they have observed and to find that one apparently saw much more than the other. The person who sees less has the harder problem in finding substance for writing, but he can practice looking for more, especially by reading, to find out where and how other writers have found their material.

See pages 224–225 and § 39a, for other approaches to choosing a subject and gathering material.

EXERCISES

A. Expand one of the paragraphs assigned on page 63 into a composition of several paragraphs; seek additional information if necessary, and think about comparisons, causes, effects, and alternatives.

B. Select the topics in the following list on which you already have sufficient information to write an informative paper of 500 or 800 words.

Figure skating	Cigarette advertising
Filibustering	National political conventions
Stamp collecting	Selective service

Tourist courts	Changes in men's clothing
Ballet dancing	Changes in automobile styles
Finger painting	Training animals

C. Select one of the topics in Exercise B on which you can get information by talking with a friend. After consulting the friend, write an informational paper of 500 to 800 words.

D. Select one of the topics in Exercise B on which you can get information by consulting an encyclopedia or other reference work. After looking up the subject, write an informational paper of 500 to 800 words.

E. Assume that the editor of your college paper has asked you to write an editorial asking for some reform which you, as an entering freshman, feel is needed at your college. Write the editorial (addressing it specifically to school authorities, faculty, or upperclass students).

F. Before attempting to write a paper on any of the topics listed below, ask yourself such questions as these: What information (demonstrable, verified facts) do I have on the subject? Will my readers accept my facts as true and relevant? Do my feelings or personal interests affect my opinions? What facts or conditions would cause me to change my attitude or opinion? Can people who are just as honest and well-informed as I disagree with my opinions?

1. The increase of crime. (Has crime actually increased? Where? What crimes? Over what period? Evidence?)
2. Subsidized athletics. (In what schools? What kinds of subsidies? Reasons for subsidies? Benefits? To whom? Evils? To whom?)
3. Complexity in art. (Does a work of art have to be complex to be good? Definition of good? In whose opinion? Are no good works of art simple? Definition of complex? Of simple? Is taste involved? Is complexity measurable? By what standard?)
4. The right to strike. (Who has the right? Who grants it? Is it limited? How? By whom? What is a right? Who enforces rights? Everywhere? At all times?)
5. The French Radical-Socialist party. (Age of the party? Platform? Who are the leaders? Size of membership? Strength in national

legislature? Growing or declining? Is the party progressive? Conservative? Source of my information?)

6. Representational art. (Must a picture accurately represent something? Why? Can a picture accurately represent? Is taste involved? What is taste? What is its origin?)
7. Happy endings. (Are stories and movies with happy endings popular? With what audiences? Why? Are happy endings unpopular? Why? With what audiences? Do all good plots have happy endings? Unhappy endings? Examples? Should the ending be appropriate to the plot? To the characters? What determines appropriateness?)
8. Minority rights. (What is a minority? How determined? Race? Meaning of race? Nationality? Occupation? Religion? Common ancestry? Skin color? Political beliefs? Common traditions? Source of rights? Are they violated? To my knowledge? Instances? Are they protected? Evidence?)
9. Propaganda. (Definition? Good? Bad? Examples? Effects? Proof of effects? Used by political parties? Charitable organizations? Churches? Nations? Candidates? Business firms? Unions?)
10. Value of the dollar. (How measured? Same from year to year? Are people better off when dollar is cheap? When it is dear? Meaning of *better off?* What people? Evidence?)

G. Other subjects which could be used, and which demand evidence and careful thinking, are as follows: man's intelligence over the past twenty centuries, lawyers' ethics, science versus religion, advertisers and editorial policy, public housing, campaign speeches, business ethics, public power development, farm subsidies, protective tariffs, jury duty, the closed shop, bombing of civilians in war, ownership of tidelands oil, poll taxes, and public medical insurance.

ORDER

In endeavoring to give form to substance, we must have before us, first and last, a definite plan. A theme of only one or two paragraphs may be planned mentally, but a longer one should always be planned on paper. Otherwise, we shall probably waste much energy in writing passages that must be discarded, in trying to move paragraphs into the positions demanded by logic, and in presenting important matter that we have forgotten, the total result being, despite our pains, a lame, straggling procession of half-formed thoughts. The easiest procedure is to prepare in advance a clear outline and to keep it before us as we write.

Suppose, to take a simple example, you were asked to write a paper on electric appliances for housekeeping. You might jot down, as you think of them, items to make a list like this:

stove	coffee maker	ironer
refrigerator	fruit juicer	vacuum cleaner
washing machine	food mixer	water heater
clothes drier	food chopper	deep freeze
waffle iron	toaster	

Obviously, such a list is merely haphazard; you could not write an orderly paper by taking up the items as they appear above. Examining the list, you would notice that some of the appliances mentioned are for the kitchen and others are for laundering and cleaning. Rearranging them, you would get the following groups:

I. Kitchen aids	II. Laundering and cleaning aids
stove	washing machine
refrigerator	clothes drier
waffle iron	ironer
coffee maker	vacuum cleaner
fruit juicer	water heater
food mixer	
food chopper	
toaster	
deep freeze	

More study would show you that the kitchen appliance group can be further re-grouped into appliances for (1) food preservation, (2) food preparation, and (3) cooking. Making this rearrangement, you would produce the following outline, which has order, system:

Electric Appliances for Housekeeping

I. Laundering and cleaning aids

A. Water heater
B. Vacuum cleaner
C. Washing machine
D. Clothes drier
E. Ironer

II. Kitchen aids
- A. For food preservation
  1. Refrigerator
  2. Deep freeze
- B. For food preparation
  1. Fruit juicer
  2. Food mixer
  3. Food chopper
- C. For cooking
  1. Stove
  2. Coffee maker
  3. Toaster
  4. Waffle iron

No matter whether your paper is a brief one-paragraph cataloguing of the appliances or a long discussion of the types and uses of appliances, following such an outline will enable you to go from subtopic to subtopic in an orderly progress, keeping related matters together and unrelated matters separated.

The principle by which one body of material is ordered may not suit another. The writer's problem each time is to find a way to break down his subject into distinct parts that relate to each other and can be arranged according to some plan. The household appliances were arranged analytically, according to types and subtypes. In another paper, say a news story or an autobiography, the order would probably be narrative, taking up events as they occurred. A similar order would be used in a paper describing a process, such as baking a cake or assembling an M1 rifle. In a paper presenting a series of arguments, as for or against college fraternities, the points might be arranged in the order of climax, from weakest to strongest.

Analytical order is the most difficult, because it offers no simple criterion like events in time or subtopics of increasing importance. It may take up a series of causes or effects, or may go from cause to effect. It may subdivide a topic or it may elaborate a statement by a series of facts or examples. Frequently it represents a combination of such arrangements.

While writing out the theme, we are to remember that there is a difference between having order and revealing order. A long theme might conceivably have order even if written without paragraph divisions or transitions between paragraphs, but its order could scarcely be apparent to the reader. To render its order obvious, we must construct a series of paragraphs which, like the parts of a living creature, shall be harmoniously adjusted and linked with one another. "A master of the art of transition," as A. S. Hill put it, "begins and ends each paragraph so as to make it grow out of the last and into the next; he moves so easily and naturally that the reader follows without being aware of the steps he is taking."[1] Every new paragraph marks some sort of step in the onward movement of the thought, but precisely what sort of step it is should be indicated by a transitional word, phrase, or sentence. If we have been discussing, for instance, the possible benefits of federal aid to state and city schools, and wish to take up the disadvantages, we should not abruptly shift the point of view but rather indicate plainly that we are leaving one phase of the subject and taking up another. The new paragraph might begin

But there are dangers in federal aid to schools.

Or In spite of these advantages, however, there are serious disadvantages.

Or These advantages must be balanced against some well known disadvantages.

If possible, link every paragraph with the one preceding.

See § 36 for instructions and examples on outlining; see pp. 64–68 and § 89 for transition.

EXERCISES

A. Plan mentally a theme of one paragraph on the topic, two reasons for studying history. Using the same topic, plan mentally a theme of two paragraphs. Then plan mentally a theme of three paragraphs on three reasons for studying history, paying due attention to the order of the reasons.

B. After a class discussion of a subject such as college loyalty,

[1] *The Principles of Rhetoric* (1895), p. 239.

jot down a list of topics that were considered, exactly in the order in which you remember them. Then write a preliminary plan by reordering these topics.

C. Rewrite the following plan in such a manner as to prevent overlapping of topics and to secure a satisfactory order of topics. Whenever possible, use the parallel construction. Rephrase at will. See § 36 for instructions on outlining.

A Campaign to Reduce Crime

I. Church recreation programs
II. Civic organizations
III. Revision of laws
IV. Churches
V. Women's club projects
VI. Sermons
VII. Improved law enforcement
VIII. Men's luncheon club projects
IX. City officials

D. Write a list of topics for a theme on an assigned subject, using the order of climax.

E. Write a list of topics for a theme on a given subject, using the chronological order.

F. Write a list of topics for a descriptive theme, using the order of progress from place to place.

G. Make preliminary plans for themes on several of the following topics, using subheadings when they appear to be needed and considering carefully the most effective order. Be prepared to name the kind of order you have chosen and the kind of reader you had in mind.

Current magazines
The Truman administration
Ballet dancing
College baseball
An ideal vacation
Labor-saving machines
Should college athletes be paid?
The best age to marry
Jim Crow laws
Euthanasia
Does television hurt football?
Does television hurt reading?

H. Write a theme of four paragraphs, giving special attention to the transitions between paragraphs. When you have finished, double underline the means of connection between paragraphs.

I. Study a given passage of prose with special reference to the transitions between paragraphs.

PROPORTION

That the parts of a composition should follow one another in orderly sequence is not enough; they must also be correctly proportioned according to their relative values. Our writing should clearly show what is important in our thinking and should subordinate the unimportant. What is slight in our estimation we should discuss briefly, perhaps merely mention; what is significant we should dwell upon till we have proved it to be significant; what is of the utmost importance we should treat so fully that the reader cannot mistake our valuation of it. A short story should not begin with an introduction out of proportion to what follows, or hasten over the situation round which the story revolves. An expository article must not spin out matters that are relatively subordinate, nor treat sketchily the facts or ideas that are fundamental to an understanding of the subject.

This law of proportion may seem simple; but in practice it offers difficulties. In the first place, importance may be of two kinds: importance in relation to the subject and importance in relation to the reader. If we are writing a piece of pure exposition, say an account (as for an encyclopedia) of the system of national government in the United States, we should treat the various divisions and subdivisions of the government in proportion to their importance in the system. If, on the other hand, our exposition is partly or wholly argumentative in purpose, as in a letter to a newspaper in favor of a certain political candidate, we should emphasize those arguments most likely to impress the readers of the newspaper in view. Or, if we are discussing convention in college life, we may safely give less space to dress (perhaps one short paragraph) than to manners (one long paragraph at least), for the former is not only less important in itself but would be so regarded by almost any audience except a convention of clothing manufacturers. Similarly, writing for student readers, we may give less space (say three paragraphs) to the topic of study than to the topic of opinion (say five paragraphs). Though our parents and a large part of the faculty might think differently, most American students are likely to be less impressed with a discussion of their habits of study and their attitude toward study than with a discussion which argued that many of their opinions and even convictions are purely imitative. Proportion would here demand an extended discussion of the latter topic, which might be conducted in this fashion: 1st paragraph, How opinion is formed (with many instances); 2nd paragraph, An example; 3rd paragraph, Another example; 4th paragraph, Another example; 5th paragraph, How opinion should be formed (with examples). Coming at the close of the theme, that is, in the most emphatic position, this final series of paragraphs should produce a strong effect.

What has just been said brings us to another practical difficulty in observing the law of proportion — the difficulty of sustaining or intensifying effort toward the close of a composition. In practice, the last third or fourth of a composition is likely to be the weakest; it is easy to rush on, without regard to proportion and emphasis, because time is short or the job is getting tiresome or boring. Try to remember that the effect of a piece of writing is normally cumulative, that we should sustain our effort and if possible intensify it as the goal looms in sight, and that a reader's final impression depends less on how you begin than how you follow through.

EXERCISES

A. Selecting three topics from the list given in Exercise G, page 81, write out plans in which each heading and subheading is followed with an indication, in parentheses, of the number of paragraphs or the number of words which would give your paper satisfactory proportion.

B. Study a piece of effective expository writing, observing the apportioning of the space, particularly in the last third or fourth of the selection. You can do this with tolerable accuracy by making a list of the paragraph topics, noting into what groups they fall, and determining how many paragraphs each topic occupies.

BEGINNING AND ENDING

Many centuries ago Aristotle pointed out that a whole is that which has beginning, middle, and end. This does not mean, however, that a whole composition must have an introduction, a body, and a conclusion — a formal scheme that is applicable only in rare cases, such as a report, thesis, or book exceptionally complex or abstruse. In most instances the introductions and conclusions of themes are not vital parts of the whole organism but merely arbitrary appendages attached mechanically. What Aristotle had in mind is, rather, that the subject must be progressively unfolded from a beginning to an end. We are to begin at the beginning, not before; to end at the end, not after.

To begin at the beginning is not so easy as to begin with an introduction or to ramble lazily into the subject. Successful writers use a variety of methods of starting, according to the nature of the subject and the audience.

1. Oftenest, they make a prompt beginning by taking up at once the first division of the subject, with perhaps a phrase referring to the subject as a whole. Thus:

> Of all the modern weapons of war, the planned spreading of disease in a civilian population is the most repugnant.

2. Often the first sentence is used to connect the topic with the reader's knowledge or experience:

> We all know that there are people who want a college degree but not a college education.

3. Sometimes the writer begins by trying to anticipate and disarm opposition:

> Although opponents of loyalty oaths for teachers are sometimes accused of being subversive, any open-minded person will have to grant that the overwhelming majority of teachers who oppose such oaths are loyal, patriotic citizens.

4. Or the writer begins by trying to rouse the reader's interest, using a startling or paradoxical statement, a quotation, or an incident involving suspense.

> The real subversives are often the loudest patriots.
>
> "All we have to fear," said Mr. Roosevelt, "is fear itself."
>
> One cold night in 1950, just after the Chinese Communists had entered the Korean scrap, a hard-eyed girl in a man's topcoat came into the diner near the campus where we usually had coffee. She was alone but she wasn't nervous She walked toward our table.

Remember that the beginning should not puzzle the reader. It should lead him by easy stages from indifference to interest; it should attract him, not repel him; and it should point clearly toward what is to follow.

The driver who signals with his hand and pulls his car over to the curb when he reaches his destination is doing more than merely stopping; he is bringing his trip to an end. Likewise the writer is expected to bring his writing to an end, not merely stop. If a reader turns your last page over, looking for what follows, you have not properly brought your writing to a conclusion. A short paper can be effectively ended with one sentence; a longer paper frequently needs a concluding paragraph. Study the following examples of sentences which indicate that there is no more to be written:

> To summarize, we recognize your problem but we insist that no agreement can be reached until the insurance rate is reduced.
>
> And these concessions should indicate the company's desire to sign a contract immediately.
>
> In the face of these objections, we cannot see how the governor could continue to insist on the appointment.
>
> In the last building the bottles are labeled and packed in cartons, ready for shipment to grocery stores all over the country.

EXERCISES

A. Examine the following books, or others assigned by your instructor, to determine whether the opening and closing paragraphs fulfill their functions: Charles Darwin, *The Origin of Species;* H. G. Wells, *The Outline of History;* Otto Jespersen, *Essentials of*

English Grammar; George R. Stewart, *Names on the Land;* Henry Adams, *The Education of Henry Adams;* H. L. Mencken, *Prejudices;* Clarence Day, *Life With Father;* Robert M. Hutchins, *No Friendly Voice;* and Stuart Chase, *The Tyranny of Words.*

B. Study and classify the methods of beginning and ending used by the authors of five articles in current magazines.

C. Write three different openings for a paper on one of the subjects suggested in Exercise F, on page 76.

D. Compare two essays from books or magazines assigned by the instructor to determine (1) how the authors obtained the substance of their writings, (2) the kinds of transition used, (3) the relative proportion of the various parts, (4) the order of the parts, and (5) the methods of beginning and ending.

E. Repeat Exercise D, using two different selections assigned by the instructor.

F. Make an outline of each of two selections assigned by the instructor to determine the order and proportion of the parts.

Book Two

A HANDBOOK OF REVISION

CORRECTNESS

EFFECTIVENESS

LETTER WRITING

PRÉCIS WRITING

To the Student

Book Two, the "Handbook of Revision," is organized under 101 rules in bold type, the titles of which are listed inside the front cover. These rules are not laws for your instructor to accuse you of violating; very few of them tell you what not to do. They are positive suggestions on details of writing, carefully phrased and illustrated to help you revise and improve your written communication.

Whenever your instructor writes a number in the margin of your paper, study the rule so numbered in this book. Rule numbers appear at the top of the pages; page numbers at the bottom. If a rule contains a term that you do not understand after reading the discussion under it, consult the Grammatical Terms, § 16.

Follow these directions in revising your papers:

1. After studying the numbered rule, rewrite the sentence or passage marked by your instructor. If the reference is to a general rule, such as 20 or 73, try to find the specific rule, such as 20b or 73a, that will help you. Add the letter for the specific rule after the number written on your paper by the instructor.

2. If after studying the rule and your sentence you do not understand how to make the revision, put a question mark by the number on your paper and consult the instructor before you attempt to make the improvement.

3. Whenever your instructor underscores the number which he writes, copy the boldfaced rule on your paper.

4. Whenever your instructor writes an Ex. after the number in the margin of your theme, you are not only to refer to the rule and revise your theme, but also to write the exercise which follows the rule or is found at the end of that section. If more than one exercise follows the rule, you are, in the absence of instructions to the contrary, to write the first exercise (lettered A). If you are to write one of the other exercises, you will be referred to that exercise by means of its letter (for example, Ex. B or Ex. C). Always enclose the exercise when you return the theme, or file it with the corrected theme in your notebook, according to instructions.

5. You should tabulate the number of times you are referred to each rule. This tabulation is almost certain to show that you need to study and restudy certain rules, and that you evidently have no trouble with numerous other matters taken up in the handbook. By identifying the points on which you should concentrate, you reduce the problem of improving your writing to a few important matters that require intensive drill.

Correctness

GRAMMAR

Grammar is the systematic description of speech habits. English grammar is the description of the speech habits of people who speak English. Since the languages of the world display great variety in their structure and often have little in common, there is no basic *grammar* applying to all languages. A grammarian who wishes to compile a grammar of a language (or a dialect) must record the language of the speakers, then analyze and codify the speech features. His description is conventionally written as a set of "rules." Since speech habits change in time, grammars have to be rewritten to keep up to date, just as maps have to be revised to keep up with shifting coast lines, changes in river beds, and the creation of lakes and canals.

Historical grammar compares the language of a people at one time with the language used at another time, for example the English of 1952 with the English of 1600, or the English of 1400 with the English of 1066. *Comparative grammar* compares the rules of two different languages of the same period or even two dialects of one language.

The scientific grammarian is expected to describe truthfully and usefully the speech habits that actually occur, not to "improve" the language, just as the map-maker is not expected to "improve" the shape of an ocean.

The college freshman who has spoken English since childhood

may well ask why he should study English grammar if grammarians do nothing more than describe speech habits. There are several valid reasons for such study, all based on the fundamental fact that there are many kinds of English. First, there are two major types, standard and nonstandard. *Standard English* denotes the language of cultivated people, the people who carry on the affairs of the English-speaking world in the arts and sciences, in business and the professions. *Nonstandard English* denotes the English of people with little formal education. Nonstandard forms like *I seen 'em* and *He ain't got none* may be emphatic and efficient in communication, but they bring on the user powerful social disapproval in standard-English circles.

In both types there are geographical varieties. Standard British has many expressions which differ from Standard American. And in both types there are numerous *functional varieties.* There are occasions when standard speakers write informally, speak formally, speak slangily, write formally, or speak informally, just as there are occasions when nonstandard speakers vary their speech from formal to informal, from pretentious to familiar. The use of language is not the same in pulpit speech, scientific writing, business letters, familiar letters, platform reading, casual conversation, school recitations, college lectures, and sports broadcasting. These and many other occasions demand different functional varieties, all of which may be standard English. What the college freshman needs to learn is not how to construct sentences like *The roof leaks* or *Did he go?* (which he already knows), but to identify and eliminate occasional nonstandard forms, and especially to recognize and use appropriately the expressions that are characteristic of certain functional varieties. It is precisely like learning what clothes to wear for such varied activities as fishing, graduation exercises, swimming, formal weddings, tea dances, church services, selling bonds, and automobile repairing.

This book does not include a full, systematic description of the English language such as can be found in the comprehensive grammars listed in the Bibliography (page 333). A comprehensive account would be necessary for foreigners learning English, but would be superfluous for a college freshman whose vernacular is English. There are hundreds of rules of English grammar, such as the requirement of *the* before river names and formation of questions like *Do you sing?* rather than *Sing you?* that are not mentioned because all of us obey these rules without ever learning them. The only rules needed by the native speaker are those covering *divided usage*, that is, expressions which differ between types or between functional varieties.

The Handbook of Revision which follows is designed to help the student (1) eliminate occasional nonstandard speech features which bring disfavor among cultivated people, (2) distinguish between forms peculiar to various functional varieties of standard English, especially between written and spoken forms, and (3) improve the effectiveness of his use of language. To analyze and discuss language, the instructor and student must have a common technical vocabulary, including such terms as *case, clause,* and *predication,* just as a golfer taking lessons needs such terms as *driver, divot,* and *par.*

Labels

In the pages which follow, numerous examples are cited to make clear the rules. These examples are preceded by labels (in italic type) of three kinds: (1) labels which refer to efficient communication or to accepted conventions of writing: *clear, vague, inaccurate, revised, right, wrong, misleading;* (2) labels which refer to style: *awkward, improved, unemphatic, emphatic, stilted;* (3) labels which indicate usage: *nonstandard, standard, colloquial, informal, formal, provincial.* The first two types are self-explanatory, but the third requires definition.

Nonstandard is applied to words and constructions which are characteristic of substandard usage and which subject the user to social disadvantage. Examples are "They brung it theirselves" and "Me and her was here." Although most such expressions are old in the language and may be in very widespread use, they are certain to handicap the user when he mingles on equal terms with speakers of standard English. A law student who works as a part-time taxi driver to earn money would not lose fares if he habitually said *I seen it,* but he would be at a serious disadvantage in law school and later in his professional and social life because of his nonstandard English. Most nonstandard English is culturally substandard, but nonstandard includes some features, such as accepted localisms, occasional archaic terms, and baby talk, which are sometimes used (ordinarily in familiar conversation) by speakers with education and cultural prestige, and which are thus not substandard. Nonstandard grammar and diction can and should be drilled out of the English of any student who expects to live and work comfortably among college graduates.

Standard English is the English used in addresses, conferences, court trials, sermons, interviews, lectures, and conversations by educated scientists, business and professional people, artists, journalists, and others who have prestige in our society. Standard written English is the normal language of our books, magazines, newspapers, reports, business letters, and similar written and printed matter. It is the kind of English which is socially acceptable and which passes unnoticed among the best-educated people. Any expression labeled *standard* in this book is one which, according to the evidence most recently collected by professional students of English, educated people can use without worry about its "correctness."

Because people who use standard English do not speak exactly as they write, and do not use exactly the same kinds of language on all occasions, it is necessary to label several functional varieties of standard English.

Formal is the label applied to standard words and expressions which are characteristic of the most dignified kinds of writing. Scientific and scholarly expositions, sober reflective and critical essays, legal documents, serious literature (except, of course, in passages of dialogue), reference books and most textbooks, and magazines edited for small, highly educated audiences are normally written in formal English. Formal expressions are always alternatives of less formal standard expressions. Both *to fix dinner* and *to prepare dinner* are standard; the latter is formal. Both *doesn't* and *does not* are standard; the latter is formal. See §§ 7b, 8b, 11, 13a, 14b, and 15 for additional examples. Remember that *formal* English is a special kind of standard English, typical of writing and some speaking about serious subjects and on serious occasions.

Informal is the label applied to standard English words and constructions which are characteristic of many books, magazine articles, and other writings addressed to the general public. Informal English is less dignified and more relaxed than formal English; it employs more contractions (especially *-n't* forms) and fewer highbrow words; and it is more likely than formal English to have short, simple clauses and more personal references. Remember that *informal* English is a special variety of standard English used when the subject and the occasion call for language which is neither highly dignified nor casual and conversational.

Colloquial is the label applied to language which is typical of easy conversation. Personal letters, dialogue in fiction, and such writings as newspaper reports of sports events and popular entertainment are commonly colloquial in tone. Many editorial writers, book reviewers, and business letter writers deliberately make their style light and intimate by the use of conversational idioms which would be glaringly out of place in sober essays on serious subjects. Some characteristics of colloquial English are loose sentence structure; slang; many contractions, such as *I've, we're, she's;* references to people by their first names; frequent elliptical constructions and fragmentary sentences; and avoidance of learned words. All terms labeled *colloquial* in this book are standard English, but are by no means appropriate in all kinds of writing.

Provincial is the label applied to expressions which are common in particular parts of the country, but which are normally avoided in writings addressed to general readers. See § 51.

Labeling a word or construction does not mean that the expression is absolutely limited to one kind of English or that it must be used in particular kinds of writing. For example, the word *cute* is usually labeled colloquial, but a serious reviewer might refer to an author's *cuteness* (meaning his inappropriate cleverness) in a formal book review. And there are many people who prefer *cunning* or *attractive* or some other word, avoiding *cute* even in intimate conversation. Some people are habitually formal in dress, manners, and speech regardless of the occasion; others are casual and informal on almost every occasion. Labels indicate the usual connotation of an expression; the writer's style often determines the appropriateness.

Standard English

Common Standard

Most of the grammar and vocabulary shared by educated speakers and writers – used for communication on all kinds of occasions – not marked with restrictive labels in dictionaries — labeled *standard* in this book

Functional varieties of written standard:

TECHNICAL	COLLOQUIAL	INFORMAL	FORMAL
Books and journal articles by experts for experts	Dialogue and writings that are conversational in tone	Books and periodicals for general readers	Serious, dignified books and articles
Informal or formal grammar, technical nomenclature, factual tone	Simple sentence structure, many contractions, popular words, much slang	Modern, relaxed sentence structure, familiar words, occasional slang, some contractions and ellipses	Conservative grammar, sober tone, learned vocabulary, rhetorical effects, no contractions, few ellipses
Typical words:	**Typical words:**	**Typical words:**	**Typical words:**
homophone	cute	doesn't	does not
isomeric	dopey	highbrow	intellectual
nodical	hipped	movie	motion picture
photoelectric	could've	run down	dilapidated
trochee	she'd	stingy	miserly
usufruct	gimmick	tired	fatigued
voltammeter	whopper		

Nonstandard English

Nonstandard and standard English share many features (else communication between many doctors and their patients, many lawyers and their clients, would be impossible), but nonstandard English has certain characteristic features: past tenses like *brung*, *throwed*, *swang*, *come*, and *done;* double negatives like *he never got nothing* and *it don't help nobody;* pronouns like *youse*, *we'uns*, and *theirselves;* numerous localisms and much archaic grammar (most of which are culturally substandard).

Sentence Defined

In English a sentence is a word or a group of grammatically related words which is not contained in a larger construction.[1] In speech it may be preceded and followed by silence; in writing it stands alone, normally beginning with a capital letter and ending with a period, exclamation point, or question mark. Scientific grammarians classify English sentences in two types: first, major sentence (commonly called *complete sentence*), which contains both a subject and a predicate and is grammatically independent; second, minor sentence (commonly called *fragment*), which may be a word, phrase, or clause that is not part of a larger construction. Examples of complete sentences (normal in written English) are:

The cost of living has risen. She left this morning.

Examples of fragments (common in spoken English) are:

Fore! Not now. Coming? Next window, please. All aboard.
The more the merrier. Two tickets to *Othello.*

Fragments are not necessarily incorrect. However, before the student can decide whether a fragment is appropriate in a piece of writing he must be able to distinguish between complete sentences and fragments. He must be able to identify phrases, verbals, dependent clauses, and independent clauses. Trying to discuss and improve writing without recognizing these elements is like trying to repair a radio without knowing the difference between a tube and a condenser.

1. Learn to distinguish readily between sentence and phrase, between sentence and clause, and between independent clause and dependent clause.

Compare the following groups of grammatically related words:[1]

Although William is registered for eighteen hours.
He can take another course.

The first group is not a complete sentence. True, it has a subject (*William*) and a predicate (*is registered*), but it is a dependent

[1] See § 16 for a definition of *related words* and other grammatical terms.

clause. *Although* and similar conjunctions always mark a dependent clause.

The second group is a complete sentence. It has a subject and a predicate: it does not have an introductory subordinating conjunction to make the clause dependent. Grammatically it does stand alone. Although the pronoun *he* refers to an antecedent outside the sentence, the context (here the preceding clause) makes the sentence complete. The antecedent may be expressed in the verbal context (as above), or it may be implicit in the situation (as when one person points to another and says, "He was here first"). Thus *He can take another course* and *He was here first* are complete independent sentences.

Except for minor sentence types considered on page 102 every sentence must contain (1) a subject and (2) a predicate. The predicate must include a verb capable of making a complete and independent assertion, that is, a *finite verb.* A finite verb must be carefully distinguished from a *verbal*, a nonfinite verb form which cannot predicate independently or completely. The difference between finite verbs and verbals may be illustrated:

The sun *rising* over the horizon (verbal — not a sentence).
Rising slowly over the horizon (verbal — not a sentence).
To rise over the horizon (verbal — not a sentence).
The sun *rises* (finite verb — a sentence).
The sun *rose* over the horizon (finite verb — a sentence).

Verbals are of several kinds. A verbal noun (*gerund* or *infinitive*) is a word derived from a verb but used as a *noun*. A verbal adjective (*participle*) is a word derived from a verb but used as an *adjective*. Verbal nouns and adjectives differ from other nouns and adjectives in derivation, not in function. To the writer of sentences, the use is what matters. Consider the use of the words printed in italics in the following sentences:

The man *runs* up the hill every morning.
Running is good exercise.
To run requires good lungs.
Running water is purer than stagnant water.

In the first sentence, *runs* is a finite verb; it makes a complete and independent assertion about the subject. In the second and third sentences, *running* and *to run* are subjects; they are used just as simple nouns, such as *baseball* or *tennis*, would be used. In the last sentence, *running* describes water in precisely the same way as the simple adjective *stagnant* does. In the last three sentences, the verbal is accompanied by a finite verb (*is*, *requires*, and *is*) that expresses the predication of the sentence. *No word ending in the suffix* -ing *or preceded by* to *can serve by itself as the verb of a sentence.* No group of words can stand alone as a major sentence unless it contains a finite verb.

A *phrase*, as distinguished from a full sentence, is a group of related words not containing both a subject and a predicate. A phrase is used as a single part of speech. Phrases may be used as conjunctions, verbs, nouns, adjectives, or adverbs. For example:

To cross the border will mean war. (Infinitive phrase used as a noun.)
A reef *of jagged granite* lay beyond us. (Adjective phrase.)
The sun rose *over the horizon.* (Adverbial phrase.)

It will be observed that phrases are not complete sentences but parts of sentences.

A *clause* is a group of words containing both subject and predicate but used as only part of a sentence. A clause may be dependent or independent. In the following sentences, the italicized clauses are dependent:

He did not hear *what I said.*
He waited *until the road was cleared.*
That he has made a mistake is obvious.
The man *who owns the farm* lives in town.

The italicized clauses express predications, but these predications are not independent. They do not stand alone, but depend upon ("hang from") some independent predication. Each is used to form only part of a sentence, and each is used as the equivalent of a single part of speech. *What I said* is used as a noun — as the object of the verb *hear. Until the road was cleared* is used as an adverb to modify the verb *waited*, and a simple adverb such as *quietly* could be substituted for it. *That he has made a mistake* is used as a noun — as the subject of the verb *is.* It is modified by the predicate adjective *obvious. Who owns the farm* is used as an adjective, to modify the noun *man.* Each of these groups of words, then, is a *dependent clause,* a group of words containing both subject and predicate, but not standing alone as a complete sentence.

A *dependent clause* expresses a predication, but the predication is dependent upon other words; it cannot stand alone as an independent assertion. A dependent clause thus differs from a sentence in this fundamental respect: A sentence contains an independent predication; a dependent clause contains a dependent predication, usually marked as such by a subordinating conjunction.

An *independent clause,* on the other hand, is a group of words containing both subject and predicate and capable of standing alone as a sentence though actually used as a part of a sentence. For example:

The heavens declare the glory of God, and the firmament showeth his handiwork.

Each of these clauses is independent, and each *could* stand alone as a simple sentence if the coördinating conjunction *and,* which merely connects the clauses, be omitted:

The heavens declare the glory of God.
The firmament showeth his handiwork.

Connected by a coördinating conjunction, these two simple sentences become a single compound sentence. In this compound sentence there are two equal and logically related parts, each of which *could* stand alone as a sentence. Whether such a group of words is a sentence or an independent clause depends entirely upon the way the writer uses it; his decision is a matter of rhetorical rather than of grammatical unity — a matter of effectiveness rather than correctness. If the independent clause begins with a capital letter and is followed by a period or other form of end punctuation, it becomes a sentence; but if it is used as a part of a larger unit, it remains an independent clause. An independent clause can readily be distinguished from a dependent clause if one remembers that an independent clause is potentially a sentence — that it *could be* punctuated as a sentence. See § 2e.

In speech, which is the primary form of language, English sentences are terminated by characteristic changes in the pitch of the voice, different patterns of change marking the ends of statements and various kinds of questions. A student who is puzzled as to whether a group of words is a sentence can sometimes solve the problem by reading the words aloud as they would be spoken. Punctuation marks such as commas, periods, and question marks are signals to the reader, indicating how the pitch of the voice should rise and fall.

EXERCISES

A. Copy the following sentences, and for each clause underscore the subject once, the predicate twice.

Example The early poems of this writer are often overlooked.

1. In America the average family of four eats more than eleven pounds of meat each week.
2. Equal opportunity for enlistment and promotion can be promised.
3. Perhaps the modesty of the senator was a disadvantage.
4. It is time for the doctor to come and examine him.
5. Who, after all these years, would recognize her?

B. Directions given under Exercise A.

1. It is more than likely that the damaged seeds will not sprout.
2. Most of those who took his advice were later disappointed.
3. Told with great narrative skill, this story indicates that the author has profited by his mistakes.
4. Whenever there was danger of icing, she always flew the plane herself.
5. Bringing a wide knowledge of dialects to his task, Professor Winston explains many hitherto puzzling developments.

C. Directions given under Exercise A.

1. One might quarrel with details in the argument at several points, but the basic logic is absolutely convincing.
2. Why is he the understudy and not playing the leading rôle?
3. Corbin and his family came from Idaho to live in a small town in Vermont, where his mother had been born.
4. Although an atomic scientist, he is pessimistic and discouraged.
5. Singing as she worked, Marie cleaned the house in a hurry.

D. Copy each of the following sentences, underscoring the independent clauses once, the dependent clauses twice.

1. It is the finest collection of butterflies exhibited since the museum was opened.

2. Wilson knew, although the speedometer was broken, that he was exceeding the speed limit.
3. I've often wondered why they call it bear grass, but no one can ever explain this name to me.
4. The barn was ideal for cockfighting but was not suited for a modern dairy.
5. When the enemy got close to Vienna, many Germans fled to Western Austria, hoping for better treatment in our prison camps.

E. Point out all the verbal nouns and verbal adjectives in the following sentences:

1. Breathless, the crowd watched the operator slowly lowering the boom.
2. Pruning roses and watering the lawn kept the old man busy.
3. They wanted to believe that Jamie had gone to the meeting.
4. Singing commercials became a popular advertising device.
5. Signs proclaiming rooms to rent began to appear next morning.

F. In Exercises A and B above, point out the phrases, the dependent clauses, and the independent clauses.

G. In Exercises A and B above, point out all the verbals.

H. Explain the function (use in the sentence) of each phrase, dependent clause, and verbal in Exercises A and B above.

Period Fault, or Sentence Fragment

2. Do not write part of a sentence as if it were a sentence.

This blunder usually occurs when the writer inserts a period before his sentence is ended, then punctuates the remaining phrase or dependent clause as if it were another sentence. The period fault is one of the most common weaknesses of the untrained writer, and it provokes the strong disapproval of more literate people. To recognize and avoid it, the student must be able to differentiate unerringly between sentences, clauses, and phrases.

What is said above does not mean that all minor sentences (fragments) are incorrect. On the contrary, as was pointed out on page 95, the minor sentence is a normal English type more commonly used in speech than in writing, but sometimes entirely appropriate in written English. See § 2f for the uses of fragments, and always be prepared to justify any fragment which you use deliberately.

2a. Do not write a noun or pronoun modified by a verbal ending in *-ing* as a complete sentence.

Fragment The virtues of our library are many. One being that smoking is allowed in the reading room on the third floor.

Revised The virtues of our library are many, one being that smoking is allowed in the reading room on the third floor.

2b. Do not write an appositive phrase as a complete sentence, even when the phrase is introduced by *namely, that is, for example,* or any other such expression.

Fragment There was only one remedy to prescribe. A remedy requiring expensive drugs.

Revised There was only one remedy to prescribe, a remedy requiring expensive drugs.

Fragment In American colleges there are four classes of undergraduates. Namely, freshmen, sophomores, juniors, and seniors.

Revised In American colleges there are four classes of undergraduates, namely, freshmen, sophomores, juniors, and seniors.

2c. Do not write as a complete sentence the second of two parallel infinitive phrases.

Fragment The President liked to take long trips by railroad. And to stop and shake hands with people in small towns.

Revised The President liked to take long trips by railroad and to stop and shake hands with people in small towns.

2d. Do not write a participial phrase as a complete sentence.

Fragment The orchestra played Beethoven's *Third Symphony* magnificently. Inspired by the conductor's confidence in them.

Revised The orchestra played Beethoven's *Third Symphony* magnificently, inspired by the conductor's confidence in them.

2e. Do not write a dependent clause as a complete sentence.

Fragment The spelling *debt* is now universal. Although *det* was once the usual form.

Revised The spelling *debt* is now universal, although *det* was once the usual form.

Note that if *although* is omitted the second clause becomes independent; but *although,* unlike *and* or *but,* is a necessary part of its clause and cannot be omitted without changing the meaning.

Fragment The editor's chief assistant is Hans Acton. Who was once the editor of an opposition paper.

Revised The editor's chief assistant is Hans Acton, who was once the editor of an opposition paper.

2f. Write minor sentences (fragments) only when you are convinced that this construction is preferable and appropriate.

Since minor sentences are common in informal spoken English, they are proper in written dialogue and in writing which attempts to give the effect of conversation. Commands, questions and answers, and exclamations are frequently fragments.

Examples "Martha!"
"Yes, Mother."
"Ready?"
"Not quite."
"Hurry up!"
"Oh! Oh!"
"What's the matter?"
"Can't find my compact."

In more formal writing fragments occur as transitional phrases and as a special device to produce desired rhetorical effects.

Transitions

Now for the second reason. Next, the effects. Then the climax.

Rhetorical use to achieve a particular effect

Down at one end, the cooking plates, pots of stew, potatoes, pot roast, roast beef, gray roast pork waiting to be sliced. Minnie or Susy or Mae, middle-aging behind the counter, hair curled and rouge and powder on a sweating face. Taking orders in a soft low voice, calling them to the cook with a screech like a peacock. Mopping the counter with circular strokes, polishing the big shining coffee urns. The cook is Joe or Carl or Al, hot in a white coat and apron, beady sweat on white forehead, below the white cook's cap; moody, rarely speaking, looking up for a moment at each new entry. Wiping the griddle, slapping down the hamburger. He repeats Mae's orders gently, scrapes the griddle, wipes it down with burlap. Moody and silent.[1]

The student in freshman English who aspires to prose as good as John Steinbeck's is to be encouraged. But he must know what

[1] From *The Grapes of Wrath*, by John Steinbeck. Copyright, 1939. Published by The Viking Press, Inc., New York.

he is doing and when and how to imitate. It is merely frivolous for the student who writes unintentional fragments to justify them by citing deliberate fragments in books and magazines.

If you use fragments deliberately, be prepared to defend your usage unless they are obviously appropriate, as in dialogue.

EXERCISES

A. Revise any of the following which contain inappropriate fragments.

1. We must preserve the principle of states' rights. Although we realize that modern conditions make the extension of federal government necessary.
2. The high school lunch room needs a thorough cleaning. And repainting from floor to ceiling.
3. Old-time automobiles fascinated him, and he collected pictures of as many as he could. Wintons, Franklins, Clevelands, Stars, Reos, Hupmobiles, and all the rest. The walls of his room were a gallery of early automobile advertising art.
4. Finally, the cost. The lowest bid was for over a half million dollars, more than this city could raise from a sales tax in twenty years.
5. Southerners who were born in the North are frequently the most provincial. Especially when they are criticized by people from another section.

B. Sometimes a sentence which is complete is broken up or revised for stylistic reasons and the result is an inappropriate fragment, which should be eliminated. Make all the changes indicated below and then eliminate the undesirable fragments.

1. Add a period after *trip*.

   Everything was right for the fishing trip, the weather being perfect, the Gulf smooth, and the boat in top condition.
2. Add a period after *us*.

   His running impressed all of us, especially his strong finishes in the dashes.
3. Add a period after *fear*.

   She felt the nausea of sudden fear, prayed that her terror did not show, and reached quietly for the alarm button.
4. Substitute *it* for *which*.

Furthermore, this tax will be very hard to collect. And now for the final reason, which is that the tax will be paid by the rural citizens who will derive little or no benefit from it.

5. Add a question mark after *revised.*

Why do the ambassadors want Point Five revised and Point Eight eliminated from the agreement?

C. Find five fragments (minor sentences) in five different publications, copy them, and explain why you think they were used.

Comma Fault

3. Learn to recognize and avoid the comma fault.

The comma fault, sometimes called the comma splice, is the use of a comma between independent clauses which are not joined by a coördinating conjunction. Compare the following sentences:

Paper binding is suitable for some books, it is not satisfactory for books which are likely to be used frequently.

Paper binding is suitable for some books, but it is not satisfactory for books which are likely to be used frequently.

The first sentence illustrates the comma fault: there is no conjunction between the clauses. The second sentence is conventionally punctuated; the comma is adequate because the conjunction *but* joins the clauses.

Since for many years writers, publishers, and printers have generally avoided the comma fault, and since generations of teachers have made students aware of it as a fault, most readers normally expect a stronger separation between independent clauses than a comma provides. It is true that some professional writers occasionally link coördinate clauses with a comma when it is not misleading and when they feel that it most accurately indicates the rhythm and movement of the sentence. But such writers do not use the comma as the normal mark of separation between independent clauses; they use it rarely and discriminatingly. (See § 3a.) Study the five methods of linking clauses listed below.

(1) *A period and a capital letter.*

Faulty The secretary was accused of subversive activity, never was there any evidence of his disloyalty.

Revised The secretary was accused of subversive activity. Never was there any evidence of his disloyalty.

(2) *A semicolon.*

Faulty Conciliation was made more difficult, fresh conflicts were made more likely.

Revised Conciliation was made more difficult; fresh conflicts were made more likely.

(3) *A comma and a coördinating conjunction.*

Faulty The time had passed pleasantly, he was surprised to find that it was nearly six o'clock.

Revised The time had passed pleasantly, and he was surprised to find that it was nearly six o'clock.

(4) *A semicolon before a conjunctive adverb.*

Faulty The contestant failed to send in a box top, therefore his entry should be disqualified.

Revised The contestant failed to send in a box top; therefore his entry should be disqualified.

(5) *A subordinating conjunction.*

Faulty Rubber cement is better for this kind of job, it doesn't soil the paper.

Revised Rubber cement is better for this kind of job because it doesn't soil the paper.

Because it doesn't soil the paper, rubber cement is better for this kind of job.

3a. Use a comma between independent clauses only when there is a clear reason for preferring the comma.

There are three types of sentences, none of them very common, in which a comma is conventionally used to separate independent clauses.

A. Three or more short parallel clauses without internal punctuation may be separated by commas.

Example It costs less, it feels better, it lasts longer.

B. Two or more independent clauses may be separated by commas to give the effect of hurry, particularly in dialogue.

Examples Come on, let's find him. Wait a minute, we want you.

C. Two grammatically independent clauses are occasionally linked with a comma when one is obviously subordinate in meaning but the subordination is not expressed for reasons of style. This is a rhetorical device known as *parataxis.* In the example below the writer evidently used a comma instead of the word *because* to make the sentence seem more conversational.

Example Bring your chair outside, the sun is shining now.

EXERCISES

A. Correct any comma faults found in the following sentences by the most effective method or methods.

1. I had never been in Omaha before, therefore I didn't know how to find the police station.
2. "Let me try," said the plumber's helper, "My hand is smaller."
3. The station joined a network in December, then we heard less local advertising.
4. The program for the meeting had already been prepared, the committee decided not to ask the dean to speak.
5. Under the quarter system the September vacation is usually longer, under the semester system there is less vacation time after the summer term.

B. Convert each of the following complex sentences into a compound sentence by omitting the subordinating conjunctions, being sure to revise (see § 3) so as to avoid comma faults.

1. Although the speaker was persuasive, he did not convince the audience.
2. William James was an influential philosopher, while his brother Henry was a popular novelist.
3. Because he has had no experience in railroad surveying, we do not recommend him for the position.
4. The *Saturday Review of Literature* is Jeffrey's favorite magazine, although he frequently disagrees with its reviewers.

5. Since the atlas was published before 1939, it does not show the present boundaries of several countries.

C. Make all the changes indicated below and then any other changes necessary to link the clauses satisfactorily.

1. Delete the word *when.*
   When Toscanini played *Dixie* in Atlanta, the audience was delighted.
2. Add *and* after *votes.*
   Late that night the tellers completed the counting of votes, the reform leaders realized that they had failed again.
3. Substitute *however* for *but.*
   The new magazine attracted many readers among business men, but the editor was anxious to build a more diversified circulation.
4. Begin the first clause with *Since.*
   Few of the students in the class could read German; the captions had to be translated by the instructor.
5. Substitute *he* for *who.*
   The members were anxious to pass a resolution supporting Mr. Grant, who always had friends in the union.

"Fused" Sentence

4. Separate your sentences. End each sentence with a period, question mark, or exclamation point.

The total omission of punctuation between sentences is a blunder that will handicap the young writer; it indicates a failure to recognize the end of one sentence and the beginning of another. The student who knows the grammatical essentials of the sentence is not likely to write fused sentences. Review Sentence Defined, § 1, p. 95. Many people who have forgotten, or who never learned, such terms as *independent clause* are said to punctuate sentence-ends correctly "by intuition." Actually, they recognize the end of a sentence by the stress and pitch pattern (which is unmistakable even when the words are read silently, when the writer "says it to himself"). But the student who cannot punctuate in this way must learn to recognize the elements of sentences.

The five ways of avoiding the comma fault may also be applied to the fused sentence. Review carefully Comma Fault, § 3.

EXERCISES

A. Correct any fused sentence below by the most effective method or methods.

1. The hero showed sudden affection for Patti it was not quite plausible.
2. A buzzing sound would announce the call by placing a small receiver to his ear the pilot would get his instructions.
3. I was without a job in the city for two months I began to think that my father had known what would happen.
4. If the committee thinks this book deserves a Pulitzer prize the members should go back to school and take a course in American literature.
5. Baseball may be the great American game for college students it isn't in the same class with football.

Agreement of Subject and Verb

If all English nouns, pronouns, and verbs had both singular and plural forms, and if everything were either single or multiple, there would probably be little trouble with subject-verb agreement. College freshmen do not write "The figure are correct" or "The problems is serious"; since *figure* is singular in form and *problems* plural, the writer unhesitatingly makes the verbs agree. Agreement is a matter of *form*. Therefore since such pronouns as *each*, *either*, and *anyone* have no plural forms but sometimes seem plural in meaning, uncertainty arises. In the sentence "Were either of the treaties opposed?" the subject of the thought is plural; if only one treaty had been asked about, the word *either* would not have been used. But *either* (the formal subject) is singular in form, and to agree in form the verb should be *was*. Obviously there is no failure in communication if *were* is used; either *was* or *were* is equally efficient in the sentence.

However, efficiency is not the only criterion. When there are two equally efficient ways of writing a sentence, the etiquette of formal English often requires that only one of the two be used, just as etiquette requires a white shirt, not a colored shirt, with a tuxedo. With certain exceptions noted below, formal Eng demands that subjects and verbs agree in form, and to violate this requirement invites the disapproval of many people who object to breaches of formal etiquette, regardless of the truth or value of what is written. *Informal English likewise has its rules of etiquette.* In informal English "Neither of the treaties were ratified" is acceptable, but "They was ratified" invites disapproval.[1]

5. Make the verb agree with its subject in person and number.

Be sure that you identify the subject of each verb. Note that some common verbs such as *can, may, will, might,* and *should* have the same form in both singular and plural, that no verb has both singular and plural forms in the past tense (except *be,* which has *was* and *were*), and that only one verb, *be,* has both a singular, *am,* and a plural, *are,* in the first person. Thus there are relatively few occasions for us to decide between singular and plural forms, and trouble spots can be isolated.

5a. Use a singular verb with a grammatically singular subject which has a plural modifier.

Nonstandard	A collection of many rare stamps are on display.
Standard	A collection of many rare stamps is on display.
Nonstandard	The vote of all the groups — union members, farmers, business men, professional people, and housewives — reveal sympathy for this new plan.
Standard	The vote of all the groups — union members, farmers, business men, professional people, and housewives — reveals sympathy for this new plan.

5b. Observe modern rules of usage of the pronouns *each, everyone, anyone, someone, anybody, somebody, everybody, nobody, either, neither, none,* and *any.*

NOTE. In formal English most of these pronouns require a singular verb; *none* and *any* may take either a singular or a plural verb. In informal English a plural verb is often used when a

none, any

[1] See p. 91 for definitions of *standard, colloquial, informal, formal,* and *nonstandard.*

comes between the subject and verb, particularly *neither*. There is a strong tendency for the verb en the meaning of the pronoun is plural.[1]

er of these proposals made by judges is acceptable.

ıer of these proposals made by judges are acceptable.

ny of those suggestions have merit?

Standard None of the paint is dry, and none of the floors have yet b sanded.

5c. Use a singular verb with a singular subject followed by a parenthetical group beginning with such words as *together with, as well as, and not, no less than, in addition to* (or revise such constructions to avoid the clash between grammar and meaning).

Standard The owner, no less than the driver, is responsible.

Awkward The piano, as well as the chairs, is in a warehouse.

Improved Both the piano and the chairs are in a warehouse. (Note that the revision makes the subject plural in grammar and in meaning.)

5d. Use a plural verb with a compound subject which is plural in meaning, a singular verb with a compound subject which is singular in meaning.

Standard Both the lecture and the demonstration were applauded.
The lecture and demonstration was in Room 212 at eight.
The secretary and treasurer is Mr. Robbins.
Bumper jack, lug wrench, screw driver, and tire iron are standard equipment.

NOTE. Two or more nouns preceded by *each* or *every* take a singular verb.

Standard Every vowel and consonant is modified by following sounds.

5e. Use a singular verb when two or more singular nouns are joined by *or, nor,* or *but*.

Standard Either *program* or *programme* is an acceptable spelling.

[1] See Russell Thomas, "Concord Based on *Meaning* versus Concord Based on *Form:* The Indefinites," *College English*, I (October, 1939), 38–45.

NOTE. When the subjects differ in number or person, make the verb agree with the nearer, or revise the construction.

Standard but awkward	Either you or I am using an outdated price list.
Improved	Either you are using an outdated price list or I am.

5f. Use a singular or a plural verb after a collective noun according to the intended meaning.

Standard	The choir was invited to the summer festival. (The invitation was extended to the group as a unit.)
Standard	The choir were invited as rapidly as he could reach them by telephone. (Individuals were invited.)

5g. Use a singular verb with most nouns which are plural in form but singular in meaning.

NOTE. Many nouns with a plural form may be either singular or plural in meaning.

Almost always singular: *economics, billiards, linguistics, logistics, mathematics, measles, mumps, news, physics, semantics.*

Almost always plural: *barracks, insignia, scissors, tactics, pliers.*

Indifferently singular or plural: *alms, headquarters, (golf) links, means.*

Determined by meaning: *acoustics, athletics, ethics, politics, statistics, data.* (Compare "Acoustics is studied by modern architects" and "The acoustics in the lecture room are bad.") For other similar words, consult your dictionary.

NOTE. Titles of publications and works of art are frequently plural in form but require a singular verb.

Standard Is *The Merry Wives of Windsor* in this collection?
The Women is still produced occasionally.
The *Times* has been very unbiased in its reports.

5h. After introductory *it* the verb is singular; after introductory *here* and *there* the verb usually agrees with the subject.

Standard	It is the officers who insist on this practice.
	Here are three specific examples of inconsistency.
	There are now four possibilities to consider.
Nonstandard	Here's three sentences beginning with expletives.

NOTE. When a compound subject with a singular first member follows, the verb after *here* or *there* may be either singular or plural, though the plural is preferred in formal writing.[1]

Standard	There was a short story and an unfinished novel among the papers found in the desk.
Formal	There were a minister and two social workers on the committee.

5i. The verb usually agrees with the subject, not the complement.

Nonstandard	The best argument for the TVA are the improved living conditions in the region.
Standard	The best argument is the improved conditions in the region.
Awkward	Our only hope is buses, which may replace the railroad.
Improved	Our only hope is that buses may replace the railroad.

5j. Distinguish carefully between *doesn't* (= *does not*) and *don't* (= *do not*).

NOTE. *He* (*it, she*) *don't,* formerly common in familiar standard English, is now generally regarded as nonstandard. Always write *he* (*it, she, a person*) *doesn't.*

5k. In formal writing use a plural verb with a relative pronoun which has a plural antecedent.

Formal	He has one of the new phonographs which play records at three different speeds.
Standard	He has one of the new phonographs which plays records at three different speeds.[2]

[1] See George O. Curme, *Syntax*, p. 55; and A. H. Marckwardt and Fred G. Walcott, *Facts About Current English Usage*, pp. 89–90.

[2] Although the plural verb is more common here, the singular is not nonstandard. See John S. Kenyon, "One of Those Who Is . . ." *American Speech*, XXVI (October, 1951), 161–165; and Russell Thomas, "Current English Forum," *College English*, XIII (October, 1951), 43–44.

NOTE. In such constructions the nearer noun or pronoun is not always the antecedent.

Standard Wilson is among the investigators who are confident of success. (*Investigators* is the antecedent of *who.*)

Standard Wilson is the only one of the investigators who is confident of success. (Here *one* is the antecedent of *who.*)

5l. Phrasal subjects describing a mass, a quantity, or a number, though plural in form, require a singular verb when the subject is treated as a unit (compare §§ 5d and 5f).

Standard Forty per cent is too small a discount on this item.
Forty per cent of those interviewed were undecided.

Note that sometimes the verb can be either singular or plural.

Standard Three and three is (or are) six.
Three times three make (or makes) nine.
The first twenty-five years is (or are) the hardest.

EXERCISES

A. Some of the following sentences are clearly formal; others are clearly colloquial. Change all verb forms that are not appropriate in the sentences.

1. Under a contract signed February 7 either the company or the union have the right to take such action.
2. The source of the weakness of the structure are the three weak girders which were not inspected.
3. It's a good thing neither of the windows were open when the rain started.
4. The committee on petitions were requested to take up this problem at its spring meeting.
5. Wasn't there a hoe and a rake here a few minutes ago?

B. Make all the changes indicated below and then any other necessary changes.

1. Change *every one* to *all.*
   It is clear that nearly every one of the applicants lacks the necessary experience in reporting public affairs.

2. Change *all* to *each.*
   When the fire bell rings all of the clerks know what to do.
3. Change *and* to *accompanied by.*
   The contest winner and her mother always get a trip to a seashore resort.
4. Change *one* to *two.*
   One visit to the southern counties was not enough for a successful campaign.
5. Change *experience* to *experiences.*
   His experience in newspaper work seems to have sobered him.

C. Change all verb forms that are not appropriate to the following formal sentences.

1. The fact that many people disagree with Mr. Pound's politics don't affect the technical excellence of his verse.
2. Neither you nor the doctor who sends you to this hospital are required to make a deposit before you are admitted.
3. The verb, as well as the subject of the sentence, are polar words, capable of many different meanings.
4. There is a dictionary, an English grammar, and a spelling book with Jackson's signature inside — possibly his whole library.
5. On this occasion the news from the war fronts are not of first concern to this audience.
6. It is unfortunate that this jury, although warned later to disregard the remarks, were allowed to remain in court while the witness was making his accusations.
7. Measles are unknown in the valley, although other childhood diseases are about as common as elsewhere.
8. Everyone in the exploring party were exhausted when the trip finally ended at the river mouth.
9. He was the first of the laboratory men who were allowed to talk to reporters after the explosion.
10. None of the characters in his stories are normal people.

D. In a short story or a novel find several violations of the rules in § 5 and explain what the constructions indicate about the characters who use them.

Agreement of Pronoun and Antecedent

6. A pronoun usually agrees with its antecedent in number and gender.

NOTE. Be sure that you can identify precisely the antecedent and the pronoun referring to it. See § 16 for the meaning of *antecedent*.

6a. In formal English use singular pronouns to refer to singular antecedents.

Pay particular attention to such antecedents as *each*, *everyone*, *anyone*, *anybody*, *everybody*, *either*, *neither*, *none*, *any*, *kind*, and *sort*. In formal English most of these antecedents require a singular pronoun; *none* and *any* may take either a singular or a plural pronoun. In colloquial English a plural pronoun is common when the antecedent is singular in form but clearly plural in meaning.[1]

Formal Each musician must defend his [not *their*] own interpretation.

Standard None of the actors had memorized their lines.

Standard Anybody who uses that elevator risks his life.

Informal Everybody in the dormitory had gone to the football game, leaving their doors unlocked.

6b. With a collective noun use either a singular or a plural pronoun according to the meaning.

Standard The class inspected its new laboratory Thursday morning. (The group acted as a unit.)

The class took their seats promptly. (The members acted individually.)

NOTE. An antecedent which takes a singular verb takes a singular pronoun; an antecedent which takes a plural verb takes a plural pronoun. See § 5f.

Standard Nobody likes to have his taste questioned.

Standard None of them want their books autographed.

6c. Use pronouns with gender appropriate to the antecedent.

Normally a masculine pronoun is used with an antecedent

[1] See p. 91 for definitions of *standard*, *colloquial*, *informal*, *formal*, and *nonstandard*.

which denotes a male being, a feminine pronoun with an antecedent which denotes a female being, and a neuter pronoun with other antecedents. However, feminine pronouns are sometimes used to refer to nouns denoting some personified inanimate things such as ships and colleges. Masculine pronouns are used with antecedents which include beings of both sexes. Neuter pronouns are used when the sex is unknown or is not particularized.

Standard	We saw that the baby had something in its mouth.
Standard	Each physician was expected to notify his patients.
Pedantic	Each physician was expected to notify his or her patients.
Standard	The big ship quivered when her bow struck the iceberg.

EXERCISES

A. In the following sentences change any pronouns which are not appropriate to the sentences.

1. This department requires that every student write their final examinations in an official examination book.
2. The committee will be asked for their report after its next meeting.
3. Don't you think everybody did their best to make him feel welcome?
4. The judge stared at the jury, and then asked them individually if they agreed on the verdict.
5. Every teacher in Hillcrest School made his or her own rules.

B. Make all the changes indicated below and then make any other necessary changes.

1. Add *has* before *sent.*
   The graduating class sent out ninety invitations to their picnic. (Formal)
2. Change *employees* to *employee.*
   Any employees caught tampering with this valve will be reported to their shop steward for disciplinary action.
3. Delete *and the precinct captains.*
   The Community Chest drive chairman wanted every block leader and the precinct captains to report their progress.
4. Change *Members* to *Each member.*
   Members of the club will have to chip in if they want us to hire a big orchestra.

5. Add *words* before *can*.
Slang can be very effective when used by a writer who knows that he is using slang and uses it with discretion.

Case

7. Use the proper case to show the relation of a noun or pronoun to other words in the sentence.

English nouns have two case forms: (1) common case (*man, horse, officer*), and (2) genitive (possessive) case (*man's, horse's, officer's*). The common case is used for a subject, object of a verb or preposition, predicate nominative, or absolute. The genitive case is used to indicate such relationships as *man's hat, horse's owner, officer's duties, boy's uncle, week's vacation, Longfellow's poems*. Six English pronouns (*I, we, he, she, they, who*) have a third case form, the objective (*me, us, him, her, them, whom*). These pronouns are said to have three cases, *subjective, objective,* and *genitive*. Since the function word *of* is frequently used to show the same kind of relationship as the genitive ending *-'s*, as in *owner of the horse, duties of an officer, color of the car, home of the professor*, such a construction is often called a periphrastic genitive, that is, a genitive formed by a phrase.

NOTE. Some English grammars employ the term *case* to indicate the function of nouns rather than the form. Such grammars describe three cases of nouns (1) nominative (subjects, predicate nouns, and absolutes), (2) genitive (possessives and similar relationships), and (3) objective (direct and indirect objects of verbs, objects of prepositions, and subjects of infinitives).

7a. Place an appositive in the same case as the word it explains.

Standard The whole family, Lois, the children, and I, were there.
He invited the whole family, the children, you, and me.

7b. Use the objective case of a pronoun as the object of a verb, a verbal, or a preposition, and as the indirect object of a verb.

Standard [1] There was no disagreement between you and me.

[1] See p. 91 for definitions of *standard, colloquial, informal, formal,* and *nonstandard.*

Nonstandard	There was no disagreement between you and I.
Standard	A number of us Progressives will support the bill.
Nonstandard	A number of we Progressives will support the bill.
Standard	Please let us know for whom the present is intended. (Here *whom* follows *for.*)
Colloquial	Please let us know who the present is intended for. (Here *who* precedes *for.*)
Formal	Whom will the Illinois delegation nominate?
Colloquial	Who will the Illinois delegation nominate?

NOTE. There is a strong tendency in spoken standard English (and hence in informal writing) for *who* to be used when it is the object of a verb or preposition that does not precede the pronoun, as in the colloquial sentences above.

7c. After the conjunctions *than* and *as* in elliptical clauses of comparison use the case which the expanded form would demand.

Standard My assistant resented my being younger than he (not *him*).

He insisted that the manager give him as much credit as [he gave] me.

He insisted that the manager give him as much attention as I [gave him].

7d. Observe standard modern usage in the case of a pronoun which functions as a predicate (subjective) complement.

Formal	It was I who first objected to this artificial separation of history and criticism. (First person)
Informal	It's me, Sister; let me in. (First person)
Standard	It is she. That was he. Was it they? (Third person)
Nonstandard	It is her. That was him. Was it them? (Third person)

NOTE. In the first person the subjective case forms *I* and *we* are preferred in formal written English, although the construction rarely occurs in formal situations. The objective case forms *me* and *us* have a long and reputable history in cultivated spoken English, and hence in many kinds of writing; they are standard English in this construction. In the third person, standard written usage prefers the subjective case forms *he*, *she*, and *they*. Although

It's her, *It was him*, and *It's them* are heard very commonly, sometimes in the speech of cultivated people, these forms are avoided in writing.[1]

7e. Insertion of a parenthetical phrase like *he said* or *I believe* does not justify *whom* where *who* is expected.

Example He tried to imitate speakers whom he thought were effective.
Revised He tried to imitate speakers who he thought were effective (*who* is the subject of *were*, not the object of *thought*.)

7f. Use *whom* and *whomever* only when the objective case is required.

Speakers to whom these words are new and foreign sometimes betray their uncertainty by using them where the subjective form is standard.

Example It could have been taken by whomever cleaned the office.
Revised It could have been taken by whoever cleaned the office. (*Whoever* is the subject of *cleaned*; the whole clause is the object of *by*.)
Standard Give this prescription to whomever you find on duty. (*Whomever* is the object of *find*; the whole clause is the object of *to*.)

7g. Use the objective case of a pronoun as the subject, the object, or the predicate complement of an infinitive.

Standard Did you take *him* to be *me*?
Did you see *them* mistreat *her*?

7h. Nouns regularly form the genitive case by adding *'s* or the apostrophe alone to the common-case form.

Examples horse's, horses', woman's, women's, city's, cities'

NOTE. See The Apostrophe, § 25, for special conditions.

7i. Personal pronouns regularly form the genitive case without an apostrophe; indefinite pronouns require the *'s*.

Examples my, mine, our, ours, your, yours, its, his, her, hers, one's, another's, anybody's, nobody's, somebody's

[1] See R. C. Pooley, *Teaching English Usage*, pp. 67–72.

7j. Use the genitive case form and the periphrastic genitive idiomatically.

Both the genitive case form and the periphrastic genitive are standard when the noun denotes an animate being (but see § 7k).

Examples general's son, son of the general; women's hats, hats of the women; turtle's mouth, mouth of the turtle

When the noun denotes an inanimate object, usage is divided. Some common phrases require the case form: *today's newspaper, pity's sake, stone's throw* (never *newspaper of today, sake of pity, throw of a stone*); many others require the periphrastic genitive: *price of milk, corner of Main and Broadway, display of paintings* (never *milk's price, Main and Broadway's corner, paintings' display*). However, the form is usually optional: *color of the sky, sky's color; height of the building, building's height; closing of the door, door's closing* (or *door closing*). When you are uncertain, the periphrastic genitive is usually safe with a noun denoting an inanimate referent.

7k. Use the periphrastic genitive, not the genitive case form, to indicate the object of an action.

Example Hatred of the Shah was widespread. (The Shah was hated.)
The Shah's hatred was concealed. (The Shah hated someone.)

7l. A noun or pronoun preceding and governing a gerund (verbal noun in *-ing*) is usually in the genitive case.

Examples The reason for the loyalty board's reviewing his case has never been disclosed.
The Senator will object to your asking that question.

NOTE. In both formal and informal English, nouns governing gerunds sometimes occur in the common-case form.

Examples There was a story in the morning paper about the debate team winning its match with Southeastern.
We heard about the golfers missing their train. (This usage is possibly common because in speech there is no distinction between *golfers* and *golfers'*.)

In formal English, pronouns governing gerunds usually are in the genitive case, but in informal English the objective case is not rare.

Formal They were pleased to learn about your joining us.
Informal Aren't you tickled at him winning the match?

The genitive case is not used when the noun or pronoun is followed by a participial construction; be sure to distinguish participles from gerunds.

Participle We heard the iceman running from the dog.
Gerund We resented the iceman's complaining to the police.

Iceman in the first sentence is more heavily stressed than *iceman's* in the second sentence.

7m. The genitive *whose* is sometimes used with a neuter antecedent, particularly when avoiding it would make an awkward construction.

Awkward This includes markers the bases of which must be set in concrete.

Revised This includes markers whose bases must be set in concrete.

EXERCISES

A. Change the nonstandard usages in the following sentences to standard English, and change the case forms of any nouns or pronouns that are not appropriate to the degree of formality of the sentence.

1. The operator should be very careful about whom he permits to handle the controls.
2. The board of directors were not aware of it being a problem.
3. No staff officer was told about the barracks' condition.
4. Ask her whether it's me she's looking for.
5. When the resort was finally opened, several other families and us rented cottages for the summer.

B. Make all the changes indicated below and then any other changes necessary.

1. Change *for* to *of*.
Commentators are agreed that there is not any chance for him to escape this time.

2. Begin the sentence with *Mr. Elton's fortune.*
The fortune was made without Mr. Elton's engaging in unethical practices or violating the law.
3. Add *we thought* after *who.*
The plan was recommended by a man who could be trusted to foresee the possible consequences.
4. After *down* insert *when Miss Temple called.*
The attendant promptly came down and escorted Miss Temple and her mother to the visitors' gallery.
5. Substitute a personal pronoun for *Miss Franks.*
We knew that it was not Miss Franks.

C. Directions given under Exercise B. Assume that the sentences are in formal English.

1. Delete *for.*
Robert's mother was very proud of him for being the best speller in the class.
2. Substitute *he, his,* or *him* for *Robert.*
She looked proudly at Robert standing on the platform.
3. Substitute *I* or *me* for *Carson,* and put *the doctor* before *wanted.*
Mrs. Bruhn thought it was Carson who wanted to see the doctor.
4. Insert *was* before *least.*
The first prize was won by an artist whom the critics thought least qualified.
5. Substitute a personal pronoun for *Miss Taylor.*
The editor suspected that McLure had more interest than Miss Taylor in writing labor news.

Subjunctive Mood

The function of the subjunctive mood is literally to indicate the speaker's mood, that is, his attitude toward the predication. Doubt, determination, hesitancy, uncertainty, wishfulness, and insistence are typical feelings expressed. Three devices are employed to indicate mood: (1) the past tense form where past time is not meant, as in "If I *had* a copy, I would sell it"; (2) modal auxiliaries, such as *can, could, may, must, ought, should;* and (3) subjunctive forms of the verb. In modern English the subjunctive function rarely requires a subjunctive form; in fact there are only a few such forms in the language.

Regular verbs in English have only one subjunctive form: the third person singular present without *-s*; compare *he takes* (indicative) with *if he take* (subjunctive). This form is now commonly used in only a few constructions, such as *God bless him, Plague take it,* and *Heaven help you,* where the subjunctive is necessary.

No irregular verb has any subjunctive forms except the verb *be,* which has two: (1) the use of *were* instead of *was* in the first and third person singular, and (2) the form *be* as an auxiliary following such verbs as *ask, agree, demand, determine, insist,* and *require,* and as a finite verb form in dependent clauses. See the examples in §§ 8a, 8b, and 8c below.

8. In a few constructions, principally confined to literary English, a subjunctive form is usual.

8a. In formal English use a subjunctive form to express a request, wish, or command, and to state a parliamentary motion or resolution.[1]

Examples God bless you.

He moved that the minutes be approved as read.

It is requested that violations be reported promptly.

8b. In formal English use the subjunctive mood to express a pure supposition or a strong improbability. In informal English the indicative mood is usual in such constructions.

Formal If it be necessary, the bishop will act.

Informal If it is necessary, the bishop will act.

Formal Let us suppose that he were still alive today.

Informal Let's suppose that he is still alive today.

8c. Use the subjunctive mood to express a condition contrary to fact.

Formal If he were the candidate, the party could get little support from the progressive faction.

Colloq. If he was the candidate, the party could get little support from the progressive faction.

Formal If I were the mayor, I would seek outside assistance.

Colloq. If I was the mayor, I'd look for outside help.

[1] See p. 91 for definitions of *standard, colloquial, informal, formal,* and *nonstandard.*

Note that the colloquial forms use the past tense to indicate the subjunctive function. Note also that inverted word order requires the subjunctive form, as in *Were I the mayor, I would seek outside assistance*, or *Were I the mayor, I'd look for outside help.*

EXERCISES

A. Make all changes in mood necessary to make the verb form in the following sentences appropriate to the style.

1. I'd be happy if this term was only beginning instead of ending.
2. We request that this paragraph is made a part of the record.
3. Resolved, that the books are audited at the end of the year.
4. If this gossip be taken seriously, it'll kill his chances to make the honor society.
5. We will demand that he pay the amount due or vacate the cottage by the end of the month.

B. Collect five sentences containing subjunctive forms from current magazines, newspapers, or books. Be prepared to explain why subjunctive rather than indicative forms were used. Note both the meaning and the style of discourse.

Tense

The tense of a verb usually, but not always, indicates the time of the predication. English verbs can be inflected in only two tenses: the present (*he laughs*), and the past (*he laughed*). There are no other tense forms; to indicate other times, we must use phrases, such as *he is laughing, he has laughed, he will laugh, he didn't laugh.* The so-called present (better, timeless present) is almost never used to indicate an action occurring at the moment; compare *he laughs* with *he is laughing.* We have seen (page 122) that the past tense form is used as a subjunctive, with no time limitation. Furthermore, several constructions other than tense forms are commonly used to indicate time. Notice the *time* of the following predications and the *method* of indicating the time:

My favorite tenor sings at the Auditorium tomorrow night.

Wilma is going to like him.

I used to listen to him on opera broadcasts.
He is to go to Kansas City after he sings in Denver.
The tenor's local admirers are about to get a surprise.
Some of them buy every record that he makes.

In these sentences past actions, habitual actions, and future actions are clearly indicated without the use of any simple past or future tense forms, and several "present tense" forms are used although none of the sentences describe present actions. Only by excluding many time-indicating constructions which raise no usage problems, and by including several phrasal constructions, can we distinguish six English tenses. Since such a classification is sometimes useful, study § 9 below.

9. Observe modern standard usage in the tense of every verb and verbal.

The following condensed paradigm displays the principal parts and the tenses of the verbs *laugh* and *take:*

	PRINCIPAL PARTS	
Infinitive	(to) laugh	(to) take
Past Tense	laughed	took
Past Participle	laughed	taken
	SIMPLE TENSES	
Present	I laugh	I take
Past	I laughed	I took
	PERIPHRASTIC TENSES	
Future	I will (shall) laugh	I will (shall) take
Present Perfect	I have laughed	I have taken
Past Perfect	I had laughed	I had taken
Future Perfect	I will (shall) have laughed	I will (shall) have taken

The verbals derived from these two verbs are as follows:

Present Infinitive	(to) laugh	(to) take
Perfect Infinitive	(to) have laughed	(to) have taken
Gerund (noun form)	laughing	taking
Present Participle	laughing	taking
Past Participle	laughed	taken

Two other present tense constructions are very common: (1) *Progressive* (I am laughing, I am taking), and (2) *Emphatic* (I do laugh, I do take). In questions and negations these are the only present tense constructions used. Note these examples:

I'm not laughing.	I don't laugh.	Do I laugh?	Am I laughing?
I'm not taking.	I don't take.	Do I take?	Am I taking?

Both of these constructions have past tense periphrastic forms:

I was (not) laughing	Was I (not) taking?
I did (not) laugh	Did I (not) take?

9a. *Present.* Use the various present tenses for the following functions:

Present action	The wind is blowing. The wind does blow. Isn't the wind blowing? Doesn't the wind blow?
Present state	It is a gale. He thinks so too. She feels good. Charles believes it is wrong.
Timeless truth	Eliot's metaphors are frequently erudite. The pine is a coniferous evergreen. Franklin believed that honesty is the best policy. (Compare *The chief justice believed that child labor laws were unconstitutional.* The past tense is used because the belief is no longer regarded as true.)
Habitual action	Professor Rowe travels in Europe every summer. The boat docks at Pier Six. He wears a homburg.
Historical present	He listens quietly to the lobbyists. He talks with party leaders. He ponders his campaign promises. Then he decides to veto the bill.

9b. *Historical Present.* Use the present in narrating past events only when it makes the action more dramatic. Do not shift aimlessly from present to past tense. See § 98b.

Faulty The quake comes at 7:03. Where there had been a few early pedestrians and a sleepy policeman, streets are deluged with rubble, and dust clouds the air. Screams of people mingle with sirens and the dull rumble of falling walls. The city exploded below the pilot of an airliner who was coasting in toward the airport.

The writer should have continued in the present tense.

9c. Present Perfect. Use the present perfect tense for an action or state that began in the past and continues into the present.[1]

Provincial Did you see the exhibit of abstract art yet?
Standard Have you seen the exhibit of abstract art yet?
Nonstandard She has been notified several times before last Monday.
Standard She had been notified several times before last Monday.
Standard She was notified several times before last Monday.
Standard She has already sent in this week's payment. (The whole of a period like *this week, this month, this year, today* may be regarded as extending at least up to the moment of speaking.)

9d. Past. Use the past tense for an action or state in past time which ended before the moment of speaking or writing.

Nonstandard His parents have lived in Arkansas until 1948.
Standard His parents lived in Arkansas until 1948.

9e. Past Perfect. Use the past perfect tense in formal English for an action or state that was completed prior to some other past action or state.

Formal The critic was an interesting and polished lecturer, but he was not the platform hypnotist that we had anticipated.
Colloq. The critic was an interesting and polished lecturer, but he was not the platform hypnotist that we anticipated.

9f. Future. Choose future tense constructions with careful regard to meaning and style of discourse.

In spoken English the most common future tense constructions are the contractions *I'll, he'll, they'll,* etc., and the expanded forms

[1] See p. 91 for definitions of *standard, colloquial, informal, formal,* and *nonstandard.*

I'm going to, he's going to, they're going to, etc., as in *I'll be there; he's going to show slides.*

In formal and literary English, the future is usually indicated by the auxiliaries *shall* and *will*, which have both time and modal significance. In all three persons, singular and plural, *will* is used for simple prediction, i.e. when the subject is assumed to be free of constraint.

Examples I will be graduated in June.
We will know more about it after the next experiment.
You will find the current *Harper's* in the reading room.
They will perform here later in the month.

Because *shall* is an auxiliary for the simple future in the first person singular and plural in the usage of many cultivated people, especially in Great Britain, and because for many years textbooks prescribed this form, usage is divided. Both *shall* and *will* are traditional and reputable auxiliaries. Since *shall*, pronounced with emphasis, is frequently used in spoken English to indicate determination, necessity, obligation, duty, or other constraint, it is often preferred in formal writing, in all three persons, singular and plural, to imply constraint.

Examples I shall expect you to make this payment promptly.
You shall report to the probation officer each week.
It shall be published three times in a local newspaper.
They shall not be liable for damage done en route.

In American spoken English *shall* is rare in the first person except in questions. In all three persons *will*, pronounced with heavy stress, may be used to express determination.[1]

9g. ***Principal Parts.*** **Use standard English forms of strong verbs.**

There are no rules for determining the past tense and past participle of strong (irregular) verbs. These forms, without exception, must be learned. They should be learned so well that they occur automatically, without the necessity for a choice between *born* and *borned, give* and *gave, lay* and *lain*, etc. Fortunately, most

[1] See C. C. Fries, *American English Grammar*, pp. 150–167.

college freshmen do use most irregular verb forms automatically according to standard usage, having learned them in childhood by imitation. However, anyone is likely to have learned a few non-standard forms; these should be discovered and replaced. Practice the standard expression repeatedly in sentences, precisely as you practice a golf stroke or a jackknife dive, until it requires no thought. The following list includes the principal parts of most of the important irregular verbs which present divided usage. For others consult your dictionary.

PRESENT INFINITIVE	PAST TENSE	PAST PARTICIPLE
bear (bring forth)	bore	born (not *borned*)
bear (carry)	bore	borne
be	was	been
begin	began	begun
bite	bit	bitten (colloq. *bit*)
burst	burst	burst (not *bursted*)
choose	chose	chosen
come	came	come
dive	dived (colloq. *dove*)	dived
do	did	done
drink	drank	drunk
drive	drove	driven
drown	drowned	drowned (not *drownded*)
eat	ate	eaten
flee	fled	fled
fly	flew	flown
forget	forgot	forgotten
freeze	froze	frozen
get	got	gotten (or *got*) [1]
give	gave	given
grow	grew	grown
hang	hung [2]	hung [2]
know	knew	known
lie (recline)	lay [3]	lain [3]
ride	rode	ridden
ring	rang (or *rung*)	rung

[1] *Got* as a past participle is preferred in British English.

[2] *Hanged* is sometimes used in reference to execution by hanging.

[3] Compare *lie* (to prevaricate), *lied*, *lied*, and *lay*, *laid*, *laid* (transitive).

rise	rose	risen
run	ran	run
see	saw (not *seen*)	seen
shake	shook	shaken
shrink	shrank (or *shrunk*)	shrunk
sing	sang (or *sung*)	sung
sink	sank (or *sunk*)	sunk
sit	sat	sat
slide	slid	slid (or *slidden*)
speak	spoke	spoken
spring	sprang (or *sprung*)	sprung
stand	stood	stood
steal	stole	stolen
swear	swore	sworn
swim	swam (not *swum*)	swum
swing	swung	swung
take	took	taken
tear	tore	torn
throw	threw	thrown
wear	wore	worn
wring	wrung	wrung
write	wrote	written

NOTE. The second principal part is always used *alone* as a past tense form. The third principal part is used with an auxiliary. Thus *I took* and *I had taken.*

EXERCISES

A. Revise the sentences that contain nonstandard tense forms.

1. It seems that he had gone to Florida and began work on a book about the Seminoles.
2. He found that his old Seminole friend was unhappy about the stock law for a long time.
3. His nurse discovered that he had accidentally tore the label off two of the bottles.
4. The halfback fell when he was hit and laid motionless after the pile-up was unscrambled.
5. Last night I called Eloise and ask her if she could type my term paper by Saturday.

B. Change any verb forms that are not appropriate to the style of the sentence.

1. Mrs. Abrams, has your baby ever bit his tongue?
2. No, but I got bit when I bought that second-hand stroller.
3. Mr. Abrams regrets that he will be unable to accept your invitation because of a previous engagement.
4. He's gotten a new automobile since we saw him in April.
5. This award for bravery is presented to Joseph Elder, who at great peril dove into Lake Alala and rescued a drowning child.

C. Change the verb form in each sentence to indicate that the action took place once in the past.

1. The farmers are burning underbrush in the peach orchard.
2. Loel is lying on the grass in the sun.
3. When the kittens have white feet she drowns the whole litter.
4. St. Louis was winning the game because of Lewis' pitching.
5. The rector was drinking his tea in a great hurry.

D. Make the changes indicated, and then make any other necessary changes.

1. Change to future tense, formal style.
   I'm very happy to have your son join our organization.
2. Insert *already* after *contract.*
   Did the actors agree to the terms of the new contract?
3. Change from colloquial to formal style.
   The doctor arrived immediately, but he didn't have the oxygen tent Maurice asked him to bring.
4. Insert *not,* making the statement negative.
   Chippendale furniture suited the room very well.
5. Change from statement to question.
   I will expect to see you at the convention next month.

E. Make the changes indicated, and then make any other necessary changes.

1. Substitute *was* for *is.*
   The book review editor is delighted that Mr. Knight has already read the book.

2. Substitute *know* for *knew*.
   We knew that she had taken a course in art in 1950.
3. Delete *had*.
   The contestant had swum the English Channel twice.
4. Substitute *thought* for *thinks*.
   Everyone thinks that he bore a heavy burden until his son was able to help him.
5. Delete *have*.
   The frames for these pictures of the past presidents have come from many parts of the world.
6. Insert *not*.
   In those days rustlers drove cattle off at night.
7. Substitute *next year* for *now*.
   The films are shown on Saturday afternoons now.
8. Change from present to future.
   I am in the library every Monday afternoon.
9. Change from present to past.
   The atomic bomb bursts with a tremendous noise.
10. Change *understand* to *understood*.
    We understand that she is a twin sister of Marie.

Sequence of Tenses

10. Make the sequence of tenses conventionally consistent: verbs and verbals in subordinate constructions depend in tense on the tense of the main predication.

Faulty Last May, Louise announced that she is leaving.

Revised Last May, Louise announced that she was leaving.

Faulty We invited him to come as soon as he can.

Revised We invited him to come as soon as he could.

10a. Timeless truths are usually stated in the present tense regardless of the tense of other verbs in the sentence.

Example Some early navigators insisted that the earth is round.

Example Physicists have said for years that the atom is fissionable.

NOTE. Occasionally the verb in such a subordinate clause is

attracted into another tense; for example, *Some early navigators insisted that the world was round.* This construction is not considered a serious flaw in writing.

10b. Participles and infinitives depend in tense upon the main verb in the sentence.

A present participle indicates time contemporary with that of the main verb; a present infinitive indicates time contemporary with or future to the time of the main verb; a perfect participle or infinitive indicates time prior to that of the main verb.

Faulty One would have expected to have heard a sound.

Revised One would have expected to hear a sound.

Faulty Trying house after house unsuccessfully, he finally gave up and resigned his position.

Revised Having tried house after house unsuccessfully, he finally gave up and resigned his position.

EXERCISES

A. Make the changes indicated below and then any other changes that become necessary.

1. Change *have liked* to *like.*
   I would have liked to be in Indianapolis for the big Memorial Day race in 1950.
2. Change *says* to *said* and *today* to *at the time.*
   General Hollis says that our coastal defenses are adequate today.
3. Delete *had.*
   Wright had insisted for years that heavier-than-air machines can fly.
4. Change *be* to *have been.*
   In that group I would be afraid to admit that I was born in New England.
5. Change *tells* to *told.*
   The contractor tells the roofers to cover as much of the roof as they can in good weather.

B. Compose five sentences in which the following are used in subordinate clauses: *have been written, will have been observed, to be protected, had improved, was prosecuted.*

Adjectives and Adverbs

11. Distinguish clearly between adjectives and adverbs both in use and in form.

An adjective is used to modify a noun or a pronoun; an adverb is used to modify a verb, an adjective, or another adverb. Frequently the form of a word does not enable one to tell whether it is an adjective or an adverb. Although most words ending in *-ly* are adverbs, this ending is not an unfailing sign of an adverb, since such adjectives as *lovely, holy, manly,* and *saintly* also end in *-ly* and since *daily, early, kindly, friendly, lowly,* etc., may be used as adjectives or as adverbs. Furthermore, there are some "flat" adverbs identical in form with the corresponding adjectives: *much, cheap, fast, first, little, straight, clean, well, ill, far.* Finally, some adverbs have two forms, usually employed with a difference in meaning: *hard, hardly; sharp, sharply; high, highly; late, lately; direct, directly; right, rightly; wrong, wrongly.* When in doubt, use the form that ends in *-ly* unless it sounds stilted.

When an adverb has two forms, one with *-ly* and one without, with no difference in meaning, the form with *-ly* is always more formal.[1] See **Comparison** in § 16.

Formal The plot moves slowly because the characters are so verbose.
Colloq. Go slow until you see the city limit sign.
Formal Melville surely could not agree with all his "interpreters."
Colloq. Sure, I'll be there at eight sharp.

11a. Some adjectives and adverbs are identical in form. Many adjectives can be converted to adverbs only by adding *-ly,* but sometimes the addition of *-ly* is a matter of choice. Observe usage differences.

Nonstandard The last sonata was considerable harder to play.
Standard The last sonata was considerably harder to play.
Colloq. Their radio is playing; we can hear it easy.
Standard Their radio is playing; we can hear it easily.

11b. Copulas like *is, seems, becomes, feels, sounds, smells, tastes,*

[1] See p. 91 for definitions of *standard, colloquial, informal, formal,* and *nonstandard.*

and *looks* are usually followed by an adjective modifying the subject, not an adverb modifying the verb. See Copula in § 16.

Examples The flowers smelled bad; they must have been decayed.
She left early, saying she felt bad.
The ice looks safe; has anyone skated on it yet?

Compare The dog smelled hungrily around our back door.
She felt cautiously in the cedar chest for her locket.

11c. Use an adjective after such verbs as *dig, hold, knock, leave, make, nail, paint, think, regard,* etc., unless the modifier clearly describes the manner of the action.

Examples He held the box high off the floor.
He held the box carefully, as if it might explode.
The flag was nailed tight against the wall of the barn.
The painter objected when Mrs. Ober wanted to paint the living room walls red.

11d. Use a phrase or revise the sentence if the use of a noun as an adjective results in awkwardness.

In all varieties of English, nouns may be used as adjectives and adjectives as nouns; examples are *rock garden, oak floor, tire rack, book store, atom bomb, college president* (nouns into adjectives), and *the private, a general, a Red, the wealthy, the revolutionary* (adjectives into nouns). Short, simple nouns are most easily used as adjectives; longer, complex nouns frequently produce awkwardness when used as adjectives.

Standard She is giving a garden party. She has a new party dress.
Awkward He is a Positivism believer.
Revised He is a believer in Positivism.
Awkward They brought back many gruesome cannibalism stories.
Revised They brought back many gruesome stories of cannibalism.

Note that a series of nouns used as adjectives may make the sentence awkward.

Awkward We need a department store personnel management expert.
Revised We need a department store expert on personnel management.

11e. In very formal writing use the comparative when comparing two things, the superlative when comparing three or more. See § 73g.

Formal Both roads are paved, but the shore road is the shorter.
Informal Both roads are paved, but the shore road is the shortest.
Standard All the roads are paved, but the shore road is the widest.

EXERCISES

A. Select the preferable form in each of the following sentences, if there is a preferable form, noting carefully the usage level of each sentence.

1. The governor proposes to make the patrol (*real, really*) effective.
2. Each student in this curriculum is required to take two (*mathematics courses, courses in mathematics*).
3. Tie it (*tight, tightly*); this trail is rough and bumpy.
4. I'd drop it (*quickly, quick*) and sign up for another course.
5. Bohemians say oysters taste (*good, well*) with sour cream sauce.

B. Make the changes indicated below and then make any other necessary changes.

1. Delete *a* and *game*.
   He played a very good game after he got over his nervousness.
2. Change *helpless* to *helplessness*.
   Such a proposal always leaves me with a helpless feeling.
3. Add *at him* after *disgusted*.
   When the policeman finally arrived, Jasper looked disgusted.
4. Change *is* to *moves*.
   The action is very fast after a leisurely first act.
5. Add *bad* before *piece*.
   The teacher said it was an intolerable piece of typing.

C. For each of the following words compose (or find) two sentences in which (1) the word is used as an adjective, and (2) the word is used as an adverb.

1. open 2. early 3. well 4. clean 5. right

D. Are the nouns *dinner, city, eagerness, speech, banker, business, friendship*, and *excitement* commonly used as adjectives? List illustrative phrases.

Conjunctions

12. Select the conjunction which best shows the relationship between the sentence elements it joins.

Coördinating conjunctions, subordinating conjunctions, and conjunctive adverbs connect words, phrases, clauses, and sentences, and show the relationship between the elements joined. See § 68 and § 69. See § 88 for correlative conjunctions.

12a. Use coördinating conjunctions to connect elements of equal grammatical rank and to show the relationship between them.

The words *and, or, nor,* and *but* are the principal coördinating conjunctions; occasionally *so, yet,* and *for* serve as coördinating conjunctions between sentences or clauses. A coördinating conjunction is used to begin a sentence only when it is a link with a preceding sentence. Unlike subordinating conjunctions, coördinating conjunctions must stand between the elements that they join.

Coördinating *The Mikado* is better known, but I prefer *Iolanthe.*
It is the Spenserian stanza or a very similar form.

Subordinating Although the smog is bad, she prefers Birmingham.
She prefers Birmingham, although the smog is bad.
When the weather gets hot, she goes to the coast.
She goes to the coast when the weather gets hot.

In the examples note that *although* and *when* (which are subordinating) do not have to stand between the two clauses. Since *for* is like *and, or,* and *but* in the place where it may appear, it is better called a coördinating conjunction, although it is usually equivalent in meaning to *because,* which is a subordinating conjunction.

12b. Use a subordinating conjunction to connect a dependent clause with a main clause. Select the conjunction which best expresses the intended meaning.

Inexact While he glanced up before the other car skidded, he could not avoid the collision.

Revised Although he glanced up before the other car skidded, he could not avoid the collision.

Colloq. Some teachers prefer Chaucer in translation so the beginning student can get the meaning immediately.

Formal Some teachers prefer Chaucer in translation so that the beginning student can grasp the meaning immediately.

Some of the most common subordinating conjunctions, including phrasal groups, are listed below, classified according to meaning:

Cause: *as, because, since, whereas, for*
Concession: *although, granted that, though, while*
Manner: *as, as if, as though*
Purpose: *in order that, so that, so*
Time: *after, as soon as, while, since, when*

Adverbs like *where, whither, how,* and *why,* and relative pronouns like *who, which, what,* and *that,* also function as subordinating conjunctions. *Directly, except, immediately,* and *on account of* are not used as subordinating conjunctions in standard English.[1]

Nonstandard The car will be ready immediately the paint dries.

Standard The car will be ready as soon as the paint dries.

12c. Distinguish between simple conjunctions and conjunctive adverbs. The latter are normally preceded by a semicolon.

An adverb used to join two independent clauses and to modify the second clause is called a conjunctive adverb, because it functions as both an adverb and a conjunction. Examples are *therefore, then, thus, still, consequently, moreover, accordingly, likewise, nevertheless, furthermore,* and *besides.* The two words *so* and *yet,* formerly always adverbs, are frequently weakened in meaning, becoming equivalent to *and* or *but,* and are then punctuated as coördinating conjunctions.

Examples Every example that he cites is spurious; therefore I cannot subscribe to his theory.
Several reviewers have pointed this out; nevertheless he continues to argue his point.

Contrast I am therefore unable to subscribe to the theory, although he continues to insist on its value.

[1] See p. 91 for definitions of *standard, colloquial, informal, formal,* and *nonstandard.*

12d. In formal English prefer *as* or *as if* (*as though*) to *like* as a conjunction. *As if* and *as though* are interchangeable.

Formal The woman began speaking quietly, as if she were telling an everyday experience.

Formal Students do not regard such matters as we faculty members do.

Colloquial Students don't look on such matters like faculty members do.

NOTE. In "He sings like a professional" *like* is a preposition.

EXERCISES

A. Replace all inexact conjunctions in the following sentences.

1. Kriss was ordinarily a docile prisoner, and sometimes he became intractable.
2. He has received six demerits for fighting in the recreation hall; also he has made two attempts to escape.
3. The new fruit looks very much like an oversized lemon.
4. The radio is out of commission although a tube is burned out.
5. The old man couldn't listen to the quiz show on account of the radio was not working.

B. List and classify all the conjunctions in Paragraph 20, page 69.

C. Identify all the coördinating conjunctions in Paragraph 12, page 59, and point out the elements which they connect.

Pronouns

13. Learn to recognize and use correctly the various classes of pronouns.

English pronouns are an arbitrary group of words which function as subject, object, complement, modifier, or connective. Usually a pronoun stands for a noun, which is called its *antecedent*. See Exercise D, page 144. A pronoun which can be inflected agrees with its antecedent in gender, number, and person, but not necessarily in case. See §§ 6, 7, 25, and 93.

CLASSES. Pronouns are classified as follows:

1. Personal. (*I, my, mine, me; we, our, ours, us; you, your, yours; he, his, him; she, her, hers; it, its; they, their, theirs, them*).

2. Compound personal, used either as reflexives — to refer to the same person as the subject — or as intensives — to emphasize a preceding substantive.

Examples He cut *himself* (reflexive).
I *myself* say it (intensive).

3. Relative, used both to refer to an antecedent and to connect a dependent clause with a main clause: *who, which, that, what, whoever, whatever,* etc.

Example The automobile *which* I bought had been run only five thousand miles. (In this sentence *which* is both a pronoun and a connective.)

4. Interrogative, used to ask questions: *who, which, what.*

Example *What* happened?

5. Demonstrative, used to point out a specific person or thing: *this, that, these, those.*

Example I never saw *that* happen before in a football game.

6. Indefinite, used to refer to a person or thing less definitely than a demonstrative does: *one, some, someone, each, either, all, few, several, many,* etc.

Example *One* should observe all the traffic rules now, for the police are arresting all violators.

7. Reciprocal, used to express mutual action or relationship: *each other, one another.*

Example The two small boys hit *each other* blow after blow.

Note. When a personal pronoun in the genitive, or when any demonstrative, indefinite, interrogative, or relative pronoun modifies a noun, it is called a *pronominal adjective.* Relatives, and sometimes interrogatives, function as subordinating conjunctions.

13a. An inflected pronoun usually agrees with its antecedent in gender, number, and person. See § 5b.

not case

Nonstandard Each patron will be given their receipt at the door.
Standard Each patron will be given his receipt at the door.

Standard	Everybody cheered when he waved to them.
Formal	Everyone is requested to remove his hat.

13b. In formal English, use *this, that, these,* or *those* only when the pronoun clearly refers to an antecedent or is explained by something which follows in the sentence.

Colloq.	And this girl who worked there fainted.
Formal	And a (or *the*) girl who worked there fainted.
Colloq.	It looks like one of those twisters.
Formal	It looks like one of those cyclones we have expected.

Note that the antecedent need not appear in the sentence. It may be in another sentence, or it may be unexpressed but made clear by pointing or other non-linguistic means. Clear reference is often more a matter of stylistic nicety in writing than a matter of clarity in meaning.

13c. In formal English, when the word *it* is used as an ordinary pronoun, be careful to make its antecedent clear.

Colloq.	Although he was very ambitious, it wasn't enough to make him a successful store manager.
Formal	Although he had much ambition, it was not sufficient to make him a successful store manager.
Colloq.	The dean's office reported that he was sick, but it wasn't serious enough to excuse his absences.
Formal	The dean's office reported that he was sick, but his sickness was not so serious as to justify his absences.
Colloq.	It says in the morning paper that high winds are likely.
Formal	The morning paper reports that high winds are likely.

Remember that *it* is sometimes used (1) as the apparent subject of a verb which lacks a genuine subject or which has a deferred subject, and (2) as the apparent object of an intransitive verb. In these constructions *it* has no antecedent.

Standard	The weather bureau reported that it was snowing. It became clear that the judge was prejudiced. Would it be possible for Mr. Abrams to come?
Standard (*but wordy*)	It was at this point that the speaker began to lose the sympathy of the audience.

Revised	At this point the speaker began to lose the sympathy of the audience.
Colloquial	"How goes it?" "The car broke down and we had to foot it." "Tell those boys to beat it."

13d. In writing, use a compound personal pronoun only in intensive or reflexive functions, or as the second member of a compound object.

Colloq.	Stephen and myself will be ushers at the wedding.
Formal	Stephen and I will be ushers at the wedding.
Standard	Does Stephen include himself when he speaks of "lucky bachelors"?
Standard	We want you to ask her yourself.
Informal	It was hard for as poor a mathematician as myself. (After *than* or *as* in a comparison.)
Formal	It was hard for as poor a mathematician as I.
Standard	Miss Thompson proposed a debate between Lippman and herself. (Second member of a compound object.) [1]
Standard	I thought you would meet Sarah and myself at the airport. (Second member of a compound object.)
Standard	She preferred to live by herself.

13e. Except in the most formal writing, use *he, his,* or *him* with the antecedents *one, everyone, anyone, etc.,* rather than repeat *one* or *one's* as the pronoun.

Stilted	One should verify one's spelling before handing in a written report.
Standard	One should verify his spelling before handing in a written report.

13f. Use *you* or *they* as an indefinite pronoun only in informal writing or in speech.

Colloq.	You can see strange things in Zamboanga.
Formal	One can see strange things in Zamboanga.
Standard	A visitor can see strange things in Zamboanga.

13g. Distinguish between *who, which,* and *that.*

Who refers usually only to persons, *which* usually only to things,

[1] See R. C. Pooley, *Teaching English Usage,* pp. 156–159.

and *that* to persons or things. However, collective nouns such as *jury, committee, council, court* take *which* when the group is regarded as a unit, and the genitive form *whose* is frequently used with things to avoid an awkward *of which*.

Who and *which* may be used in both restrictive and nonrestrictive clauses; *that* is used only in restrictive clauses. See § 17c.

Examples The pronunciation which (or *that*) I prefer is the older.
In my dialect, which (not *that*) is Midland, the words "horse" and "hoarse" are homophones.

Aimless shifting between *who* and *that* (referring to persons) and *which* and *that* (referring to things) should be avoided, particularly in parallel constructions.

Example Oneonta, which is a town name in Alabama, and that is also a town name in New York, has two pronunciations.

Revised Oneonta, which is a town name in Alabama, and which is also a town name in New York, has two pronunciations.

EXERCISES

A. In the sentences below change any pronouns which are not appropriate to the sentences.

1. The tribe to whom we were sent had been in Oklahoma many years.
2. Yourself and Ratchford will be the nominees.
3. Attendant, how does one find one's locker in this gym?
4. The third point is that they rarely know, in city councils, how the suburban citizens think about such matters.
5. These flying saucers that we read about can be explained.

B. Make the changes indicated and then any other necessary changes.

1. Add *chairman of the* before *commission.*
   The commission, which has disagreed with the governor, will be under heavy pressure to accept the regulation.
2. Change *person* to *one.*
   Each person was assigned to a lifeboat near his stateroom.
3. Change to very formal style.
   I'd like to know what they do for amusement at State College.

4. Change *fish* to *people.*
   Are animals and fish which have been inoculated entirely immune to this disease?
5. Change to formal style.
   Wilma's asked everybody to bring their bathing suits.

C. Find all the pronouns in Paragraphs 1 and 2 on pages 44–45 and classify them according to the types listed on pages 139–40.

D. Identify the antecedents of the pronouns in the following sentences. Note the expressed antecedents, the implied antecedents, and the pronouns without an antecedent.

1. Before coming to this high school as principal, she was dean of girls at Oak High School in Cedarcrest.
2. He is one of those self-satisfied people with good jobs who never understand why anybody else needs unemployment insurance.
3. Governor Dewey called in the reporters and told them that he would not be a candidate.
4. When we left nobody thought that it would rain that day.
5. Does anyone think that his real wages have declined in value?

Confusion of Clauses

14. Learn to distinguish between a noun clause and an adverbial clause.

Noun clause as subject:

That he is angry amuses me. (The clause *that he is angry* has the same function here that a simple noun would have: *Comedy* amuses me, *Skelton* amuses me, *Fiction* amuses me.)

Noun clause as object:

We saw *that it was snowing.* (The clause *that it was snowing* has the same function here that a simple noun would have: We saw *wheat,* We saw *men,* We saw *Skelton.*)

Adverbial clause (of place):

We sat *where it was cool.* (The clause *where it was cool* has the same function here that a simple adverb would have: We sat *there,* We sat *inside,* We sat *here.*)

Adverbial clause (of time):

We came *when she called.* (The clause *when she called* has the same function here that a simple adverb would have: We came *then,* We came *later,* We came *early.*)

14a. Make the structure and function of subordinate clauses absolutely clear.

In the sentence *We know* [*that*] *he was angry* the conjunction *that* can be omitted without misleading the reader. Sometimes, however, the omission of the conjunction makes the sentence misleading or confusing. The use of a noun clause without *that* as the subject of a verb is particularly annoying to readers. Study the examples below.

Confused	Milton considered the purpose of evil was to teach the nature of good by contrast. (The reader is annoyed by misreading *the purpose* . . . as the object of *considered,* and not as the subject of *was.*)
Improved	Milton considered *that* the purpose of evil was to teach the nature of good by contrast.
Confused	I had an accident is the cause of my being late
Improved	I am late *because* I had an accident.
Confused	The greatest benefit I received from my course in psychology was it taught me to concentrate when I study.
Improved	The greatest benefit I received from my course in psychology was *that* it taught me how to concentrate when I study.

NOTE. A quoted sentence, however, may be used as a noun clause:

"Every beginning is hard" is the translation of a German proverb.

Although such conjunctions as *when, where, since, while,* and *because* normally introduce adverbial clauses, remember that the function of the clause, not the conjunction alone, determines whether it is noun, adjectival, or adverbial.[1] Furthermore, conjunctions are used in different ways in different varieties of English. In the sentence "This is the place *where Lincoln delivered a famous address*" the *where*-clause is adjectival. In formal definitions, where *is* serves as a copula, a substantive follows the verb: "A conserva-

[1] See Russell Thomas, "When-clauses After Is (Was)," *College English,* X (April, 1949), 406–408.

tive is a person who wishes to preserve existing conditions." (Compare nonstandard "A conservative is when a person wishes. . . .") However, *is* sometimes means "takes place" or "comes about" and can be followed, especially in informal English, by an adverbial clause: "A hassle is when baseball players get in a quarrel."

14b. In formal writing do not use an adverbial clause as a noun clause or as an adjective clause.[1]

Colloq. The reason I had an automobile accident was because I had lost a great deal of sleep.

Formal The reason I had an automobile accident was that I had lost a great deal of sleep.

Colloq. Only because I don't think the idea fair is why I object so strenuously.

Formal I object so strenuously because I do not think the idea fair.

Colloq. A dramatic monologue is where only one person speaks to an audience.

Standard In a dramatic monologue only one person speaks to an audience. A dramatic monologue is a poem in which only one person speaks to an audience.

EXERCISES

A. In the following sentences revise any constructions that are not appropriate. Note that sentences 3 and 5 are clearly colloquial.

1. One can find evidence in many magazines of the 1920's where writers realized that the economic situation was not healthy.
2. A conjunctive adverb is when an adverb is used to connect two clauses in a compound sentence.
3. The reason why I want you to bring those books up from the basement and put them in the attic is because the basement gets damp in wet weather.
4. The principal difference between the two professors was they held divergent opinions on the "new criticism."
5. Because I don't think the decision good is why I spoke so strongly.

B. Make the changes indicated, then any other necessary changes. In revising, prefer complex sentence structure.

[1] See p. 91 for definitions of *standard, colloquial, informal, formal,* and *nonstandard.*

1. Delete *this*.
   The reason many students misspell *affect* and *effect* is this: both words are pronounced alike in most American speech.
2. Change *occurs* to *is*.
   Metathesis occurs when two sounds are transposed, as in the pronunciation *whipser* for *whisper*.
3. Delete *that*.
   His mother came from eastern New England; that is why he has some pronunciations that sound strange here in Idaho.
4. Begin the sentence with *The reason*.
   It is hard to indicate pronunciation with our alphabet because we have three times as many vowel sounds as vowel letters.
5. Begin the sentence with *The reason*.
   We got here so much sooner than we expected to because we found a short cut that saved ten miles.

Double Negative

15. Avoid redundant and nonstandard double negatives.

Constructions in which two negatives make an affirmative, such as *not unclean, never illogical, not infrequently,* are standard English. The use of two negatives modifying different words, once standard English, is now nonstandard. Such sentences as *I didn't say nothing* and *He hasn't got none* are unambiguous and emphatic, but are serious errors in linguistic etiquette. They are regularly regarded as nonstandard.

Nonstandard He didn't interview none of the victims at the time.
Standard He didn't interview any of the victims at the time.

The words *but* (meaning *only*), *hardly, scarcely,* and *only* are negative in meaning, so that *can't help but, wasn't hardly, couldn't scarcely, haven't only,* etc. are double negative constructions. This type of double negation is common, even in cultivated speech, but is generally avoided in formal written English.

Formal Your handwriting is so illegible that we could hardly read what you had written.

Informal	Mr. Truman couldn't help but veto this bill.
Formal	Mr. Truman could not help vetoing this bill.
Formal	The once proud nation could not but surrender unconditionally. (Idiomatic.)

EXERCISES

A. Revise any of the following sentences which contain inappropriate double negatives.

1. Tests showed that the water in the pool was not impure.
2. Scarcely nobody was ready when the warning buzzer sounded.
3. We are not certain that the playground won't be graded and equipped by the time school opens in the fall.
4. No fishing nor swimming is allowed on these premises.
5. The United Nations couldn't hardly ignore the Arab argument.

B. Directions given under Exercise A.

1. The driver pushed down the accelerator. "Cain't nobody catch us once we get past the river bridge," he yelled.
2. They could not see in the dim light of early evening whether no one was sitting on the library steps.
3. She couldn't leave that night; neither the train nor the bus could get out because of the flood.
4. You can't but admire the way the old man keeps on working.
5. Mother, I don't see but one box of cereal in the cabinet.

General Exercises in Grammar

A. Sentences in this exercise are presumed to be in formal English. Make the changes indicated, and then any other necessary changes.

1. Insert the proper form of *suppose* after *is*.
   Taps are blown at ten o'clock and everyone is to be in bed.
2. Substitute *who* or *whom* for *that*.
   Every young idealist is prone to follow the lives of those that they deem better than themselves.

3. Change *master* to *mastery.*
   The first requirement, I believe, is that the instructor be a thorough master of his subject.
4. Substitute *such as* for *we saw.*
   There were all kinds of actors. We saw horseback riders, clowns, tightrope walkers, and tumblers.
5. Insert *but* before *two.*
   The company did not have two actors who knew their parts on the night of the dress rehearsal.
6. Insert *anxiety, and tension* after *worry.*
   Man fully realizes the important part which worry plays in his life in the twentieth century.
7. Substitute a period for the comma after the first *it.*
   Industrial waste is dumped into this stream, the city sewage system empties into it, and heavy rains subject it to flash floods every spring.
8. Substitute *move* for *hope.*
   I hope that the treasurer of this organization is instructed to refund $50.00 to Mr. Lawley after tonight's meeting.
9. Begin the sentence with *Johnson knew that.*
   The manager has eliminated all the candidates for art editor except Christie and Johnson.
10. Change *is* to *was.*
    Since she is over seventy, one expects to find a feeble old lady who cannot move or act quickly.

B. Sentences in this exercise are presumed to be in informal English. Make the changes indicated, and then any other necessary changes.

1. Substitute *was* for *is.*
   The hero's sudden affection for Madeline is not made quite plausible. Though he shows pity when he discovers her poverty.
2. Substitute *it* for *that.*
   Paul suddenly discovered an unusual knock in the motor that caused him to wonder whether he had put in oil recently.
3. Substitute *neither* for *both.*
   Both of the fishing holes you told me about are now open to the public.
4. Substitute a personal pronoun for *Menner.*
   Aren't you upset about Menner being left off the guest list?

5. Add *already* after *association.*
   The state editors' association held its annual summer meeting at a resort hotel in the mountains.
6. Change the verb in the main clause to past tense.
   She lies on a sun deck two hours every morning trying to get a sun tan because people expect a vacationer to be sunburned.
7. Insert an adverb indicating that the stop was sudden.
   The child stopped halfway across the street when he heard a dog barking on the other side.
8. Change *the audience* to *everybody.*
   The announcer encouraged the audience to clap their hands and stamp their feet when a speaker was introduced.
9. Add *had* after *speaker.*
   The speaker forgot his manuscript, but he gave the speech so often that he could do it from memory.
10. Begin the sentence with *Last year.*
    The football team wins the hard games without many injuries but in the breathers half the players seem to get hurt.

C. Change any nonstandard constructions in the following sentences to standard, but do not change the style from informal to formal.

1. The sun was shining very bright, so we ask the neighbors if they'd lend us straw hats.
2. The woman resented her husband and his brothers setting on the porch all morning talking while she worked at housekeeping.
3. The reason she missed the bus and had to take a taxi to town was because she'd laid in bed with a headache till after ten o'clock.
4. Most of his impressions of doctors he's had and those who he's met at the hospital have been favorably.
5. Between you and I there will be no misunderstanding of this contract, but the man whom I think will succeed me doesn't know how we have interpreted the price formula.

D. Rewrite the sentences in Exercise C in formal English.

E. In the story below, which is written in informal English, you will find much nonstandard grammar. Copy the narrative *line by line* so that you will have fifty lines as in the original. Write *Colloq.* above any expression which would not be appropriate if the discourse were written in formal English. Change all non-standard expressions to standard English.

BUILDING A RADIO-PHONOGRAPH

On account of everybody in our family like to listen to
records and our old radio didn't have a player, last summer
Mother asks me to install one. Which I was glad to do, since
I had a couple of weeks with nothing to do before going to
5 National Guard camp.

The old cabinet wasn't big enough was why I had to look
for another one, neither of the radio shops sell empty cabi-
nets. Looking all over town, finally I found a big one in a
second hand furniture store. With no works in it. I bought
10 it we spent four days scraping and varnishing it till it
looked real good, like it was a new cabinet. You couldn't
hardly tell it had been did over, also the old radio fit in
it pretty well after I'd sawn off some braces in the cabinet.

Mother and me went down town and got a player, one of the
15 33-1/3 r.p.m. long play jobs. And several platters, which I
would have liked to have heard before we had got them, but
we had to hurry, being that it was near closing time. After
I'd mashed two fingers with the hammer, broke Father new
screwdriver and bent the pliers' handle, the player has been
20 put in the cabinet.

We tried the radio first, it picked up London and Montreal
but couldn't tune in none of the local stations. Mother said
something must be wrong. Then she tried to use the
vacuum cleaner in her bedroom and it picked up music
25 very faint from a local station. After I'd shook the set once
or twice and reversed a few connections when the radio began to
work all right, probably I was lucky. After having had several
experiences like that, we got the player connected also some
records on the changer. If I was to tell all the troubles we'd
30 had, you wouldn't hardly believe me.

Then Father decided the LP discs sound better in the store
then on our set, we must have had a poor radio in the first place.
I next gotten a speaker which was nearly new but didn't fit a
radio a neighbor had had and hooked it up in our cabinet. That
35 was better, but neither Father or I were satisfied. Hoping to
get wider range performance. We put in a pre-amplifier and a

fancy new cartridge. Father become satisfied but Mother begun to feel different. She said so many songs she wanted to hear wasn't on LP, She argued so much until I give up and swapped our
40 player for a two-speed machine. It was air-cooled and had a little broom to sweep the records off but weren't equipped with no time clock to turn it on every morning.

Two days before my two weeks is up, Father, a real music lover, found out about 45 r.p.m. players and here we go again. Soon as
45 he brung one home I went into the cabinet again, broke a finger nail and three vases doing it, and founded space for the newest turntable. Connecting it was something else. All the time Mother complaining because she couldn't listen to Arthur Godfrey while we had the machine tore down. Fortune for me, the thing run good
50 just before I left so my name ain't mud yet at home.

Grammatical Terms

16. Learn to analyze a sentence into its component parts.

More specifically, learn to recognize the *framework* of a sentence (subject, predicate, complement, and modifiers); the parts of speech; and learn to distinguish clearly between a sentence, a clause, and a phrase.

Absolute An *absolute* expression is a grammatically independent element, one with no syntactical relation to any other word in the sentence. *Absolute phrases* consist of a noun or a pronoun and a participle. *The day being chilly*, we put on our coats. (*Day* is called a *nominative absolute*.) Do not confuse the absolute construction with the construction consisting of a noun or a pronoun modified by a participial modifier: "The day, *having dawned clear and chilly*, was just the kind we had been waiting for." (In this sentence the italicized expression is a participial modifier of *day*, the subject of the sentence.) See **Independent Element.**

Adjective A word used to limit or qualify a noun or a pronoun. Typical limiting adjectives are *third*, *the*, and *certain*. Typical qualifying adjectives are *pretty*, *sour*, and *risky*. See **Comparison,** page 154, and Adjectives and Adverbs, § 11.

Adjective Clause A subordinate clause introduced by a relative pronoun or relative adverb and used like an adjective, to modify a noun or a pronoun: "The house, *which was old and deserted*, stood near the road." Note that an adjective clause stands after the substantive which it modifies.

Adverb A word used to modify a verb, an adjective, a verbal, or another adverb. Relative and interrogative adverbs are like subordinating conjunctions in that they serve to join a main clause and a subordinate clause: "I do not see the place *where* he put the box." "I do not know *why* he came." See Conjunctions, § 12, and Adjectives and Adverbs, § 11.

Adverbial Clause A subordinate clause used as an adverb. Adverbial clauses express ideas of time, place, purpose, manner, result, etc. See § 12.

Agreement Correspondence in form between two parts of speech, as a verb and its subject or a pronoun and its antecedent. See §§ 5, 6.

Antecedent The substantive to which a pronoun refers. In "The chemist must revise his atomic table," *chemist* is the antecedent of *his*. See Pronouns, § 13.

Appositive A substantive used both to limit or explain another substantive and to refer to the same person or thing: "John Smith, *my uncle*, wrote the editorial." (*Uncle* is in apposition with *John Smith*.) "The novelist *Steinbeck* wrote *The Grapes of Wrath*." (*Steinbeck* is in apposition with *novelist*.) Phrases and clauses may also be used as appositives. See § 17h.

Article *The* is the definite article; *a* and *an* are indefinite articles. *A* is used before words beginning with a consonant sound, *an* before words beginning with a vowel sound. See § 66 under **A, An.**

Auxiliary A verb of incomplete predication used with another verb to form a verb phrase indicating voice, mood, or tense. *Have, may, can, be, shall, will, must, ought*, and *do* are common auxiliaries. "I *have* lost my purse." (The verb phrase here is *have lost*.) Most auxiliaries are also used as independent verbs: "I *have* no brothers." An auxiliary is a type of **Function Word,** q.v.

Case In modern English *case* usually refers to form, e.g. *man* (common case), *man's* (genitive case), *he* (subjective case), *his* (genitive case), *him* (objective case). However, some grammarians use *case* to indicate function, describing *Wilson* and *manuscript* in "Lane sent Wilson the manuscript" as in the objective case, and *Lane* as in the subjective case. See Case, § 7.

Clause A group of words which contains a subject and a predicate but which is a part of a larger construction (a sentence). By structure, clauses are independent and dependent; by function dependent clauses are noun, adjective, and adverbial. See §§ 1 and 14.

Collective Noun See **Noun.**

Colloquial Referring to features of language which are characteristic of speech (and writing which imitates speech) rather than of deliberately formal writing. See pages 91–94.

Common Noun See **Noun.**

Comparison The modification of an adjective or adverb to indicate degrees of superiority and inferiority in quantity, quality, or intensity. The three degrees are positive (*high, quickly, good*), comparative (*higher, more quickly, less quickly, better*), and superlative (*highest, most quickly, least quickly, best*).

Normally the shorter and more common words are compared by inflectional endings: *cooler, weakest;* and longer or less common words by *more* and *most: more satisfactory, most talkative.* See § 11.

Complement A word or group of words necessary to complete the meaning of a verb. "He is a *lawyer*." (*Lawyer* is a subjective complement, or predicate noun.) "The lawyer is very *aggressive*." (*Aggressive* is a subjective complement, or predicate adjective.) "We should elect him *mayor*." (*Him* is a direct object; *mayor* is an objective complement, or predicate objective.)

Complex Sentence A sentence made up of one independent clause and one or more dependent clauses. "If you compare the grammar of today with Shakespeare's grammar, you will find that a number of changes have taken place."

Compound-complex Sentence A sentence made up of two or more independent clauses and one or more dependent clauses: "Although he is seventy years old, he goes to work every day and his health is very good."

Compound Predicate A predicate containing two or more coördinate verbs or verb phrases. Hopkins denied saying "We will tax and tax, and spend and spend, and elect and elect."

Compound Sentence A sentence made up of two or more independent clauses. "This dictionary lists nearly a million words, but it does not include many terms heard on college campuses."

Conjugation The inflections (and sometimes the phrasal constructions) of a verb used to indicate person, number, tense, mood, and voice.

Conjunction A word used to connect words, phrases, clauses, and sentences. See § 12. See also **Preposition.**

Conjunctive Adverb An adverb used as a conjunction. See § 12c.

Construction A combination of forms in a grammatical unit. Constructions involving affixes (jump*ed*, loud*ly*, *un*done) are called morphological; those involving words (*will go, of wood, for you*) are called syntactic or periphrastic.

Coördinate Of equal grammatical rank; not subordinate. In "Steel and concrete are expensive, but beams made of them are strong and last forever" there are two coördinate clauses; the first clause has coördinate nouns, and the second has coördinate verbs.

Copula, Copulative Verb, Linking Verb A verb used to link a subject with a predicate complement. *Is, was, are, seems, becomes, looks, smells, tastes,* (and sometimes *sounds* and *feels*) are common copulas.

Correlative Conjunction A conjunction used as a member of a pair; examples are *either . . . or, neither . . . nor, both . . . and.* See § 88.

Declension The inflections of a noun or a pronoun for case, number, or person.

Demonstrative See Pronouns, § 13.

Dependent Clause See page 98.

Direct Address See **Vocative.**

Direct and Indirect Discourse Direct discourse is the quoting of the exact words of another person: John said, "I am sorry that I cannot come."

Indirect discourse is summarizing in your own words what another person has said or written: John said that he was sorry he could not come. See §§ 27, 28.

Ellipsis The omission of a word or words easily implied from the context. "These are the books [that] I bought." "He is taller than I [am]."

Expletive *It, here,* or *there* when used to introduce a verb that precedes the subject. "*It* is true that he is not coming." "*Here* comes the parade." "*There* are many men present."

Finite, or Predicative, Verb A verb that changes in form to agree with the subject in person and number; a verb form that is capable of making an independent assertion concerning the subject. The nonfinite forms of the verb — infinitive, gerund, and participle — are incapable of making an independent assertion. See pages 96–97.

Formal See pages 91–94.

Function The way in which a word or a word-group is used in a sentence. There are only five important functions: subject, verb (predicate), complement, modifier, and connective (conjunctions and prepositions).

Function Word A word which has no concrete meaning and which is used principally to indicate relations between other words.

Examples son *of* mine, *will* go, *to* sing, *didn't* try, *get* sick, hold *up*, *is* cool

Gender The classification of such nouns as *father, maid,* and *pen* and third person singular pronouns (*he, his, him; she, her, hers; it, its*) as masculine, feminine, or neuter. "Maleness" is a part of the meaning of *father* and *he* just as "loudness" is a part of the meaning of *roar* and *shout.*

Genitive Case The inflected form of a noun (*son's, women's, thieves'*) or of a pronoun (*my, his, its, whose*) used to indicate various relationships such as possession. See § 7.

Gerund A verb form in *-ing* which is used as a noun, but which can have an object and which can be modified by an adjective or an adverb: "Rapid *typing* is her forte." "*Typing* rapidly does not seem to tire her." "*Typing* a thesis in German is hard work." See **Participle.** See also pages 96 and 97.

Govern A verb or a preposition is said to "govern" its object; that is, the verb or preposition requires the substantive object to assume a form showing its relation to the governing word.

Likewise, a clause on which another clause depends is said to "govern" the dependent clause.

Homophone A word which is identical in sound (but not in meaning) with another word. Examples are *bread* and *bred*, *been* and *bin*, *frees*, *freeze*, and *frieze*. Some homophones, such as *affect* and *effect*, *accept* and *except*, may be pronounced differently for contrast, but in normal speech they are identical.

Idiom See § 52.

Indefinite Pronoun See Pronouns, § 13.

Independent Clause See pages 97–98.

Independent Element A word or a group of words not having any grammatical connection with the sentence in which it stands. Vocatives, interjections, absolute phrases, and strongly parenthetical expressions are independent elements.

Indirect Discourse See **Direct Discourse.**

Infinitive The first principal part of a verb (usually preceded by *to*), frequently used as a noun. The infinitive is a verbal noun. It resembles a verb in that it may have an adverbial modifier and can take a subject, an object, or a predicate objective; it resembles a noun in that it can perform the chief functions of a noun. It may be used as subject of the verb, as direct object, as complement, as appositive, etc. The infinitive may also be used as a modifier, as in "The water is not fit *to drink*." The infinitive (without *to*) is used with function words to form many verb constructions: He will *go*, I don't *swim*, Can't you *swim?* Another common type is "They helped him *work* the problem."

Inflection The change in the form of a word to show a change in meaning or a change in relationship to another word or word group. English nouns are inflected for case and number; pronouns for case, number, and person; verbs for tense, number, and person. See **Declension, Conjugation,** and **Comparison.**

Informal See pages 91–94.

Intensive Pronoun See Pronouns, § 13.

Interjection An exclamatory word or phrase used independently in a sentence.

Intransitive, Transitive A transitive verb has an object; an intransitive verb does not have an object. A verb in the passive voice is transitive only if it has a *retained object.*

Examples She plays the piano. (Transitive.)
She plays beautifully. (Intransitive.)
She was given the piano. (Transitive, with retained object.)

Most verbs can be used either transitively or intransitively, but copulas are always intransitive. *Lie, sit,* and *rise* are normally intransitive; *lay, set,* and *raise* are normally transitive. See **Voice.**

Limiting Adjective An adjective, such as *tenth, this, some,* which restricts rather than qualifying or describing. Contrast such qualifying adjectives as *good, strong, happy.*

Linking Verb See **Copula.**

Main Clause An independent clause. See page 98.

Major Sentence A complete, independent utterance. See § 1.

Minor Sentence An utterance lacking a verb or a subject or an independent predication. See § 1 and pp. 5–6, 102.

Modal Auxiliary An auxiliary verb used to form a verb phrase indicating mood. "He *may* come." "I *should* have come sooner." See Subjunctive Mood, § 8.

Mode See **Mood.**

Modification Limiting, defining, qualifying, or describing the meaning of a word or a group of words. "Stagnant water is unwholesome." *Stagnant* modifies the noun *water* and gives it a meaning not possessed by the unmodified noun.

Modifier A word or group of words used to limit, define, qualify, or describe the meaning of other words in the sentence. A modifier may be a single word, a phrase, or a dependent clause. A dependent clause used as a modifier has the function of an adjective or an adverb. For examples of properly punctuated modifiers, see § 17c.

Mood A change in the inflection of a verb to indicate the manner in which the speaker views or conceives the action or state of the verb.

The *indicative* mood states or questions a fact: "He came." "Did he come?"

The *subjunctive* mood views the action as conditional, possible, doubtful, desired, supposed, or unreal. "If he *were* here, we *could* go on with the program."

The *imperative* mood is used to give a command or an entreaty. "Bring your dictionary to class." "Trade at Blank's Store." "Buy savings bonds." The "polite imperative" may be in question form with or without a question mark: "Will you please call on our auditor."

See also § 8.

Nominative Absolute See **Absolute.**

Nonessential Modifier, Nonrestrictive Modifier See § 17c.

Nonstandard See pages 91–94.

Noun One of the major parts of speech in English. Nouns are usually inflected for plural number (*desk, desks; tooth, teeth*) and for genitive case (*man, man's; month, month's*), can be modified by adjectives (big *desk;* pretty *teeth;* long *month*), and fill the office of substantives (*men* change; the *tooth* hurts; the *dentist* pulled her *tooth*). The traditional definition of a noun as the name of a person, place, or thing is of little use in analyzing sentences; only *after* we determine that a word is a noun (by observing its form or function) do we know that it names something. For instance, in the sentence "This little smud contains three gorps" we instantly identify *smud* as a noun because it is in subject position and is modified by adjectives; we identify *gorps* as a noun because it is in object position, is modified by an adjective, and has plural form, agreeing with the plural adjective. If we say that these words are nouns because they name something, we actually mean "have noun form and function" when we say "name something."

A *proper* noun usually is not modified by an article, is singular in number, and is definite. It refers to a particular person, place, or thing: *Joseph, Palo Alto, Cuba, Baltimore.* See § 32c.

A *common* noun usually may be modified by an article, is singular or plural, and is definite or indefinite. It refers to a class or a member of a class of persons, places, or things: *calliope, judge, egg, democrat, bronze.*

A *collective* noun refers to a group or collection, not a single person or thing: *jury, council, family, flock, covey.*

An *abstract* noun refers to something (its referent) which cannot be perceived by one of the five senses: *hate, patriotism, goodness, truth, mind.*

A *concrete* noun refers to something (its referent) which can be perceived by one of the five senses: *fish, piano, egg.*

A *compound* noun is a substantive formed by uniting two or more words: *postman, post office, son-in-law.*

Noun Clause See **Substantive Clause.**

Number The form of a noun or of a pronoun, which indicates whether its referent is one (*singular*) or more than one (*plural*). The form of a verb which indicates whether its subject is singular or plural. See §§ 5 and 6.

Object A word, phrase, or subordinate clause used to indicate the person or thing affected by the action of a transitive verb; or the substantive following a preposition.

The noun, pronoun, or clause which is the immediate goal of the action of the verb is called the *direct object:* "He repairs *furniture.*" "She called *him.*" "Please tell *whoever answers the telephone.*" The direct object normally comes after the verb in a sentence.

The noun, pronoun, or clause which is the ultimate goal of the action of the verb is called the *indirect object:* "He sold the *lawyer* a desk." "The lawyer sent *me* a bill." "Please tell *whoever answers* that she is sick." The indirect object normally follows the verb and precedes the direct object. However, when the ultimate goal is the object of a preposition in an adverbial phrase modifying the verb, it follows the direct object: "The captain sent a message to *me.*"

The noun or adjective referring to the same person or thing as the direct object is called the *predicate objective,* or *objective complement:* "The men elected Harry (direct object) captain" (predicate objective, or objective complement). See **Intransitive.**

Objective Complement See **Object.**

Parenthetical Element An expression interrupting a sentence that would be grammatically complete without it. See **Independent Element** above. For the punctuation of parenthetical expressions, see pages 171–177.

Parse To analyze and describe the form and use of a word or a group of words.

Participle An adjective derived from a verb and sharing the nature of both adjective and verb. A participle differs from a verb in not being used to make an assertion. It resembles a verb in that it may be modified by an adverb and may take an object. It resembles an adjective in that it may modify a substantive and be modified by an adverb. The participle has two forms: *walking, walked; beginning, begun.* The present participle and the gerund both end in *-ing*. See **Gerund** and also page 96.

Parts of Speech The classification of words according to their forms and functions. The eight parts of speech are *noun, pronoun, adjective, adverb, verb, preposition, conjunction,* and *interjection.* These are all discussed in their proper alphabetical order in this section. To determine what part of speech a word is, ask yourself what its forms are, and how it is used in the sentence. Nouns have characteristic forms (*speaker, speaker's, speakers*) as do verbs (*relieve, relieved, relieving*). However, since a very large number of words can be either noun or verb (*head, hand, walk, run, light, strike, review, test, subject, object*) you would have to examine such a word in a sentence (to learn whether it is a subject or object or predicate, or whether it is modified by an adjective or an adverb) to determine its part of speech in the sentence.

Passive Voice See **Voice.**

Past Perfect A verb construction used to indicate an action completed before another action that occurred in the past: *had gone.*

Past Tense A verb inflection (*laughed, took*) or verb construction (*was laughing, did take*) used to indicate an action that occurred in past time.

Perfect See § 9.

Periphrastic Denoting a phrasal construction. "Meter *of the poem*" is a periphrastic genitive; contrast "*poet's* meter," which is an inflected genitive. "We *didn't call*" is a periphrastic verbal construction; contrast "We *called,*" which is an inflected verbal construction.

Person The form of a verb or pronoun indicating whether one is speaking, is spoken to, or is spoken about: "I sing, you sing, he sings."

Phrase A phrase is a group of related words not containing a subject *and* a predicate.

In respect to function, phrases may be used as the equivalent of verbs, nouns, adjectives, or adverbs: "He *has gone*." (Verb phrase.) "The roof *of the house* was blown off." (Used as a noun, as the subject of the sentence; *of the house* is an adjective phrase.) "The man *with red hair* is his brother." (Adjective phrase.) "He stood *at the door*." (Adverb phrase.)

In respect to form, phrases are classified as (1) prepositional: *over the fence;* (2) participial, made up of a participle and its modifiers or object: *Slowly mounting the steps,* he turned and gazed silently at the scene; (3) gerund, made up of a gerund and its modifier or object: *Mounting the tire* is the next step; (4) infinitive: *To entertain* some people is very difficult. See also **Absolute, Preposition,** and page 173.

Plural See **Number** and §§ 5, 6.

Positive Degree See **Comparison.**

Predicate The verb of a sentence or clause (or the verb and its modifiers or complements). The predicate may be either a single word or a group of words: "He *slept*." "He *has been sleeping*." The *simple predicate* is the predicate verb or verb-phrase. The *complete predicate* is the predicate verb or verb-phrase together with all its modifiers and complements. See also **Compound Predicate.**

Predicate Adjective See **Predicate Complement.**

Predicate Complement, Predicate Nominative, Subjective Complement The word or words used to complete the meaning of a linking verb (copula) and to describe or identify the subject of the verb. The predicate complement may be a noun, a noun clause, an infinitive, a gerund, a pronoun, an adjective, or an adjective phrase. These kinds of predicate complements are illustrated in the following sentences:

John is my *brother*. (*Brother* is the predicate complement or predicate nominative.)

My suggestion is *that we leave at noon*.

To see is *to believe*.

Seeing is *believing*.

It is *he*. (Predicate complement or predicate nominative.)

I am *tired*. (Predicate adjective.)

He is *out of sight*. (Predicate complement or predicate nominative.)

Predicate Nominative See **Predicate Complement.**

Predicate Noun See **Predicate Complement.**

Predicate Objective See **Object.**

Predicate Verb See **Predicate.**

Predication A combination of subject + finite verb, found in every clause or sentence. See also **Ellipsis** and page 4.

Predication, Reduction of See **Reduction of Predication.**

Predicative See **Finite.**

Preposition A word or words used with a substantive to form a phrase and to show the relation of the substantive to another word in the sentence. A phrase introduced by or formed with a preposition is called a *prepositional phrase.* "He rode *over the hill.*" (*Over the hill* is a prepositional phrase introduced by the preposition *over.*) The substantive following the preposition is called its direct object and is in the objective case. Some prepositions (*phrasal prepositions*) contain more than one word: "I carried out the plan *according to* your instructions." Distinguish carefully between prepositions and conjunctions. A conjunction is used merely to connect words or word-groups. A conjunction does not have an object; a preposition does. "No one *but* him deserves the applause." (*But* is a preposition in this sentence.) "We invited him, *but* he did not come." (*But* is a conjunction here.)

Present Perfect See § 9.

Principal Clause An independent clause. See page 98.

Principal Parts of a Verb The principal parts of a verb are the three forms from which the complete conjugation of the verb is derived. The principal parts are the present infinitive, the past tense, and the past participle. For the principal parts of many irregular verbs and a synopsis of verb forms, see §§ 9 and 9g.

Progressive Present, Past, Future, etc. The form of the verb used to represent the action as going on at the time referred to. The progressive forms are made up of some form of the verb *be* + the present participle: *He is singing, he was singing, he will be singing. He is singing* is the progressive present; *he sings* is the timeless present. For the conjugation of a verb, see § 9.

Pronominal Adjective See Pronouns, § 13.

Pronoun See Pronouns, § 13.

Proper Noun See **Noun.**

Reduction of Predication Changing the expression of an idea so as to put it in a more subordinate grammatical form; changing principal clauses to subordinate clauses, subordinate clauses to phrases, and phrases to single words. Note the progressive reduction of predication in the following sentences:

We gazed at the water of the lake, and it was as clear as crystal.
We gazed at the water of the lake, which was as clear as crystal.
We gazed at the crystal-clear water of the lake.

Referent The nonverbal meaning of a word. You can feel and inspect a referent of the word *page* in any book; you can observe a referent of the word *eat* by watching people at a meal. See § 57.

Related Words Words which are normally used in connection with each other. Typical examples are (1) noun and its modifiers, (2) verb and its modifiers, (3) adjective and its modifiers, (4) subject and verb, (5) verb and object, (6) verbal and subject, object, or modifiers, (7) preposition and object, (8) subordinating conjunction and subordinate clause or phrase. In the sentence "Yes, she brought them" *she* and *brought* are related (subject and verb); *brought* and *them* are related (verb and object); but *yes* is not related to any other word in the sentence.

Relative Pronoun See page 140.

Restrictive Modifier See § 17c.

Retained Object See **Intransitive, Transitive.**

Sentence For a definition see Sentence Defined, § 1. For different types of sentences see **Simple, Complex, Compound, Compound-complex, Major,** and **Minor.**

Sentence Element Subject, predicate, complement, or modifier — one of the separable parts into which a sentence may be analyzed.

Sentence Modifier Some adverbial modifiers are used to modify the complete sentence rather than a single word in the subject or in the predicate. These sentence modifiers, instead of describing the action, rather reveal the writer's attitude toward the statement made in the sentence. Some of the more common sentence modifiers are *thus, therefore, undoubtedly, of course, certainly, surely, to be sure, I am sure, all things considered, in fact, clearly,* *fortunately*, and *obviously*. For the punctuation of sentence modifiers, see § 17f.

Simple Predicate See **Predicate.**

Simple Sentence A sentence containing a single predication. Either the subject or the predicate, or both, may be compound, but there must be only one combination of subject and verb, only one clause. "John has come." (Simple subject and simple predicate.) "John and his brother have come." (Compound subject and simple predicate.) "John has come and will stay several days." (Simple subject and compound predicate.) "John and his brother have come and will stay several days." (Simple sentence with compound subject *and* compound predicate.) Distinguish between a simple sentence with compound predicate and a compound sentence. Compare the sentences given above with this compound sentence: "John has come, and his brother came with him." See **Compound Predicate.**

Simple Subject See **Subject.**

Standard See pages 91–94.

Strong Verb A verb that forms its last two principal parts by a change of vowel and without the addition of *-ed*, *-d*, or *-t*: *sing*, *sang*, *sung*. Strong verbs are sometimes called *irregular*. See **Weak Verb.**

Subject A noun or its equivalent (pronoun, noun clause, or other substantive) about which an assertion is made, and with which a present tense verb agrees in person and number. The *simple subject* is a noun or its equivalent. The *complete subject* is the simple subject with all its modifiers.

Subjective Complement See **Predicate Complement.**

Subjunctive See Subjunctive Mood, § 8, and **Mood.**

Subordinate Clause See pages 7 and 98.

Substantive A noun or any other word or word-group used as the equivalent of a noun. Nouns, pronouns, gerunds, infinitives, clauses, and sometimes phrases are all used as substantives.

Substantive Clause A dependent clause used like a noun, as subject, direct object, appositive, etc. "*That he will come* is certain." (The substantive clause is used as the subject of *is*.)

Syntax That part of grammar which deals with the mutual relationships of words in a sentence; the structure of a sentence.

Tense Tense indicates the time of the action of a verb. See Tense, § 9.

Transitive See **Intransitive.**

Verb One of the major parts of speech in English. Verbs are inflected (*skip, skips, skipped, skipping; teach, teaches, taught, teaching*) and fill the office of predicate in clauses and sentences. A verb asserts an action, condition, or state.

Verb-Adverb Combination A periphrastic verb such as *break up, put off, take out,* and *come upon.* See **Up** in the Glossary of Diction, § 66.

Verb Phrase A verb used with a function word or words to form a syntactic unit: *have seen, can see, look over, to have looked.*

Verbal A verb form that cannot be used to make an independent assertion. See **Gerund, Infinitive, Participle,** and § 1.

Vocative, Direct Address A noun or a pronoun used to show to whom a speech is addressed: "My friends, it is clear that we must reconsider our position." "Officer, where is Oak Street?"

Voice The verb construction which indicates whether the subject acts (active voice: *he bites*) or is acted upon (passive voice: *he was bitten, he gets bitten*).

Weak Verb A verb that forms its past tense and past participle by adding *-d, -t,* or *-ed* to the infinitive: *jump, jumped, jumped; burn, burnt, burnt; tie, tied, tied.* Weak verbs are sometimes called *regular,* although weak verbs such as *buy, catch,* and *keep* are irregular. See **Strong Verb.**

PUNCTUATION

Punctuation has two uses in present-day English: (1) significant, and (2) conventional. Periods, commas, and other marks are used significantly when they supplement the letters of the alphabet to represent spoken language in writing. Consider the word-sequence *Governor Warren is a Republican* as it is printed here. These five words alone do not make a complete sentence until we put a question mark, exclamation point, or a period after *Republican.* Any one of the marks enables the reader to reproduce in speech what the writer intends, and the three marks make three quite different sentences. Put a comma after the word *Republican* and the reader expects something to follow. Automatically the reader stresses, pitches, and times the words and pauses as the punctuation marks signal him. This is the significant use of punctuation marks.

The other use of punctuation is to satisfy custom, much like shaking hands as a greeting or standing up at the seventh inning of a baseball game. For example, a colon, a comma, or a dash is not needed after the salutation of a letter for meaning; no one would read a letter differently without such a mark, but convention requires one of the three, and letter writers must conform.

It might be possible to tell students to use certain marks to indicate certain patterns of intonation (pitch, time, pause, and stress), but we are not accustomed to analyzing our speech in these terms, and furthermore some conventional punctuation does not correspond to intonational patterns. Therefore rules of punctuation must be stated in terms of sentences and sentence elements. Again, grammatical nomenclature is necessary for the handbook writer to communicate with his readers.

There are two styles of punctuation, commonly called "open" and "close." Close punctuation, characteristic of nineteenth century English, with its formal style and involved sentences, uses more marks. The trend today is to use more direct sentences and fewer punctuation marks. To punctuate sentences effectively, the student should be able to recognize the breaks between principal sentence elements, to remember the situations which conventionally require punctuation marks, and to decide when the meaning is affected by the use or omission of particular marks.

The Comma

17. Use a comma within the sentence to indicate the least emphatic separation of elements.

The comma is used to separate various sentence elements. By separating main clauses from each other, and often from subordinate clauses, the comma helps make clear the relation between different parts of the sentence. By taking the place of voice inflection in spoken English, the comma makes written sentences easier to grasp.

17a. Use a comma to separate independent clauses connected by a coördinating conjunction.

And, but, or, nor, and *for* between clauses are regularly preceded by a comma unless the clauses are short and clearly separated. *So* and *yet* between clauses are preceded by a comma if the relationship is close, by a semicolon if the relationship is loose.

Examples A question mark is not pronounced like a vowel or a consonant, but listeners always recognize spoken questions. (Note that *but* connects clauses here, and *or* connects two nouns.)

They provided a new typewriter, and an adding machine was ordered for us. (The clauses are short but the sentence would be momentarily misread without the comma.)

They provided a new typewriter and ordered an adding machine. (Comma unnecessary; the predicate is compound, but there is only one clause.)

17b. Use a comma after an introductory adverbial clause or phrase when the clause or phrase is long or is in danger of being misread.

There is no ironclad rule which will tell you when a clause or phrase is long enough to need a comma. The closeness in meaning between the introductory adverbial expression and the main clause will often determine whether the comma is desirable. As a rule, introductory adverbial phrases containing an infinitive, a gerund, or a participle are followed by a comma. A study of the examples below and of the practice of good modern writers will give you a clearer idea of when to use a comma.

Long clause	As I entered the front door of my fraternity house on the designated Saturday morning, I was told to find the lawn mower and to give it some exercise.
Long phrase	With such an extremely large group of workers, the country can withstand an attack indefinitely.
Misreading	Next morning while I was shaving, the cat ran into the room.
Verbal phrase	After being without a job in New York for almost three months, I found myself compelled to think of returning to Moundville.
Misreading	To begin with, my cousin decided to see how fast the automobile would go. (Introductory phrases containing a verbal may easily be misread.)

Caution. Do not use a comma after a short introductory phrase or clause:

Examples In the afternoon he usually took a long walk.
If I come I shall be able to stay only a few minutes.

17c. Use commas to set off nonrestrictive modifiers (words, phrases, and clauses). Do not use commas to set off restrictive modifiers.

Relative Clauses

Relative clauses may be used in two ways:

(*a*) To *describe* an antecedent; such clauses are known as *nonrestrictive,* because they do not restrict or limit the meaning of the antecedent. They are parenthetical in nature.

(*b*) To *define* or *identify* an antecedent; such clauses are known as *restrictive* because they restrict, identify, or narrow the meaning of the antecedent.

To determine whether a relative clause is restrictive or nonrestrictive, apply the following tests:

Test I. Read the sentence without the relative clause to determine whether the omission of the clause changes the meaning of the antecedent.

Example Motor cars, which are both numerous and efficient, have become necessary to modern life. (The main predication *Motor cars have become necessary to modern life* is unchanged by the omission of the relative clause. The same statement, *have become necessary*, is made about the same subject, *motor cars*. The information given by *which are both numerous and efficient* is lacking, but the antecedent *motor cars* does not denote any larger or smaller or different referent. The relative clause is nonessential and should be set off by commas.)

non-restrictive

Example Motor cars which have defective brakes should not be allowed on the highways. (The main predication in this sentence is not made about *motor cars*, but about a particular class of motor cars, those with defective brakes. The omission of the relative clause *which have defective brakes* changes the reference of the antecedent from a special class of motor cars to all motor cars. *Motor cars should not be allowed on the highways* is not the same predication, because the meaning of the antecedent has been changed. The relative clause restricts the antecedent; hence it is not set off by commas.)

Restrictive

Test II. For the relative pronoun substitute *and* + a personal pronoun which agrees with the subject of the main clause.

Example Motor cars — and they are both numerous and efficient — have become necessary to modern life. (The inserted *and* clause merely gives additional, somewhat parenthetical information about all motor cars; it resembles an afterthought interpolated within the main clause; the relative clause is therefore nonessential.)

Example Motor cars — and they have defective brakes — should not be allowed on the highways. (Since the *and* clause in this sentence does not give information about all motor cars, the sentence does not make sense; the clause is therefore restrictive. The antecedent *motor cars* must be limited to those particular cars which have defective brakes.)

The two tests which we have applied to relative clauses may likewise be applied to a phrase or other modifier. For example, note the effect of eliminating the italicized phrases in these sentences: "Motor cars *with defective brakes* should not be allowed on the highways" and "Motor cars, *now both numerous and efficient*, have become necessary to modern life."

Adverbial Clauses

Adverbial clauses, like relative clauses, may be restrictive or nonrestrictive. Remember that a relative clause is used as an adjective, and an adverbial clause is used as an adverb. Thus an adverbial clause may restrict a verb, adjective, or adverb.

Examples We practiced indoors *whenever it rained.* (Restrictive.)

Early in December, *when we were preparing for Christmas*, the warehouse was burned. (Nonrestrictive.)

He climbed as high *as he could.* (Restrictive.)

Words and Phrases, Especially Participles

Examples *Determined to kill a few marsh hens*, we rowed the small boat far into the marshes. (Nonrestrictive.)

Walking towards the building, I suddenly discovered that I was late. (Nonrestrictive.)

Laws *threatening freedom of speech* have been proposed. (Restrictive.)

For the use of the dash and parentheses, see §§ 24c and 26a.

17d. Use commas to set off an inserted sentence-element, such as a transposed, emphatic, or suspended expression.

Transposed or Inserted Expressions

Examples The house, *old and deserted*, was said to be haunted. (Adjectives regularly precede the noun they modify; here they are transposed.)

The rain is over, I am glad to say. (This noun clause would normally follow the verb *say*.)

My brain, *though partially numbed by fear*, managed to convey the thought necessary to start my feet moving.

He kept making comments which, *although intended to be amusing*, were merely silly.

The moccasin, *or cottonmouth as it is often called*, is a common water snake.

He will, *at the slightest provocation*, fly into a rage.

EMPHATIC ELEMENTS

Example He is a leader, *not only among fraternity men*, but also among non-fraternity men.

SUSPENDED EXPRESSIONS

Examples Before, *and immediately following*, World War I the great mass of German people were very poor.

The author could eliminate two characters, *he thought*, without changing the plot.

Exception He had an idea which he thought would save the world. (A parenthetical *he thought*, etc., after a relative pronoun is not usually set off by commas.)

NOTE. For the use of the dash with inserted elements, see § 24c; for parentheses, see § 26a.

17e. Use a comma to emphasize a contrast between coördinate sentence-elements.

The comma is often used before *but, not, and not,* and *yet* to emphasize a contrast, and before *or* to emphasize an alternative.

Examples I called John, not Tom. (Contrasted nouns.)

He entered rapidly, yet noiselessly. (Contrasted adverbs.)

He tried, but failed miserably. (Contrasted predicate verbs.)

17f. Use commas to set off sentence modifiers.

Many words or expressions modify a whole sentence or predication rather than a single word or word group. Such sentence modifiers as *accordingly, then, therefore, on the other hand, in the first place, yes, no, well, indeed, certainly, finally, perhaps, in fact,* etc., often mark a transition or summary, or direct the reader's attention to a turn in the thought of the paragraph. Such sentence modifiers are set off by commas so that they may not be mistaken for modifiers of some single word or sentence element.

Examples The best professional baseball players, *of course,* make their way into the major leagues.

My joy was short, *however,* for the ship kept sailing away from us.

Consider, *for example,* our recent elections in student government.

Every young boy, *I am sure,* is faced at one time or another with the problem of securing a job.

Yes, I am willing to ride in your new automobile.

17g. Use commas to set off absolute phrases.

An absolute phrase is an independent element consisting of a noun or pronoun + a participle.

Examples *The time limit being up,* we all went back to the farmhouse.

My lantern having slipped from my hand, I found myself in complete darkness.

17h. Use commas to set off a nonrestrictive appositive. Restrictive appositives require no commas.

An appositive is restrictive if it is part of a proper name, if it is quoted or italicized, or if it is used to identify its antecedent.

Examples He is very fond of my favorite author, Mark Twain.

Spivey, a man of great ability, was elected chairman.

Sinclair Lewis's novel *Main Street* has been widely read in America. (*Main Street* is here a restrictive appositive.)

The word *burgle* and the expression "He gets my goat" are not accepted in formal English. (Restrictive appositives.)

My brother Alton is very fond of O'Neill's play *The Emperor Jones.* (Restrictive appositives.)

The idea that you are qualified for this position is unwarranted. (Restrictive appositive.)

In the year 1941 we actively entered the war. (Restrictive appositive.)

NOTE. When *namely, that is, viz.,* and *i.e.* introduce an appositive or illustration rather than an enumeration or a clause, they are preceded *and followed* by a comma. For the use of a colon, see § 20a.

Example I have only one favorite sport, *namely*, baseball.

NOTE. When *such as, as, especially, e.g.*, or *for example* introduces an example or a series of examples, the whole phrase should be set off by commas except when *such as* is restrictive.

Examples Many hitherto unimportant sports in college, *such as archery, golf, and polo*, are now attaining great popularity.

Poems such as these are difficult to memorize.

17i. Use commas to set off dates and geographical expressions and initials or titles following a personal name.

Examples On Tuesday, July 4, this bank will be closed.

December 2, 1927, was the birthday of the Model A.

In March, 1932, Roosevelt was inaugurated.

Talladega County, Alabama, was named for a battle.

Booker Tee, Oklahoma, was named for Booker T. Washington.

Maxwell, A. E., Rawson, H. E., and Jackson, L. O., were cited for bravery under fire.

Samuel Dale, A.M., Litt.D., LL.D., died yesterday. His address was 2310 Sherman Avenue, Atlanta, Georgia.

Commencement will be on August 24th. (No parenthetical element.)

Note that in "open" punctuation there is an increasing tendency to omit the comma after the year in a date: "On June 9, 1950 he graduated from the state university."

17j. Use commas to set off words used in direct address (vocatives).

Examples Please answer the telephone, Ruth.

You realize, Major Whipple, that such tactics are dangerous.

17k. Use a comma after a mild interjection.

Examples "Oh, perhaps you are right," she said.

"Well, hurry if you want to be on time."

17l. Use commas to separate a series of coördinate words, phrases, or clauses. A series means three or more items.

Note the two common types of series: (1) A, B, C; A, B, C, D, etc. The comma is necessary in this type of series. (2) A, B, and C; or A, B, or C.

SERIES OF THE TYPE A, B, C

Examples He is known to be upright, faithful, honest. (Coördinate adjectives separated by commas.)

I often met him on the street, in his office, at church. (Coordinate phrases.)

CAUTION. If the members of a series A, B, C consist of independent clauses, semicolons may be used before items B and C. But see §§ 3 and 19.

Example He went to look for his clothes; I sorted out the papers; she returned to the kitchen.

SERIES OF THE TYPE A, B, AND C

In a series of the type A, B, and C; A, B, C, or D, the comma before *and* (*or*) is usually optional. Although the use of the comma before *and* (*or*) is preferred by some writers, it is often omitted by reputable writers, except where it is needed for immediate clearness, as in such sentences as these:

The statement showed the amounts spent for storage, billing, wrapping, and mailing. (The third comma makes it clear that wrapping and mailing charges were listed separately.)

Modern women do not wish to sweep and scrub, cook, and nurse children.

In cases where no misreading is possible, the comma before *and* is optional.

Examples She possessed beauty, poise, and courage. (Coördinate nouns.)

She possessed beauty, poise and courage.

Rapidly we bathed, dressed, and hurried back to the cabin. (Coördinate verbs.)

Rapidly we bathed, dressed and hurried back to the cabin.

A week passed, a heavy rain fell, and the roof collapsed like cardboard in a steam press. (Coördinate clauses.)

A week passed, a heavy rain fell and the roof collapsed. . . .

NOTE. When the last two items form a unit, the comma before *and* should be used in a series of the type A, B, and . . . and. . . .

Example He played tennis, shot two rounds of golf, and then swam and dived.

NOTE. A comma is always used before *etc.* at the end of a series.

17m. Use a comma between adjectives in abnormal order or in reversible order. A comma is not used between adjectives in a normally fixed order.

Examples with normally fixed order (*no commas*):

The coach wants eleven healthy young men.
Her attractive gray eyes were wide open.
The little old ladies did not hear the announcement.
He had an impressive British stage accent.

Examples in abnormal order (*commas required*):

The coach wants eleven young, healthy men.
Her gray, attractive eyes were wide open.

Examples in reversible order (*commas required*):

The brightest, biggest, coolest room was hers.
The coolest, biggest, brightest room was hers.
He has an intelligent, sensitive taste in literature.
He has a sensitive, intelligent taste in literature.

Note that when adjectives have reversible (not normally fixed) order, the conjunction *and* can be substituted for the comma:

The biggest and brightest and coolest room was hers.

17n. Use a comma to prevent misreading or a delay in reading. It is often wiser, however, to recast the sentence than to depend solely upon punctuation for clearness.

Examples Ever since, I have read many historical novels.

For him, accepting certain traditional doctrines meant acquiescence in ignorance and superstition.

I had to wait, for my brother had been delayed.

Exactly what sort of a man he is, is hard to say.

The more I worked on that problem in algebra, the more perplexed I became.

You will join us in this trip, won't you?

Inside, the rooms were brightly lighted.

NOTE. A comma may be used to mark an omission.

Examples "To share with you his last crust was a part of his religion and to eat alone, a crime."

"If there are daggers, the likelihood is that sooner or later there will be stabbing; if armaments, wars; if tools, trade; if rhetoric, argument." (L. P. Jacks.)

"A danger call means flee; a call for help, approach." (Pillsbury.)

17o. Use commas to set off *he said, she replied,* and similar expressions from direct quotations.

Examples "We are ready to leave," he said.

He said, "We are ready to leave."

"I am ready," he said, "to leave now."

See Dialogue and Quoted Matter, § 28, for a full treatment of this subject.

See pages 179–184 for exercises on the comma.

Unnecessary Commas

18. Avoid the use of unnecessary commas.

Be able to justify every comma you use. When in doubt, omit the comma.

18a. Do not use a comma between a subject and a verb, or between a verb and a direct object or a predicate nominative, except to prevent misreading.

Wrong The sight of the prancing horses with their daring riders, made me breathless with wonder.

Another change I would make, is the abolition of comprehensive examinations.

It has been shown, that as a small boy Landor had a very vivid imagination.

NOTE. Although the commas in sentences like these represent a pitch pattern of spoken English, they are omitted in writing.

18b. Do not use a comma after a short, introductory, essential adverbial modifier.

Distracting In this college, there were students from twenty-five states.

(See also § 17b.)

18c. Do not use a comma before the first or after the last member of a series.

Wrong She gave the child, ripe, fresh, red, apples. (Commas after *child* and after *red* are both wrong.)

Our state needs a well-planned, scientifically designed, economical, network of paved highways. (Comma before *network* is momentarily misleading.)

18d. Do not use a comma before an indirect quotation or before a quoted or italicized literary title except when the title is a nonrestrictive appositive.

Wrong He said, that he would sign the contract.
I have just finished, *The Return of the Native.*

But I have just read a very interesting novel, *The Last Stand.* (Comma is right here because the title is a nonrestrictive appositive.)

Wrong He had recently sung, "Sylvia" at a concert.

18e. Do not use commas to set off restrictive modifiers or restrictive appositives.

Wrong The man, whom you met in the hall, is Dr. Kipton.
The information is furnished by the characters, themselves.

(See also §§ 17c and 17h.)

18f. Do not use commas between correlatives joining single words or between the elements of the compound conjunctions *so . . . that, so . . . as, as . . . as,* or before *than* or *rather than* in comparisons.

Wrong The average athlete is so tired when he returns home from practice, that he is sometimes tempted to put his lessons aside for a future time.

Professor Cranford seems much more feeble, than he did a year ago.

Neither armaments, nor treaties have protected some countries.

18g. Do not use a comma between adjectives when the adjectives occur in a normally fixed order before a noun.

Wrong Longfellow was a vigorous, young man at this time.

18h. Do not use a comma between parts of a compound predicate unless the two verbs are contrasted (see § 17e) or are widely separated.

Wro[illegible] [illegible] was very careful to remove all carbon, and finished by wiping [illegible]linders with a clean cloth soaked with gasoline.

18i. Do not use a comma before a coördinating conjunction which connects two dependent clauses unless the second is an afterthought or an interpolation.

Wrong As the play progresses, and the pursuing natives gain on the fleeing Emperor Jones, the tom-toms beat louder and louder. (*As* governs both dependent clauses, and since the second is not an afterthought or interpolation, no comma should be used before *and.* The comma after *Jones* sets off an introductory dependent clause.)

GENERAL EXERCISES IN THE USE OF THE COMMA

A. Supply commas where they are needed in the sentences below, and (if your instructor so directs) write above each comma the number of the appropriate rule (i.e. § 17b, etc.)

1. Programs such as the "Ford Theater" on Friday the "Theater Guild" on Sunday and the "Radio Theater" on Monday were highly recommended.
2. This study of the Japanese in America from 1844 when they first came to this country to the present time is a sound book.
3. When the plane got close to the end of the runway and still didn't begin to rise Jones began to sweat.
4. "Oh tell that creep to drop dead."
5. The word *stooge* which is about fifty years old and the word *jazz* which is perhaps even older are of unknown origin.

6. My uncle although a lifelong Democrat disapproved the farm price program.
7. While I was out hunting my brother suddenly decided that he wanted to go back to the ball park.
8. She thought it was bad for example to keep a dog in the city.
9. She likes to have pets around the house but she said a dog should not spend his life in apartments and on concrete pavements.
10. I was born February 29 1932 in Scooba Mississippi.
11. In tennis track and baseball my school always did better than in football.
12. She said "Sara how do you turn on the porch light?"
13. In basketball his hands were too small his feet too big.
14. Friday July 13 is a day I'll never forget.
15. The girls made sandwiches pies cookies and lemonade.
16. We wanted fruit juice toast milk and ham and eggs.
17. The professor knew I hadn't made very good grades played on any athletic team or taken part in school activities.
18. With a lot of help from the Chamber of Commerce the census takers finally located enough people to put the population slightly over 2500.
19. The scared little girl was crying stumbling and calling for her mother.
20. At our house parties were never much trouble and my mother was always glad for us to invite friends in.

B. In the sentences below, add any needed commas, put a circle around any unnecessary commas, and be prepared to cite the rule for each comma that you think should be used.

1. But in the universities if anywhere *Hamlet* and *Lear* must be read understood, and appreciated.
2. This type of word tells or more exactly implies, a story.
3. When you can use the typewriter because I cannot read your handwriting very easily.
4. One hears too much discontent, over the present system of distribution.
5. Mother who had gone riding in the family automobile did not return at the specified time.
6. The stores downtown were having a busy day, for I had to drive around for fifteen minutes, before I could find a place to park.

7. By the time the pistol was fired for the game to end the spectators were yelling frantically for another touchdown.
8. It is almost unbelievable that a man who was not over twenty-three and had never seen service in the army could draw a picture of a soldier on the battlefield so vividly that old soldiers would praise it for its accuracy.
9. If, we believe, certain advertisements motion pictures are on the whole our best entertainment.
10. Sir Galahad was with the Round Table not of it.
11. The fall of the year having come we planned to spend a week in the mountains of North Carolina.
12. Any classic novel such as *Silas Marner* or *Ivanhoe*, will be acceptable for a book report.
13. Father decided that he a friend and I would go to Miami Beach Florida for a vacation.
14. "Where is the fire young man?" said the policeman revealing his lack of originality in repartee.
15. Germany Italy and Japan flooded America, with all kinds of propaganda.
16. His laugh was a deep hearty chuckle that shook his gigantic young frame.
17. When the sun went down however it was decidedly cooler.
18. The warm weather had melted the snow higher up on the mountain causing the brook to rise very rapidly so rapidly in fact as to carry away all of our equipment including our matches.
19. To many, Americans today the danger to future democracy lies not in invasion from abroad but in a breakdown of rugged individualism.
20. Jack who was then acting as our leader said "This seems to be a good place to camp, for the night."

C. Directions given under Exercise B.

1. As Father remembers it our home town was very different in his youth from what it is today.
2. There were no paved streets no concrete sidewalks and no traffic signs or lights.
3. The "downtown" section has probably changed most as you would expect.
4. Forty years ago there were livery stables blacksmith shops and

general stores which have disappeared to make room for service stations cafes women's clothing stores radio and appliance dealers and self-service grocery places.

5. Although there were drug stores and barber shops Father says they didn't resemble the ones we patronize now.
6. Beauty shops were unknown, there were no power company or gas company offices, and the undertaker's principal business was running a hardware store.
7. The doctors, lawyers, and dentists who practiced in the town all had offices upstairs over stores on the main street.
8. Wide sheds to protect people from the sun and rain extended in front of every store out over the brick sidewalk so that you could walk any downtown block protected from the weather.
9. Watering troughs and hitching racks which were provided by the merchants to attract trade were numerous along the street.
10. Not a single sign over a business firm is the same as when my father was a schoolboy, forty years ago.
11. However not all the changes have taken place downtown.
12. There are differences although they may not be so obvious in the residential sections.
13. The houses used to be bigger with wider lawns and more trees.
14. The architecture was different too: most houses were frame instead of brick and more of them were two and three storied.
15. Although some people had open lawns the typical home had a fenced front yard to keep chickens and children in and neighbors tramps and dogs out.
16. Evergreens which are standard today must have been rare because Father says almost everybody had flowers in the front yards and barns and vegetable gardens in the back.
17. Drinking water came from cisterns which were filled by pipes from roof gutters or from wells that tapped underground water fifteen or twenty feet deep.
18. To pull up the well buckets or cistern buckets there were windlasses and usually the kitchen had a hand pump over the sink.
19. If the boys wanted to play ball they used somebody's vacant lot since public playgrounds were unknown in those dark days.
20. No neon signs, no juke boxes no taxis or busses no motorcycle cops no swimming pools except in country creeks no street lights and no television aerials — it surely must have been different.

D. Explain the reason for the use of each comma in Paragraphs 3 and 4 on page 52.

E. Make the changes indicated, and then make all other necessary changes.

1. Substitute *furthermore* for *and*.
   The drivers were not notified that a new type of carburetor was being installed; and they were not instructed to keep a record of gasoline consumption.
2. Delete *Because* and insert *thus* before Wilton.
   Because the paintings had not been exhibited in recent years, Wilton was not very well known in art circles.
3. Make the third clause a separate sentence.
   Girls are now taking engineering courses, men are enrolled in home economics, and the campus is not what it used to be.
4. Delete *however*.
   If the price of aluminum continues to drop, however, many articles now made of steel will be made of aluminum.
5. Combine in one sentence.
   Let me have it quick. The sink is almost running over.
6. Delete the first *and*.
   The furniture is being repaired and the interior will be redecorated and a new roof will be put on.
7. Insert *that time* after *since*.
   The new highway was opened to traffic last week, since the old highway has been closed for repairs.
8. Delete *but*.
   British movies are becoming very popular; but I like them because I like to see new and unfamiliar actors.

EXERCISES ON RESTRICTIVE AND NONRESTRICTIVE MODIFIERS

Make the changes indicated below and all additional changes that are necessary.

1. Omit the word *the*: The Winston Churchill who was a popular American novelist died in 1947.
2. Insert *the* before *John Rose*: The police are trying to find John Rose, who was seen late last night at a news stand on the corner of Canal and Tenth streets.

3. Omit the article *a*: After studying art all through high school, in 1937 he entered a college where many social activities and harder courses forced him to give up the hobby.
4. Insert *father's* before *house*: She hurried to his house, which was just two blocks away, and beat frantically on the door.
5. Change the punctuation to show that he has only one son: Coach Hamilton wrote immediately to his son who was in the army, suggesting that he try to get a leave for the week end of the family reunion.
6. Insert *although it was out of date* after *Sandburg*: Professor Wallis liked his edition of the poems of Sandburg and determined to have a binder put a new cover on it.
7. Change *saw* to *seeing* and omit *and*: My nurse saw how feverish I was and called the doctor at his home.
8. Insert *she thought* after *which*: The psychiatrist assured her that the elephants which she saw were imaginary.
9. Substitute *a* for *Eglin*: After driving along the coast for three hours, they finally reached Eglin Beach which looked clean and not too crowded.
10. Omit *the* after *into*: We ran into the Gil Ferris who had played shortstop for Gorgas University leaning against the soda fountain in a drug store.
11. Insert *a former all-American* after *Smart*: We were encouraged when we heard that Paul Smart would be in town and would help coach the team.
12. Insert *wearing shorts* after *girls*: The dean of women ruled that girls could not appear on the quadrangle or any public street.
13. Insert *nine* before *professors*: The professors who made up the starting line-up of the faculty team had all played college or semipro baseball.
14. Delete *thirty-four-ounce*: Robinson preferred a thirty-four-ounce bat which was too heavy for most of the players.
15. Delete *engineering*: Students in engineering colleges where mathematics is a required course cannot avoid college algebra.

The Semicolon

19. Use the semicolon to indicate more of a break than the comma, but less than the period.

The semicolon has well-defined uses of its own and should not be regarded as a loose substitute for the comma or the period.

19a. Use a semicolon between two independent clauses not joined by one of the simple coördinating conjunctions (*and, but, or, nor, for, yet*).

This rule explains the use of the semicolon in the following types of compound sentences:

When no connective of any sort is used between the independent clauses:

Example Clothing is by no means the only subject of interviews; the company for which I worked makes surveys on almost every business in this country. (A comma here would produce a *comma fault*; no mark here would result in a *fused* sentence.)

When no conjunction is used but an explanatory expression introduces the second clause:

Example A boy should choose his profession as early as possible because of the long period of training required; for example, seven or eight years are required beyond high school before one can practice medicine. (A comma after *required* would create a comma fault.)

In such a case the punctuation is just the same as it would be if the explanatory expression — *namely, for example, that is, i.e., viz.* — were omitted entirely.

When the clauses are connected by a conjunctive adverb. (See § 12c for a list of such adverbs.)

Examples We heard the officers go into the tent next to ours and say that it was not in satisfactory order; consequently we became very nervous when they entered ours.

He turned and asked us if we were ready to leave; then he started the motor.

19b. The semicolon may be used to give greater emphasis to the separation between two clauses or to make the word-grouping clearer.

huh?

see 17f

EMPHASIS. Since the semicolon marks a greater degree of separation than does the comma, it gives greater emphasis and independence of meaning to each of the two*clauses. The semicolon is also used to balance or contrast two*clauses more sharply than can be done by a comma. *independent

Example Then came the time to pay the bill; but I reached for my wallet in vain.

CLEARNESS OF WORD-GROUPING. When any elements of a sentence are loosely related, are long, or are complicated in structure (especially when they contain interior punctuation), it is often advisable to employ semicolons to indicate clearly the chief divisions in the sentence. In the following sentences commas would not indicate the chief divisions so clearly as the semicolons do:

Examples Among the most important characters of the story are Kory-Kory, Melville's guard and servant; Nehivi, chief of the Typees; Fayaway, a beautiful maiden of the tribe; and Marheyo, the aged father of Fayaway. (The semicolons clearly separate one subject and its appositive from the next subject and appositive.)

I learned that Susan Vickers, a senior at Hilton College, was traveling in Europe; that her sister, a striking brunette, accompanied her; and that Robert, their young brother, was in a summer camp in Massachusetts.

19c. Do not use the semicolon as a loose equivalent of the comma or the period.

Especially avoid these three common misuses of the semicolon:

As a substitute for the comma or the colon after the salutation in letters or before a direct quotation. See §§ 20a and 17o.

As a substitute for the comma between a dependent clause and a main clause or before a participial phrase.

Wrong When one is compelled to sit up all night and the cold winds howl steadily outside his cabin; he is likely to find that he cannot keep his imagination under control. (Change the semicolon to a comma.)

Wrong For about an hour after lunch, we remained in our tents; resting, playing bridge, and listening to the radio. (Substitute a comma for the semicolon.)

Before an adverb or before an appositive at the end of a sentence.

Wrong It is; unfortunately, too late to change our decision.

Wrong All the sports writers made the same prediction for that football game; an overwhelming victory for Minnesota. (Substitute a comma, a colon, or a dash for the semicolon.)

EXERCISE

Punctuate the following sentences and be prepared to explain why you insert or delete each semicolon. Where the use of the semicolon is optional, explain the effect of the use or omission.

1. Skiing seems to be a rather dangerous sport furthermore very few people are able to ski close to home.
2. English words are of three types: simple which cannot be analyzed complex which are made up of a root plus one or more affixes and compound which are made up of two or more words joined together.
3. The compound *postman* is written as one word; but the compound *Terre Haute* is written as two separate words.
4. They met; he proposed; and she accepted; all in two weeks' time.
5. The bat was two inches longer than he was used to consequently he had trouble getting set at the plate.
6. We were encouraged to establish a school newspaper the principal thought the students should have an outlet for their writings; both news and opinions.
7. Samson could write very good English however he was timid and wouldn't write editorials about the foul cafeteria meals.
8. Ralph who knew a lot about athletics was so illiterate that we had to rewrite the sports page every week Alice who could turn out a perfect society page in two hours was lazy and always late with her copy; and the humor editor didn't know a good joke from a sack of corn.
9. The crew consisted of A. W. Rosen pilot Carl Weeks navigator O. P. Koski engineer and several others who cannot be identified.
10. Catch the ladder quick it's slipping.

The Colon

20. Use the colon as a formal mark of anticipation and in the conventional ways listed below.

The colon usually serves to introduce a list, a series of examples, a formal appositive, or a formal or extended quotation. The colon indicates a greater degree of separation than the semicolon and puts very strong emphasis on what is to follow, except when it is used as in §§ 20b, 20c.

20a. Use a colon to stress a word, phrase, or statement that is to follow.

Examples There was only one answer to such scandal as this, namely: resignation. (The colon is used before a single word only to mark an emphatic appositive.)

After a moment the speaker began as follows: "Some words about the responsibilities of citizenship are unquestionably needed in the light of recent crimes in our community."

The question is: What will the grand jury do with such statements? (For the use of capitals after the colon, see § 32a.)

Awkward The men nominated were: Brown, Earhart, and Fowler. (A colon between verb and complement is awkward.)

Improved The men nominated were Brown, Earhart, and Fowler.

NOTE. A comma is used before a short or informal quotation except when the quotation is paragraphed separately. (See § 17o.)

20b. Use a colon between two independent clauses if the second clause gives a concrete example or an amplification of the statement in the first clause.

Examples Everything was perfect for our hunting trip: the weather was cool, our dogs were the best in the county, and our party consisted of six excellent huntsmen.

If politicians believed in my utopia, they would do more than be content with the boundaries of their own countries: they would boycott any country which invaded another.

In such sentences as these the semicolon — the mark of balance or sharp contrast — may be used instead of the colon. Or if stronger separation of clauses is desired, the colon may be replaced by a period. But in such sentences a comma is not used. (See § 3.)

20c. Use the colon in references to separate the title of a book from the subtitle, the chapter from the verse in Biblical quotations, and the place of publication from the name of the publisher. A colon is also used after the formal salutation of a letter and between hour and minute figures.

Examples *Charlotte Temple: A Tale of Truth.*
John 3:16.
Boston: Houghton Mifflin Company.
Dear Sir:
6:45 P.M.

EXERCISE

Punctuate the following sentences. Be able to explain each colon that you use. (For the use of capitals, see § 32.)

1. The backfield was composed of the following L. Miller quarter Lewis fullback J. Miller left half and O'Toole right half.
2. There was one box that he wouldn't let anybody touch the one containing his collection of old *Esquire* calendars.
3. We made up our minds however to tell him one thing we would not any longer put up with the goat in our front yards.
4. The chief advanced with dignity across the stage bowed gravely three times and in the best movie manner said Ugh.
5. Finally came the words everybody had been nervously waiting for Congress declared war today.
6. Mississippi has many place-names of Indian origin in California Spanish place-names are more common.
7. Gentlemen Please send me one corkscrew with a left-hand thread.
8. Precisely at 643 every morning that rooster sounded off at 702 a freight engine blew for a grade crossing nearby.
9. The entry is as follows Robert C. Pooley *Teaching English Usage* New York D. Appleton Century 1946.
10. The rebellious football team wanted just one thing more money.

The Period

21. Use the period as the ordinary end-stop mark and as a mark of abbreviation.

21a. Use a period after every declarative sentence.

This rule applies to sentence fragments used deliberately (see Sentence Defined, page 95), to unemphatic imperative sentences, to indirect questions, and to imperative sentences phrased as questions.

Examples "Will you have some buttermilk?" he asked.
"Yes."
"Waiter, two glasses of buttermilk."
I wonder what made him think of buttermilk.
Will you please itemize this statement so we can look up our purchase orders. (A question mark could be used here; punctuate such a sentence to indicate how you expect it to be read aloud.)

21b. Use a period after every abbreviation except those which conventionally require no period.

Examples Mrs., Jr., i.e., etc., j.g., 3 lbs., p.m.

Contractions, such as *can't*, *don't*, *I'll*, roman numerals (*I*, *II*, *IV*, *XII*, etc.), forms like *1st*, *3rd*, *9th*, and shortened words such as *percent*, *taxi*, *lab*, are not abbreviations and require no period. Certain abbreviations of names such as *CIO*, *CYO*, *CBS*, *NBC*, particularly names of government agencies (*FBI*, *NLRB*, *TVA*, *CAA*) are officially written without periods, and many abbreviations have optional periods (*AAUP*, *A.A.U.P.*, *BPOE*, *B.P.O.E.*, *OED*, *O.E.D.*, *MS*, *MS.*). When in doubt, consult a dictionary

Note. Within a sentence the period after an abbreviation is always followed by any other mark of punctuation that would have appeared if no abbreviation had been used. Note, for example, the commas between the series of abbreviations just above. But at the end of a sentence one period serves to mark the abbreviation and to end the sentence. A question mark or exclamation point, however, follows an abbreviation period at the end of the sentence.

NOTE. Always put the period inside quotation marks. Put the period inside parentheses or brackets when the matter inclosed is an independent sentence; otherwise put it outside.

Examples Browning's "My Last Duchess."

The President of the Rushton student body sent for the five boys accused of hazing. (The officials of the college had given him their names.)

I enclose a check for forty dollars ($40.00).

21c. Use three periods to indicate an omission (or ellipsis) within a quoted sentence or passage.

Examples "Although we ought to think and talk about the matters of large intrinsic worth and least about things of relative value . . . there is abundant evidence to the effect that . . . native mental tendencies are quite the reverse. . . ." (An additional period is necessary here at the end of the sentence.)

"What on earth . . . ! And why . . . ?" I gasped. (Note that a question mark or an exclamation point may follow ellipsis periods.)

He mumbled and moaned for a time. . . . Then came no sound. (The fourth period after *time* marks the end of the sentence.)

The Exclamation Point

22. Use the exclamation point to show strong feeling or surprise.

Do not overwork this mark.

The exclamation point may be used at the end of an exclamatory sentence, or, more rarely, after an exclamation or interjection within a sentence. In the latter case the comma is used for all except very strong exclamations. (See § 17k.)

Examples Ha! You have given your money for nothing?

Come, speak the truth!

What! Here in my own home, under my very eyes, somebody has taken your money! — the only money we have! — and I'm not to know who took it!
You hear me — go!
A fine remark, that!

NOTE. Place the exclamation point inside the quotation marks or parentheses when it is a part of the quoted or parenthetical matter; otherwise place it outside.

Examples The lady shouted, "Save my child!"
What a pile of "mazuma"!
In that musical (*Oklahoma!*) are several interesting characters.

The Question Mark

23. Learn to use the question mark according to the three special rules below.

23a. Use a question mark at the end of every direct question, whether original, quoted, or inserted in a declarative sentence.

Examples Are you going?
"Are you going?" he asked.
Can the applicant do successful work in college? is the only question before us.
He asks whether this applicant can do successful college work. (Here no question mark is used because the sentence is an indirect, not a direct, question.)
You are going? (Question in the form of a declarative sentence.)

The "polite imperative" (see page 159) has interrogative word order, but a question mark is not necessary. Usage varies.

Examples Will you please report at our Detroit office May 31.
Will you please report at our Detroit office May 31?

23b. Use a question mark at the end of each interrogative element in a compound question if separate emphasis is to be given to each of the elements.

Examples What do you think now of his boasted honor? his integrity? his upright character? (Here separate emphasis is given to each interrogative element.)

What do you think now of his boasted honor, his integrity, his upright character? (Without separate emphasis upon each interrogative element.)

23c. Use a question mark within parentheses to show that you are uncertain or doubtful as to the correctness of the preceding word or fact.

Example Chaucer was born in 1342 (?) in the city of London.

NOTE. Place the question mark inside the quotation marks or parentheses only when it is a part of the quoted or parenthetical matter.

Examples Let us consider this question: "How can the United States remain neutral?" (A declarative sentence ending with a quoted question.)

Who now knows the song "Where Is My Wandering Boy Tonight"? (This question mark serves a double purpose.)

This excellent propaganda against war (*What Price Glory?*) might well be revived at this time.

CAUTION. Do not use a question mark to label your own irony or humor.

Ineffective The comic (?) books bored Dr. Green.

EXERCISE

Put the necessary punctuation in the following sentences. Indicate any optional punctuation by placing the alternative mark in parentheses above your first choice.

1. He inquired whether his daughter could get a special diet at the school or not
2. Who wrote "The Cherry Orchard"
3. "Are you ready Isabel" asked her impatient husband
4. "Certainly" she screamed "are you"
5. Will you please read the enclosed recommendation carefully and indicate your decision as soon as possible
6. Is the trouble with the hot water heater or is it with the faucet

7. What language is spoken in Thailand (Siam)
8. Was it Pilate who first said "What is truth"
9. What is his height weight color of hair color of eyes
10. Will this reorganization plan save money was the only question asked by some congressmen, who were not concerned with improving administrative efficiency

The Dash

24. Use the dash, ordinarily in informal writing, to mark a break or shift in thought.

24a. Use the dash to indicate a decided interruption, such as a sudden or unexpected shift in the construction, or a marked break in the thought, or uncertainty or hesitation on the part of a speaker.

Examples "She behaved like ——" and then he refused to go further in his condemnation. (Interruption.)

"Ah! Mr. Sheppard, how — you up from the country? How's your friend — the — er — painter?" (Sudden shift of construction; hesitation.)

Read the note under § 24c.

NOTE. In typing, space properly and make the dash twice as long as the hyphen.

24b. Use the dash to heighten the suspense and so emphasize an appositive, an afterthought, or a summary of a preceding statement.

Examples She felt the turmoil of sudden fear, wondered whether she was showing it, lost it in unnatural alertness — all in the second before she answered. (Summary.)

When, therefore, I say that I have no ear, you will understand me to mean — for music. (Heightened suspense and increased emphasis.)

To give the phrase, the sentence, the structural member, the entire composition, song, or essay a similar unity with its subject and itself — style is right when it tends toward that. (Emphatic conclusion.)

I then saw the answer to my problem — I would ask my father to lend me the money. (Long and emphatic appositive.)

The camera not only sees things that are visible to the human eye, but sees them a thousand times clearer than does the best human eye — even when aided by a powerful microscope. (Afterthought.)

24c. Use the dash to emphasize a parenthesis.

If the parenthesis is long, is informal or emphatic, or contains commas, the dash is preferred to commas or parentheses. (See § 26a.)

Examples Society — she knew, she must know — cared little for the forms, the outside of things.

My father bought that house — can you believe it? — for only eight thousand dollars.

The row of houses had large wooden pillars and wide pilasters holding up the balcony — the ever-present balcony! — over which trailed green vines.

Editorial writers have severely criticized our policy — or lack of it — in the treatment of our colonies.

NOTE. When a sentence ends with a dash, the period is always omitted. An exclamation point or a question mark may be used with a dash, however, if the meaning demands it.

Examples I do not like the idea; but of course if you really want to —

The house was good enough, but as for the family — !

"Your father disapproves — are you listening to me? — but go ahead and learn by experience if necessary."

24d. Use the dash sparingly in formal writing.

The dash is not to be used to conceal an ignorance of other marks of punctuation.

Childish and Monotonous At night I went out in the canoe — the moon was just rising — I paddled far out — there was not a sound to be heard — I came in about midnight.

EXERCISE

Insert dashes and other marks of punctuation wherever they

are needed in the following sentences and be able to explain your use of each dash.

1. He shows us how Leeuwenhoek supposed to be a very ignorant man accidentally invented the microscope.
2. If the mines turn out to be valuable but who knows anything about their future his winnings will be enormous.
3. Glamorous posters and signs, handsome uniforms, brass bands playing military marches all these are used to make men want war.
4. "I will offer you er er fifty dollars for that automobile," said the old farmer to the salesman.
5. Such violations of American liberties and rights could have only one end war.
6. "Gentlemen if you please" but the orator's voice was lost in the shouts of the crowd.
7. In the fight for he yielded only to force Robert Shipton was cut on the head by a sword.
8. Thus the problem remains shall we have a censorship of our radio system by the central government, by one person, by one class of people, or by the people as a whole?
9. Then came breathless silence, a silence one could feel, a silence of mingled fear and hope broken suddenly by a woman's scream.
10. For our government to control the radio would be a direct conflict with a fundamental American ideal the right of free expression.

The Apostrophe

25. Use the apostrophe according to the special rules below.

25a. Use the apostrophe and *s* to form the genitive (possessive) of both singular and plural nouns not ending in *s*.

Singular woman's, child's, month's, Dali's
Plural women's, children's, mice's, geese's

25b. Use the apostrophe alone to form the genitive (possessive) of plural nouns ending in *s*.

Examples months', girls', horses', friends'

25c. Usage varies in the formation of the genitive (possessive) of singular nouns ending in *s*.

Examples	Wallace Stevens'	or	Wallace Stevens's
	O. W. Holmes'	or	O. W. Holmes's
	Roger Williams'	or	Roger Williams's
	mistress' home	or	mistress's home

NOTE. It is generally the practice (1) to use the apostrophe alone to avoid three sibilant sounds: *Moses'*, *Jesus'*, *Ulysses'*, *Kansas'*, and (2) to use the apostrophe and *s* to avoid any danger of misunderstanding: *Ricks's* (in contrast to *Rick's*). When in doubt use the apostrophe and *s*.

25d. Add the apostrophe (or apostrophe and *s*) to the last member of a group when the group is regarded as a unit.

Separate Keats' and Byron's poetry, Lincoln's and Douglas's speeches

Group unit Park and Tilford's label, boys and girls' tennis court

NOTE. Use the apostrophe and *s* also to form the genitive (possessive) of a phrasal compound or similar group of words.

Examples Somebody else's hat, my brother Tom's rifle, my son-in-law's home

25e. Add the apostrophe and *s* to form the genitive (possessive) of indefinite pronouns.

Examples One's, another's, nobody's, anybody's, everybody's, somebody's

NOTE. This rule does *not* apply to the personal pronouns: *its, his, yours, whose, ours, hers, theirs.*

25f. Use the apostrophe to show that letters or figures have been omitted.

Examples Cap'm, doesn't, 'em, the class of '56

25g. Use the apostrophe and *s* to form the plural of letters, figures, or words referred to as such.

Examples There are two *a's* in *separate.*
Dot your *i's* and cross your *t's*.
His *3's* are too much like his *5's*.
He uses too many *and's* and *so's*.

25h. Put the apostrophe in the right place.

Right isn't (not *is'nt*), Keats' (not *Keat's*).

25i. The apostrophe is frequently omitted in the names of organizations, institutions, and places.

Examples State Teachers College, Merchants Protective Association, Harpers Ferry, Queen Annes County, Kings Mountain

Martha's Vineyard, *Bedloe's Island*, and *Land's End* are examples with the apostrophe. When in doubt about a place-name, look it up in *Webster's Geographical Dictionary*, *ACD*, or *NCD*.

EXERCISES

A. Use the apostrophe correctly in the following sentences.

1. Lets glance back and observe somebody elses situation.
2. The people of England, and of the whole world, in fact, eagerly awaited Chamberlains decision.
3. I should like to buy a girls bicycle.
4. If it is a Siamese its eyes will remain blue.
5. Uncle Eph was so argumentative that he wouldnt agree with a casual remark about the weather.
6. The *3s*, *5s*, *7s*, and *9s* in this type are not descending figures.
7. Lets organize a students coöperative store.
8. Neither ones views on Chiang suited the President.
9. A weeks vacation and a months separation pay were granted.
10. Nobodys going to hold anybodys hat and coat in this fight.

B. Form the genitive (possessive) of each of the following.

1. man
2. men
3. Phyllis
4. it
5. Burns
6. ox
7. oxen
8. lice
9. Sophocles
10. Ross
11. George the Fourth
12. mother-in-law
13. Professor Hiss
14. Norfolk and Western
15. The AFL
16. The *New York Times*
17. Truman and Barkley (campaign)
18. goodness (sake)
19. Archimedes
20. Adam and Eve (quarrel)

Parentheses and Brackets

26. Use parentheses and brackets to enclose supplementary or interpolated material.

26a. Use parentheses to enclose material which is connected only loosely with the main thought of the sentence.

Such material may be used to explain, amplify, or interpret. Commas, dashes, and parentheses are all used to set off parenthetical or interpolated sentence-elements. The choice among these three marks of punctuation depends upon the closeness of the relation between the parenthetical sentence-element and the sentence in which it stands. Commas indicate the closest continuity; dashes reveal a greater and more emphatic break; parentheses are used to enclose the most loosely connected insertions. The writer must determine the degree of closeness he wishes to express and punctuate accordingly. (See §§ 17 and 24c.)

Example If there are wet leaves lying around (and there are sure to be thousands of them) we shall probably skid.

In consequence of the many stories that were told about the lady (I can only remember a few), I expected to find her a subversive character.

26b. Use parentheses where numerical accuracy is essential.

Example I enclose a check for fifty dollars ($50.00).

This is not usually necessary in printed or typed matter.

26c. Use parentheses to set off figures indicating the divisions of an enumeration within a sentence.

Example The speaker referred to two important tendencies: (1) the tendency toward centralization in government, and (2) the trend toward a better understanding between the different social classes.

26d. Do not put any punctuation before the first parenthesis mark within a sentence. Punctuate after the second mark just as you would if the sentence contained no parentheses.

No capital or period is used with a parenthesis which is inserted within a sentence, but a question mark or an exclamation point may be used. A parenthetical sentence not inserted within another sentence follows the regular rules of punctuation.

Example As the automobile swung sharply round the corner (it was an eight-cylinder car), the policeman blew his whistle. (No period or capital is used because the parenthetical sentence is inserted in the body of another sentence.)

If you decide to come with us, bring your gun (you have it at your house, haven't you?) and meet us at the station. (Note that a question mark is used in the parenthetical sentence.)

26e. Never use parentheses to cancel anything you have written. Draw a line through the word or passage which you wish to delete.

26f. Use brackets to mark an interpolation you have made in quoted material or to enclose a parenthesis within a parenthesis.

This interpolation may be an explanation, a comment, a correction, or *sic* to point out that the original has been quoted exactly.

Examples "This poem [*Piers Plowman*] is thoroughly characteristic of the age [second half of the fourteenth century] in which it was written. The author [or authors, as some scholars would have us believe] was widely imitated by other writers."

The poem he quoted (Gower's *Confessio Amantis* [Macaulay's edition]) contains some tales told by Chaucer.

EXERCISE

Make the changes indicated, using brackets and parentheses wherever needed.

1. Add *$60.00.*
   The lessee agrees to make a monthly payment of sixty dollars.
2. Add *you remember him as editor of the college paper.*
   Don Sprague is writing sports for a Chicago newspaper.
3. Add *sic* after the date, indicating that it is wrong in the original and not your error.
   "Edgar Allan Poe was born in 1890 in Boston."
4. Add *now Mrs. L. P. Ward* after *Neeley.*
   Frances Neeley was the first girl elected to the office.

5. Insert *1*, *2*, and *3* to emphasize the enumeration.
   Kurath divides American English into three principal regional types: Northern, Midland, and Southern.
6. Add *formerly Christiania* after *Oslo.*
   Oslo was founded about the middle of the eleventh century.
7. Add *at least so I thought* after *expert.*
   He was the local expert on frog gigging and coon hunting.
8. Add *Ann Arbor* before the date, and indicate that you are supplying information which is not in the book.
   See Hans Kurath, *A Word Geography of the Eastern United States*, 1949, Figure 3.
9. Insert *Victor Hugo* after *he.*
   This book (written before he was thirty) is my idea of a good novel for the movie producers to consider.
10. Add *actually, she was born in 1880* after *Dickinson.*
    She claims to be a twentieth century Emily Dickinson.

Quotation Marks

27. Use quotation marks to set off direct quotations and words which you wish to call attention to.

27a. Use quotation marks to enclose words which you wish to call special attention to, such as technical terms in non-technical writing, markedly colloquial words out of context, nicknames, slang, coined, or humorous words.

Technical words require quotation marks only when they are written for readers who are not familiar with them; quotation marks are not used in technical writing addressed to readers familiar with the technical terms.

Examples He automatically looked at the "ears" of the morning paper for the weather report. (newspaper jargon)

In those good old days teen-agers called people "drips" and "creeps." (slang which the writer of the sentence does not use)

My beautiful snapshot came back from the yearbook office with "crop marks" on it. (technical term)

NOTE. If such a word is repeated, there is no necessity for using quotation marks again. If the word is in your own vocabulary and your reader's, there is no necessity for quotation marks at all. Do not call attention to words which honestly and efficiently convey your meaning.

27b. Use quotation marks before and after every separate direct quotation.

Do not put quotation marks around verbs of saying, indirect quotations, or well-known quotations which any reader can recognize. Study the examples below.

Examples He said, "Will you come?"

I replied, "Yes."

"My father wants to meet you," he said. "Will you call tonight?" (Note that the verb of saying is not enclosed within quotation marks.)

He said, "My father wants to meet you. Will you call tonight?" (This single, uninterrupted quotation requires only one set of quotation marks.)

Do unto others as you would have them do unto you was his motto, and he actually practiced it. (The saying is too well known to need quotation marks.)

Faulty He said that "he would be happy to meet us."

Revised He said that he would be happy to meet us. (No quotation marks are used here because the exact words of the speaker are not given.)

He said, "I shall be happy to meet them." (Here the exact words of the speaker are given.)

27c. Use quotation marks to enclose direct quotations, but not indirect.

Examples Professor Craig opened his lecture by saying, "The Revolutionary War had four chief causes."

Professor Craig opened his lecture by saying that the Revolutionary War had four chief causes.

CAUTION. *Be sure to use quotation marks to acknowledge your indebtedness to other writers for all words you borrow from them.* This is a matter of fundamental literary honesty.

27d. A quotation within a quotation should be enclosed by single quotation marks.

Example The witness testified: "I heard the defendant say, 'I had no idea that my uncle was in the city that day.' "

27e. Use quotation marks to enclose the title or name of a poem, a short story, a play, or an essay — if such a literary work is not printed separately in book form — an article, a song, a motion picture, a lecture, or a chapter or section-heading of a book.

Either quotation marks or italics may be used for works of art and names of ships and aircraft.

Examples Browning's "My Last Duchess" (short poem)

Poe's "The Gold Bug" (short story)

O'Neill's "The Emperor Jones" (play not published separately)

Emerson's "Self-Reliance" (essay)

Alan Devoe's "The Mystery of Migration" (article in the *American Mercury*)

"O Promise Me" (song)

"The Life of Émile Zola" (motion picture)

"American Humorists" (lecture)

"The Dandy and the Squatter" (Chapter IV of DeVoto's *Mark Twain's America*)

Gainsborough's "The Blue Boy" or *The Blue Boy* (painting)

Rodin's "The Thinker" or *The Thinker* (statue)

"Franconia" or *Franconia* (ship)

"The Spirit of Saint Louis" or *The Spirit of Saint Louis* (airplane)

(See also §§ 28e, 28f, and 29.)

27f. Use quotation marks to define or translate words.

Examples *Depend* once meant "hang down."

Gothic *taihuntaihund* is translated "hundred."

27g. Never employ quotation marks without good reason.

Instead of using quotation marks to apologize for the words you have used, search until you find words which need no apology. Rarely use quotation marks to label your own humor. Do not enclose the title of your theme in quotation marks unless the title itself is a quotation. A too frequent use of quotation marks gives the impression of undue self-consciousness.

(For the Exercise, see page 206.)

Dialogue and Quoted Matter

28a. In writing dialogue, make a separate paragraph for every change of speaker.

The explanatory words of introduction including the author's or editor's comments are ordinarily put in the same paragraph with the speech. But a paragraph of explanation or narration by the author must not be included in the paragraphs of dialogue. When the explanations or comments introduce a long uninterrupted quotation, they may be placed in one paragraph and the quotation itself in another.

Example "You must resign," said Governor Holmes.
"Must I?" queried Fleming Mitchell.
The Governor shouted at him vehemently:
"Here are at least a dozen reasons. . . ." (A long, uninterrupted quotation is to follow.)

For the colon with quoted matter, see § 28c.
For the quoting of verse, see § 34g.

28b. When quoting several consecutive paragraphs from the same author, place quotation marks at the beginning of each paragraph, but at the end of the last paragraph only.

NOTE. It is also permissible to omit quotation marks and set off the quoted matter typographically. In typing a quotation of several lines, center and single-space the quotation (except in a manuscript to be printed, which should be double-spaced throughout for legibility).

(See § 40f.)

28c. Always separate the words introducing the direct quotation from the quotation itself.

The comma is used unless the quotation is long or formal, is paragraphed separately, or is not preceded by a verb of saying, in which cases a colon is preferred to the comma.

Examples He said, "Certainly."

She said, "I see that you have an engagement."

"I see," she said, "that you have an engagement."

Very slowly he replied, "I'll do it," and then walked hesitatingly toward the cabin.

His words may well be repeated here: "I have full confidence in the judgment of the committee."

28d. Use a semicolon after *he said, she replied,* and similar expressions when they are inserted between two independent clauses, provided the second independent clause does not begin with a coördinating conjunction.

Examples "Blanche, I have brought a friend to see you," said the old man; "turn around and speak to him." (A comma after *man* would result in a "comma fault.")

"The trip today has been a very long one," said Mr. Thaxton; "therefore I must retire very early." (If sentence unity demands it, the second clause of a divided quotation should be written as a separate sentence.)

28e. Place the comma and the period inside closing quotation marks.

Examples "If I lend you the book," he said, "you must be sure to return it within a week."

The last word in the stanza is "forlorn."

28f. Place the question mark, the exclamation point, the colon, the semicolon, and the dash outside the quotation marks, except when they are a part of the quotation.

Examples "Go!"

"Where?" (In these two cases the mark of punctuation is part of the quotation. Note the omission of a verb of saying.)

The crowd yelled, "Save the game, Duke!"; but the mighty batsman swung in vain.

Did he say, "I have an engagement"?

"Have you an engagement?" he said.

"I was just getting into the car —" he began, but stopped in sheer surprise.

How furious he was at the simple words, "Call again"!

28g. Do not place a comma or a period after a question mark or an exclamation point.

Unnecessary "What are we waiting for?," said the priest.
"Stop!," shouted the policeman to the disappearing boys.

EXERCISES

A. Punctuate and paragraph the following passage, paying especial attention to the dialogue.

Kay batted her green eyes at the traffic policeman and asked innocently did I do something wrong not much he said wetting the point of his pencil with his tongue speeding reckless driving running four red lights attempting to avoid arrest lets see your drivers license she pouted then smiled sweetly and began rummaging in her oversize handbag why officer it isn't here what will I do when did you have it last I must have left it in the bag that I lost down at Quindo Beach yesterday did you report the bag lost just then the radio in his car began droning number thirteen number thirteen watch for a yellow Cadillac convertible driven by a blond young woman license Georgia 61C43 repeat Georgia 61C43 last figure 3 or 8. Driver left scene of an accident on highway 78 six miles south of Booton fifteen minutes ago at first the cop listened automatically, but as the details came sing-song out of the speaker he stepped nearer his car to hear better, meanwhile looking straight at Kay her eyes widened as the message droned on why that could be me, except that I was at Quindo Beach fifteen minutes ago; there must be another Cad convertible around here if you got here from Quindo Beach in fifteen minutes lady you had to average sixty-five and there are six traffic lights to slow you in that stretch suppose you follow me back to the station have it your way mister she said, still sitting quiet and working her ninety-watt smile overtime then as he turned to get in his car she suddenly gunned the Cadillac and was a hundred yards down the highway before he was under the wheel headquarters he yelled into his microphone as he slammed the gearshift into low and stomped on the throttle.

B. Directions under Exercise A.

the master of ceremonies bounced up and down on the balls of his feet and smiled his gooey toothy smile now the little lady who has the most box tops tries the Qunchies Quiz-Quiz he shouted what's your name mam miss agnes tooson the contestant said and giggled looking out at the studio audience well well miss twosome welcome to our microphone it's always crowded when you have a date isn't it I don know why and my name's tooson well a twosome and a boy friend makes three and three's a crowd ha ha ha now miss twosome here's your first question think hard now what is a rectrix it's a big feather from a birds tail so sorry youre wrong much hand waving and headshaking from eight or ten young men who hadn't seemed to be listening they must have been producers of the show oh youre right I must have got my cards mixed up youre absolutely right now the next question who wrote *Didon* can you tell me miss tooson giggled some more bit off two fingernails and said firmly Etienne Jodelle youre right youre absolutely right why did you decide to enter our super-Qunchies quiz-quiz miss newsome the girl ducked her head shyly and wadded the damp handkerchief in her left hand well we listen to you every Monday through Friday at eleven and mama said to me last night aggie that's what she calls me but my name's agnes why don't you collect those box tops out behind the back steps and go down to that quiz-quiz I didn't much want to but she said go on take a chance so here I am well good that's great now here's another question what is the population of Llangefni in Wales do you know miss toomey Oh yes its 1782 right you are now here is the jackpot question are you ready miss miss what was your name agnes tooson and not was it still is yes I'm ready all right here we go with the grand prize question what state is New York City in yes New York City what state is it in why I guess its New York after we had gotten out of the crowd coming out of the studio jack said lets wait around a minute I want to see what some of those people look like when theyre not working.

MECHANICS

Certain conventions of English writing and printing, pertaining mainly to italic type, quotation marks, capital letters, syllable division, and abbreviation, are commonly called mechanics. Although most matters of mechanics are dictated by custom and are subject to changes in fashion, literate people have come to expect certain consistencies which pass unnoticed when observed, but which distract attention when violated.

Italics

29. In longhand or typewritten copy, underline a word to indicate that if printed it would be in italics (slanting type).

29a. Use italics to mark foreign words and abbreviations of foreign words.

Examples of words occasionally used in English but still regarded as foreign: *outré, glacé, Gesundheit, Lebensraum.*

Examples of words imported from foreign languages (note the diacritical marks) but now regarded as English and not italicized: café, début, élite, canyon, rodeo, hara-kiri.

Examples of abbreviations that require italics are *ibid., id., loc. cit., op. cit., q. v.* (Foreign terms.)

Examples of abbreviations that do not require italics are A. D., B. C., a.m., p.m., cf., and e.g.

Since there is no rule to guide you in this use of italics, consult your dictionary when in doubt.

29b. Use italics to refer to a word or a letter or a number as such.

Examples Care should be taken to distinguish between *accept* and *except*, between *ac* and *ex*.
The *7's* are longer than the *4's*.

29c. Only rarely use italics to emphasize a word.

Although nineteenth-century authors were fond of italicizing for emphasis, modern writers usually prefer other means of obtaining stress and force.

29d. Italicize the word *Resolved* in formal resolutions.

29e. Prefer italics to quotation marks in indicating the titles of books, newspapers, magazines, operas, and other musical compositions.

29f. Use either italics or quotation marks for literary titles.

Good usage differs widely in the representation of literary titles. The best practice in formal writing is to prefer italics in writing the titles of books (except the Bible and the books in it), newspapers, magazines, operas, and symphonies. Quotation marks are used to enclose the titles of poems, stories, plays, essays — if they are not printed as separate books — articles, paintings, songs, lectures, motion pictures, and subdivisions of books. The complete work should always be distinguished from its parts.

NOTE. Newspapers frequently use quotation marks instead of the more formal italics for all the titles and names listed above. Sometimes they omit both italics and quotation marks and treat such titles as ordinary propery names.

Examples Margaret Mitchell's *Gone with the Wind* (book)
the *New York Post* (Some writers do not italicize the name of the city in the title of a newspaper. Either practice is acceptable.)
the *Saturday Evening Post* (magazine)
Beethoven's *Eroica* (symphony)
Wagner's *Lohengrin* (opera)
Rodin's *The Thinker* or "The Thinker" (statue)
the *Queen Mary* or the "Queen Mary" (ship)
the *Spirit of Saint Louis* or the "Spirit of Saint Louis" (airplane)

NOTE. Italics are not usually used for the title of the Bible or its books.

NOTE. For the proper use of titles in footnotes and bibliographies, see § 40.
(For models, see pages 269–271.)

NOTE: In manuscript to be printed, italics are frequently used for contrast, as in formal rules and sub-titles.

EXERCISES

A. Place the necessary italics and quotation marks in the following sentences.

1. She said tell him to stop making those snide remarks about me.
2. Darrow's cartoon showed an old capitalist asleep with a copy of the New York Sun over his face.
3. Expressions like oldie and goodbye now get tiresome very soon.
4. Aubrey Burns is the author of Segregation and the Church in the Southwest Review.
5. DuBose Heyward's short story The Half Pint Flask is one of the best I ever read.
6. Gens du monde means people of fashion.
7. The words movie and photo are not in some older dictionaries.
8. Berrey and Van den Bark's American Thesaurus of Slang is the most interesting book we have used in this course.
9. He wanted to carry me to the dance, as they say in the South.
10. If Aunt Elsie read anything besides the Saturday Evening Post it must have been the Sears Roebuck catalogue.

B. Directions given under Exercise A.

1. Since he took English 151 he thinks Eliot's The Wasteland is the only first-rate poem in the English language.
2. Mencken's The American Language interested me more than any other book on the reading list.
3. It may have been a phony war to some people, but in 1940 it was serious enough to my family.
4. The senator is a phony; not one of his claims is valid.

5. The tune Third Man Theme from the excellent movie The Third Man could be heard all up and down Fraternity Row every night.
6. The person who wants to read the best of Emerson's essays must read The American Scholar, The Divinity School Address, and Self-Reliance.
7. We learned that a tazza is a kind of bowl, not a dance.
8. Who said these are the good old days you'll be reminiscing about twenty years from now?
9. The suffix ish means one thing when added to nouns, another when added to verbs.
10. A chapter entitled "Footless" Questions is reprinted in Lee's The Language of Wisdom and Folly.

Representation of Numbers

30. Write figures or spell out numbers consistently.

30a. Do not spell out the numbers in dates, hours when *a.m.* or *p.m.* is used, pages or sections of books, room or street numbers, or cardinal numbers (one, two, etc.) preceded by a word of enumeration or a word indicating a division of a section.

Examples July 25, 1888
1693 University Avenue
Pages 13, 18, and 40
Part II, section 3
Lower 13 in Car 64H

30b. Follow a consistent system of writing numbers.

One widely used (rather formal) system is to use figures for all numbers which cannot be written in one or two words: *fifty-five players, 5,870 students, eleven coaches, six thousand seats, 840 tickets.*

Another (less formal) system is to use figures for all numbers above nine: *eight students (20 per cent of the class), seven dormitories with 70 rooms, housing 210 students.*

NOTE. These rules apply to sums of money also. The dollar sign is not normally used for sums of less than a dollar.

30c. Do not begin a sentence with a figure.

Undesirable 21 days later he went home.
Standard Twenty-one days later he went home.

30d. Except in cases where extreme accuracy is desired, do not repeat a number in parenthetical figures.

Undesirable We killed ten (10) birds.
Standard We killed ten birds.

But see § 26b.

30e. Except in dates, page and verse numbers, street and telephone numbers, use commas to set off figures in groups of three.

Standard 1,789,678
4200 B.C.
page 1007
6020 Drexel Avenue
Dearborn 5636

30f. Use a hyphen in compound numbers for sums less than a hundred.

Standard Twenty-five, eighty-seven

30g. The abbreviations *st, nd, rd, th* after days of the month are unnecessary and are avoided in most writing.

Undesirable June 1st; October 4th, 1929
Standard June 1; October 4, 1929

EXERCISE

In the following sentences rewrite any numbers that should be changed.

1. 60 pounds was the proper pressure for this model in 1947.
2. That book was too long; it had six hundred eighty-five pages.
3. It was a nineteen forty Buick, license no. D87966.
4. On September 1st there will be over 25,000 applications.
5. The percentage of errors was only 0.9 after two weeks.

Syllabication

31. If a word must be broken at the end of a line, observe conventional rules of syllabication.

Although there are many rules for syllabication, those given below will prove to be the simplest and the most helpful.

31a. Always place a hyphen at the end of the first line, not at the beginning of the second.

31b. Divide only between syllables, and then be sure that the part of the word on each line is pronounceable by itself.

Consult your dictionary if you have any doubt about how a word is divided into syllables.

Examples *pro-fes-sor, meas-ure, gra-cious, o-ri-en-tal, go-ing*

31c. Do not divide a word so that a single letter stands alone as a syllable; and, except for prefixes and suffixes, rarely write two letters as a separate syllable.

Examples *many* (not *man-y*), *across, only, ever*

31d. Never divide monosyllables.

Although *stepped* and *missed* look like two-syllable words, remember that they are pronounced *stept* and *mist*, obviously monosyllabic. Be guided by the pronunciation, not the spelling.

31e. Two consonants or double consonants are usually divided except in such words as *call-ing*, where the base word ends in a double consonant, or in words like *fa-ther*.

Examples *com-mit, per-mit*, but *tell-ing, spell-ing, spell-er, moth-er*. (*Th* in *fa-ther* and *moth-er* is a digraph, two letters representing a single sound, like *ch* in *ma-chine* and *sh* in *cash-ier*. The digraphs go with the syllables in which they are pronounced.)

31f. Three or more consonants are divided so that the consonants that are pronounced together stand in the same syllable.

Examples *dem-on-strate, mael-strom, per-spec-tive*

31g. Compound words are divided between their component parts.

Examples *black-board, over-take, battle-ground*

31h. Prefixes and suffixes are usually treated as separate syllables.

But *-ed* stands alone only when it is pronounced as a separate syllable. Where the rule for doubling a single final consonant gives two consonants, the additional consonant goes with the suffix.

Examples *oc-cur, oc-cur-ring, man-ly, re-duce, ante-date, start-ed, tak-ing;* but *gnarled, walked*

EXERCISES

A. By putting in hyphens, indicate the points at which the following words can be broken at the end of a line.

segmental	kissed	pre-scientific
coughed	disappoint	dwelling
referred	compounds	prism
language	biography	inquire
anti-vivisection	differential	principle
tremble	dictaphone	trailed
African	graphic	calling

B. Directions given under Exercise A.

groused	implicit	italicize
kinsman	presidential	rapacious
trouble	trucked	spilling
mountain	agency	patience
rebellious	bishop	gauche
programme	hungry	bronzed
semester	resignation	satin

Capitals

32. The two ordinary uses of capitals are (1) to mark the beginning of a sentence and (2) to mark a noun or adjective as proper and not common.

32a. Capitalize the first word of every sentence, whether original or quoted, and of every formal resolution, salutation, or question.

Standard He said, "Let us go."

"No! No! Of course not." (Fragmentary sentences.)

His statement was as follows: "Never begin a task unless you know that you can complete it."

He told us what the secret of success is: patience at all times.

These three reasons prevented us from winning the pennant: our coach was new; our backfield was inexperienced, and our captain was severely injured in the first game.

"Now one asks, 'What types of progress did the poet advocate?'"

With the remark "Will he come if we ask him?" he left the room.

The question: Which of these two men is better fitted for the position? would be hard to answer. (Formal question.)

Benjamin Franklin says that "the sleeping fox catches no poultry."

(In the last sentence the quoted matter is necessary to the grammatical completeness of the sentence in which it stands. Thus a quotation incorporated in a *that* clause does not begin with a capital letter even though the original quotation began with one.)

EXCEPTION. He sailed for Europe — this was his first trip abroad — on May 14. (A parenthetical sentence inserted in another sentence does not begin with a capital.)

32b. Capitalize the first word of every line of conventional poetry.

The time and my intents are savage-wild,
More fierce and more inexorable far
Than empty tigers or the roaring sea.

NOTE. Some modern poets do not capitalize the first word in each line. When quoting them, follow their practice in every detail.

32c. Capitalize all proper names.

Proper names are of three types: (1) genuine proper nouns, (2) common nouns conventionally capitalized, and (3) noun phrases containing a proper noun or adjective.

(1) Proper nouns (which can be recognized in spoken English) may be defined as nouns which are always singular, always definite,

and never modified by a limiting adjective (*some*, *twenty*, *oldest*, etc.). Examples are *Cincinnati*, *Franklin Roosevelt*, *Pope Pius*, *Cranford*, *Saturn*, *Buddha*, *America*, *Mark Twain*. The referent of a proper noun is always a unique specimen.

When a proper noun is occasionally used to refer to a class of objects instead of a unique specimen, it becomes a common noun in spoken English (takes plural form and limiting modifiers), but in writing the capital letter is retained. Examples: "He's a modern Mark Twain," "Other countries have their Shakespeares and Miltons, too," "The Joneses once lived here."

When such a noun is used regularly to refer to a class of objects, dictionaries list it as a common noun, and in this usage no capital letter is required. Examples: *babel*, *vandal*, *sandwich*, *boycott*, *watt*, *china*, *hamburger*, *quisling*, *morocco*, *turkey*.

(2) Some nouns which are treated as common nouns in speech (take limiting modifiers or plural form) are conventionally capitalized because of custom, or to show courtesy or respect. Examples (note the articles): *the Pope*, *the Koran*, *the North Pole*, *the Old Testament*, *the Pleiades*. Contrast *recent popes*, *the poles of a magnet*, *a testament*, *Pope Pius*, *Saturn*, *Genesis*. Such nouns must be memorized (see lists below); no rule identifies them.

(3) Numerous proper names consist of a noun phrase containing a proper adjective. Examples: the *Hudson* River, the *British* Empire, the *Pacific* Ocean, the *Augustan* Age, the *Presbyterian* Church, the *Washington* Monument, the Gulf *of Aden*, the Shah *of Iran*.

Proper adjectives are (1) derivatives of proper nouns (*Mexican*, *American*, *Semitic*, *Episcopal*) or (2) proper nouns used as adjectives or as members of adjective phrases (*Jefferson* Memorial, *Populist* Party, *Missouri* River, *Holland* Tunnel, University *of Alabama*, Straits *of Dover*, Governor *of Nebraska*).

When two or more proper adjectives modify a noun in the plural, the noun is not capitalized (*the Tombigbee and Yazoo rivers*, *the Suez and Panama canals*, *Princeton and Colgate universities;* contrast *Princeton University* and *Colgate University*.)

In terms of meaning, the most important classes of proper names are the following:

(*a*) Names of individuals, languages, and social groups: Mary Martin, William the Conqueror, "Dizzy" Dean, Man o' War, Father (but not *my father*), Spanish, Cherokee, Mongol, Baptist, American Bar Association, United Electrical Workers, Odd Fellows, Rotary Club.

(*b*) Names of institutions and particular artifacts: Howard University, Bellevue Hospital, Bankers Trust Company, Brooklyn Bridge, Statler Hotel, Skyline Drive, Rodin's "The Thinker," Boulder Dam, Eiffel Tower, Fifth Avenue (sometimes Fifth avenue).

(*c*) Geographical names and names of political units: Grand Canyon, Pikes Peak, Chesapeake Bay, the South (or the south), Delaware, Tuscaloosa County (or county), Ithaca.

(*d*) Names of days, months, and holidays: Saturday, January, Armistice Day, Fourth of July.

(*e*) Names of historical events and epochs: the Crimean War, the Battle of the Bulge, the Renaissance, the Industrial Revolution.

(*f*) Names of religious personages, ceremonies, and writings: the Virgin Mary, the Holy Ghost, Easter, Yom Kippur, the Talmud, the Apostles' Creed, High Mass.

(*g*) Titles of literary and musical compositions.

When you are in doubt about a particular word, look it up in *ACD* or *NCD*. Titles like *president* and *chairman of the committee* are not capitalized unless you can substitute a person's name for the title in the sentence.

Examples The president of the college should be an educated man.
The President was born in Virginia.

32d. Capitalize titles of honor preceding a proper name and all degrees following a name.

Examples President Jefferson
ex-President Hoover
We saw the President yesterday. (If a title is used alone, only titles of great respect should be capitalized.)
We are going to elect a president and a secretary this afternoon.

(Capitals are never used unless the reference is to a particular person.)
the Crown Prince of Italy
Jasper Maxwell, Ph.D., F.R.S.
May I go now, Father? Are you going too, Auntie? (but *my father*, *your aunt*.) (Use no capitals when a word is used as a common noun; the limiters [*my* and *your* here] show that *father* and *aunt* are common nouns and not substitutes for proper nouns.)

32e. Capitalize *I*, O (but not *oh*), *No.* (number), *B.C.*, *Jr.*, *Sr.*, *A.D.*, and *Esq.*

A.M. and P.M. may be written either with or without capitals.

32f. Capitalize the words *Whereas* and *Resolved* in formal resolutions and the first word following either of these words.

32g. Capitalize the first, last, and every important word in the titles of your themes.

32h. Capitalize the first, the last, and all important words in the titles of books, sections or chapters of books, poems, plays, stories, newspapers, magazines, essays, articles, lectures, works of art, motion pictures, and songs.

Articles, prepositions, and conjunctions are not capitalized unless they stand first in the title. If the article *the* stands first in the title of a newspaper or magazine, however, it need not be capitalized.

Examples the *Saturday Evening Post*
the *New York Times*
the *Atlantic Monthly*
The House of the Seven Gables
"The Vision of Sir Launfal"
"Under the Lion's Paw"

32i. Avoid the unnecessary use of capitals.

Do not capitalize for emphasis.
Do not capitalize the names of the seasons.
Do not capitalize *north*, *northern*, *east*, *south*, *west*, etc., when these words merely indicate direction. (See § 32c.)

Do not capitalize the first word after *he said* when this expression is inserted between two parts of a single quoted sentence. (See § 28d.)

Capitals are not regularly used in such terms as *the gymnasium, the post office, the war, town, the library*, etc., unless they are used as substitutes for proper names: "Are you going to town or to the library?"

Do not capitalize the *second* part of hyphenated words unless they are proper nouns or proper adjectives: *Thirty-seventh Avenue* (but *Anglo-French relations*).

Do not capitalize the names of studies in the curriculum unless they are proper nouns or adjectives (English, Latin, Indian, German, etc.) or unless they form part of the official title of a specific course, such as Mathematics 104, Chemistry 171. "Wilson registered for courses in economics, geography, Russian, and history."

EXERCISES

A. Supply necessary capitals in the following sentences.

1. permission to take advanced courses in french must be secured from the head of the department.
2. my father had german, chemistry, history, and greek his first year.
3. where do the tennessee and ohio rivers come together?
4. the secretary of state hurried to washington when news of the invasion reached him.
5. i think there was a national bank near the corner of winston and bullock streets.

B. Directions given under Exercise A.

1. margaret ralston then said, oh, let captain scuttle sing it.
2. this book is published by houghton mifflin company of boston.
3. after visiting the canal zone we spent a week in colombia.
4. at 6 a.m. the first northbound bus leaves camp slocumb for omaha.
5. the university club at 421 queen city avenue was damaged, although the manager extinguished the fire very quickly.

Abbreviations and Contractions

33. Use abbreviations and contractions sparingly.

33a. In connected writing, use only abbreviations of the kinds listed below.

Such common abbreviations of titles as Mr., Mrs., Messrs., Hon. (unless *the* precedes), Rev. (unless *the* precedes), Col., Dr. before proper names, and Esq., Jr., Sr., D.D., LL.D., Ph.D., and other titles after proper names — No. or $ before figures, St. (Saint), A.M., P.M. (or a.m., p.m.) used with other words or A.D. and B.C. used with dates.

Also, i.e., etc., cf., viz., vs., but not & for *and.* (Some writers spell out even these words in formal writing, using *that is, and so forth, compare, for example,* and similar expressions.)

33b. Avoid the abbreviations of Christmas, proper names, titles not followed by a proper name, Christian names, names of months, days of the week, states, countries, and studies (mathematics, economics, English, etc.).

Such words as *company, incorporated, brothers,* and *railroad* are sometimes abbreviated in the official names of business firms. In writing such names, follow precisely the official form.

The names of states, and words like *avenue, street,* and *road* are conventionally abbreviated in mailing addresses, but the abbreviation is a short cut that does not flatter the addressee. When you abbreviate a state name, use the approved Post Office abbreviation, which you can find in *ACD* or *NCD.*

33c. In connected writing, spell out the words *volume, chapter, page, line, company, association,* etc.

33d. Capitalize an abbreviation if the unabbreviated word would be capitalized.

33e. In formal writing avoid contractions: words written with an apostrophe to indicate the omission of a letter from the body of a word, such as *won't, don't, he'll, they'd.*

In informal writing, which has become increasingly colloquial in recent years, contractions of *not*, as in *won't*, *isn't*, *doesn't*, and *shouldn't*, occasionally occur. Other contractions, such as *I'll*, *we've*, *they're*, *she's*, *you'd*, and *they'd* are strongly colloquial in flavor and are used only in clearly colloquial passages, such as dialogue.

NOTE. No period is required after a contraction. For the period after abbreviations, see § 21b.

33f. Do not use ditto marks except in the most informal writing, such as lecture notes.

EXERCISE

In the following sentences spell out all abbreviations that are inappropriate.

1. Dr. John Simmons, Jr., of the coroner's office, wrote DOA on the report form, indicating that the victim was dead on arrival.
2. Some Americans believe that certain foreign countries have excellent forms of gov't., but the form here in the U.S.A. suits me perfectly.
3. The druggist came back from a fishing trip in Wis. with ninety lbs. of assorted lake fish.
4. Stop! R. R. Crossing!
5. For many yrs. the G. & C. Merriam Co. has published *Webster's* dictionaries.

General Manuscript Form

34. Pay careful attention to all matters of manuscript form.

This section deals with the form of all papers. See § 40 for a special treatment of form in the research paper.

34a. Legibility. Do not run letters or words together or leave a space between letters of the same word.

Use a typewriter if possible; if not, write with a good pen, use black or blue ink, and make every word legible. Do not let the loops of letters overlap between lines. Take care to avoid the omission of end punctuation, of the dot over an *i* or *j*, and of the cross of a *t*. Take especial pains to write proper names correctly and to distinguish in form and size between capitals and small letters.

34b. Paging. Number and arrange the pages of your manuscript in proper form.

Use Arabic numbers in the upper right corner (or middle) of the page. Use white paper of a standard size ($8\frac{1}{2} \times 11$ unless otherwise instructed) and write on one side only.

34c. Spacing. Leave a margin of one inch on all sides of the page.

Do not crowd your writing at the bottom of the page; leave the last line blank. Do not leave part of a line blank except at the end of a paragraph or before a quotation placed below the words introducing it. Leave one letter-space between words, two between sentences. If the paper is to be stapled into a folder, leave $1\frac{1}{2}$ inch margin on the left instead of the normal 1 inch. If you use a typewriter, be sure to double-space your composition except in footnotes and centered quotations.

34d. Indention. Indent paragraphs uniformly — five spaces on the typewriter or the equivalent (about one inch) in handwritten manuscript. Take care to indent quotations and verse correctly.

34e. Erasures and Corrections. Do not leave unsightly erasures or blots on your paper.

To cancel a word draw a single straight line through it. Do not use brackets or parentheses to cancel.

To insert an omitted expression use a caret (∧) below the line at the point of omission and write the inserted words either between the lines above the caret or in the margin opposite the caret. Rewrite a page rather than leave it full of unsightly blots, blurs, or corrections.

34f. The Title. Center your title on the first page, and capitalize the first word, the last word, and every important word. Leave a space of one inch between the title and the first line of the theme.

Do not repeat the title on succeeding pages. Ordinarily, prepositions, articles, and conjunctions are not capitalized unless they stand first or last. If the paper has printed lines on it, put the title on the first line, leave the second blank, and begin your theme proper on the third. No period follows the title, but a question mark or an exclamation point may be used. Do not use quotations or italics for the title of a theme unless you are using a quoted title. The first sentence of the theme proper must be intelligible without reference to the title.

Right My Job Last Summer
A New Process for Making Pottery

For choice of title, see § 39a.

34g. In quoting verse, follow exactly the mechanical arrangement of the original. Center the quoted passage inside the margins of your own manuscript.

Right When I entered Jack's room I found him dolefully declaiming some lines from William Cullen Bryant's most popular poem:

So live that when thy summons comes to join
That innumerable caravan, which moves. . . .

He had to memorize the passage for his next English class. Jack much preferred working in the chemistry laboratory to struggling with poetry.

If another sentence of your own composing follows the quotation and belongs in the same paragraph with the matter preceding the quotation (as above), do not indent the first line which follows the quotation.

34h. Do not begin a line with a punctuation mark.

The only exceptions are quotation marks, the opening mark of a parenthesis, and the dash.

34i. Unless otherwise directed, put the pages of your theme in sequence and fold lengthwise. Then with the crease to the left, use the form suggested by your instructor on the outside of the last page. The forms below are typical.

Right Allgood, John
My Job Last Summer
October 1, 1954
Paper 2
Professor Hansen

Allgood, John
English 1d M.W.F. 11
October 1, 1954
My Job Last Summer

COMPOSITION

The six sections which follow deal with the larger problems of the writer: planning, paragraphing, using libraries and printed sources, and writing substantial papers.

Choosing a Subject

Some instructors, particularly in the beginning weeks of the composition course, assign specific subjects for student papers; some assign types of subjects, such as autobiographies, explanatory papers, or narratives, leaving the student to select his particular subject; and others require the student to select his own subject.

When you face the problem of choosing a subject to write a paper on, you may be able to solve it easily. Students who are preparing for professions, such as engineering, business, social work, law, teaching, or journalism, usually know what kinds of writing they will have to do in their professional life and can begin their training by writing reports, letters, case histories, or news stories of the kind that they will write later, finding subjects without any trouble.

Many students, however, have not settled on a particular profession, or are not sufficiently advanced to know what kinds of writing will be required of them. Such students have several alternatives. They may write about themselves — their personal experiences, interests, tastes, friends, families, likes and dislikes. Or they may choose subjects that will be of value in their most immediate future: subjects of the kind they must write on in their courses. Every college student will be faced time after time with the problem of writing answers to examination questions which ask him to *define, explain, compare, point out, analyze,* or *summarize* something, and with the problem of writing reports and notes on outside reading.

The best way to learn how to write on topics which occur in college courses is to find such topics and use them for subjects of themes in English composition. Examine your textbooks and reading lists for subjects; talk with other students taking the same courses; consult your instructors for suggestions; and look up books and magazine articles pertaining to courses you are taking. If you are studying government and select "The Powers of Presidential Electors" as the subject of a paper for your English class, you will enlist the aid of your English instructor in obtaining and organizing knowledge which will be useful in a course in government.

The following list of subjects is intended to be suggestive, to indicate the kinds of subjects that you might select when you are given a free choice:

Personal Experience

How I learned to tell the truth
My favorite enemy
The greatest fright of my life
My darkest moment
Why I came to college
The reading I like

Opinion

Why I like (or dislike) football (or any activity)
My views on extracurricular activities
Fraternities have their uses
Politicians and politics

Information

Resources of Iran
Mound builders
Advertising in 1850
Airmail rates

Analysis

The UN veto power
Tideland oil ownership
Whitman's diction
Outdoor advertising

Narration

Building Hoover Dam
The Boston Tea Party
The Battle of New Orleans
A polar expedition

A Process

How to mothball a ship
How to glaze pottery
How to survey public opinion
How to plan a radio program

Summary

A chapter or section of a chapter in a textbook

Definition

A technical term or concept in a special field

35. Choose a subject on which you can write an interesting paper.

The subject should be one in which you are interested because you know something about it or because you are curious about it. It should be one which you can make interesting to your readers.

35a. Choose a subject on which you can get information.

It may be something which you already know about or which you can learn about from reading or discussion. Do not choose a subject so remote that you can do nothing but generalize vaguely.

35b. Limit your subject.

Do not try to explain communism in a paper of 800 words or narrate the life of George Washington in 500 words; narrow such subjects to special aspects which can be covered thoughtfully in the space you are allowed. Remember, however, that you should practice condensed writing of the kind that you will use in answering examination questions.

Review the discussion of selecting a subject on pages 73–75.

Outlining

An outline is a blueprint of a composition. Just as an architect's blueprint reveals the lines, proportions, and relations between the parts of a structure, so does an outline reveal the plan of a piece of writing. To carry the analogy further, the architect can make alterations or even fundamental changes in the design of a structure much quicker and cheaper on a drawing board than he can after construction has started; similarly a writer can alter and improve the organization of a paper much more conveniently in an outline than he can in a paper which he has already partly written.

36. Learn how to outline a paper before writing it.

There are three types of outline.

The *Topic Outline*, useful in planning short or long papers, consists of phrases.

The *Sentence Outline*, which consists of complete sentences stating the main ideas, is probably the most useful, for it reveals clearly the organization and coherence of the paper.

The *Paragraph Outline*, which consists of topic or summary sentences representing the thought of the successive paragraphs, is sometimes used in planning short papers. The sentences are indented as if they were so many paragraphs.

36a. In a topic outline, indent and capitalize as in the following model:

NEW WORDS IN AMERICAN ENGLISH

Thesis: There are three main sources of new words in American English.

I. Importations from foreign languages
    A. Spanish
    B. German
    C. American Indian
    D. French
II. Composition and derivation
    A. Compounding
    B. Prefixing and suffixing
    C. Coinage
    D. Blending
III. Functional change
    A. Common nouns
        1. From proper nouns
        2. From other parts of speech
    B. Verbs
    C. Other parts of speech
        1. Adjectives
        2. Adverbs

36b. In a sentence outline, indent exactly as in this model:

Thesis: There are three main sources of new words in American English.

I. Americans frequently import words from foreign languages.
    A. Mexican Spanish has supplied many such words.
    B. German words have come from European German and from Pennsylvania German.
    C. Not many recent words have come from American Indian languages.

D. Many French words naming luxuries have been imported.

II. New words from native materials are numerous.

A. Lists of new words show many new compounds.

B. Prefixing and suffixing are popular sources.

1. Standard English prefixes and suffixes are used freely.
2. New prefixes and suffixes are developed, such as *-cade*, *-eroo*, etc.

C. Few new words are coined, except as trade names.

D. Blending produces a surprising number of words.

III. Functional change continues to furnish new words.

A. Common nouns are probably the most numerous products.

B. Verbs are usually made from nouns.

C. Other parts of speech are less frequently changed.

1. Adjectives are made from nouns.
2. Occasionally a new adverb is produced.
3. Rarely are connectives initiated.

36c. Do not make coördinate any matter that is logically subordinate.

Faulty C. New words from sports
1. From baseball
2. From boxing

D. From other sports

Revised C. New words from sports
1. From baseball
2. From boxing
3. From other sports

36d. Do not make subordinate any matter that is logically coördinate.

Faulty B. New compound words
1. Nouns like *afterburner*
a. Verbs like *double-park*

Revised B. New compound words
1. Nouns like *afterburner*
2. Verbs like *double-park*

36e. Remember that subdivision always means division into at least two parts.

Faulty D. Words made by prefixing
1. For example, *decontaminate*

E. Words, such as *isolationist*, made by suffixing

Revised D. Words like *decontaminate,* made by prefixing
E. Words like *isolationist,* made by suffixing

36f. In outlines as well as in other writing, express parallel thoughts in parallel form.

Faulty 1. Coinage of new trade names
2. How trade names become common nouns

Revised 1. Coinage of trade names
2. Change of trade names to common nouns

Or 1. How trade names are coined
2. How trade names become common nouns

The Paragraph

37. Master the principles of paragraph construction.

See pages 43–67 for a discussion of the writing of paragraphs.

A paragraph, according to the *ACD,* is "a distinct portion of written or printed matter dealing with a particular point." The heart of this definition is the phrase *distinct portion.* Just as a house or a layer cake is made up of separate parts, so a piece of writing is made up of distinct portions. A book, for instance a textbook in history or chemistry or mathematics, is made up of chapters, each of which is a complete unit. Similarly, a chapter is made up of paragraphs, each a group of sentences (rarely one sentence) making a unit. Good paragraphs are not made by indenting at the end of every 150 or 200 words; every good paragraph is made by combining a group of sentences dealing with one particular point.

It is very hard to read a whole page of unbroken print; the eye tires and the attention wanders. But a carefully constructed series of paragraphs will develop the whole topic in a series of steps so that the reader can grasp the whole in easy stages.

37a. Indent your paragraphs uniformly: an inch in hand-written manuscripts and five spaces in typed manuscripts. Do not indent unless you are beginning a new paragraph.

37b. Make the length of a paragraph suit the nature of the topic and

the educational level of the audience. Be careful to avoid short, choppy paragraphs except in news-reporting. As a rule, a paragraph should contain at least 100 to 150 words.

A vividly told story may call for a short paragraph form; a scientific essay will tend toward the longer type of paragraph. A paragraph of introduction, transition, summary, or especial emphasis is usually shorter than other types of paragraphs. Guard against a series of short, choppy paragraphs, for they suggest a lack of substance, a bad organization or grouping of ideas, and a disregard for unity or for the relative emphasis to be placed on the different aspects of the subject the theme deals with; on the other hand, paragraphs which are too long become heavy and diffuse. Furthermore, they are often hard to follow because they contain more than one topic. Generally, the paragraph should avoid undue shortness by containing a group of related sentences — not *one* sentence; on the other hand, it should avoid undue length by not exceeding 250 to 300 words. Paragraphs in formal writing for highly educated readers are usually longer than paragraphs in writing for a general audience, for example, in newspapers and general magazines.

The best way to secure the right kind of paragraph is (1) to study the methods of good writers; and (2) to prepare a careful outline of what is to be written. Then see to it that each paragraph contains the material which should come in at that place, and no more. As a simple example, the following outline for a composition on kinds of taxes might indicate what each paragraph should contain:

I. Income
II. Property
III. Sales
IV. Licenses
V. Gasoline

If each paragraph contained from 250 to 300 words, the whole essay would include 1600 to 1700 words. For examples of choppy paragraphs, see Exercise A at the end of this section.

37c. Make your paragraphs unified.

A paragraph should contain some clearly perceived kind of unity.

In the descriptive paragraph the unity is singleness of impression. In the narrative paragraph unity is achieved by grouping details of each event. In the expository paragraph unity is achieved by developing a single topic. If a paragraph contains matter which is irrelevant to the general topic, it violates the principle of unity. An example of such violation is seen in the following paragraph:

For some mysterious reason people always fill iced tea glasses too full. I never am served a glass of tea, either at home or at a restaurant, that isn't full to the brim, with the ice cubes sticking up in the air. If I try to put a spoonful of sugar in, the tea runs over and spills on the table. The only solution is to drink a sip of tea first and lower the level so the sugar can go in. But I don't like the taste of unsweetened tea. *Tea is the favorite beverage of China, and all our tea is imported.* I simply cannot understand why people have to run their iced tea glasses over on the tablecloth or swallow an unpalatable mouthful without sugar before being able to enjoy a glass of a very fine summer drink.

Unity is shown in the following paragraph, from Bret Harte's "The Outcasts of Poker Flat":

As Mr. John Oakhurst, gambler, stepped into the main street of Poker Flat on the morning of the 23rd of November, 1850, he was conscious of a change in its moral atmosphere since the preceding night. Two or three men, conversing earnestly together, ceased as he approached, and exchanged significant glances. There was a Sabbath lull in the air, which, in a settlement unused to Sabbath influences, looked ominous.

37d. Use a topic sentence to indicate the unifying thought of the paragraph, especially of the expository paragraph.

The topic sentence usually — though not always — comes at the beginning of the paragraph, as in the following from Macaulay's essay on Milton:

The Puritan was made up of two different men, the one all self-abasement, penitence, gratitude, passion; the other proud, calm, inflexible, sagacious. He prostrated himself in the dust before his maker, but he set his foot on the neck of his king.

Here, the topic sentence is followed by a general illustrative statement, after which Macaulay develops his topic by means of a series of cumulative details that build up a long and strongly unified paragraph.

37e. Make your paragraphs coherent.

The sentences composing a paragraph should follow some definite order; they should form a sequence, and not a mere unrelated group. Coherence is secured by clear sentence order and by the use of reference words and transitional words and phrases. Transition — the orderly progress from topic to topic — is the secret of coherence. Within the paragraph it is found from sentence to sentence; in the whole composition, from paragraph to paragraph. Review pages 57–67.

Coherence secured by transition:

1. Within the paragraph:

> Even at that exciting moment it carried me back to the old "Admiral Benbow" in a second; *and* I seemed to hear the voice of the captain piping in the chorus. *But* soon the anchor was short up; *soon* it was hanging dripping at the bows; *soon* the sails began to draw, and the land and shipping to flit by on either side; *and* before I could lie down to snatch an hour of slumber the *Hispaniola* had begun her voyage to the Isle of Treasure. (STEVENSON, *Treasure Island.*)

2. From paragraph to paragraph:

> Thus it becomes clear that all living powers are cognate, and that all living forms are fundamentally of one character. (Summary of what has preceded.) The researches of the chemist have revealed a no less striking uniformity of material composition in living matter. (Suggestion of what is to follow.) (HUXLEY, *On the Physical Basis of Life.*)

Coherence secured by sentence order:

> Theoretically, of course, one ought always to try for the best word. But practically, the habit of excessive care in word-selection frequently results in loss of spontaneity; and, still worse, the habit of always taking the best word too easily becomes the habit of always taking the most ornate word, the word most removed from ordinary speech. In consequence of this, poetic diction has become latterly a kaleidoscope, and one's chief curiosity is as to the precise combinations into which the pieces will be shifted. There is, in fact, a certain band of words, the Praetorian cohorts of poetry, whose

prescriptive aid is invoked by every aspirant to the poetic purple. Against these it is time some banner should be raised.

Coherence secured by reference words and phrases:

Some hold that education without theology is worse than none. *Others maintain*, quite as strongly, that education with theology is *in the same predicament. But* this is certain, that those who hold *the first opinion* by no means agree what theology should be taught; *and* that those who *maintain the second* are in a small minority.

37f. In writing dialogue, make a separate paragraph for every change of speaker.

(See § 28a.)

EXERCISES

A. Combine these short, choppy units into unified paragraphs:

Those who express astonishment at the lack of reading skill on the part of older students or of their older children should remember that learning to read is a lifelong process; that those who have completed their reading lessons have completed all of life's lessons.

Parents sometimes express concern that their first-grade youngsters "haven't even learned the alphabet." The letters have by no means been abandoned in the modern teaching of reading. We have noted, however, that interest ranks at the top as a factor in learning to read.

Few students are overcome with the interest stirred by twenty-six irregular little characters that have no meaning until they are fitted together to make a word. Children forced to learn the alphabet first may learn to read in spite of it, but not as a result of it.

It was once widely contended that, since mental development proceeds from the simple to the complex, letters should be learned before their complicated assembly into words. Those who supported this principle would never have applied it in teaching objects.

The child was shown a horse, and he learned it as a whole horse — all at once — not as an assembly of withers, fetlocks, pasterns, mane, etc. If the child was around horses long enough he learned to call these anatomical parts by name, but there have always been many estimable persons who could recognize a horse a block away who never did know the withers from the fetlocks.

Children who continue as students will live a long time with words. They will learn the letters of which the words are compiled. In the meantime it is about as easy for them to learn the whole word "strawberry" or the whole word "kitchen" as it is for them to distinguish a whole horse from a whole cow.

B. 1. Achieve coherence and unity in the following passage by selecting the important topics in it and developing each into a unified and coherent paragraph:

Metal furniture is easy to clean and should last much longer than wooden. Many people like the atmosphere of mellow old wood furniture, and nobody can make an aluminum table or desk look as handsome as an old walnut or cherry piece. Only in the past few years has metal furniture become popular.

2. Rewrite the following paragraph to make it unified and coherent:

Some place names, such as New York, Maryland, and Baltimore, are of English origin. Indian names for rivers are common: Delaware, Mississippi, Potomac, Coosa, etc. American place names are of varied origins. Many cities are named for people; Washington, Lincoln, Jackson, Hamilton, and Columbus are all over the map. Mountain names, like the Smokies, Rockies, White, Blue Ridge, etc., are descriptive. French, Dutch, Spanish, and German names appear in scattered parts of the country.

C. The topic sentences of the following paragraphs have been omitted. Supply them.

1.

Automobiles cannot be used because there are no roads past the foothills. The streams are too shallow and rough for boats. There isn't a spot within twenty miles level enough for landing even a light plane. Horses are out because the surface is too steep, rough, and rocky for a horse to get footing. Burros might do, but the climate isn't suitable.

2.

He must, first of all, know the principles of sound esthetic design. This involves a thorough study of two and three dimensional form, texture, and color. Essentially, his job is to make a product or package better looking — more appealing than its competitors, thereby increasing sales. In order to design adequately for industry, the designer must be familiar with the various manufacturing materials and the processes whereby these materials are given their final form. This means that the designer must be aware of the limitations as well as the possibilities of such processes as die casting, plastic molding, sand casting and others. The industrial designer must have his finger on the public's pulse. He must be conscious of the major trends of public thought and style and be able to interpret these in terms of what the public is most likely to approve and buy.

3.

We just take it for granted because it has been handed down to us from our ancestors. But do we really appreciate it? Put yourself in a foreigner's shoes. It is very probable that your foreign friend has never been free from the time of his birth. He probably has had his whole life dictated to by his leader. We in America have a tendency to forget that freedom is not universal.

4.

French loan words began to come into the language after the Norman Conquest and continued to be borrowed steadily through the fourteenth century. Other periods of great borrowings from French were the Renaissance and the modern period. The borrowings from the Scandinavian languages, on the other hand, were introduced in large measure only during the period from 800 to the Norman Conquest, since when there have been relatively few borrowings. The borrowings from these two languages differ also in other respects. For example, the borrowings from French consisted in general of words needed to express ideas relating to law, government, property, and manners, whereas the borrowings from Scandinavian were more homely, everyday words. Again, many French words have been introduced from French literature, whereas the Scandinavian loan words came in almost exclusively through direct contact between the English and the Scandinavian settlers in England.

D. Break each of the following selections into paragraphs. The first should be in three paragraphs, the second in five.

1. Since definitions are not statements about things, but are notifications about words, they cannot be verified and cannot be called either true or false. A definition tells the reader how the writer uses a word. For example, when a person defines sound as a sensation in the hearing organs, he is notifying his readers of how he uses the word *sound.* Another person may define sound as vibrations in the air, and thus notify his readers of his usage. Neither definition can be called either true or false, since the two writers can differ at the same time, and since

either can change his usage at a later time. *Deer* once meant "animal"; now it means a particular kind of ruminant mammal; in the future it may come to mean something else. Obviously we are wasting our time when we argue that a particular definition is or is not true; but we can very usefully discuss the usefulness or intelligibility of a definition. Sometimes a statement in the form of a definition is actually a report of the usage of certain people at a certain time; such a statement can be verified. If, for instance, a political science teacher says that *bicameral* means "having two houses or branches" he may be telling us that political scientists now use the word in that sense. We can test the truth of his report by examining the usage of political scientists, but we have no assurance that they will not legitimately use the word in a different sense tomorrow. Making people understand our definitions — actually understand them, not merely say they understand — is sometimes easy, sometimes hard, depending on the words being defined. Easiest to handle are words which can be defined by having people look at (or smell, taste, feel, hear) something; examples are *shoe, red, rain, bitter, shrill.* Slightly more troublesome are words which require an action or operation; examples are *to twist, to walk, a nod, a shrug.* Much harder are words which have to be defined by citing other words, for instance *misunderstand, honest, irony,* and *charity.* When such words, which we call abstractions, are defined by other words which are equally abstract, as when *charity* is defined as "almsgiving" or "benevolence," we have no way of being sure that we have made the meaning clear. If, however, we define *charity* as "giving money, food, or clothing to poor people," we have at least used words in the definition which can be defined by pointing and by going through actions. People can understand exactly what we mean and may even agree to use our definition when it can be put in concrete words, but some terms are so hard to translate into concrete words that we never define them satisfactorily.

2. U. S. Commissioner of Education Earl J. McGrath made it clear that "television like radio has the advantage of timeliness and immediacy. Like motion picture film, it combines photographically accurate visual representations with animation to give living reality to the subject. But television's great contribution to education will be the combination of these advantages of timeliness, immediacy, and realism in one medium, plus its ability to teach people without requiring their assembly in a classroom." The hearings made it quite clear that the educators do not condemn commercial broadcasting as such. They are insisting that educational stations are needed to supplement the

largely entertainment fare which commercial stations provide and that the two types of stations can exist amicably side by side. But they did hammer home the idea that commercial television stations could not do the educational job that needed to be done. Mr. James Marshall, member of the Board of Education of New York City, said that his school system had already put on nearly seventy television programs through the facilities of CBS and NBC. And then he added this revealing sentence: "But it is significant that at least sixty-five of the seventy were done between the fall of 1945 and the fall of 1947; in the past three years, our opportunities for coöperation with the local commercial stations in the 'capital city of television' have become almost non-existent." Kermit Eby of the University of Chicago warned about the use of mass media when used manipulatively, particularly if used independently of discussion. "True education," he said, "can take place only when the following conditions prevail: (1) full presentation of the facts; (2) unlimited and free discussion; (3) complete responsibility for the personality in the process; and (4) ample time for the fermentation of ideas." Belmont Farley, appearing for the National Education Association, pointed out that the channels applied for could not all immediately be used. Indeed, he said, "Needs cannot be measured by the ability immediately to meet them. It may be decades before all television channels set aside for educational use are employed for that purpose in every community in which they are available."

Using the Library: Finding Material

38. Learn how to use the library.

A knowledge of how to use the library is essential for successful college work. From your first course in college to your last you will be expected to investigate special topics and to find information for yourself. Hence you cannot get far in your studies without knowing how to use the library easily and efficiently.

A library is an orderly storehouse of books and other printed material. Its contents are catalogued and arranged, and the best ways to get at them are carefully mapped and charted, so that you need waste no time in futile rummaging. The contents of a library are of two main kinds. The first kind is the material you usually wish to get at: informational books on special topics, literature and literary criticism; magazines; bulletins and pamphlets; and newspapers. To most of this material you will have no direct access, since most libraries use a closed shelf system; that is, users of the library are not allowed to wander at will among the stacks. But libraries contain a second kind of material, tools to help you find the information and the books you want, and these are available to everyone. These tools are of three sorts: (1) reference books, (2) bibliographies, and (3) the card catalogue. Skill in the use of these aids is the first step toward efficient use of the library.

38a. Make a special visit to your library and examine the Reference Room, the Bibliography Room (if there is one), and the card catalogue.

Find out what the shelves in the Reference Room contain. A half-hour so spent will save you many hours later. Handle the books, page through them, and form at least a bowing acquaintance with them. Find out how the contents are arranged, what special aids such as indexes, cross-references, prefaces, and tables of contents they contain. Then examine the card catalogue. The more you know about the physical make-up of the library, the more efficient you will be in your later work.

Reference Books

38b. Begin the search for information on most subjects by examining reference books: encyclopedias, almanacs, yearbooks, and dictionaries.

These works are usually shelved in the Reference Room or Main Reading Room of the library and may not be taken from that room. Articles in encyclopedias generally give concise information and often append brief bibliographies of special works on the subject. Hence they often furnish your best starting point. If the encyclopedia has an index, begin your work with that. Write down all the pertinent articles which the index lists; then go through the articles, one by one. If you are to write a report or a research paper, list each article on a bibliography card (§ 39b). A few of the most useful general encyclopedias are:

Encyclopaedia Britannica. 14th ed.; Chicago: Encyclopaedia Britannica Corporation. 24 vols. Reissued annually. One should always try to use the latest reissue.

The largest and most dependable encyclopedia in English, this work gives information on almost every topic of general interest. Unless your subject is very recent or technical, you may well begin work on it by consulting this encyclopedia. The index and bibliographies are especially useful. For topics of less recent interest, the 11th edition (Cambridge: University Press, 1910–11. 29 vols. Index) is more complete and exhaustive. An annual supplement is titled *Britannica Book of the Year.*

The New International Encyclopaedia. 2d ed., revised; New York: Dodd, Mead and Company, 1929. 23 vols. Supplement, 2 vols., 1930.

This work also treats most subjects of general interest, but the articles are shorter than those in the *Britannica.* There is no index, but numerous cross-references make the material easily accessible. If you are in haste, or want only concise information, *The New International* will be more useful to you than the *Britannica.* Bibliographies follow important articles. An annual supplement is titled *New International Yearbook.*

Encyclopedia Americana. 1945 edition; New York and Chicago: Americana Corporation, 1945. 30 vols. Index. Annual reissues.

This work also covers most subjects of general interest, but particularly stresses topics such as government, industry, business, and science. Many important articles have bibliographies. The *Americana Annual* is an annual supplement.

Besides these general works there are also a number of special encyclopedias which cover limited fields of learning. Some of the most important of these are:

The Catholic Encyclopaedia. New York: Universal Knowledge Foundation, 1928. 17 vols. Revised and enlarged edition in 16 vols.; New York: The Gilmary Society, Inc., 1936– .

This work gives much useful information not only on the Catholic Church, but also on medieval history, literature, philosophy, and art.

The Jewish Encyclopaedia. New edition; New York: Funk and Wagnalls Company, 1925. 12 vols.

This work contains scholarly and dependable signed articles on Hebrew culture, religion, philosophy, literature, and history from their beginnings to the present.

Hastings, James, editor, *Encyclopaedia of Religion and Ethics.* New York: Charles Scribner's Sons, 1911–28. 13 vols. Index. Reissued in 7 vols. in 1931.

This work contains information on most religions and systems of religious philosophy. Its articles treat of persons and places important in religious history; systems of ethics and philosophy; religious customs, practices, and doctrines.

Bailey, L. H., editor, *Cyclopaedia of American Agriculture.* New York: The Macmillan Company, 1907–09. 4 vols.

This work subdivides its material by volume: I, farms; II, crops; III, animals; IV, the farm and the community.

Monroe, Paul, editor, *Cyclopaedia of Education.* New York: The Macmillan Company, 1925. 3 vols.

This work contains articles on different systems of education, noted educators, particular colleges and universities.

Seligman, Edwin R. A., and Alvin Johnson, editors, *Encyclopaedia of the Social Sciences.* New York: The Macmillan Company, 1930–35. 15 vols. Index. Reissued in 8 vols. in 1937.

An authoritative work in its field. Articles concern philosophy, ethics, political science, economics, sociology, education, and allied subjects. The bibliographies are useful.

There are many other specialized encyclopedias besides those we have listed. Often they provide invaluable suggestions for further investigation of a topic in a limited field.

38c. If you want information on a historical, literary, or biographical topic, consult reference works of the following kinds.

Hart, James D., *The Oxford Companion to American Literature.* New York: Oxford University Press, 1941.

Johnson, Allen, and Dumas Malone, editors, *Dictionary of American Biography.* New York: Charles Scribner's Sons, 1928–37. 20 vols. Supplement, 1944. Index.

This work closely corresponds, for American persons, to the one listed below for English.

Langer, W. L., editor, *Encyclopaedia of World History.* Boston: Houghton Mifflin Company, 1940; revised edition, 1948.

A revision of the Ploetz *Manual of Universal History,* which gives in concise, usable form all the important and many of the minor facts of world history.

Spiller, Robert E., and others, *Literary History of the United States.* New York: The Macmillan Company, 1948. Bibliography, Vol. III.

Stephen, Sir Leslie, and Sir Sidney Lee, editors, *The Dictionary of National Biography.* New York: Oxford University Press, 1937–39 reprint. 24 vols. Indexes. Supplements.

This is considered the standard work for brief authoritative biographies of well-known English persons not living. Good bibliographies. The work now needs revising.

Who's Who. London: A. and C. Black, Ltd., 1849 to date.

An annual work listing well-known persons. The compact biographies are supplied by the biographees themselves.

Who's Who in America. Chicago: A. N. Marquis Company, 1899 to date.

An American biennial similar to the one listed above.

Ward, A. W., Sir G. W. Prothero, and Sir Stanley Leathes, editors, *Cambridge Modern History.* New York: The Macmillan Company, 1902–26; 2d ed., 1926. 13 vols. and atlas.

Ward, Sir A. W., and A. R. Waller, editors, *The Cambridge History of English Literature.* New York: The Macmillan Company, 1931. 15 vols. Index, 1933. Bibliography, 1941. 4 vols.

Such works as the last two have important bibliographies at the ends of chapters, at the ends of volumes, or in separate volumes.

38d. Remember that dictionaries also are invaluable reference books.

The most useful are the historical dictionaries, which cite dated evidence for all words and meanings entered.

Murray, Sir James A. H., and others, editors, *A New English Dictionary on Historical Principles.* Oxford: The Clarendon Press, 1888–1928. Corrected reissue, 1933, with the title *Oxford English Dictionary.* 10 vols. Supplement, 1933.

The most comprehensive English dictionary, this work traces the history of words and their meanings from the earliest English records to the time of compilation.

Craigie, Sir William, and James R. Hulbert, *A Dictionary of American English on Historical Principles.* Chicago: University of Chicago Press, 1938–1944. 4 vols.

Mathews, Mitford M., *A Dictionary of Americanisms.* Chicago: University of Chicago Press, 1951. 2 vols.

Dictionaries of more general nature, both abridged and unabridged, are listed in § 65a, p. 318.

38e. Other reference books of miscellaneous kinds are useful. Find out which ones your library has.

A few of them are the following:

Bartlett, John, compiler, *Familiar Quotations.* 12th ed., revised and enlarged; Boston: Little, Brown and Company, 1948.

Quotations are arranged chronologically according to the date of the author's birth. An index of quotations, keyed by important words, is at the back of the book.

Lippincott's New Gazetteer; A Complete Pronouncing Gazetteer or Geographical Dictionary of the World. Angelo Heilprin and Louis Heilprin, editors; Philadelphia: J. B. Lippincott Company, 1906; with conspectus of 15th census, 1931.

A reasonably detailed geographical dictionary, containing accounts of countries, important rivers, cities, and mountains. Now in need of revision.

Rand McNally Commercial Atlas and Marketing Guide. 81st ed.; Chicago: Rand McNally and Company, 1950. Index. Supplements.

This work contains excellent maps and detailed information about population, transportation, manufacturing, markets, railroads, steamship lines, and so on.

Peck, Harry T., *Harper's Dictionary of Classical Literature and Antiquities.* New York: The American Book Company, 1897.

A valuable work for brief descriptions of persons, characters, books, historical events, and places prominent in Greek and Roman history and mythology.

Webster's Geographical Dictionary. Springfield: G. & C. Merriam Co., 1949. Maps and tables.

A desk dictionary providing spelling, pronunciation, and geographical information on important places in the world.

World Almanac and Book of Facts. New York: The New York World-Telegram (Now World-Telegram-Sun), 1868 to date. Index.

An important annual containing valuable miscellaneous information, chiefly American, including social, political, and commercial statistics, recent laws and lists of important events.

Bibliographical Guides

Information in reference books is necessarily concise, and so are bibliographies in such works. Hence, unless you wish only general information, you will want to carry your search further.

38f. Go next to bibliographical guides, which list reference works and also books and articles on special subjects.

These guides also are usually on open shelves in one of the reading rooms of your library. The most useful guides to reference works are:

Barton, Mary N., and others, *Reference Books: A Brief Guide for Students and Other Users of the Library.* Baltimore: Enoch Pratt Free Library, 1947.

Hutchins, Margaret, Alice S. Johnson, and Margaret S. Williams, *Guide to the Use of Libraries.* 5th ed., revised; New York: H. W. Wilson Company, 1936.

Mudge, Isadore G., *Guide to Reference Books.* 6th ed.; Chicago: American Library Association, 1936. Supplement, *Reference Books of 1935–1937.* Chicago: American Library Association, 1939. Supplements.

This work does not furnish information on your subject, but lists and describes the reference books where information can be found. See Table of Contents and Index.

Other guides list informational books and literary works of all kinds. Among them the most useful are:

Bateson, F. W., *Cambridge Bibliography of English Literature.* New York: The Macmillan Company, 1941. 4 vols.

Evans, Charles, *American Bibliography.* Chicago: Privately Printed, 1903–. 12 vols.

A chronological dictionary of books, pamphlets, and periodicals printed in the United States from 1639 to 1820. Not yet completed.

United States Catalog. 4th ed.; New York: H. W. Wilson Company, 1928.

Lists books in print at the time of publication. Listings are arranged by subject, author, and title.

Cumulative Book Index. New York: H. W. Wilson Company, 1928 to date.

This list includes works published in English throughout the world. Monthly supplements (except in August) keep it up to date.

Books in Print. New York: R. R. Bowker Co., 1948–.

An annual author-title-series index to the *Publishers' Trade List Annual*, a master catalogue of the principal publishers in the U. S.

38g. For subjects of recent or current interest consult guides to periodicals and newspapers.

The most useful of the periodical guides are:

Readers' Guide to Periodical Literature, 1900 to date. New York: H. W. Wilson Company, 1905–.

This work lists important articles on a wide variety of subjects from over 100 non-technical periodicals. Material is arranged under subject, author, and title in a single listing. Monthly supplements keep the work up to date. It is the most important guide for current general use.

Nineteenth Century Readers' Guide to Periodical Literature. New York: H. W. Wilson Co., 1944. 2 vols.

Poole's Index to Periodical Literature, 1802–1906. Boston: Houghton Mifflin Company, 1882–1908. 7 vols.

This work lists articles mainly in general literature, chiefly of the nineteenth century, both American and English. Entries are under subject and title in a single listing.

International Index to Periodicals, 1907 to date. New York: H. W. Wilson Company, 1913–.

This work lists more technical periodicals than the *Readers' Guide*, some in foreign languages. Listings are under subject and author. Monthly supplements keep the work up to date.

There are a number of more specialized indexes, typical of which are the following:

Annual Magazine Subject Index. Boston: The Boston Book Company, 1908–.

This work specializes in the arts, travel, history; it includes many less well-known American and English periodicals.

The Industrial Arts Index. New York: H. W. Wilson Company, 1913–.

Lists articles on business, trade, and engineering, but provides only a subject listing.

To save space, entries in these guides are often reduced by a kind of shorthand which you must be able to read, since all details are necessary if you are to get the material you want. Thus typical entries in the *Readers' Guide* are:

> WORDS, New
> Thirty thousand new words. J.F. Bender. il.
> N Y Times Mag p 22 D 2 '45
>
> READ, Allen Walker
> Word harvest of '45. Sat R Lit 29:5–6 Je 22 '46

The first of these entries is a subject entry. It includes (1) the title of the article (with no capitals except the first word); (2) the author's name; (3) *il.*, indicating that the article is illustrated; (4) the name of the magazine; (5) the page number; and (6) the date. The second entry is an author entry. It includes (1) the title of the article; (2) name of the magazine; (3) the volume and page numbers; and (4) the date. See § 39c for an expansion of these entries into bibliographical form.

38h. **Use one of the two principal newspaper indexes to find material in the newspapers indexed or in any newspaper.**

If you should be interested in a well-known person and want to find all you can about him in newspapers, it would be an impossibly tedious job to page through issue after issue of a newspaper looking for mention of his name. By consulting one of the big indexes you can learn the dates on which he was in the news; then you can quickly look in the available newspapers of the same dates to find your material. Neither of the big indexes, however, will help you find items that were not sufficiently important to be reported in the newspapers issuing indexes. The two principal indexes are:

New York Times Index, 1913 to date. New York: New York Times Co., 1913–.

The Official Index to the [London] *Times*, 1914 to date. London: The Times Publishing Company, 1914–.

The Card Catalogue

Reference books and guides help you find material on your subject.

38i. To find more material, and to find how much of it your library possesses, go to the card catalogue.

This catalogue lists every book and magazine or newspaper file your library owns, but it does not list separate magazine or newspaper articles (see the guides discussed above, §§ 38g, 38h). The catalogue uses a single alphabetical listing, under which entries are made according to (1) author, (2) title, (3) subject. To facilitate your search, nearly every book in the library is listed at least twice, under author and title, and many are listed under as many as six or eight subject cards besides. Hence part of your success in finding material in the library depends on intelligent use of the card catalogue, and particularly on your skill in finding the appropriate subjects.

The most usual kind of "author" card looks like the following, a specimen of the Library of Congress cards, which are printed by the thousands and distributed to libraries throughout the United States:

> PE1574.M25
> McKnight, George Harley, 1871–1951
> English words and their background, by George H. McKnight . . . New York, London, D. Appleton and company, 1923
> x p., 1 l., 449p. 21^{cm}.
> "References for further reading" at end of most of the chapters.
> 1. English language. 2. English language — Semantics. 3. English language — Etymology. I. Title.
> 23–1006
> Library of Congress
> ——— —— Copy 2
> [36i2]

This card contains much pertinent information about the book.

It lists (1) author, last name first, with date of birth (date of death is also included if the author is not living); (2) the full title and subtitle of the book, followed by the author's name given in the normal order; (3) the place of publication, name of publisher, and date; (4) information about the pagination, use of diagrams and illustrations, and size of the book; (5) mention of bibliographies which may be useful to you; (6) subject headings under which the book may be listed; (7) the Library of Congress call number of the book.

A subject or a title card may be a duplicate of the one above with the appropriate subject heading or the title of the book typed across the top. On the other hand, it may be a special typed card prepared in your library and containing most (though not all) of the information given on the Library of Congress card.

Whichever kind it is, each card also contains, in the extreme upper left corner, the call number, a set of symbols by which the library has classified the book and by which the location of the book in the library is indicated.

By the time you consult the card catalogue, if you have used reference books or periodical guides first, you may already have a stack of bibliography cards of your own (§ 39b). Your first task, then, will be to look up these items to see whether your library has them. If it has, be sure to take down the call number of each item on your card. If the item is not listed, cancel your card or try to find the item in another library.

Your second task will be to find other material. Make a list of all the pertinent subject headings you see on the cards you consult in the catalogue, and check through those subjects for new references. Check all the entries given under the name of each of your authors to see whether he has other works related to your subject.

When you have examined the reference books and periodical guides which may help you, and have gone through the card catalogue, you will have used the three main aids every library can offer. Next, for every book, bound magazine, or newspaper you wish to use, you must make out a call slip, provided by the library at the circulation desk. Present these slips to the attendant at the desk and the volumes you ask for will be brought to you there.

Preparing the Research Paper

39. Remember that a good research paper requires thorough investigation, careful recording, and logical organization of material.

The research paper, also called the term paper, or the course paper, is longer, more exhaustive, and more objective than the other types of writing usually included in the composition course. It is not simply an expression of the writer's opinions, feelings, or experiences; it is a thorough, balanced, and truthful presentation of some small segment of knowledge, based largely on published works. It is not a mere summary of one or two books or articles; it is the writer's own organization and expression of a body of facts which he has assembled from a number of reliable sources.

The preparation of a research paper will teach the student how to use a library, how to evaluate sources, how to take notes, how to plan and write a substantial expository paper with documentation, and most important, how to establish a small body of knowledge upon facts discovered by independent investigation, free of bias and hearsay. A knowledge of certain useful mechanical principles and the ability to investigate thoroughly, organize logically, and write clearly are essential.

Choosing a Subject for Research

39a. Select a suitable subject.

The first step in the process of writing a research paper is choosing a subject. In advanced classes the nature of the course will automatically limit the general field in which the paper is to be written; in a composition course the student may be free, with his instructor's advice, to select his own subject. A few principles should be observed at the beginning to ensure a successful paper. The subject should be one of interest to the writer and to possible readers. It should be a narrow, limited, specific subject which can be explored intensively, not a broad subject which would have to be covered superficially. It should be some aspect of a topic which involves the use of several sources. It should be a subject that calls for library reading, not a study involving only first-hand observation or laboratory investigation. Finally, it should be a subject that can be investigated within the library facilities available to the writer and that can be handled within the space-limit prescribed by the instructor.

The following list of subjects may be helpful to a student who needs suggestions. Even if no one of these appeals to him, the list will suggest the general type of subject which can be handled (usually after some narrowing) in a research paper.

- The Atlantic Pact
- Miracle drugs
- The "New Criticism"
- Peacetime uses of radar
- Experimental colleges
- Loyalty oaths
- Color television
- The Pentagon
- Lemon culture
- The TVA
- Weather cycles
- Church membership
- Universal military training
- Japan since 1945
- Air express
- Guided missiles
- Abstract sculpture
- U. S. Department of Defense
- Government reorganization
- Inland waterways
- Rainmaking
- Rare Bibles
- Election forecasting
- Oil field jargon
- Changes in dictionaries
- English Channel swimming
- The Olympic Games
- Television and the movies
- Television and sports
- Canadian airlines
- The Pulitzer prizes
- Anti-segregation laws
- A city political machine
- Farm subsidies
- Dorothy Parker
- James Thurber
- The Southern agrarians
- Veterans hospitals
- Allen Tate
- Writers' conferences
- Summer theaters
- Ralph Bunche
- Rocket warfare
- The Dixiecrat revolt
- William Faulkner's reputation
- French Indo-China

Once the subject has been selected, the preparation of the paper will involve three principal steps: (1) gathering material; (2) assembling and organizing material; and (3) writing and documenting the paper. These three steps are described in detail in the remainder of § 39 and in § 40. All the illustrations and examples are from a paper on "New Words in American English."

Gathering Material: Bibliography[1]

After you have chosen a subject, your next step is to find and list the books, magazine articles, pamphlets, and newspaper accounts that may provide information on the chosen topic. (See Using the Library: Finding Material, § 37.)

39b. In making your bibliography, use 3 x 5 or 4 x 6 inch cards and place only one item on each card.

Use the form illustrated below unless your instructor directs otherwise. Adopt one form and use it consistently.

The figure below illustrates the usual form used in a bibliography card for a book by one author:

PE1574.M25

McKnight, George H., _English Words and Their Background._ New York: D. Appleton and Company, 1923. 449 pp.

Notice that only one entry is made on a card, and that the following items are included, in this order: (1) the author's surname; (2) the author's given name or initials; (3) title of the book; (4) place of publication; (5) publisher; (6) date; (7) number of pages. The title of the book is underlined (italicized). Commas follow the author's surname and given name or initials and the publisher's name; a colon follows the place of publication; periods follow the author's initials, the title, the date, and the number of pages. Every fact contained on a bibliographical card should be checked at least twice to insure completeness and accuracy.

NOTE. It will save time later if you place the library call number on the bibliography card as in the illustrative card shown above.

Slight modifications of this form are used for publications which differ in some way from the standard book entry illustrated. The following are the most common:[1]

(1) A book by two authors:

Starnes, De Witt T., and Gertrude E. Noyes, *The English Dictionary from Cawdrey to Johnson.* Chapel Hill: University of North Carolina Press, 1946. 299 pp.

(2) An edited anthology:

Caffee, Nathaniel M., and Thomas A. Kirby, eds., *Studies for William A. Read.* University, La.: Louisiana State University Press, 1940. 338 pp.

(3) A translation:

Paul, Hermann, *Principles of the History of Language.* Translated by H. A. Strong. New York: Macmillan & Co., 1889. 512 pp.

(4) A book in a series:

Kurath, Hans, *A Word Geography of the Eastern United States.* Studies in American English, 1. [Ann Arbor:] University of Michigan Press, 1949. 88 pp., 164 plates. (The brackets indicate that the enclosed matter is not on the title page of the book.)

(5) A signed article in a magazine or journal:

Redman, Ben Ray, "Arthur Koestler: Radical's Progress," *College English,* 13: 131–136, December, 1951. [Or use this form: XIII (December, 1951), 131–136.]

(6) An unsigned magazine article:

"Air Talk," *New York Times Magazine,* p. 4, March 28, 1948. [Or use this form: (March 28, 1948), p. 4.]

[1] See also William Giles Campbell, *A Form Book for Thesis Writing* (Boston: Houghton Mifflin Company, 1939), pp. 24–33, or the *MLA Style Sheet* (New York: Modern Language Association of America, 1951).

(7) A newspaper:

Christian Science Monitor, August 24, 1952.

(8) An encyclopedia:

Encyclopaedia Britannica. 14th ed. Chicago: Encyclopaedia Britannica Corporation, 1948. 24 vols.

39c. You should begin making bibliography cards with the first pertinent name, book, or article you find as you go through reference books and guides.

(See § 38b–g.)

Bibliographies appended to encyclopedia articles usually give the briefest possible entries: "Spengler, *Decline of the West.*" Take these down as you find them and later, when you go through the card catalogue, add the author's first name or initials and the required facts of publication. By the time you have gone through the card catalogue, your bibliography cards for books should be complete. Most guide books, such as the *Readers' Guide*, also use special entries briefer than the full bibliographical forms you will want. Thus the brief entries given in § 38g (page 245) would be transferred onto your cards as:

Bender, J. F., "Thirty Thousand New Words,"
New York Times Magazine, Dec. 2, 1945, p. 22.
[Or: (Dec. 2, 1945), p. 22.]

Read, Allen W., "Word Harvest of '45,"
Saturday Review of Literature, 29:5–6, June 22, 1946.
[Or: XXIX (June 22, 1946), 5–6.]

Sometimes the guide book entries will not give all the facts you need to know about a magazine article. If so, you must wait until you see the magazine before you can fill in the details. Cards for books, however, can be completed from the card catalogue, which contains all the information you will require (§ 38i). Be sure each card is as complete as you can make it before you stop working with the catalogue. Authors' names are written on bibliography cards with the surname first as an aid to the alphabetical filing and listing.

Gathering Material: Reading for Information

39d. **In working on a research project, learn to read rapidly and selectively, availing yourself of all the aids a book has to offer.**

If you read every word in every item listed in your bibliography, you would never be done. Hence, you must learn to read quickly, economically, and selectively. Decide what to read first. If your subject is "New Words in American English," for instance, it will be best not to start with an article listing the new words of 1950; it will be best to start with a comprehensive discussion of vocabulary change. Fill in the background first. Details can come later, when you will be better able to understand their significance and to evaluate them. Your first step, then, should be to get from your library several of the books that you believe will give you a picture of the whole subject. Then go through the books rapidly and discard those which are not satisfactory.

Like a library, a book also has special guides to save you time and effort. Going through a book, finding what it contains, and spotting the material you want by means of these guides will save you many hours. The first of these aids is the Table of Contents. Read that carefully to find whether any particular chapters or sections look promising and whether others may be disregarded. Suppose you want a few helpful hints on intelligent reading and you go to Mortimer J. Adler's *How to Read a Book*. The Table of Contents tells you that Part I concerns "The Activity of Reading," Part II "The Rules," and Part III "The Rest of the Reader's Life." Obviously the eight chapters of Part II will be most likely to give you what you want. After you have examined the Table of Contents, look at the Preface. Professor Adler begins by saying, "I have tried to write a light book about heavy reading." That statement by itself tells you the purpose of the work: that it is non-technical, probably fairly general, and should be easy reading.

Most informational books also have indexes. If, for instance, you want to learn about Jack Straw and the Peasants' Revolt of 1381, you need not look through all of a history of England or even all of one chapter. You may find that the material you want covers less than a score of pages and is indexed under "Peasants' Revolt."

Often, too, material on a particular topic is scattered through a book of some length, even through several volumes. When it is, the index is your best guide to the pages you want. Many informational books contain bibliographies at the beginnings or ends of chapters, the ends of sections, or the ends of volumes. These may lead you to material which your previous search had not revealed. Often works so found prove to be mines of valuable information. A bibliography grows like a snowball. The longer you work on a topic the more sources you discover. Part of your work in reading should be to look for additional material.

Remember always that you are reading for information. Even in the particular chapters and sections you go through, you need not read and understand every word on every page. Learn to glance quickly down a page and to stop for thorough reading only when you come upon pertinent material.

Finally, learn to distinguish between what is fact and what is opinion. Both types of statement will be pertinent to your research, but your basic material should always be fact. If, for instance, a writer states that Herman Melville wrote *Moby Dick*, a story of whaling, in 1851, you may take that as fact. It is a thing which happened, is easily verifiable, and is generally accepted. On the other hand, if a writer states that *Moby Dick* is the greatest American novel, that is opinion, for it is not a matter which can be proved or disproved, and other authorities, on equally reasonable grounds, may disagree. The dividing line between fact and opinion is often blurred, but it is part of the research worker's task to be alert for the distinction, and never to cite opinion as fact.

Gathering Material: Taking Notes

After some preliminary reading and thinking about the subject, the student should decide, at least tentatively, on the scope and purpose of his paper. To do this, he must consider his potential readers. Are they highly educated people who can be expected to know something about the subject already, or specialists who will know a great deal about the subject, or general readers who are literate but uninformed? It is unnecessary to include detailed material which the audience can be expected to know already. Is the purpose to provide an orderly body of information which is new to the audience, or to present known facts in a new or different light? A clear definition of the scope and purpose should enable the student to take notes economically. He should read his sources attentively, making a note of every item of information that seems likely to be useful in informing his particular audience about his selected subject.

Although research papers may vary greatly in subject, length, scope, and purpose, they are all alike in being independent investigations based on library reading. For this reason the reading, note taking, and outlining that precede the actual writing are of primary importance. No writer of a research paper should read his sources and depend on his memory alone for the facts discovered in the reading. He should take full, detailed, and scrupulously exact notes on what he reads so that when he comes to write the paper every fact of importance will be before him on a note card, accurately identified. He should never have to return to a source after he has once read it and taken notes on it. A useful manual on note taking found in most libraries is E. W. Dow, *Principles of a Note System for Historical Studies* (New York: Century Company, 1924).

39e. Fix in your mind the form and content of a note card.

Every note card [1] should contain three items:

1. A heading at the top, indicating the topic and subtopic of the note (not the title of the paper or the source).
2. The note itself, which may be a summary of what you have read, a comment on what you have read, or a quotation from the reading (to be copied — *within quotation marks* — when you wish to include in your paper a strikingly worded or especially important passage).
3. The precise source of the note, containing the author's name, the title of the work, and the exact volume and page number.

[1] Stationery stores carry 3 × 5, 4 × 6, and 5 × 8 inch cards which fit into standard boxes and drawers.

Two typical note cards, one containing a quotation, the other containing a summary, are illustrated below.

In your initial reading of encyclopedia articles (§ 38b) you should have noticed many of the smaller topics (subdivisions) of your general subject. These small topics will usually be the headings or subheadings of your first note cards; as you read you will prob-

> Words from Chinese
> "Chinese immigration has made almost a negligible impression on American speech; of words from this channel, perhaps only _chop-suey_ (which is questionable), _fan-tan_, _joss_, _kowtow_ _tong_, and the slang _yen_ (strong desire) are at all generally familiar."
> Stuart Robertson, _Development of Modern English_, p. 341

> Words imported twice
>
> Mathews says some words have been taken into British English from a foreign language, and then later taken into American English independently from the same foreign language. Examples are _chile_ and _ocelot_.
> M. M. Mathews, _Some Sources of Southernisms_, pp. 17-21

ably add more, discard some, and change others. For example, in writing on "New Words in American English" you might have such headings as Aviation Terms, Medical Words, New Slang, Radar Terms, Political Neologisms, and Trade Names. If a large number of cards have the same heading you are not properly subdividing the material; if almost every card has a different heading you are not properly relating your material or you are including too many diverse facts.

39f. Take notes on all statements of opinion and on all statements of fact that are not a part of common knowledge.

It is not necessary to make a note on the statement that in World War II Americans came in contact with speakers of many different languages, or on any such generally known facts.

39g. Make direct quotations in your notes only when you think it will improve your paper to have the exact words of your source.

When you do make a quotation, copy the passage exactly as it appears, not changing a word, a letter, or a mark of punctuation. Be sure to enclose every quotation in quotation marks on your note cards. (See § 21c for indicating omissions in quoted matter.) Check every quotation twice to avoid having to return to the source later to verify it.

39h. Make only one note on each card, never two or more.

If a note is too long for one card and too unified to be put under several headings, use consecutively numbered cards. (It is not advisable to write on both sides of a card.)

Under no circumstances should two notes appear on one card. Restricting each card to one note will allow you to try many possible plans of organization by merely rearranging the cards without recopying any notes.

39i. Do not take notes which duplicate those that you have already taken unless you are piling up evidence on one side of a controversial question.

Much of the reading for a research paper may be repetitious. For example, a student investigating new words will find many discussions which cite the same processes and examples. Certain striking changes will be described almost identically by several writers. Once a fact has been noted, that fact need not be recorded from other writings unless the matter is controversial and the additional citations support an argument.

The student should remember that not everything in print is necessarily true or reliable; he should ask his instructor for assistance in evaluating sources.

Arranging the Material

39j. Collect your cards when you have finished your reading, and arrange them in several related piles, using the headings on the cards to guide you. When you have found a satisfactory arrangement, these piles will correspond to the chapters or sections of the paper.

This process, which is made possible by the use of one card for each note, is of inestimable value in organizing the paper. There will probably be no one inevitable arrangement, but by shuffling the cards and trying various combinations you should find a logical grouping. For example, suppose you have a number of cards on new words in politics. You might arrange them according to part of speech: nouns, verbs, and adjectives. Or you might arrange them according to source: new coinage, compounding, foreign importation, derivation, and functional change. Or you might possibly want to group them according to time of origin: 1901–1920, 1921–1940, 1940–. After the first grouping is made, you should then arrange in logical order the cards within each pile.

Finally, you must decide the order of the separate piles, by a process similar to that used within the piles. This is actually deciding the order of the sections or chapters of the whole paper. For example, if you have main sections by periods of time, you would logically put the earliest period first, the latest period last. Or if your main sections are by types of source, you might put the most important first and the least important last. Any order should be satisfactory provided it is logical and coherent. Shuffling and rearranging piles of cards is much easier than rewriting the whole paper.

39k. Make a full outline of the paper, based upon the final grouping of the note cards.

See § 36 for instructions on making an outline.

39l. Collect ample material before undertaking to plan your paper, and add to your material if it is insufficient.

Do not hesitate to discard notes that do not fit into the most satisfactory plan. You will probably find when you begin outlining that some of the notes you took before planning the paper are not useful. Discard them. Decide finally on the scope and purpose of the paper.

Style and Mechanics in Research Writing

40. Remember that a good research paper must be clearly written and correctly documented.

The writer of a research paper should remember that this paper is informational, not primarily entertaining or argumentative. Clarity is the prime quality to be sought. Precise and exact diction, close-knit and clear sentences, order and proportion in paragraphs, chapters, and the whole paper — these are the requisites of a clear expository paper. The grammar, diction, and sentence structure should be formal or cultivated informal, not colloquial or slangy. The style should be rather dignified, but not bookish or dull. The writer's individuality should be apparent, but in this type of paper it is better to be distinctive by being clear and accurate than by being eccentric or smart.

The documentation of a research paper (citation of exact sources of the material) is very important, for two reasons. First, honesty demands that a writer show precisely where he got his material. Since a research paper is largely drawn from published writings, common decency requires that the writer acknowledge the sources of his information. Second, the validity or truthfulness of the paper should be objective. The statements made in a research paper are not the opinions of the author, but are facts discovered by him. He should make it absolutely clear where he got his evidence, so that a reader may verify his statements in any library.

In addition to these special demands of the research paper, the student should remember all he has learned about unity, coherence, and emphasis in organization, and all he has learned about good English in expression.

The following rules describe the process of orderly writing and documentation in a research paper.

40a. With the note cards and outline before you, write rapidly and freely a first draft, using the note cards for content and the outline for a guide.

40b. At the end of each portion of the paper that is written directly from a note card, indicate in a note at the bottom of the page the exact source of the information, keying the passage in the paper to the note with an arabic superscript numeral placed at the end of the passage and repeated before the note.

For examples see pp. 269–70.

Some instructors prefer that students insert the notes in the first draft directly after the relevant passage, separating the note from the text by horizontal lines, as in the following example:

Trade names like Socony, from Standard Oil Company of New York, were probably the first new words made up from initials.[19] However,

---

[19] Margaret Bryant, Modern English and Its Heritage, p. 312.

---

initials have been used instead of words for many years in America: examples are OK, YMCA, COD, FOB, and JP. OK is a genuine word, which can be spelled okay.

40c. Write the first draft rapidly, concentrating on the ideas rather than on the punctuation, mechanics, and paragraphing.

The first draft should be written if possible at one sitting, to ensure consistent attitude and style, and to enable the writer to keep the parts in proper relation to the whole. Some students may work better by writing slowly, revising as they write; but most people are distracted from the progress of thought in the whole paper if they pause frequently to consider minor points of mechanics or wording.

40d. Rewrite the paper in final form, paying close attention to clear expression, appropriate grammar and usage, and good paragraphing and mechanics.

If you use a typewriter, double-space the body of your manuscript; single-space footnotes and long indented quotations.[1]

40e. Place all source references in footnotes at the bottom of the page, observing a consistent standard form for footnotes.

Single-space footnotes of more than one line, but leave two spaces between consecutive footnotes. See pp. 269–70 for sample pages from a research paper illustrating proper footnoting.[2]

A footnote should be given for every statement of fact or opinion taken from another writer or work. A workable test is this: Ask yourself which passages in the paper might cause a reader to say, "How do you know this?" Then anticipate the reader's question by citing the exact source of every such passage. As a matter of course you will make a footnote for every note used in the writing.

Observe the following conventions in footnoting:

(1) At the *end* of every passage or quotation to be footnoted, place an Arabic numeral after and slightly above the passage you are footnoting. No period follows these numerals. Footnote numbering may run consecutively throughout the paper or throughout each chapter. The form preferred by the instructor should be used. Place each footnote at the bottom of the page on which ends the passage or quotation referred to, with a solid line separating footnotes from the last line of the text, as on pp. 269–70.

[1] In papers which reach their final form in typescript, single spacing serves to set off footnotes and inserted quotations. In papers which are to be printed, however, no single spacing should be allowed, because it is hard for the typesetter to read. The editor marks footnotes and long quotations to be set in appropriate type.

[2] See the "MLA Style Sheet" (printed in the April, 1951, issue of *Publications of the Modern Language Association*, pp. 3–31, and also available separately in pamphlet form) for the standard footnote styles followed by most university presses and most scholarly journals in language and literature. Practices in the social sciences and the natural sciences differ somewhat from the recommendations of the MLA Style Sheet.

(2) Begin the footnote by placing the key numeral on (or just above) the line three spaces from the left margin. Then insert the author's name, the title of the book, the volume and page number, giving the exact page from which the passage was taken. Since footnotes are not arranged alphabetically, the author's surname is not put first.

Some instructors may wish to have publication data included in the footnote. Such information is usually given in the first footnote reference to a book, magazine, or other work if the paper does not include a formal bibliography.

If the reference is to an article in a periodical, the title of both the article and the periodical and the date must be included. Note the following examples:

8 Lorenzo Turner, Africanisms in the Gullah Dialect, p. 232.

9 I. Willis Russell, "Among the New Words," American Speech, 24: 225-228, October, 1949. [Or, XXIV (October, 1949), 225-228.]

(3) Certain abbreviations are conventional in footnotes. When a work is referred to more than once in the same chapter *without any intervening references,* the word *ibid.* followed by the page number is used instead of a repetition of the full citation. *Ibid.* is always italicized (underlined) and followed by a period and a comma. When a work is referred to more than once *with references to other works intervening,* the full reference need not be repeated after the first citation. The abbreviation *op. cit.* after the author's name, and the new page number are sufficient. When two or more works by an author are included, *op. cit.* cannot be used; the titles must be repeated. When a citation immediately following on the same page is to the same volume and same page, *loc. cit.* may be used. See page 270 for examples of the use of these abbreviations. Other abbreviations are:

Chaps. or *chaps.*, "chapters"
ff., "and the pages following"
l., "line"
ll., "lines"
p., "page"
pp., "pages"
Vol. or *vol.*, "volume"
Vols. or *vols.*, "volumes"

40f. **Insert short quotations in the text, always enclosing them in quotation marks. Indent four spaces to the right and single space long quotations (four lines or more in length), without using quotation marks.**

For the quoting of verse, see § 34g.

40g. **Arrange the first page of each chapter (if the paper is long enough to be divided into chapters) according to the following conventions:**

The legend CHAPTER I (or II, III, etc.) in capital letters should be centered two inches from the top of the sheet. Three lines below, insert the title of the chapter, also in capital letters. The first paragraph should begin one inch below the chapter title. No page number appears on the first page of a chapter, but such pages are counted in the numbering. The page number is simply not put on the page.

40h. **Number the pages consecutively, beginning with the first page of the body of the paper.**

Use Arabic numerals, placed in the upper right-hand corner or center of every page (except the first page of chapters. See § 40g).

40i. **Include in the format of the paper (1) a title page; (2) a table of contents; (3) the body of the paper; and (4) a bibliography.**

The title page and table of contents should be prepared according to the models shown on pp. 265 and 267, with any modifications required by the instructor.

The bibliography is a complete list, alphabetically arranged, of the works read or consulted in the preparation of the paper. Every work you cite in your footnotes must be included. If only a few works are used, they may be placed in one list. If more than a dozen are used, it is better to classify them in a way to make the bibliography easy to consult. A conventional form is a bibliography in two divisions: (*a*) Books, Bulletins, and Pamphlets; (*b*) Magazine and Newspaper Articles. Another common form has the two divisions: (*a*) Primary Sources; and (*b*) Secondary Sources. The nature of the list will determine the best form.

Within each group, the items are arranged alphabetically according to the first letter of the authors' surnames. Anonymous works are entered according to the first letter of the title (disregarding *A* and *The*). When there is more than one work by one author, the author's name need be given but once; in subsequent entries place a one-inch unbroken line where the name would otherwise appear.

A model bibliography is given on p. 271. Notice particularly that the form of the entries is exactly the same as that used on the bibliographical cards (except that library call numbers are never included in the bibliography).

NEW WORDS IN AMERICAN ENGLISH

by

Howard L. Robbins

Term Paper for English 100

Walker College

May, 1952

TABLE OF CONTENTS

CHAPTER		PAGE
I.	THE CHANGING AMERICAN VOCABULARY	1
	Why new words are needed	1
	History of American neologisms	3
	American and British differences	8
II.	NEW WORDS FROM FOREIGN LANGUAGES	13
	American Indian and Mexican-Spanish	14
	European and Oriental sources	17
	Minor foreign-language sources	20
III.	NEW WORDS FROM NATIVE MATERIALS	22
	Compounding and derivation	22
	Functional change	31
	Original creation	36
	BIBLIOGRAPHY	40

CHAPTER I

THE CHANGING AMERICAN VOCABULARY

When new things are invented, such as television, bulldozers, and fluorescent lighting, or new things are discovered, such as neutrons, folic acid, and penicillin, it is obvious that they must be named. Americans are known as active inventors, discoverers, and developers of new gadgets, medicines, ideas, conveniences, and ways of doing things. New kinds of music, art, government, communication, manufacturing, and amusement are constantly appearing in the United States and have to be named. It is said that the words a nation uses are an index to its history and culture.[1]

Such words as automobile, phonograph, delicatessen, cafeteria, fraternity, radio, co-ed, atomic bomb, jet pilot, air-mail, and motorcycle were not known to Americans a hundred years ago because they had no need for such words. The things that the words stand for did not exist. Most of these things are products of science, and science has been very important in changing our civilization to its present form.[2] All around us we can see and hear about things produced by science that had to be named when they came into use. This scientific activity has changed our vocabulary greatly, and is still changing it.

---

[1] Mitford M. Mathews, ed., A Dictionary of Americanisms (Chicago: University of Chicago Press, 1951), p. v. [Material within parentheses may be omitted if it is given in the bibliography.]

[2] Albert C. Baugh, A History of the English Language (New York: D. Appleton-Century Company, 1935), p. 367.

that although functional change does not produce a new form, it does virtually produce a new word.[19] For example the noun <u>needle</u> has been changed to a verb <u>to</u> <u>needle</u>, meaning to goad or excite.[20] The form is still <u>needle</u>, but as a verb it is really a new word in our dictionaries. Likewise the use of the noun <u>panic</u> in theatrical language as a verb is so well established that dictionaries list it as a new word.[21] This changing of the part of speech of a word is an old practice in English, frequently used by poets for special effects in verse.[22]

Sometimes writers convert a noun into a verb because they do not know a perfectly good verb which would serve; for example <u>to</u> <u>chairman</u> instead of <u>to</u> <u>preside</u> <u>over</u>, and <u>to</u> <u>pressure</u> instead of <u>to</u> <u>press</u>, but usually these shifts are to fill needs.

Mr. Mencken lists a number of verbs which began as nouns, for example <u>to</u> <u>audition</u>, <u>to</u> <u>intern</u>, <u>to</u> <u>model</u>, <u>to</u> <u>alert</u>, <u>to</u> <u>accession</u>, <u>to</u> <u>sabotage</u>, and <u>to</u> <u>blueprint</u>.[23] This kind of word invention is especially popular in slang, and Mencken cites a number of examples from the magazine <u>Variety</u>.[24] But serious writers vary frequently from the

---

19 Bryant, <u>Modern</u> <u>English</u> <u>and</u> <u>Its</u> <u>Heritage</u>, p. 309.

20 "New Words Section," <u>Webster's</u> <u>New</u> <u>International</u> <u>Dictionary</u>, p. cvi.

21 <u>Loc</u>. <u>cit</u>.

22 Bryant, <u>op</u>. <u>cit</u>., p. 308.

23 H. L. Mencken, <u>The</u> <u>American</u> <u>Language</u>, <u>Supplement</u> <u>I</u>, pp. 385-386

24 <u>Ibid</u>., p. 387.

BIBLIOGRAPHY

I. Books

Baugh, Albert C., A History of the English Language. New York: D. Appleton-Century Company, 1935. 509 pp.

Bloomfield, Leonard, Language. New York: Henry Holt and Company, 1933. 564 pp.

Bryant, Margaret, Modern English and Its Heritage. New York: The Macmillan Company, 1948. 407 pp.

Craigie, Sir William, and James R. Hulbert, A Dictionary of American English. Chicago: University of Chicago Press, 1938-44. 4 vols.

Mathews, Mitford M., A Dictionary of Americanisms. Chicago: University of Chicago Press, 1951. 2 vols.

Mencken, Henry L., The American Language. 4th ed. New York: Alfred A. Knopf, 1936. Supplement I. 1945. Supplement II. 1948.

Webster's New International Dictionary. 2d ed. Springfield: G. & C. Merriam Co., 1934.

II. Articles

Cary, D. M., "Words from Surnames," Word-Lore, 3:103-105, February, 1928. [Or: III (February, 1928), 103-105.]

Elton, William, "A Glossary of the New Criticism," Poetry, 73:153-162, December, 1948. [Or: LXXIII (December, 1948), 153-162.]

Matthews, Brander, "The Art of Making New Words," Unpopular Review, 9:58-69, 1918. [Or: IX (1918), 58-69.]

Pound, Louise, "Vogue Affixes in Present-Day Word Coinage," Dialect Notes, 5:1-14, 1918. [Or: V (1918), 1-14.]

Read, Allen W., "The Word Harvest of '45," Saturday Review of Literature, pp. 5-6, 46-49, June 22, 1946. [Or: (June 22, 1946) pp. 5-6, 46-49.]

Russell, I. Willis, "Among the New Words," American Speech, 24:302-307, December, 1949. [Or: XXIV (December, 1949), 302-307.]

Shulman, David, "Whence 'Charley horse'?" American Speech, 24:100-104, April, 1949. [Or: XXIV (April, 1949), 100-104.]

SPELLING

Misspelling is a serious social and professional handicap. Like egg on a man's tie, it prejudices people against the offender regardless of the cogency of his thought. There are many reasons for the general regard for correct spelling. Editors and printers demand a dependable standard; for many people it is an easy accomplishment, just as dancing or juggling is easy for some; it is one of the subjects long taught in every elementary school and encouraged by spelling bees; and misspellings are subject to simple judgment by reference to dictionaries and spellers.

There are two principal reasons for misspelling. First, English words are spelled inconsistently and unphonetically. It is impossible to determine how an English word is spelled by hearing it or pronouncing it (compare *receive, recede; tee, tea; quay, key; seize, sees*, and *seas*). Every word must be remembered visually. Second, some people are weaker than others in "visual memory"; certain individuals, for reasons yet obscure, can easily remember how words sound but have difficulty recalling how they are written.

Unless you are a rare pathologic case, you can improve your own spelling.

If you misspell words in spite of the precautions recommended below, check the misspelled words if they occur in the list in § 49, page 287. In a special section of your notebook also record, in the correct form, every word you misspell. Put a cross mark for every subsequent misspelling of a word. Write the words alphabetically or group them according to spelling (*ei* words, *ie* words, dropping the final *-e*, etc., and the other spelling rules presented in §§ 41–48). Find out in each case whether a knowledge of some spelling rule would have prevented the error you made. A study of your own errors is much more important than the study of a general list compiled by another person.

After making your list, study and review the words according to some sound method of learning how to spell. The following method is good because it enables you to *see* the letters and syllables in a word (accurate visualization is the most important aid to spelling), to *hear* the word, and to *feel* how it is pronounced and written. Study only five to ten of the most troublesome words at a time.

After learning the pronunciation and common meanings of the word, study it by the following plan: (1) Look closely at all of the letters while you pronounce each syllable slowly and distinctly. (2) Look away from the word and try to see each letter in the right order as you again pronounce the word syllable by syllable. (3) Now look back at the word to make sure that you have visualized it correctly. (4) Without looking at the word again, write it plainly and without hesitation, and think of each letter and look at it closely as you write it. Whispering the letters is helpful to some students. Then check your spelling. (5) If you write the word correctly, cover up what you have written and write the word three or four times without looking at any previous spelling of it. If you make any mistakes, start all over again.

Pronunciation and Spelling

Many present-day spellings represent the way words used to be pronounced, not the way they are pronounced today. Examples are *business, loved, forehead, handsome,* and *write.* Some spellings have been adopted from foreign languages; examples are *prophet, troupe, heir,* and *suite* (compare *profit, troop, air, sweet*). Furthermore, we have about forty vowel and consonant sounds which we must spell with only twenty-six letters; thus it is impossible for spelling to represent the sound of English words accurately with the conventional English alphabet.

Trusting to pronunciation causes the misspelling of such words as *accommodate, amateur, disease, fourth, government, it's, minute, occurred, success,* and *tragedy.* Occasionally a misspelling may reflect a nonstandard pronunciation; common examples are *athlete, cavalry, column, geography, library, perform,* and *secretary.* Learning the standard pronunciation may help the student learn the correct spelling and thus eliminate two faults at once. Deliberate mispronunciation of words like *dEspair*, *educatOr*, *labOratory*, *sepArate*, *sophOmore*, and *stationAry* may help you remember the spelling, but be sure not to use these mispronunciations except as memory aids.

EXERCISES

A. In which of the following words does the spelling seem to indicate more syllables than you actually pronounce?

Aerial, aspirin, chocolate, different, everybody, familiar, general, governor, history, interesting, literature, memory, miniature, positively, privilege, rabies, referee, separate (adj.), *series, several.*

B. Which of the following words are spelled with "silent" consonants? (In case of doubt, look up the pronunciation in your dictionary.)

Arctic, attacked, chalk, column, diphtheria, fellow, flight, February, gnash, height, incidentally, hiccup, mortgage, often, paradigm, phrase, professor, which, Windsor, wrestle.

Confusion of Similar Forms or Sounds

41. Avoid the confusion of words similar in form, or similar or identical in sound.

The following groups of words are often confused. Look up the pronunciation and the meaning of all unfamiliar words in this list.

accent, ascent, assent
accept, except
adapt, adopt
affect, effect
all right (never *alright*)
all together, altogether
awhile, a while
berth, birth
born, borne
breath, breathe

canvas, canvass
capital, capitol
cavalry, Calvary
censor, censure
choose, chose
coarse, course
complement, compliment
conscience, conscious
costume, custom
council, counsel, consul

dairy, diary
decent, descend, descent
deprecate, depreciate
desert, dessert
dining, dinning
dying, dyeing
earnest, Ernest
emigration, immigration
euphemism, euphuism
fare, fair
foreword, forward
formally, formerly
forth, fourth, forty
freshman, freshmen
guard, regard
hear, here
holy, wholly
instance, instants
irrelevant, irreverent
its, it's
Johnson, Jonson
knew, new
know, no
later, latter
lead, led
loath, loathe
loose, lose
luxuriant, luxurious
mind, mine
moral, morale
of, off
ought, aught
past, passed
pastime, pass time
peace, piece
plain, plane
precede, proceed
presence, presents
prevalent, prevail
principal, principle
prodigy, progeny
prophecy, prophesy
quiet, quite, quit
respectively, respectfully
reverend, reverent
rite, right, write
sense, since
shone, shown
sight, cite, site
sleight, slight
speak, speech
Spenser, Spencer
staid, stayed
stationary, stationery
stature, statue, statute
straight, strait
suit, suite
their, there, they're
therefore, therefor
threw, through
till, until
to, too, two
troop, troupe
vain, vein, vane
weak, week
weather, whether
which, witch, sandwich
who's, whose
woman, women
your, you're

EXERCISES

A. Choose ten of the groups given above and compose sentences to illustrate the correct spelling and meaning of the words in each group. Write a separate sentence for each word in the group.

B. Do the same for ten other words given above.

C. Do the same for ten more words given above.

Etymological Kinship

42. If you have studied a foreign language, use your knowledge of etymology to guide you in spelling.

A knowledge of the etymology (origin) of a word will often help to recall the spelling. Form the habit of looking up the etymology of words and of following the cross-references good dictionaries give to words that are of the same origin.

Study the explanation of etymological data in your dictionary (pp. xxiii–xxiv in *ACD*, p. xix in *NCD*) and the abbreviations used in etymologies (bottom of left-hand pages in *ACD* and p. xxi in *NCD*). Simple words, such as English *feel*, *big*, *clean*, *roll*, are words which cannot be analyzed into meaningful parts. Complex words, such as *feeling*, *biggest*, *unclean*, *unrolled*, are words which can be analyzed into meaningful parts, called *bases*, *prefixes*, and *suffixes*. *Biggest* is made up of the base *big* and the suffix *-est; unclean* is made up of the base *clean* and the prefix *un-; unrolled* is made up of the base *roll*, the prefix *un-*, and the suffix *-ed*. Prefixes (which precede the base) and suffixes (which follow the base) are called *affixes*. The bases of foreign words cited in etymologies are called *roots* and *stems*.

Distinguish carefully between the following pairs of prefixes:

ante, "before": *antedate*, *antecedent*

anti, *ant*, "against": *anticlimax*, *antarctic*

dis, "apart, away, not": *disappear*, *disown*, *dissect*

de, "from, off, down": *decease*, *deduce*, *depose*

dis, *di*, "twice": *dissyllable*, *digraph*

dys, "ill, hard": *dyspepsia*

hyper, "above, excessive": *hypersensitive*, *hyperirritable*

hypo, "under, slightly": *hypodermic*, *hypoactive*

inter, "between, among": *intercollegiate*, *interurban*

intra, *intro*, "within, inward, in": *intramural*, *intramuscular*, *introduce*, *introspection*

per, "through, thoroughly": *pervade, percolate, perfume*

pre, "before": *precede, prevent, predict*

Note the three words in *-ceed: exceed, proceed, succeed.* Except for *supersede* most other words of this class are spelled *-cede: precede, concede, recede, secede,* etc.

EXERCISES

A. Write several derivatives of each of the bases which are listed below. Draw a slanting line between the base form and the prefix or suffix: *con/cede.*

Agri-, ali-, dent-, esti-, liber-, luci-, manu-, merge-.
Aud-, clam-, corp-, credi-, dic- (dict-), divi-, domi-, migra-.
Milli-, min-, mult-, nomi-, omni-, ord-, sent-, voc-.

B. Supply *cede, ceed,* or *sede:*

ex-, con-, inter-, pre-, pro-, re-, suc-, super-.

C. Look up the etymologies of several words which you have misspelled and separate all that you can into prefixes, bases, and suffixes.

Ei and Ie[1]

43. Do not confuse *ei* and *ie*.

The following rhyme may help you to remember the spelling of some words:

Write *i* before *e*
Except after *c*,
Or when sounded as *a*
As in *neighbor* and *weigh*.

The first half of this rhyme applies only when *ei* or *ie* has the *e* sound heard in *he*.

[1] This treatment owes much to the excellent discussion in C. O. Sylvester Mawson's *The Dictionary Companion* (Garden City, New York: Doubleday, Doran and Company, Inc., 1935). This material has been used with the permission of Mrs. Mawson and the publishers.

Examples of *ie* after any consonant except *c:*

achieve, belief, believe, brief, chief (cf. *handkerchief, mischief, mischievous*), *field, fiend, grief, grievance, niece, piece, priest, relief, relieve, shield, series, siege, species, wield, yield.*

Examples of *ei* after *c:*

ceiling, conceit, conceive, deceitful, deceive, perceive, receipt, receive.

COMMON EXCEPTIONS. *Either* (*neither*), *leisure, seize, weird.* Note also the *ei* in *height, heir, their, foreign, sleight* and the *ie* in *fierce, fiery, friend, ancient, patient, sufficient,* and other words having a *sh* sound in the unaccented syllable.

The last two lines of the rhyme mean that you are to write *ei* always if the sound is that of *a* in *ale.*

deign, eight, eighteen, eighty, freight, heinous, inveigh, neigh, neighbor, reign, rein, seine, sleigh, veil, vein, weigh.

EXERCISES

A. Insert *ei* or *ie* correctly in the following words:

bel. .ve, conc. .ted, financ. .r, forf. .t, fr. .nd, fr. .ght, l. .sure, misch. .-vous, n. .ce, perc. .ve, rec. .ve, r. .gn, s. .ge, s. .ze, sl. .ght, th. .r, w. .ld, w. .rd, v. .n.

B. Get a friend to dictate twenty-five of the *ei* and *ie* words in this section; then check your spelling by the words listed above and compute your score.

Doubling a Final Consonant

44. Before a suffix beginning with a vowel (*-ing, -ed, -er, -est, -ish,* etc.), double a single final consonant (1) if it is preceded by a single vowel and (2) if the consonant stands either in a monosyllable or in a word accented on the last syllable. Unless both of these conditions are fulfilled, do not double the consonant.

Apply the rule to *drag* and *occur.* (1) Both end in a single consonant preceded by a single vowel, and (2) one is a monosyllable and the other is a word accented on the last syllable. Thus when we add a suffix beginning with a vowel, we know that the final consonant must be doubled:

drag+ing=dragging *occur+ing=occurring* (Note that the accent of *occur* is not shifted when the ending is added.)

quit+ing=quitting (u and i are two vowel letters, but *quit* has only one vowel *sound.*)

NOTE. Derivatives in which the accent is moved toward the front of the word do not have a doubled consonant: *prefer'* (*preferred'*), but *pref'erence; confer'* (*confer'ring*), but *con'ference.*

NOTE. Because there are many exceptions to the rule for doubling the final consonant, use your dictionary when in doubt.

EXERCISES

A. Add *-ed* or *-er* to the following words:

box, refer, travel, stir, question, big, float, sweet, top, fix, permit, benefit, picnic, model, quiz.

B. Look up in your dictionary the spelling of the inflected forms of the following verbs:

bus, chagrin, combat, worship, revel, label.

Dropping Final -E

45. For words ending in silent -e, drop the -e before a suffix beginning with a vowel, but retain the -e before a suffix beginning with a consonant.

Examples of final *-e* dropped before a vowel suffix:

arrange: arranging
change: changing
desire: desirable, desirous
fleece: fleecy
force: forcing
guide: guidance
imagine: imaginary, imaginable
love: loving, lovable
please: pleasant, pleasure
use: using, usable, usage

Examples of *-e* retained before a suffix beginning with a consonant:

arrange: arrangement
excite: excitement
fate: fateful
stale: staleness
sole: solely

Exceptions. *Dyeing* and *singeing* retain the *e* to distinguish these words from *dying* and *singing*. *Shoeing* and *hoeing* always, *eyeing* and *mileage* sometimes retain the *e*.

Since *c* and *g* followed by the back vowels *a*, *o*, and *u* usually have the "hard" sound, as in *call* and *go*, the *e* is retained after *c* or *g* when the suffix begins with a back vowel, as in *-able*, *-ous*, etc. The retaining of the *e* indicates the "soft" sound of *c* and *g* which generally occurs before *e*, *i*, and *y*, as in *gem*, *ginger*, *gypsy*, *cent*, *cigar*, and *cylinder*.

Examples with *e* retained: *advantageous*, *changeable*, *noticeable*, *peaceable*, and *serviceable*. Note that *e* is dropped in *argument*, *awful*, *duly*, *ninth*, *truly*, and *wholly*.

EXERCISES

A. Write the present participle (the form in *-ing*) of each of the following words.

Admire, agree, argue, arrive, change, come, die, din, dine, dye, eye, grace, grieve, hope, lose, love, move, please, prepare, prove, range, receive, separate, serve, shoe, singe, slope, take, use, write.

B. Add *-able*, *-ible*, *-ful*, or *-ous* to each of the words below. Add more than one of these suffixes if you can.

Accept, admire, change, courage, credit, desire, fame, force, live, love, mistake, notice, outrage, peace, sale, sense, service, trace, trouble, tune.

C. Form derivatives of the following words by adding *-ment*, *-ly*, or *-ty*.

Able, acknowledge, amaze, argue, commence, content, develop, entire, general, god, great, judge, like, love, nine, partial, polite, prince, safe, sick, special, subtle, sure, true, vague, wasteful.

Final -Y

46. In words ending in *-y* preceded by a consonant, change the *y* to *i* before any suffix except one beginning with *i*; words ending in *-y* preceded by a vowel regularly retain the *-y* before all endings.

Examples of *-y* preceded by a consonant:

ally: allies *busy: business*
mercy: merciful *study: studious*
embody: embodied *easy: easily, easier, easiest*

Examples of *-y* retained before a suffix beginning with *i:*

embody: embodying study: studying hurry: hurrying.

Examples of words with final *-y* preceded by a vowel:

stay: stayed alley: alleys employ: employed.

But note the exceptions:

day: daily *say: said*
lay: laid *slay: slain*
pay: paid

NOTE. When *'s* is added the *-y* is never changed: *lady: lady's.* Note the spelling of *beauteous, piteous,* and *plenteous.*

EXERCISES

A. Write the third person singular present indicative, the past tense, and the present participle of each of the verbs below.

Example *try: tries, tried, trying*

Accompany, annoy, busy, carry, convey, cry, deny, envy, ferry, hurry, lay, marry, pay, play, rely, say, spy, study, supply, tarry.

B. If you are better than the average in spelling, read section 8, p. 1196 in *NCD.*

Plurals

47. Follow these rules for spelling plurals.

a. Plurals in -s or -es. For most nouns, form the plural by adding *-s* to the singular: *bells, boys, capes, cups, seas, trees.* Since nouns ending in a sibilant sound (*s, sh, ch, x, z,* etc.) require a vowel to make the plural pronounceable, add *-es* to such words: *axes, buzzes, marshes, quizzes* (the *z* of *quiz* is doubled according to

§ 44). Be sure to add *-s* to form the plural of words such as *tourist, dentist, scientist, physicist,* and *psychiatrist,* which end in *-st* in the singular.

b. Plurals of nouns ending in -y. Nouns ending in *-y* preceded by a consonant generally change the *y* to *i* and add *-es: armies, cries, flies, ladies, skies, studies.* Nouns ending in *-y* preceded by a vowel usually add *-s* only: *joys, keys, monkeys, plays, quays.* (See § 46.)

c. Plurals of nouns ending in -fe or -ff or -f. For nouns ending in *-fe* change the *fe* to *ve* and add *-s: knife: knives; wife: wives.* Nouns ending in *-ff* merely add *-s: bailiff: bailiffs; sheriff: sheriffs.* Nouns ending in *-f* are so variable in the plural (*loaf: loaves,* but *chief: chiefs; dwarf: dwarfs; elf: elfs* or *elves*) that one should be guided by the pronunciation of the plural, or, better still, should consult a dictionary when in doubt. (The note under *plural* in a Merriam-Webster dictionary contains much valuable information about the formation of plurals.)

d. Plurals of nouns ending in -o. Nouns ending in *-o* preceded by a vowel add *-s: cameos, folios, radios.* For nouns ending in *-o* preceded by a consonant, the plural forms are so variable that one should consult a dictionary whenever in doubt. The following nouns, however, have a plural ending in *-s: autos, bamboos, dynamos, pianos, quartos, solos.* The following have a plural ending in *-es: echoes, heroes, mosquitoes, Negroes, noes, tomatoes, torpedoes, vetoes.*

e. Plurals of proper nouns. Follow the regular rules for *-s* and *-es* plurals: three *Toms* in the family and two *Charleses,* the *Browns,* the *Davises,* the *Joneses.*

f. Irregular English plurals. The following irregular plurals are survivals of different Old English noun declensions: *oxen, children, brethren, geese, feet, mice, men, women, sheep, deer, swine.*

g. Plurals of words borrowed from French, Hebrew, Latin, or Greek. Many words derived from foreign languages retain the plural of the language from which they were borrowed. Many words of this class have been partly naturalized and have a second (anglicized) plural. The present tendency is to anglicize (and regularize) the plural of foreign nouns.

alumna: alumnae (feminine)
alumnus: alumni (masculine)
analysis: analyses
basis: bases
beau: beaux or beaus
cherub: cherubim or cherubs
crisis: crises
datum: data
focus: foci or focuses
formula: formulae or formulas
gladiolus: gladioli or gladioluses
hypothesis: hypotheses
index: indices or indexes
insigne: insignia
medium: media or mediums
memorandum: memoranda or memorandums
phenomenon: phenomena
radius: radii or radiuses
seraph: seraphim or seraphs
stigma: stigmata or stigmas
stratum: strata or stratums

h. Plural of compounds. Compound nouns usually form the plural by adding *-s* or *-es* to the important word in the compound: *sons-in-law, courts-martial, bystanders, passers-by, poets laureate, attorneys general* or *attorney generals.* But if the component elements are so closely joined as to be felt as a simple word, the suffix is added to the end of the word: *cupfuls, handfuls.* In a few words both elements are pluralized: *menservants, womenservants.*

i. The plural of letters, figures, signs, etc. See Apostrophe, § 25g.

EXERCISES

A. Write the plural or plurals of twenty of the following words, and then check your spelling by the dictionary or by your instructor's dictation. List the words that have more than one plural form.

Alias, alibi, alumna, alumnus, analysis, appendix, banjo, beau, beauty, belief, brother-in-law, buffalo, bus, canto, cattle, Chinese, cloth, crash, crisis, cuff, cupful, day, deer, die, dilettante, donkey, echo, fish, fly, gas, glass, hero, index, lady, lady's-maid, man-at-arms, man-eater, manservant, mass, Miss Smith, Mr. Brown, mouse, Negro, ottoman, passer-by, piano, poet laureate, potato, quiz, rabbi, radio, radius, runner-up, shelf, sky, soliloquy, staff, stratum, strife, teaspoonful, tree, trout, valley, waltz, 10, and *a* (as in: There is one *a* in *pare* but two . . . in *separate*).

B. Directions given under Exercise A. Do the same for twenty other words listed in Exercise A.

C. Write the singular of each of the following and then check your spelling by a dictionary or by your instructor's dictation. (Not all of the words have a separate singular form.)

Alleys, allies, alumnae, alumni, bacteria, banditti, bases, cherubim, crises, criteria, data, dicta, exempla, fabliaux, genera, genii, insignia, measles, memoranda, messieurs, mumps, phenomena, radii, seraphim, series, species, strata, tableaux, theses, valleys, wolves.

Compound Words

48. Learn the conventions which govern the writing of compounds.

There are no hard-and-fast rules to be followed in the writing of compounds. But although dictionaries and reputable publishing houses differ widely in their practice, they agree, in the main, on the following rules. When you have to guess, write the words without a hyphen. Keep your dictionary always at hand to consult when you are in doubt. It will be less confusing and you will gain consistency in your writing of compounds if you take only one dictionary as your guide.

48a. Use the hyphen in writing the following classes of words:

1. Two or more words used as a single adjective *preceding* a noun: *first-class* sailors, *worn-out* books, *four-footed* animals, *salmon-pink* in color, *light-colored* clothing, *well-known* man, a *so-called* error, *two-story* houses, *up-to-date* information.
2. Compound numerals less than a hundred: *sixty-five, forty-nine, forty-ninth.* But when a fraction is used as a noun (*Two thirds* of the men are unemployed), omit the hyphen.
3. Compounds containing a preposition or a noun followed by a prepositional phrase: *off-color, off-chance, jack-in-the-box, jack-o'-lantern, father-in-law, passer-by, runner-up.*
4. Words that may be misinterpreted or that are difficult to read: *re-form, re-creation, re-cover* (to distinguish these words from *reform, recreation, recover*); *bell-like, anti-imperial, ante-evolutionary.*
5. Usually after *self-*: *self-conceit, self-confidence, self-sufficient,* etc., but *selfsame*; usually *selfhood*; after words ending in *'s: dog's-tail* (a kind of grass), *cat's-paw*; and when the second part of the

compound is capitalized: *ex-President Hoover, pro-German, anti-British, Sino-Japanese.*

NOTE. *Good-by* (*good-bye*) is hyphenated.

48b. Write the following classes of words solid:

1. A compound word which is normally accented as a single word (usually with the accent on the first syllable and no accent or a very light one on the second) and which expresses a meaning different from the meaning of the first word plus the meaning of the second. Note the accent in *forehead, freshman, gunwale, postman. Redeye, firecracker, overdrive,* and *roundworm* have a specific meaning which is not the same as the meaning of the adjective plus the meaning of the noun. If, however, the first word is used as an adjective to modify the second, the two words are written separately: a *red cross*, a *red deer*, a *red oak*, a *fresh pear*, a *round dish.*
2. Most compounds consisting of *any, every, no, some,* and *body, thing, where: anybody, anything, anywhere.* Compounds with *one* may be written solid or separately: *anyone, any one.*
3. Compound personal pronouns and prepositions: *myself, oneself, itself, into, within, upon, towards.*
4. Words consisting of a root plus a prefix or a suffix: *ahead, beside, outdoor, overtake, upstairs, goodness, kingdom,* but *ex-President, pro-German.*

48c. Write separately the following classes of words:

1. Two or more words which have the same meaning in unconnected succession as they do when they are hyphenated or written solid: *boy scout, a high school, good night, a good time, pipe clays, pipe line, pipe organ;* he needed two *black boards* and two *red ones.* Compare a *classroom blackboard.*
2. *All right, any time, by and by, et cetera, every time, in spite of, inasmuch as, some day, some way.* But: *nevertheless, someone, southwest, today, tomorrow, tonight.*

EXERCISES

A. Classify twenty of the following forms as (1) those written solid, (2) those written with a hyphen, and (3) those written as two words. Be prepared to report how your dictionary writes these typical expressions.

allAmerican	interdenominational	out standing
allright	judge advocate	overdraft
antebellum	Knownothing	overwhelming
antiaircraft	lighthouse	Pan Slavism
antifreeze	logrolling	peacemaker
anyone	longsuffering	percentage
attorneyatlaw	maneater	post man
audio visual aids	meaningful	post office
basketball	Middleages	psycho somatic
breakdown	motherinlaw	publicspirited
bricabrac	nambypamby	shellless
chowmein	name sake	sixtythree
coaxial cable	nature study	somebody
cradle song	nonintervention	spokesman
crossexamine	north eastward	square toed
farreaching	offprint	stage struck
foot hills	on looker	still hunt
halftone	open minded	supernatural
hangover	openshop	sweat shop
headstrong	out of doors	tenderhearted

B. Directions given under Exercise A.

C. Directions given under Exercise A.

Spelling List

49. Master the list of most frequently misspelled words given later in this section.

49a. Proofread your papers to discover every word about whose spelling you have the slightest doubt and then consult your dictionary for the correct spelling.

While you are writing the first draft of your paper, simply check or query the words about which you have any doubt. Do not let mechanics interfere with the spontaneity of your writing. But when you are revising, read aloud (for this enables you to detect many kinds of errors) and also look closely at every letter of doubtful words in order to detect any misspellings. When you consult a dictionary on the spelling of a word, learn also its pronunciation and commonest meanings.

The following are suggested as reliable for spelling and are reasonably priced (around $5.00): *American College Dictionary*, Funk and Wagnalls' *New College Standard Dictionary*, *Webster's New Collegiate Dictionary*, and the *Winston Dictionary*, College Edition. See also § 65.

49b. Record all words you misspell and when you have mastered them study the following list.

The following list contains nearly all of the common words that are frequently misspelled by college students. After you have learned to spell all the words on your individual list, learn to spell the words in the list below, for by doing so you will eliminate eighty-five to ninety per cent of the common errors in spelling. Do not study more than five to ten words at a time. The preferred spelling is given for words spelled in two or more ways. No simplified (or reformed) spellings are listed.

absolutely
absurd
accept
accidentally
accommodate
accomplish
accumulate
accusative
accustom
achievement
acknowledge
acquaintance
acquitted
across
address
adjectival
adverbially
advice
advise
adviser
aeroplane
affairs
affect
aggravate
alley
allotted
allowed
all right
ally
almost
already
altar
alter
although
altogether
alumna (æ)
alumnus (i)
always
amateur
ammunition
among
amount
analysis
analyze
angel
angle
annual
another
anxiety
anything
anywhere
apartment
apparatus
apparent

appearance
appropriate
arctic
argument
arising
arithmetic
around
arouse
arranging
arrival
artillery
ascend
ask
asked
association
athlete
athletics
attempt
attractive
audience
authorities
automobile
auxiliary
awkward

balance
balloon
barbarous
baring
barring
baseball
based
battalion
bearing
because
becoming
before
beggar
beginning
believe
beneficial
benefited
border
borne
boundaries
break
breathe
brilliant
Britain
Britannica
Briton
buoyant
bureau
business
busy

calendar
candidate
can't
capital
capitol
carburetor
cemetery
certain
changeable
changing
characteristic
chauffeur
choose
chose
chosen
clause
cliff
climb
clothes
coarse
colloquial
column
coming
commission
committed
committee
companies
comparatively
compel
compelled
competent
competition
complement
completely
compliment
compulsory
concede
conceivable
conceive
conjunction
conquer
conqueror
conscience
conscientious
consensus
considered
continuous
control
controlled
convenient
corner
corps
country
course
courteous
courtesy
cozy
cries
criticism
criticize
cruelty
curiosity
curriculum
custom
cylinder

dealt

debater
deceive
decide
decision
declarative
deferred
deficient
definite
democracy
dentist
dependent
descend
describe
description
desirable
despair
desperate
destruction
develop
device
devise
dictionary
difference
digging
dining
dinning
disappear
disappoint
discipline
discussion
disease
dissatisfied
dissipate
distribute
divided
doctor
doesn't
dormitories
dropped
drunkenness
dying

ecstasy
effect
efficiency
efficient
eighth
eliminate
embarrass
eminent
employee
encouraging
enemy
engineer
enthusiastic
entirely
equipped
equivalent
erroneous
especially
etc.
every
everybody
everything
everywhere
exaggerate
exceed
excel
excellent
except
exceptional
exercise
exhaust
exhilarate
existence
expected
expense
experience
explanation
extension
extensive
extremely
extremity

familiar
fascinate
February
fiery
finally
financial
financier
football
foreign
foremost
foresee
forest
forfeit
formally
formerly
forth
forty
forward
fought
fourth
frantically
fraternities
freshman
friend
frightened
fulfill
furniture
further

gaiety
generally
genitive
genius
glorious
good-by
government
governor
grammar
grandeur
grievous
guard

guest
guidance

harass
haven't
having
height
heroes
hesitancy
hoping
horde
humorous
hundred
hundredths
hurries
hypocrisy

imaginary
imagination
imagine
imitative
immediately
impromptu
incident
incidentally
incredible
indefinitely
independent
indispensable
inevitable
influential
innocent
instance
intellectual
intelligence
intentionally
intercede
interested
invitation
involve
irresistible
isn't
its
it's
itself

knew
knowledge
known

laboratory
laid
later
latter
lavender
lead
led
liable
library
lightning
likely
literature
loneliness
loose
lose
losing

magnificence
maintenance
maneuver
manual
manufacture
mathematics
mattress
meant
medicine
militarism
miniature
minute
mischievous
misspelled
modifier
modifies
modifying
momentous
morale
mosquitoes
motor
murmur
muscle
mysterious

naturally
necessary
necessity
Negroes
neither
nervous
nevertheless
nineteenth
ninetieth
ninety
ninth
nominative
no one
northeast
noticeable
noun
nowadays

obedience
oblige
obstacle
occasionally
o'clock
occurred
occurrence
off
officer
omission
omitted
oneself
opinion

opportunity
optimistic
ordered
organization
original
ought
ourselves
outdoor
outrageous
outside
overrun

paid
parallel
parliament
participial
participle
particularly
partner
passed
pastime
peaceable
perceive
perform
perhaps
permissible
perseverance
personal
personnel
persuade
phrase
physical
physically
picture
piece
plain
planned
pleasant
politics
possess
possession

possessive
possible
potatoes
practically
practice
prairie
precede
precedence
precedents
preceding
prefer
preference
preferred
prejudice
preparation
prepositional
prevalent
principal
principle
privilege
probably
proceed
profession
professor
prominent
pronunciation
propaganda
propeller
prophecy
prophesy
proudest
prove
pursue
pursuing
putting

quantity
quarter
questionnaire
quiet
quite

quiz
quizzes

raised
realize
really
recede
receive
receiving
recognize
recommend
reference
referring
regard
religion
religious
remembrance
rendezvous
repetition
replies
representative
restaurant
rheumatism
ridiculous

sacrifice
sacrilegious
safety
sandwich
scarcely
scene
schedule
scrape
secretary
seized
sense
sentence
sentinel
separate
sergeant
service

several
severely
shining
shipyard
shone
shown
shriek
siege
significant
similar
slight
soliloquy
sometimes
sophomore
source
southwest
speak
specimen
speech
speed
statement
stationary
stationery
statue
stature
statute
stopping
stops
straight
strength
strengthen
stretch
struggle
studying
subordinate
succeed
success
successful
sunrise
superintendent
supersede

sure
surprise
suspense
swimming
syllable
symmetry

tasting
temperament
tenant
tendency
than
their
themselves
there
thereabout
therefor
therefore
they're
thorough
thought
threw
through
throughout
tired
to
together
too
tournament
toward
track
tract
tragedy
tries
truly
Tuesday
two
typical
tyrannical
tyranny
tyrant

unanimous
undoubtedly
unnecessary
until
use
useful
using
usually

valuable
vegetation
vengeance
victorious
village
villain
volunteer

warrant
warring
weak
weather
week
weird
welfare
where
wherever
whether
which
whither
whom
who's [= who is]
whose
without
woman
women
wonderful
won't
writing
written

your
you're

Effectiveness

DICTION

Diction is choice of words. Although every speaker selects words from his vocabulary every time he speaks, even in such set expressions as *Albany is the capital of New York*, and *Water boils at 212 degrees Fahrenheit*, improving diction usually refers to (1) learning new and more precise words, or (2) using the most effective words for particular purposes. The student may thus improve his diction by (1) choosing words from the extensive English lexicon to add to his vocabulary, or by (2) choosing from his own vocabulary the best words for particular occasions.

A considerable amount of vocabulary improvement goes on constantly in college classes, when students learn about *osmosis, quatrains, pan-Hellenism, syndromes, unilateral treaties, siblings, peneplains,* and *dualism*. As the student learns new things or learns more precise names for familiar things his vocabulary is automatically (and more or less painlessly) improved. This process, however, helps only with the nomenclature of particular "subjects." It is exactly the same as the vocabulary improvement that a boy enjoys when he takes a job in a hardware store and has to learn the names of hundreds of articles on the shelves. Words of more general and nontechnical application are not systematically taught; they may be picked up from teachers, classmates, and reading, but most students cannot rely on casual contacts for genuine improvement of their diction. Sections 58, 59, 64, and 65 advise the student how to enlarge his vocabulary.

The second type of vocabulary improvement, choosing the best words for particular occasions, may also involve learning new words, but it is usually a matter of learning when to use and when not to use certain words. Fortunately most common words like *water*, *eat*, *think*, *can*, *under*, *blue*, and *happy* are used by standard and non-standard speakers on formal and informal occasions in all varieties of English. But some words are used characteristically by certain types of people or in certain special situations. Readers and listeners are quick to notice the inappropriate, out-of-place use of such words, and may punish the user, regardless of the importance of what he is saying. A notice reading PLEASE EXTINGUISH THE ILLUMINATION in a dormitory would be inappropriate diction; so would the phrase "You guys and gals" in a college president's address to a coeducational student body. There is nothing "wrong" with the *words* in either example, but in both the words are not suitable to the occasion.

As a part of social experience we unconsciously and automatically associate certain words with particular types of people or situations. Novelists and short story writers make use of this fact by having their characters speak "in character," that is, in words that will identify the educational level, or occupation, or social class, or geographical origin of the characters. Conversely, we all grow up learning the vocabulary of the people around us, and we all are likely to use some words that are not in universal use, words that some people will associate with particular groups or places. It is the problem of the student to learn which words in his vocabulary have restricted use, and how to avoid them when they are inappropriate.

Some of the following sections are designed to help the student identify words of limited usage and become aware of their restrictions. With the aid of his instructor and his dictionary, the average college freshman can learn very easily to avoid serious violations of fitness in the use of words. Very young children learn that some words are acceptable at some times and taboo at other times; the problem of the college student learning when to write *bankrupt* instead of *broke* is no different. But the avoidance of inappropriate words is a negative virtue; it is something that we take for granted in educated people. The positive virtue of using precise, meaningful, and effective words is harder to acquire and properly has greater rewards.

Standard Usage

50. In writing for a general audience use standard English words.

This means that you should normally avoid words that a good dictionary labels with some restriction, words that are too new to be immediately recognized, and the affected use of old-fashioned words (marked *archaic* or *obsolete* in your dictionary). Naturally the use of technical words in a technical paper for specialists or dialect words in conversation in a story would not violate this rule.

Examples of nonstandard English:

Archaic words — *forfend* for "prevent," *mark* for "frontier," *noise* for "rumor," *thou* for "you," *whiles* for "at times," *save* for "unless."

Obsolete words — *endull, exceptless, falsage, gome, inflexure.*

Dialect — *garden sauce* (vegetables), *power* (a multitude), *stoop* (pillar), *tight* (shapely), *piece* (a short distance).

Examples of technical terms:

petticoat (as in electricity), *definition* (as in television), *pan* (as in motion pictures), *generation* (as in mathematics), *osculant* (as in zoology).

National Use

51. Use words which have national currency.

A person who has lived mainly in any one section of the United States is almost certain to use a few expressions which are not used nationally. These are very hard to identify, since all of us tend to think that we speak English, while people from other sections speak dialects. Our diction is taken for granted as normal, while that of other regions sounds outlandish. For example, any one of the following expressions may seem ordinary, or may sound dialectal to you, depending on your own regional type of English: *sick to the stomach*, *I want off*, *light bread*, *school gets out*, and *Dutch cheese*. When you learn that a term you use is regional, find the national equivalent for use in writing that is addressed to people from other sections.

EXERCISES

A. Make a list of ten expressions that you have heard or read which are not common in your section of the country.

B. Find in your dictionary twenty words or meanings which are labeled as restricted geographically.

C. List the national terms which can be substituted for the provincialisms listed in Exercise A. In Exercise B.

Idiom

52. Use idiomatic words and constructions.

An idiom is an expression described by a special rule, a rule that does not apply to any (or many) other constructions. The rule that English adjectives precede the nouns they modify is a *general* rule: it applies to an infinite number of adjectives and nouns. The rule that requires *in bed* (compare unidiomatic *on bed* and *at bed*) is a *special* rule: it applies to the two words *in* and *bed*. Such a rule is so particular that it is never expressed as a rule; we simply tell foreigners and children to say *in bed*, not *on bed* or *at bed*.

When a person learns new words or phrases in the normal manner, that is by hearing or reading them in sentences, he automatically learns their idiomatic use: college students do not have to be taught such idioms as *attorney-at-law*, *mother-in-law*, *student of law*, and *forbidden by law*. But when a person learns a new word without learning how it is used, he may write such unidiomatic expressions as *aversion of* (on the model of *dislike of*, *hatred of*, *fear of*) instead of idiomatic *aversion to;* and *desirous for* (on the model of *eager for, hopeful for, anxious for*) instead of idiomatic *desirous of.* When you look up a word in your dictionary, be sure to note its idiomatic use if this is given.

Some idioms are not common to all varieties of English. For example, *different to* is common in British, rare in American English. *Wait on a signal* is provincial, *in back of* is informal, *entertain to dinner* is nonstandard. Be sure that your idioms, like your grammar and your vocabulary, are appropriate to your subject and your readers.

Study the pairs of idioms listed below, and add to the lists any expressions called to your attention in your own writing.

Not Preferred	*Preferred*
amount of things	number of things
complected	complexioned
couldn't scarcely	could scarcely
equally as good as	just as good as
identical to	identical with
identify to it	identify with it
inferior than	inferior to
in regards to	in regard to
might could	possibly could
on account for	on account of
Reverend Dow	Reverend Mr. Dow
reverse to	reverse of
take sick	get sick
to home	at home
treat on	treat of

EXERCISES

A. In the following sentences change all the idioms which are inappropriate to the sentences. In case of doubt, consult a dictionary.

1. Students without a B average are prohibited to audit courses.
2. Music students are invited to listen at the opera broadcasts in the small auditorium on Saturday afternoons.
3. Who put my tennis racket in back of the dresser?

4. The chairman of the board is reported to be planning on appealing the decision of the lower court.
5. Criminals try to blame their troubles to policemen.
6. This one's identical to the kind we used to sell.
7. It is difficult to reconcile the older officers with the new plans.
8. Jason went on a long journey in search for the golden fleece.
9. The result from the experiment was entirely unexpected.
10. If you listen at the door you can hear him breathe.

B. Use each of the following words in two sentences, showing how the words are used with different prepositions:

accused, adapt, agree, authority, averse, disagree, part (verb), *suitable, treat* (verb), *subscribe.*

C. Look up each of the following words in your dictionary to determine what idiomatic meanings or uses it has with particular prepositions:

ask, call, comply, crack, differ, drive, ease, get, go, hold.

D. Make a list, from speech you have heard or from your reading, of idioms which are different from your own. Examples might be *quarter of* (or *to*) *six, angry at* (or *with*) *someone,* to *stop in* (or *at*) a town. Try to determine whether the differences are regional, social (standard or nonstandard), or functional (formal, informal, technical, slang, etc.). Compare your conclusions, as far as possible, with what your dictionary says about these idioms. See § 65i, page 322.

Correct Diction

It is important to understand exactly what "correct" and "incorrect" mean when applied to diction. Everyone knows that many people who have little schooling, and whose contacts are mainly with people of their own local group, use such expressions as *a apple, clumb a tree, I seen it,* and *he set down,* yet make themselves understood with no difficulty. They are not "making mistakes" in the sense that one makes mistakes in singing or in subtraction. The person who says *set down* is not trying to say *sit down* and failing; he is very successfully using words which are normal in his native speech. But in the speech of more privileged people *sit down* is the normal form, and to such people *set down* connotes a lack of formal education. Regardless of the origin, age, or efficiency of an expression, if it connotes illiteracy to educated people they will consider it "incorrect" precisely as they consider sport shoes "incorrect" with an evening dress, and the person who wishes to become identified with the educated group must break the habit of saying *set down* and learn *sit down*. If the habit of saying *I seen it* is fixed by years of repetition, it will be hard to break (but no harder than for a person who first learns *I saw* to change to *I seen*). Fortunately the average college freshman who has such "illiteracies" in his speech is likely to have only a few and can concentrate on eliminating them.

53. Substitute standard for nonstandard expressions.

The most common examples are matters of grammar as well as matters of word choice: they are (1) cases of pronouns, as in *Us Democrats should help him*, *Me and her saw the accident*, and *Them people are on thin ice*, and (2) verb forms, such as *He run away*, *She brung it*, *He done more than I did*, and *He ain't qualified*. There are also occasional examples like *hisself*, *irregardless*, *They was a man here*, and *Please borrow me a handkerchief*.

EXERCISES

A. Revise the following sentences, making the diction standard.

1. He learned me how to play tennis.
2. The plasterers have went to another job.
3. The speaker come over from Jacksonville by bus.
4. He showed we freshmen how to light a Bunsen burner.
5. Leave them do it theirselves.

B. Find ten examples of nonstandard diction in short stories or a novel, and note what kinds of characters use the expressions.

54. Avoid improprieties. **An impropriety in standard English is the use of a word in a meaning, a form, or a function that is nonstandard.**

1. Improprieties in meaning: *dialect* for *dialogue*, *expect* for *suspect*, *later* for *latter*, *colloquial* for *nonstandard*.

NOTE. Many homophones, pairs of words which are identical in sound, are confused in writing. Examples are *effect* for *affect*, *except* for *accept*, *capitol* for *capital*, *principle* for *principal*. Such improprieties in writing are simple misspellings.

2. Improprieties in form: *Between you and I*, *Whom was it?*, *somebody's else*, *He has did it*. Forms of this type usually are not native to any variety of English, but frequently occur as a result of confusion when speakers attempt to change their grammar.

3. Improprieties in function: *immediately*, *also*, and *without* as conjunctions, *shelf* and *half* as verbs, *against* as a conjunction. It is useful to remember that many people object to *contact* as a verb, *like* as a conjunction, and *good* as an adverb, although these usages have long been common in standard English.

The observant student who reads current newspaper editorials, magazines, and books may notice words used in new senses that are not in dictionaries, new forms, and new functions, and may reasonably ask why these are not improprieties. The answer is that an innovation may go unnoticed or even be applauded if it serves a useful purpose and its creator commands respect, but an equally useful innovation may be labeled nonstandard if it becomes associated with people of little schooling.

Functional Varieties

We have many varieties of getting about, such as walking fast, tiptoeing, running, trotting, marching, ambling, and walking slowly. All are good and proper ways of moving, but any one may be wrong on certain occasions. Occasionally we are told how to go: to walk (not run) to a fire escape, to tiptoe in a sickroom, or to walk slowly in a wedding procession; yet no textbook could possibly tell everyone precisely how to move in all possible situations. Similarly, no dictionary could possibly indicate precisely when any word is appropriate and when inappropriate. Some ministers use informal language in certain sermons, before certain congregations, and very formal language in different sermons. Salesmen learn when to use easy, colloquial language and when to use formal, solemn language, just as they learn to be jovial on some occasions, deadly serious on others, depending on the place, the listener, and the occasion. The subjects we talk about, our reasons for talking, the age, sex, education, occupation, personality, and standing of our listeners, the circumstances of our talking — all are so variable and shifting from day to day and hour to hour that we must learn adaptability, learn when to be respectful, friendly, positive, playful, sympathetic, firm, scornful, amused, or excited. Effectiveness in diction is much like tact in talking.

Some words are used so normally and regularly at dances, horse races, and sporting events, in comedy performances, on college campuses, and by unconventional speakers that the words become automatically associated with informal and light speaking. Such words are inappropriate in wills, obituaries, and treaties. Effective writers choose their words to fit the occasion. Since lexicographers cannot anticipate every possible occasion on which words may be used, they label many words and meanings *colloquial, literary, popular, archaic,* etc., to indicate roughly the kind of association the words are likely to make. See pages 91–94.

55. Use formal words in a formal style, informal words in an informal style, keeping the diction appropriate to the occasion.

Formal He dived headforemost into the water.
Informal He took a header into the water.
Formal Appointments with the doctor must be made in advance.
Informal You can't get a date with her by asking at the last minute.
Formal Coin-operated phonographs are manufactured in Ellboro.
Informal They make juke boxes in Ellboro.

EXERCISE

Find the words which are inappropriate in the following sentences and select appropriate substitutes. Note that sentences 3, 7, and 9 are obviously conversational.

1. Governor Smith's pal, Franklin Roosevelt, nominated him for the presidency.

2. A serious accident occurred today in Enid, a jerkwater town in southern Delaware.
3. Can I borrow your fountain pen to take a quiz next hour?
4. The defendant agreed to remove his old lady immediately from the almshouse, and thus received a suspended sentence.
5. Municipal ownership of the waterworks will be discussed at a confab between the council and a citizens' committee.
6. It is necessary to have a refrigerator in which food will save.
7. Aren't they fed up with that bonehead in the governor's office?
8. After mixing thoroughly, bring to a boil; then dump in salt.
9. When he gave me a D in trig, I was fit to be tied.
10. While trade is roaring, the bank should not discourage loans.

Slang

56. Use slang only when it is fully appropriate.

Slang is undignified language, usually good-humored, and more or less disrespectful. When new and fresh, slang expressions are either bold innovations, such as *razz*, *beaut*, *flivver*, *what gives?*, *flunk*, and *hooey*, or striking figures of speech like *highbrow*, *bonehead*, *knockout*, *lame-brain*, *pop-quiz*, and *punch-drunk*. Slang may be produced by any of the normal processes of linguistic change: original creation (*burp*, *oomph*), compounding (*jaywalker*, *pantywaist*), importation from another language (*calaboose*, *kibitzer*), shift of stress (*broTHER*, *posiTIVEly*), functional change (*what goes?*, *make with music*), change of meaning (*corny*, *jerk*, *tomato*), affixing (*debunk*, *unlax*), clipping (*babe*, *prof*), reduplication (*boogie-woogie*, *heebie-jeebies*), and blending (*veep*, *bohunk*). When an innovation is made in a serious situation (for example *insulin*, *betatron*, *televise*) it is not slang; thus much slang has such non-serious origins as the sports world, jazz musicians, college life, and the underworld, where flippant attitudes call for flippant expressions.

Many slang terms enjoy a burst of popularity and then disappear; examples are *jellybean* and *cat's pajamas* of the 1920's, *blueskin* and *dumfoozled* of the nineteenth century. Other terms of slang origin, such as *highbrow, jaywalker*, and *debunk* lose their slang connotation and become part of the general colloquial vocabulary (although dictionaries continue to label such expressions *slang* long after they have lost their slanginess). Rarely does an expression of slang origin lose its original connotation completely and become formal English. The use of outdated slang is typical of dull people; the use of any slang where formal English is more appropriate shows a lack of tact.

EXERCISES

A. In the following sentences substitute more appropriate English for all slang that is out of place. Note that sentences 1, 6, and 10 are not likely to occur in serious writing.

1. You wouldn't go to the dance with a creep like him?
2. Dr. and Mrs. Humel request the pleasure of Mr. Adamson's company at a blowout for their daughter Yvonne.
3. The prosecutor is evidently assuming that no law-abiding citizen would carry that much lettuce in his wallet on a fishing trip.
4. Police reported that a tall joker wearing glasses had been threatening the manager earlier that day.
5. The counselor's staff have found that your son is spending very little time studying, and we recommend that he make with the books more seriously or withdraw from college.
6. Joe is dating a mighty slick chick in Louisville weekends.
7. Many excellent pieces of writing have come from authors whose living depended on lousy potboilers and pulp fiction.
8. Did President Lincoln's murderer surrender or take it on the lam after the assassination?
9. This poet impresses me, after a careful study of his works, as a screwball who cannot distinguish positivism from Fabian socialism.
10. So you were taken for a month's pay? Didn't you know the match was fixed?

B. Make a list of ten expressions which you might use in talking with a college professor, but which you would not use in writing an examination paper.

C. If your library keeps bound back issues of popular magazines like the *Saturday Evening Post*, examine some stories published in the 1920's and list at least five slang expressions used in dialogue which are now trite or which are not used today.

D. Watch for and list effective uses of slang in editorials, picture captions, headlines, and other printed matter. Try to decide what in the subject-matter, context, or writer's attitude makes the slang appropriate.

Connotation and Denotation

57. Be careful to use words which connote as well as denote exactly what you mean.

The referent (non-verbal meaning) of a word is something which you can point to, or smell, or taste, or hear. For example, the referent of the word *face* can best be defined by pointing to a certain part of a person's head. The denotation of *face* is "the front part of the head, from chin to forehead." Other words, such as *countenance*, *mug*, and *visage*, have the same denotation (can be strictly defined in the same words), but differ in connotation, because they are accompanied by different associations. When a person hears or reads a word, it automatically stirs up fleeting memories of past occasions when he has heard or read it. Since *countenance* and *mug* are not likely to have been met in similar circumstances, they are not likely to have the same connotation. Compare the associations made for you by the words *girl*, *damsel*, *maiden*, *babe*, and *lass*, or *nag*, *horse*, and *steed*, or *cheat*, *defraud*, *chisel*, and *swindle;* synonyms always differ, though sometimes only slightly, in connotation.

The writer should remember that a word may have different connotations for different readers, depending on their past experiences. To some people *cotton* connotes green and white fields, to others surgical dressings, to others fabrics, and to others financial transactions.

Writers commonly express their attitudes and attempt to produce desired effects by choosing words for their connotations. Compare *fat, red-faced bureaucrat* and *portly, ruddy-faced public official*, or *slender, well-groomed college girl* and *skinny, dressed-up coed*, or *eat heartily* and *stuff like a glutton.* Synonym notes in dictionaries and special books of synonyms are helpful when you wish to distinguish fine shades of connotation, but the best way to learn the connotation of words is to observe their usage in the English you read and hear.

Slang, archaic terms, nonstandard English, and other such varieties of vocabulary differ from standard English only in connotation, but they are treated separately because they make up large classes of expressions that have common characteristics.

EXERCISES

A. Write a description of the appearance and clothing of a person you have seen or might have seen recently, giving as many facts as possible, but not indicating by the connotation of a single word that you like or dislike, approve or disapprove this person.

B. Rewrite Exercise A, using exactly the same details, but substituting words to let your reader know that you do not like or approve the person.

C. Rewrite Exercise A, using exactly the same details, but indicating that you approve or like the person described.

D. Repeat Exercises A, B, and C, describing a building, or a ball game, or a speech, or a movie, or a book.

GENERAL EXERCISES IN DICTION

A. Change the wording of the following sentences wherever necessary to make them suitable for formal English, such as in a letter applying for a position.

1. My high school teachers gave me swell grades.
2. I was fourteen when my old man moved to Tuscaloosa.
3. Sundays I carried a paper route to make spending money.
4. Did the records office send over my credentials yet?
5. During the depression my pater made a valiant effort to ward off the vicissitudes of pennilessness by purveying pencils on city thoroughfares.

6. I had not planned on looking for work until late in May.
7. Biology, math, and physics were my favorite courses in college.
8. The day I graduated my grandfather made a killing on the stock market.
9. If you would like for me to come in for an interview, please phone.
10. You can take it for sure that I am interested in the job.

B. Improve the diction of the following sentences.

1. Before long she had learned to make supper for her father.
2. Did your billing department correct the statement already?
3. Enjoy a Noise-O radio when you stay to home nights.
4. The group recommends that Mr. Wilson be selected to administrate this program.
5. It behooves one always to do one's utmost.
6. Our representative reports that your public relations staff made his visit a real pleasant one.
7. The school board decided to take action against the bookies who hang around the gymnasium.
8. I have but one life to donate to my country.
9. Department heads paid fulsome tribute to the revered dean.
10. The postman was proud of his ponderous beard and curvy hair.

C. Make the changes indicated and any other necessary changes.

1. Change *look* to *listen*: Duson wanted to look at the speaker.
2. Change *Hills* to *Street*: Ellis has bought a house in Druid Hills.
3. Change *Agnes* to *be done*: This does not belong to Agnes.
4. Change *close* to *in harmony*: The effect is not close to what the designer intended.
5. Change *bear* to *treat*: The chapter doesn't bear on hagiology.
6. Change *to look* to *in search*: The men went to look for Johnny.
7. Change *attend* to *comply*: Ask him to attend to the regulations.
8. Change *know* to *knowing*: There was no way to know when he came.
9. Change *confidence* to *respect*: Young poets have confidence in the opinions of some newspaper reviewers.
10. Change *effect* to *attraction*: The dusty old room has a strange effect on the neighborhood children.

Exact Diction

58. Choose the exact word.

In some circumstances, such as casual conversations between friends, vague language is common. Such remarks as *The play was good*, *He has a new car*, *Rex is writing a book* are suitable for many occasions. At other times it would be more effective to say that the play was *hilarious* (or *absorbing*, or *entertaining*, or *superbly staged*, or *competently acted*). Sometimes it is better to say that he has a *big 1952 yellow Plymouth station wagon*. It may be useful to know that Rex is writing a *domestic comedy* (or a *historical novel*, or a *biography*, or a *cookbook*). Knowing when to use exact words is a part of the art of thinking.

To determine whether words you have used are sufficiently exact there are two tests. First, ask yourself whether a reader will understand precisely what you mean, nothing more, nothing less, and nothing different. Second, look up synonyms for doubtful words in a dictionary (such as one of those listed in the footnote on page 41) and pay particular attention to the distinctions in meaning made by the dictionary. See the exercises following this section and also Exercise *I* on page 326.

The student should always remember that his hearers and readers respond to the words he uses, not the words he should have used; the best examination paper is one which answers exactly and precisely the questions asked. Such pairs of words as *voiceless* and *speechless*, *pale* and *pallid*, *poetry* and *verse*, *ratify* and *confirm* are synonyms, but they are not identical. No one can use such words to the best effect without knowing their shades of meaning.

EXERCISES

A. Study the synonym note under each of the following words in your dictionary: *drag*, *disgrace*, *feeling*, *fault*, *level*. (The synonym note may appear under any one of a group of synonyms, with cross references under the others; for example the *ACD* treats the synonyms of *drag* under *draw*, the *NCD* under *pull*.) After studying these synonyms, substitute more exact words in the following sentences.

1. The bank clerk's infamy is known to only a few people.
2. His greatest vice is his tactlessness.
3. A claw hammer is used to drag nails out of boards.
4. His emotions on the subject are too well known in Congress.
5. Tugging and straining, the horse slowly drew the heavy log down to the river bank.
6. A passion of nostalgia saddened the refugees as they left.
7. The pasture is so smooth that it doesn't drain well.
8. Envy is a foible that makes many people needlessly unhappy.
9. The surface of this light bulb is not level, but it burns.
10. Judson thought of the dishonor which his family would suffer if he should be caught accepting a bribe.

B. Substitute a more exact word for each italicized expression:

1. The butler had committed a *homicide.* (Indicate that the act was unlawful, malicious, and planned.)
2. The woman *trembled* when the door opened. (Indicate that the weather was cold.)
3. He is very *modest.* (Indicate that his modesty is exaggerated.)
4. I have *learned about* a weakness in that argument. (Indicate that the weakness had been concealed.)
5. The boy *obtained* enough money to spend a week at camp. (Indicate that he worked for the money.)
6. His handwriting can be recognized by one *feature.* (Indicate that this characteristic is peculiar to his handwriting.)
7. The judge is a man of *honesty.* (Indicate that he cannot be swayed or bribed.)
8. After a long conference the negotiators *decided* to end the dispute at the next meeting. (Indicate that the decision was positive.)
9. The professor has a *new* solution to the problem. (Indicate that the solution is unusual.)
10. His *theory* has not been precisely defined. (Indicate that the proposed explanation has not been tested.)

C. Substitute one of the following words for each italicized expression in the sentences below: ***belfry, bellicose, chesterfield, con-***

cise, cutting, dialect, dialogue, fraternal, glider, incredible, incredulous, movable, pondered, portable, reflected, stalactites, stalagmites, stethoscope, thermometer.

1. This company produces typewriters *that can be carried about.*
2. The doctor wanted a *thing to measure temperature.*
3. Hanging from the roof of the cave were many *things like icicles.*
4. The old lady sat in a *kind of porch swing like a couch.*
5. They are twins *that are not identical.*
6. The *part of the church enclosing the bell* was blown away.
7. That explorer's story was *hard to believe.*
8. Sarah *weighed* the problem *in her mind* for a week.
9. The argument was not very *sharp and clear-cut.*
10. Good *conversation between two people* is not easy to write.

Emphatic Diction

59. Make your important words emphatic.

One of the best ways to give prominence to important parts of a sentence is to choose emphatic diction. You may improve your wording in several ways:

a. Use words that are intense in meaning. In many sentences *wail* is better than *cry, plummet* better than *drop, demand* better than *ask, jubilant* better than *happy, furious* better than *angry.*

b. Use fresh and striking words, but be careful not to over-use unusual words. In some contexts *front-running* is better than *leading, eye-opening* better than *amazing, black out* better than *obscure.* Be sure that new expressions (which frequently begin as slang) are appropriate to the context.

c. Use specific, exact words; see § 58.

d. Use concrete words rather than abstract words whenever possible. Thus *open-mouthed* is more emphatic than *astonished, dripping* more emphatic than *very wet, fire-engine red* more emphatic than *bright red.*

e. Use simple and direct words rather than pretentious words. Ordinarily, prefer *hearse* to *funeral coach, janitor* to *custodian, beauty* to *pulchritude, fighter* to *pugilist, letter* to *epistle.*

f. Use figurative rather than literal words when appropriate; see § 96.

EXERCISES

A. Make the important words in the following sentences more emphatic (and appropriate to the sentences).

1. The plant was closed by a workers' organized refusal to work.
2. Many, many lives are lost in vehicular traffic mishaps yearly.
3. The motel room was so warm that we could hardly sleep.
4. The headwaiter angrily told the sailor to leave the place.
5. The catcher stooped and said, "Come on, Fred; throw the ball!"
6. There was a highly amusing scene when an intoxicated man tried to catch a hog that went out on the frozen pond.
7. Give me liberty or let me lose my life.
8. All we have to be afraid of is being afraid.
9. 'My child is within the burning structure," said the woman.
10. Citizens, let us replace these dishonest officeholders with reputable men and women of our party!

B. Write a mild ten-sentence editorial suggesting that some public facility or service be improved. Rewrite the editorial, demanding an immediate improvement.

C. Find a more emphatic synonym for each of the following words:

hungry, walk, embezzler, unclear, loud, unhappy, hurry, nervous, poor. diminish.

Triteness

60. Avoid trite (over-used, stale) expressions.

Expressions that have been worn out by excessive use are boring and ineffective. You must learn to distinguish terms like *foot of the mountain, calendar year, fly swatter, to head a committee,* and *drop of water* (which are very common, but not trite) from clichés like *black as pitch, cheap as dirt, genial mentor, goes without saying,* and *last but not least.* The expression *drop of water* does not become trite because it is not a substitute for anything; the expression *thin as a rail* is trite because it is overworked as a substitute for *very thin.* If you will read and listen attentively you will learn to recognize hackneyed, trite expressions. See page 40.

Examples

abreast of the times
birds of a feather
breakneck speed
clear as a bell
cool as a cucumber
dry as dust
fair sex
fit as a fiddle
good as gold
green with envy
hard as nails
heavy as lead
imposing structure
mine of information
nipped in the bud
pure and simple
quick as a flash
raving beauty
sadder but wiser
wee small hours

EXERCISES

A. Make a list of ten trite expressions gathered from newspapers or magazines.

B. Write a paragraph of about fifteen sentences, using as many clichés as possible, then rewrite the paragraph, eliminating all trite expressions.

C. Substitute fresh expressions for all the clichés in the following paragraph:

The blushing bride was put to the acid test when, although green as grass as a cook, she had to prepare a sumptuous repast for her husband's proud parents. The table groaned when they began to partake of the refreshments, but they did justice to the occasion and left her cupboard bare. It goes without saying that she was tired but happy when she proved equal to their expectations and gave a brilliant performance as a budding genius of the culinary department. That night with a sigh of relief she fell into the arms of Morpheus to sleep the sleep of the just.

Fine Writing and Pretentious Writing

61. Avoid affected and unnatural diction.

Young writers frequently pick up high-flown, pretentious expressions from literature and use them inappropriately. This is the same kind of bad taste as wearing an evening dress to a bargain-basement sale. A related fault is the use of artificial, bookish diction. Blunders like *She looks badly*, *somebody's else*, *behind John and I*, and *irregardless* are made by people who have imperfectly learned certain rules about English words. Note the forced elegance in these sentences:

When the lucent orb ascended (meaning *when the sun rose*).

Manifold assistance (meaning *much help*).

Manacled malefactor (meaning *handcuffed criminal*).

He did rightly in coming (meaning *he did right in coming*).

EXERCISE

Revise the fine writing and artificial writing in the following sentences.

1. He is a contender for political office who will be difficult to vanquish in an electoral contest.
2. The nurse informed the child that her parturition occurred in the Commonwealth of Virginia, A.D. 1942.
3. It was her intention to disavow her earlier oration to the youthful newspaper salesman.
4. Most of James' tomes make my paternal parent somnolent.
5. The little boy seemed rapidly to have disappeared.
6. Night had gathered around her her sable robes as my wingless chariot of the air sped through the shoreless waves of silver cloudlets brushed with the silver glint of the moon and myriads of flashing jewels in the dome above.
7. Because concussion from the big guns of the Pacific fleet thirty miles at sea has been cracking plaster, breaking dikes, and assailing residents of Santa Monica, California, the bulldogs of the deep will do their barking henceforth ten miles farther out.
8. The Gods of Fate set before the sterling sons of swat of Jonesville the

golden opportunity — and how ravenously they partook of it is gloriously described in the gripping details of that glittering 4-to-3 triumph Saturday that wound up when Billy Reese, battling behemoth of the day, clubbed a low-hanging liner just out of reach of Bigelow, and Tim Poole came spurting home to do a roundhouse slide and elude Jordan and brought forth a flood of cushions and the few remaining straw hats that had not been hurled to the diamond during previous rallies.

9. Gay costumes were clinging clammily to rain-chilled shoulders; hats were bedraggled — and shoes and fur pieces were waterlogged. Spirits generally were at a pretty low point when the race started, and when Blackwood took the lead with Misstep trailing, a mighty moan rose.

10. But if thy poor pate be incapable of daring, even in expression, then grope dubiously in the dismal swamps of verbiage, and let thy mind's fingers feel after spongy and dropsical words, out of which little sense can be squeezed, and arrange the cozy epithets and unsubstantial substantives into lines, and out of the very depths of pathos thou shalt arise a sort of mud-Venus, and men shall mistake thee for her that rose from the sea, and the coin shall still clink in thy fob, and thou shalt be called Beautiful.

Wordiness

62. Use only enough words to say what you mean.

In our desire to make ourselves clear we often unnecessarily repeat words or ideas. Repetition is good when it is essential to clearness or emphasis, bad when it adds nothing to what has already been said. Using too many words actually retards communication.

Study the following types of wordiness.

a. The use of a word or phrase not grammatically necessary.

Napoleon *he* was one of the world's greatest military geniuses.

Keep off *of* the fence. Where is he *at*?

Whatever he tries to do he does *it* well. (This fault is called *redundancy.*)

b. The repetition of an idea in the same or in different words.

This sort of wordiness is due to a scarcity of ideas and too many words.

It was a clear, starry night, *and not a cloud was to be seen.*

He was an *instrumental* factor in bringing about changes in building, sanitation, lighting, *and* etc.

He was a talkative, loquacious, garrulous old man. (The three adjectives mean the same thing. Choose the strongest adjective and omit the other two. This fault is called *tautology.*)

c. A general expansiveness of style that can be corrected only by entirely rewriting the sentence or paragraph. This type of wordiness (*verbosity*) is often due to the use of syntactical constructions which contain more words than are necessary for the clear and emphatic expression of one's thought, such constructions as:

(1) *Straggling compound sentences:* We watched the fish swimming in the water of the lake, and it was very clear.

(2) *Choppy sentences:* Mark Twain often had a bitter sting in his humor. He did not enjoy life. His stories may be interpreted as satire.

(3) *Impersonal constructions:* There were five of us who went to the theater.

(4) *Piled up adverbs and prepositions:* He lives away back yonder up on Little River.

(5) *Absolute phrase containing a noun which refers to the subject of the main clause:* The garden being very wet, it could not be plowed today.

d. The introduction of trivial, obvious, or irrelevant details that add nothing to the meaning of the sentence and leave nothing to the reader's imagination. (This fault is called *prolixity.*) Select the important details and omit the others. See § 67.

"Is this Mr. Dougan's coat?" the detective asked the trembling maid.

"Yes, that is certainly his coat, the one he wore every Sunday he went into Booneville to attend church. He was a regular church-goer, sir, and always wore this coat, which was made for him by a Booneville tailor and which I always brushed carefully and hung in the small closet every time he took it off."

Caution. In your zeal for conciseness in expression, do not fall into a telegraphic style. Do not let elliptical clauses dangle, and do not omit the subject or the verb of a sentence. There is a vast difference between being economical and being stingy.

EXERCISE

Shorten the following sentences without sacrificing any essential meaning.

1. There is need for temporary housing for people to live in near this dam while it is being constructed.
2. This amendment is irrelevant and off the subject.
3. Whatever additional books are needed for the course, they should be bought in time for them to be catalogued.
4. The new reporter wrote a feature story on the subject of the aardvark which had recently been bought by the zoo.
5. They need some training along the lines of radio repairing.
6. An autobiography of one's life may not be interesting at all.
7. Some of the redundant words are not essential.
8. There was not an empty pew; they were all occupied.
9. Green's letter which came from his publisher mentioned the possibility of selling the story to a movie studio for a picture.
10. This hospital shortage, with respect to which we are all concerned, is a community problem.
11. At that moment the cattle were surrounded on all sides by yelling cow hands.
12. That drink used to cost five cents in the currency of the United States anywhere in the country.
13. On the other hand, however, taking everything into consideration, we do not approve the plan which has been proposed.
14. The station plays classical records of music composed by Bach and Brahms and other classical composers every afternoon at 4.
15. Our broadcast on the air starts at 5. It lasts thirty minutes. Many school children listen. They write us letters about it.
16. There was a poem omitted that I would like to see in every collection of his works. It is "When Lilacs Last in the Dooryard Bloomed."
17. This dictionary has a gazetteer of place names.
18. She stood with arms akimbo and her hands on her hips.
19. Consider the case of General Graydon. He knew the city as a boy when his parents lived there in his childhood.

20. The gear shift lever which changes the gears is mounted on the left hand side of the steering wheel in this car.

Euphony

63. Avoid harsh combinations of sounds.

The word *euphony* is derived from two Greek words meaning "well" and "sound." Euphony is concerned with avoiding unpleasant combinations of sounds. In the writing of prose, it requires (1) the avoidance of rhymes in close succession, such as "day" and "decay," or the use of a too regular meter, (2) the avoidance of unconscious puns, and (3) the avoidance of like sounds in close succession, especially sibilant or hissing sounds, such as *s, sh, z* and endings like *-ing* and *-tion.*

Bad On the boat she wore a coat that was out of style.
His mother thought the airline stewardess was too flighty.
We must turn our attention to the prevention of the convention.

Reading aloud is an excellent means of detecting harsh and unpleasant combinations of sounds.

EXERCISE

Revise the following sentences to avoid any unpleasant combinations of sounds.

1. He tried to sell his cellmate shares in a salt mine.
2. After seeing the prints, the prince was convinced.
3. The publication of new texts strengthened his argument.
4. Do these prophets profit from their own prophecies?
5. Caesar seized the opportunity and began the battle.
6. The governor's investigation of education was a sensation.
7. When the Ku Klux Klan climbed to power, minorities began to worry.
8. You can can vegetables late in the summer and store them.
9. Those swans swim on the pond all day without tiring.
10. The mayor's secretary's indexes were very useful.
11. Her singing was exceptionally supple and spontaneous.
12. Those tame deer? We caught 'em last autumn.

Enlarging the Vocabulary

64. Enlarge your vocabulary for broader understanding and more effective use.

When you begin a new subject in college, such as chemistry or psychology, when you take up a new hobby, such as stamp collecting or chess, or when you get interested in a topic of importance in the news, such as inflation or atomic fission, nobody has to tell you to learn the terminology of the subject. You learn new words and new meanings of familiar words as a part of learning about the subject. This is genuine vocabulary enlargement. But the practice of systematically memorizing new words, regardless of their frequency or importance, is a useless exercise, except possibly to crossword puzzle addicts.

The people who use words most successfully (e.g. students who make high marks on examinations and intelligence tests, experts of many kinds, successful lawyers, executives, speakers, and writers) have usually built up their vocabularies in two ways: (1) by deducing meanings from contexts, asking other people the meanings of new words, or looking up meanings of new words *in order to understand what they read and hear;* and (2) by finding new words and new meanings of familiar words *to make their own language more effective.*

If you read in an editorial, "This unilateral proposal is chauvinistic," you can understand what the writer means only by knowing what the words mean. If you look up *unilateral* and *chauvinistic* you are enlarging your vocabulary. The process is completed when you recognize the words in other contexts and become familiar with them, especially by using them when they fit. Or, if you write, "It is free of lawyers' dialect," then realize that *dialect* is not exactly the word you want, you could look up the synonyms under *dialect* in a dictionary and find *jargon,* which is used to describe the special language of a trade or profession. This is enlarging your vocabulary.

Be sure to find out the meaning of every word that you encounter more than once in your reading; its frequency is an index to its importance. Making lists of new words (especially technical words in college courses) and repeatedly studying the lists will help you improve your vocabulary and thus increase your knowledge of the subjects. Making a habit of looking for more precise synonyms in your own speaking and writing will help you improve your expression.

EXERCISES

A. Make a list of twenty words which you have read or heard but cannot define precisely. Learn the spelling, pronunciation, part of speech, and commonest meanings of each.

B. Pick ten of the words listed in Exercise A and write two sentences for each word to illustrate two different meanings of each of the ten.

C. Repeat Exercise A, listing twenty additional words.

D. Repeat Exercise B, using words from Exercise C.

E. Keep a list of new words which you encounter frequently and turn it over to your instructor when required.

Using a Dictionary

65. Buy a good dictionary and get in the habit of using it systematically. Learn how to find and interpret the information your dictionary provides.

Pocket size and high school dictionaries do not give enough information for use in college work. Your instructor will recommend a "desk" or "college" dictionary.

65a. Get the latest edition of a reputable dictionary. There are several on the market in different price ranges.

College level desk dictionaries:

American College Dictionary. New York: Random House, 1947; Harper and Brothers, 1948. (Abbreviated *ACD*)

Webster's New Collegiate Dictionary. Springfield: G. & C. Merriam Co., 1949. (Abbreviated *NCD*)

Webster's New World Dictionary of the American Language, College Edition. Cleveland: World Publishing Company, 1953. (Abbreviated *NWD*)

Unabridged dictionaries:

Webster's New International Dictionary. Springfield: G. & C. Merriam Co., second edition, 1934.
New Standard Dictionary. New York: Funk and Wagnalls Co., 1947.

For the fullest information about words, consult the historical dictionaries listed on page 241.

65b. Become familiar with the arrangement of material in the dictionaries you use and with the abbreviations used in the word-entries.

This information is given in the *American College Dictionary* on p. xl; in *Webster's New World Dictionary* on pp. ix–xiv; in *Webster's New Collegiate Dictionary* on pp. xviii–xxii. To locate this guide in other dictionaries, consult the table of contents.

65c. Learn how to find any word in the dictionary as quickly as possible.

Use the thumb index if your dictionary has one, and learn how to use the guide words printed in boldface at the top of each page, two to a page. If, for example, you are looking up *genocide* in *NCD,* you can open the volume at p. 338 (where words beginning with G start) by using the thumb index. Then turn pages, looking only at the guide words, until you reach the page with *genial* and *genus* as guide words; since *geno-* comes between *geni-* and *genu-*, you will find *genocide* on this page. This is much faster than looking at the word entries in the columns.

65d. Learn how to find and interpret the information dictionaries give about spelling, syllabication, and compounding.

See also § 48.

Although most English words have only one conventional spelling, many words are correctly spelled in two or more ways. Any spelling entered in a desk dictionary is correct; otherwise the editors would not list it. If one spelling is indicated as "preferred" this means that the editors find it most common in general American usage; see Section 7 on p. xl of *ACD*, or Section 1 on p. xviii of *NCD*. Dictionary editors do not decide which of two spellings is better; they keep close watch on books, magazines, and newspapers, and for the benefit of dictionary users report which spelling is most common in general use.

Since it is necessary to know how to divide words between syllables at the end of a line, dictionaries show how words are broken into syllables in writing. See Section I on p. xl in *ACD* or Section 1 on p. xviii in *NCD* for an explanation of the system. Note that some compounds are written solid, some are written as two words, and some are hyphenated, e.g. *topcoat*, *top hat*, and *top-heavy*.

65e. Learn to find and interpret the information dictionaries give about the pronunciation of words.

Two things about pronunciations in dictionaries should be learned: (1) what a dictionary can tell you about the pronunciation of a word, and (2) how the information is presented.

(1) No dictionary editor presumes to decide how a word ought to be pronounced. He listens carefully to the way people pronounce words and reports the pronunciations actually used by educated people. "The authority of a dictionary is based completely upon the actual speech . . . of the community of effective citizens . . ." (*ACD*, p. xxii). "The function of a pronouncing dictionary is to record as far as possible the pronunciations prevailing in the best present usage, rather than to attempt to dictate what that usage should be. In so far as a dictionary may be known and acknowledged as a faithful recorder and interpreter of such usage, so far and no farther may it be appealed to as an authority" (*NCD*, p. ix).

By listening carefully to the speech of educated people, students of English have found that there are regional differences in the pronunciation of such words as *on*, *vary*, *hurry*, *house*, *dog*, *art*, *ask*, *new*, *third*, and thousands of others. Only by deciding arbitrarily that the pronunciation prevailing in some one section (such as New York, or South Carolina, or Indiana) is "correct" could dictionaries report one pronunciation for such words; since such a decision would not be accepted nationally, the dictionaries show several "correct" pronunciations for many words. Furthermore, many educated people, regardless of their origin, differ in their pronunciation of such words as *ration*, *diphtheria*, *adult*, *February*, *government*, and *envelope;* no dictionary has any basis for choosing just one correct pronunciation for such words. Another factor is the style of speech represented. A word pronounced with emphasis in a formal address may be very different from the same word in ordinary spoken usage. Be sure to find out how your dictionary indicates these differences in pronunciation.

(2) Since English spelling cannot be trusted to indicate the pronunciation of a word, every English dictionary has to spell every word twice: once for writing and once for pronunciation. First, the primary and secondary accent (stress) marks must show the syllable stress. Second, the vowels and consonants must be unmistakably indicated. Study the pronunciation key in your dictionary and learn the sounds represented by diacritic marks, which are interpreted in key words. If you look up *gaoler* you will find *gaol* respelled (jāl); the *j* is pronounced as in *just* (*ACD*) or *joke* (*NCD*), the ā as in *able* (*ACD*) or *ale* (*NCD*), and the *l* as in *low* (*ACD*) or *late* (*NCD*). The stress in *gaoler* is on the first syllable. Thus you learn that the word is pronounced exactly like *jailer*. Do not be bothered by the fact that different people may pronounce some of the key words (e.g. *here*, *out*, *urn*, *burn*) differently; there is no national standard way of pronouncing these words.

Do not worry if your pronunciation of a word is not the "preferred" one. When a word has two pronunciations, one must obviously be printed before the other; if the editors have evidence that one is more common among educated people than the other, they put the more common in first (preferred) position. But any pronunciation that is sufficiently common to be recorded in a desk dictionary is unquestionably "correct." The notion that some pronunciations are inherently better than others is regarded as an old wives' tale by linguistic scientists.

65f. Learn the order in which various dictionaries list the meanings of a word.

The Webster dictionaries list meanings in chronological order;

hence archaic, obsolete, and special meanings may precede common modern meanings. The *ACD* lists the present central meaning first, followed by transferred, special, and out-of-date meanings.

65g. Learn where your dictionary shows the etymology of a word and how to interpret the abbreviations in the etymologies.

The etymology is a condensed history (so far as is known) of a word. It usually shows the earliest known form of a word; rarely is this the "original" form. Since all civilizations have had words long before they began writing, most of our words have come ultimately from prehistoric (hence unrecorded) forms. Knowing the etymology of a word may help you *remember* its spelling, its meaning, and its kinship with other words, but the etymology does not *determine* the spelling or meaning, which are fixed by usage.

65h. Learn where to find and how to interpret the grammatical information your dictionary gives about words, especially the parts of speech, irregular inflectional forms, combinations, and idiomatic phrases.

After the phonetic respelling following a word-entry, you will find the abbreviation the dictionary uses to show what part of speech the word is. Sometimes, as in "run-on" entries, a word used as more than one part of speech will be entered only once, but will be followed by abbreviations of the other parts of speech it represents.

If the plural of a noun, the principal parts of a verb, or the comparison of an adjective is irregular or if the spelling of an inflectional form is exceptional, the irregular form or forms are entered after the abbreviation of the parts of speech.

65i. Learn the meanings of the labels, such as *Colloq., Brit., Geol., Obs.,* which frequently restrict particular spellings, pronunciations, meanings, and usages.

It is very important not to assume that you understand these labels because the words seem familiar. No one can use a modern dictionary such as the *ACD* or *NCD* intelligently without knowing how that particular dictionary defines such terms as *colloquial*.

65j. Learn where your dictionary enters names of real people, fictitious characters, names of places, abbreviations, proofreader's marks, etc.

Examine carefully the front matter preceding the alphabetical word entries, and the back pages following the word entries (including the end papers inside the front and back covers). Many students waste hours looking elsewhere for useful facts which are conveniently presented in desk dictionaries.

EXERCISES IN THE USE OF A DICTIONARY

There is no one book which we can call "the dictionary." Any publisher who desires can publish a dictionary, and several different publishers do. For these exercises do not use a dictionary smaller than a desk or college edition, such as the *NCD*, *NWD*, or *ACD*. Before preparing an exercise, review the appropriate paragraphs in § 65.

A. Spelling.

Determine which of the following spellings are restricted in use and which are not listed in your dictionary:

Adviser, advisor; all right, alright; altho, although; carburator, carburetor; catalog, catalogue; disc, disk; enclose, inclose; gray, grey; hiccup, hiccough; Holinshed, Hollingshead; judgement, judgment; night, nite; Nebuchadnezzar, Nebuchadrezzar; Peking, Peiping; stogie, stogy; tho, though; traveler, traveller.

B. Pronunciation.

How are the different functions (parts of speech) of the following words shown by a difference in accent, in pronunciation, or in both?

Absent, conduct, desert, house, invalid, present, rebel, recall, refuse, subject.

What syllable does your dictionary mark with a primary accent in the following words?

Adult, cement, cigarette, deficit, inquiry, inspect, mischievous, organization, positively, recess, research, theater.

Find the pronunciation or pronunciations of each of the following words:

Again, breeches, chic, data, drama, drought, exquisite, everybody, February, gala, genuine, grievous, hospitable, hundred, irrelevant, quinine, recognize, route, status, victuals.

C. Proper Names and Place Names.

First find where your dictionary enters the names of all real persons and the names of places — whether all in the main vocabulary, all in separate sections, or some in one place and some in another. Then look up the following names, learn the pronunciation of each, and be able to tell who each person was and where each place is:

Asunción, Walter Bagehot, Bikini, Chiang Kai-shek, Eamon De Valera, André Gide, Iran, Munchausen, Niagara, Nietzsche, Poitiers, Saar, Schumann, Seoul, Sinkiang, Teheran, Tel Aviv, Worcester, Yangtze, Zwingli.

Identify each of the following:

Chimera, Dolly Varden, El Dorado, Gambrinus, Ganymede, Hector, Jason, Jonah, Paul Bunyan, Pythias.

List ten place names that are currently in the news; learn the identity, location, and pronunciation of each.

D. Pronunciation.

Copy the phonetic respelling of the following words: *arouse, bevel, claret, atom, porpoise, supreme,* and *datum.* Read the discussion of the symbols used to indicate the unstressed vowel in your dictionary (p. xxii in the *ACD*, pp. x–xvii in *NCD*, pp. x–xi in *NWD*). Learn the meaning and use of the word *schwa.*

Read the discussion of styles of pronunciation (normal and formal) in the front pages of your dictionary. Make a list of ten words which would be pronounced one way in a sermon, another way in conversation.

E. Meaning.

Write out what you think each of the words in the next paragraph means. Be sure to define the words in the form of a clear statement instead of using synonyms. Then compare your definition with that given in your dictionary. A word like *present, substitute,* or *insult* may be entered more than once in your dictionary or followed by two or more abbreviations to show that it is used as more than one part of speech. You need to define only one function (part of speech) of each word below.

Armistice, catharsis, flair, inflammable, livid, fascism, moron, purvey, manslaughter, tortuous.

Find what label or labels your dictionary attaches to each of the words in the next paragraph or to certain of its meanings. Copy the words or definitions to which labels are attached and be able to explain the meaning of each label you find. See Section 5 on p. xl of *ACD*, pp. xviii–xx in *NCD*, V. B., pp. xiii–xiv in *NWD*.

Carry (verb), *clarabella, cute, enthuse, highjacker, low-down, pack* (meaning "to carry"), *pack* (noun), *traumatic, worm* (verb).

F. Meaning.

List ten strange or unfamiliar words that you have found in any book or magazine article. Try to define each word from the context in which it occurs. Then compare your definition with the definitions given in a good modern dictionary.

G. Etymology.

Turn to the specimen dictionary pages (328–331 in this book) and find from what languages at least ten words for which etymologies are given were derived. Be sure to distinguish between words which came into English directly from a foreign source and those which came through one or more intermediate languages.

Look up the etymology and earliest known meaning of the following words, checking the words whose etymology helps you remember the pronunciation, spelling, or meaning:

Blizzard, bloomer, carnival, cello, cliché, coupé, curfew, educate, flatter, hazard, insulin, jalopy, parasite, pediatrics, podiatrist, quarantine, smash, spaghetti, trite, vernacular.

Explain why your dictionary has more than one etymology for each of the following forms: *base, dumb, firm, junk, mush.*

Does your dictionary give the etymology *before* the first definition or meaning of a word or *after* the last definition? What is the relation between the position of the etymology and the order in which dictionaries give the various meanings of a word?

H. Prefixes and Suffixes.

Copy the following words and draw a slanting line between the base (root or stem) and the prefix or suffix: *trans/late, re/lat/ion, mean/ness.* Then look up each prefix and suffix and determine from what language it was derived and what it means.

Antecedent, circumscribe, contradict, diameter, export, glorious, holiness, imposition, intercollegiate, kingship, laryngitis, laudable, megaphone, orphanage, patriarch, precedent, produce, spinster, subconsciousness, tantalize.

I. Synonyms.

Look up the following words in your dictionary and find which have synonym studies at the end of the entry: *broad, care, close, deny, face, foreign, forward, idiomatic, kind, material.* If a word does not have a synonym study (or a cross reference to the synonyms under another word), explain why.

List ten trite words (for suggestions see § 60) and find as many synonyms as you can for each. Use five of the words you discover in sentences which show that you understand the exact meanings.

J. Parts of Speech.

Consult your dictionary and answer the following questions about each word listed below. Is the word used as more than one part of speech? How many times is the word listed in your dictionary? If it is listed only once, what different abbreviations, such as *n.*, *v.*, *adv.*, etc., do you find in the paragraph containing the word? Are the different functions of the word revealed by a difference in accent or pronunciation?

Absent, alternate, effect, duplicate, English, lie, near, round, set.

K. Irregular Inflectional Forms.

Consult your dictionary and answer the following questions about each word listed in the paragraphs below. Does your dictionary give the plural or plurals of nouns or the second and third principal parts of verbs? Does it give the comparative and superlative forms of some adjectives? For what kinds of words is such information given? Are any of these double plurals or double verb or adjective forms labeled? Does your dictionary point out any difference in meaning between the two plurals or two sets of principal parts?

Nouns: *bandit, attorney-general, goose, house, brother, sheaf, agendum, index, ellipsis, thesis, billet-doux, fish, opus, axis, oats.*

Adjectives: *bad, foremost, old, swift, much, far, economical.*

Verbs: *bid, have, dare, dive, drink, learn, leap, burn, sit, go.*

L. Idioms, Phrases, and Combinations.

Consult an unabridged dictionary under the first word or the key word in each of the following idioms and combinations, and after each write the meaning your dictionary gives:

By and large, gone for good, head over heels, on all fours, spic and span.

M. Capitals.

Consult your dictionary to determine which of the following words (1) are always capitalized, or (2) are capitalized in certain meanings but not in others:

Amazon, arabic, bible, Dutch, English, italic, madras, ottoman, southern.

N. Abbreviations and Symbols.

Where does your dictionary list commonly used abbreviations, signs, and symbols? Tell what each of the following abbreviations, signs, or symbols stands for:

A.A.A., CIO, dial., e.g., i.e., Pharm., Q. E. D., ℞, £, *c/o.*

O. Foreign Words and Phrases.

Find out whether your dictionary lists foreign words and phrases in the main vocabulary, in a special section, or common foreign phrases in the main vocabulary and rarer phrases in a special section. Then learn the pronunciation and the meaning of the following foreign expressions:

Cherchez la femme, nolo contendere, reductio ad absurdum, Floréal, lusus naturae, honi soit qui mal y pense.

P. Write a short paper explaining why some dictionaries supplement their verbal definitions with illustrations. Cite examples in your dictionary.

mo'sey (mō'zĭ), *v. i.;* MO'SEYED (-zĭd); MO'SEY·ING. *Slang.* To go or move in a strolling, shuffling manner; esp., to depart.

Mos'lem (mŏz'lĕm; -lĕm; mŏs'-), *n.; pl.* MOSLEMS (-lĕmz; -lĕmz) *or collectively* MOSLEM. [Ar. *muslim* a believer in the faith established by Mohammed, fr. *aslama* to surrender (to God).] A Mussulman; an orthodox Mohammedan. — **Mos'lem,** *adj.*

Mos'lem·ism (mŏz'lĕm·ĭz'm; mŏs'-), *n.* Mohammedanism.

mosque (mŏsk), *n.* Also **mosk** [F. *mosquée*, fr. It., fr. Ar. *masjid*, fr. *sajada* to bow down, adore.] An Islamic place of public religious worship.

Mosque of Omar at Jerusalem.

mos·qui'to (mŭs·kē'tō), *n.; pl.* -TOES (-tōz). [Sp., fr. *mosca* fly, fr. L. *musca.*] **1.** Any of certain insects (order Diptera, family Culicidae), having, in the females, needlelike organs in the proboscis with which they puncture the skin of animals to suck their blood. Certain mosquitoes are the only transmitting agents of various diseases, as malaria and yellow fever. See AËDES, ANOPHELES, CULEX, WIGGLER, WRIGGLER. **2.** [*pl.* -TOES or -TOS] A light, speedy British twin-engined long-range bomber.

mosquito boat. = MOTOR TORPEDO BOAT. See PT BOAT, *Illust.*

mosquito net. A net, screen, or curtain for excluding mosquitoes. — **mosquito netting.**

moss (mŏs; 74), *n.* [AS. *mos* a marshy place.] **1.** *Chiefly Scot.* A bog; swamp; esp., a peat bog. **2. a** Any bryophytic plant (class Musci) characterized by the small, leafy, often tufted stems bearing sex organs at the tips. **b** A clump of these plants. **3.** Hence: **a** Any of numerous mosslike lichens, as Iceland *moss*, rock *moss*, etc. See ICELAND MOSS. **b** Any of several pteridophytic plants of a mosslike habit, as club mosses (genus *Lycopodium*). See CLUB MOSS. — *v. t.* To cover or overgrow with moss.

moss agate. *Mineral.* A variety of agate, containing brown, black, or green mosslike markings.

moss'back' (mŏs'băk'; 74), *n.* *Slang, Chiefly U.S.* An ultraconservative person; a fogy.

moss'bunk'er (-bŭngk'ẽr), *n.* [D. *marsbanker.*] The menhaden.

moss'–grown', *adj.* Overgrown with moss; antiquated.

moss hag. *Scot.* A pit or slough in a peat bog.

‖**mos'so** (môs'sō), *adj.* [It., past part. of *muovere* to move.] *Music.* Literally, moved; rapid; — in directions; as, ***meno mosso,*** less rapid.

moss pink. A low, tufted plant (*Phlox subulata*) of the phlox family, of the eastern United States, with pink or white flowers.

moss rose. A variety (*Rosa centifolia muscosa*) of rose having a mossy calyx and flower stalk.

mother church. **2.** Derived from or as from one's mother; native; as, one's *mother* tongue.

Moth'er Car'ey's chick'en (kâr'ĭz). Any of several species of small petrels, esp. the stormy petrel (which see).

Mother Goose. **1.** The feigned narrator of a volume of fairy tales by Charles Perrault, first published in 1697. **2.** The pretended writer of the ancient nursery rhymes known orig. as *Mother Goose's Melodies* but usually entitled in modern editions **Mother Goose's Nursery Rhymes,** first published in London about 1760.

moth'er·hood (mŭth'ẽr·ho͝od), *n.* **1.** State of being a mother; character, qualities, or spirit of a mother. **2.** A body of mothers; as, the *motherhood* of the nation.

Moth'er Hub'bard (hŭb'ẽrd). **1.** The subject of a well-known nursery rhyme. **2.** A type of loose full gown worn by women.

moth'er–in–law', *n.; pl.* MOTHERS-IN-LAW. **a** Mother of one's husband or wife. **b** A stepmother; — now not in standard use.

moth'er·land' (mŭth'ẽr·lănd'), *n.* **a** A country regarded as a place of origin. **b** = FATHERLAND.

moth'er·less, *adj.* Destitute of a mother.

moth'er·ly (mŭth'ẽr·lĭ), *adj.* Like, suitable for, or characteristic of a mother. — **moth'er·li·ness,** *n.*

Mother of God. *Eccl.* The title of the Virgin Mary, sanctioned by the Council of Ephesus (A.D. 431), in opposition to the Nestorians.

moth'er–of–pearl', *n.* The hard pearly internal layer of several kinds of shells, esp. of pearl oysters, river mussels, and the abalone shells; nacre. — **moth'er–of–pearl',** *adj.*

Moth'er's Day (mŭth'ẽrz). *U.S. & Can.* A day appointed for the honoring of motherhood and the loving remembrance of one's mother, — observed on the second Sunday in May, or in schools the preceding Friday.

mother tongue. **1.** One's native language. **2.** A language from which another language originates.

mother wit. Natural or native wit or intelligence.

moth'er·wort' (mŭth'ẽr·wûrt'), *n.* A bitter Old World mint (*Leonurus cardiaca*) with dentate, wedge-shaped leaves and axillary whorls of small purple flowers.

moth'y (mŏth'ĭ), *adj.;* MOTH'I·ER (-ĭ·ẽr); MOTH'I·EST. Full of moths.

mo·tif' (mō·tēf'), *n.* [F.] **1.** In literature and the fine arts, a salient feature of a work; esp., the theme, or dominant feature. **2.** *Music.* = MOTIVE, *n.*, 3.

mo'tile (mō'tĭl; 56), *adj.* [See MOTIVE.] *Biol.* Exhibiting, or capable of, spontaneous movement. — *n.* *Psychol.* One whose mental imagery takes the form of inner feelings of action, as muscular movements, etc. Cf. AUDILE, VISUALIZER. — **mo·til'i·ty** (mō·tĭl'ĭ·tĭ), *n.*

mo'tion (mō'shŭn), *n.* [OF., fr. L. *motio*, fr. *movere, motum* to move.] **1.** Act, process, or instance of changing place or position; movement; — opp. to *rest.* **2.** Action of a machine with respect to the relative movement of its parts. **3.** Mental act, or impulse to any action; inclination. **4.** A proposal looking to action; esp., a formal proposal made in a deliberative assembly. **5.** *pl.* Movements; actions. **6.** *Obs.* A puppet show or puppet. **7.** *Law.* An application

freebooter. — **moss′troop′er·y,** *n.* — **moss′troop′ing,** *n. & adj.*

moss′y (mŏs′ĭ; 74), *adj.;* MOSS′I·ER (-ĭ·ẽr); MOSS′I·EST. **1.** Overgrown or edged with moss or something like moss; as, *mossy* trees. **2.** Resembling moss; as, *mossy* green. — **moss′i·ness,** *n.*

most (mōst), *adj.; superl.* of MORE. [AS. *mǣst.*] **1.** Greatest in number, quantity, size, or extent; — often as superlative of *many, much.* **2.** Greatest in degree. **3.** Nearly all; as, *most* men. — *adv.* **1.** In the greatest degree or to the greatest extent; — used with an adjective or adverb to form the superlative degree; as, *most* wicked; *most* rapidly. **2.** [Short for *almost.*] *Colloq. & Dial.* Almost; nearly. — *n.* **1.** The greatest or largest quantity, amount, etc. **2. a** The greatest number or part; preponderating portion. **b** Most persons; as, cleverer than *most.* **3.** The utmost value, degree, result, etc.

-most (-mōst; *in familiar words also* -mŭst). [AS. *-mest.*] A suffix forming superlatives of adjectives and adverbs, as in hind*most*, fore*most*, etc.

most′ly (mōst′lĭ), *adv.* For the greatest part; chiefly.

mot, *n.* [F. See MOTTO.] **1.** (*pron.* mō) A pithy or witty saying. **2.** (*pron.* mŏt) *Archaic.* A note of a bugle.

mote (mōt), *v. i.; past tense* MOSTE (mōst). [See MUST, *v.*] *Archaic.* May; might.

mote, *n.* [AS. *mot.*] A small particle, as of floating dust.

mo·tel′ (mō·tĕl′), *n.* [From *mo*torists' ho*tel.*] An inn or group of cabins along a highway, in which motorists may spend the night.

mo·tet′ (mō·tĕt′), *n.* [F., dim. of *mot* word. See MOTTO.] *Music.* A polyphonic choral composition on a sacred text, usually without instrumental accompaniment.

moth (mŏth; 74), *n.; pl.* MOTHS (mŏthz; mŏths). [AS. *moththe.*] **1.** Any of several small yellowish or buff tineid insects (esp. *Tinea pellionella*) whose larvae eat woolen goods, furs, feathers, etc.; — called also CLOTHES MOTH. **2.** Any of certain insects (order Lepidoptera), distinguished from butterflies by generally stouter bodies, smaller wings, less brilliant coloring, and usually nocturnal habits. In the larval or caterpillar state most moths feed upon plants, many being destructive (see GYPSY MOTH, BROWN-TAIL MOTH, etc.), and few (see SILKWORM) of any direct use to man. See PUPA, SILKWORM, *Illusts.*

moth ball. A ball, formerly of camphor, now of naphthalene, for keeping moths from clothing.

moth′–eat′en, *part. adj.* Eaten into by moths; like moth-eaten cloth. — **moth′–eat′,** *v. t.*

moth′er (mŭth′ẽr), *n.* [Prob. after *mother* parent, fr. MD. *modder* filth, mud.] A slimy membrane composed of yeast cells and bacteria which develops on the surface of alcoholic liquids undergoing acetous fermentation. It is added to wine or cider to produce vinegar. Called also **mother of vinegar.**

moth′er, *n.* [AS. *mōdor.*] **1. a** A female parent, esp. one of the human race. **b** Ancestress. **2.** That which has produced or nurtured anything; source of birth or origin. **3. a** A woman in authority or dignity like a mother's; — used specif. as a title of a woman head of a religious house; as, a *mother* superior. **b** An old or elderly woman, esp. of humble station; as, *Mother* Hubbard. **4.** Maternal tenderness or affection. — *v. t.* **1.** To adopt or care for as a child. **2.** To acknowledge that one is the mother of. — *adj.* **1. a** That is a mother or a mother's; as, *mother* love. **b** Bearing the relation of a mother; as, a

Melodic progression, as a change of pitch in the successive tones of a voice part. — *v. i.* To make a significant movement or gesture, as with the hand. — *v. t.* To direct or invite by a motion.

mo′tion·less, *adj.* Without motion; unable to move. — **mo′tion·less·ly,** *adv.* — **mo′tion·less·ness,** *n.*

motion picture. a A series of pictures, usually photographs taken with a **mo′tion–pic′ture cam′er·a** presented in very rapid succession, with objects represented in successive positions slightly changed, and producing, because of the persistence of vision, the optical effect of a continuous picture in which the objects move. **b** Specif., a photoplay. A machine for projecting motion pictures on a screen is a **mo′tion–pic′ture pro·jec′tor** (or *cinematograph*). — **mo′tion–pic′ture,** *adj.*

motion sickness. Nausea, dizziness, etc., caused by motion, as of an airplane, automobile, or ship.

mo′ti·vate (mō′tĭ·vāt), *v. t.* To provide with a motive; to impel; incite. — **mo′ti·va′tion** (-vā′shŭn), *n.*

mo′tive (mō′tĭv), *n.* [OF. *motif,* fr. ML. *motivus* moving, fr. L. *movere, motum,* to move.] **1.** That within the individual, rather than without, which incites him to action; any idea, need, emotion, or organic state that prompts to an action. **2.** A theme or dominant feature, as of a literary composition; a motif. **3.** *Music.* The theme or subject; a leading phrase or passage which is reproduced and varied through the course of a composition or a movement.

Syn. **Motive, spring, impulse, incentive, inducement, spur, goad** mean a stimulus to action. **Motive** implies any emotion or desire operating on one's will and driving it to action; **spring** (or more commonly *springs*), the basic motive, often unrecognized; **impulse,** an impetus or driving power either as given by another or arising in oneself; **incentive,** a motive developed through extraneous influences; **inducement,** one prompted by enticements or allurements; **spur,** one that stimulates the mind or increases energy or ardor; **goad,** one that keeps one going even in spite of drawbacks.

— *adj.* **a** *Now Rare.* Moving or tending to move to action. **b** Relating to motion or the causing of motion; as, *motive* power. **c** Pertaining to a motive or motives.

— *v. t.* **1.** To prompt or incite by or as by a motive or motives. **2.** To connect with the guiding or controlling idea of a work, as in art, literature, etc.

motive power. Any power, as water, steam, wind, electricity, etc., used to impart motion to machinery.

mo·tiv′i·ty (mō·tĭv′ĭ·tĭ), *n.* The power of moving or producing motion; available energy.

‖**mot juste** (mō′ zhüst′). [F.] The exactly right word; precisely expressive phrasing.

mot′ley (mŏt′lĭ), *adj.;* MOT′LEY·ER; MOT′LEY·EST. [ME. *motteley.*] **1.** Variegated in color; parti-colored. **2.** Hence: **a** Diverse; heterogeneous. **b** Composed of varying parts; discordantly composite. **3.** Wearing motley. — *n.* **1.** A woolen fabric of mixed colors, made in England between the 14th and 17th centuries. **2.** A garment of such cloth; the characteristic dress of the professional fool. **3.** *Obs.* A jester; fool. **4.** Any mixture, esp. an incongruous mixture, as of colors.

mot′mot (mŏt′mŏt), *n.* Any of numerous jaylike nonpasserine birds (subfamily Momotinae) confined to tropical forests from Mexico to Brazil. The color is chiefly green and the tail is long and peculiarly shaped.

en·cour·age (ĕn kûr′ĭj), *v.t.*, **-aged, -aging. 1.** to inspire with courage, spirit, or confidence. **2.** to stimulate by assistance, approval, etc. [ME *encorage(n)*, t. OF: m. *encoragier*, der. *en-* EN-[1] + *corage* COURAGE] —**en·cour′ag·er,** *n.* —**en·cour′ag·ing·ly,** *adv.* —**Syn. 1.** inspirit, embolden, hearten. **2.** urge, abet, second; foment, promote, advance, foster. —**Ant. 1.** dishearten.

en·cour·age·ment (ĕn kûr′ĭj mənt), *n.* **1.** act of encouraging. **2.** state of being encouraged. **3.** that which encourages. —**Ant. 1.** disapproval. **2.** depression.

en·crim·son (ĕn krĭm′zən), *v.t.* to make crimson.

en·cri·nite (ĕn′krə nīt′), *n.* **1.** a fossil crinoid. **2.** any crinoid. [f. EN-[2] + m.s. Gk. *krínon* lily + -ITE[1]]

en·croach (ĕn krōch′), *v.i.* **1.** to advance beyond proper limits; make gradual inroads. **2.** to trespass upon the property or rights of another, esp. stealthily or by gradual advances. [ME *encroche(n)*, t. OF: m. *encrochier*, der. *en-* EN-[1] + *croc* hook] —**en·croach′er,** *n.* —**Syn. 1, 2.** See **trespass.**

en·croach·ment (ĕn krōch′mənt), *n.* **1.** act of encroaching. **2.** anything taken by encroaching.

en·crust (ĕn krŭst′), *v.t.* incrust. —**en′crus·ta′tion,** *n.*

en·cum·ber (ĕn kŭm′bər), *v.t.* **1.** to impede or hamper; retard; embarrass. **2.** to block up or fill with what is obstructive or superfluous. **3.** to burden with obligations, debt, etc. Also, **incumber.** [ME *encombre(n)*, t. OF: m. *encombrer*, der. *en-* EN-[1] + *combre* barrier (g. LL *combrus*, t. Gallic: m. *comberos* a bringing together)] —**Syn. 3.** oppress, overload.

en·cum·brance (ĕn kŭm′brəns), *n.* **1.** that which encumbers; something useless or superfluous; a burden; a hindrance. **2.** a dependent person, esp. a child. **3.** *Law.* a burden or claim on property, as a mortgage. Also, **incumbrance.**

en·cum·branc·er (ĕn kŭm′brən sər), *n.* *Law.* one who holds an encumbrance.

-ency, a noun suffix, equivalent to **-ence,** as in *consistency, dependency, exigency.* [t. L: m.s. *-entia*]

ency., encyclopedia. Also, **encyc.**

en·cyc·li·cal (ĕn sĭk′lə kəl, -sī′klə-), *n.* **1.** a letter addressed by the Pope to all the bishops of the world in communion with the Holy See. —*adj.* **2.** intended for wide or general circulation; general. Also, **en·cyc′lic.** [f. s. LL *encyclicus* (r. L *encyclios*, t. Gk.: m. *enkýklios* circular, general) + -AL[1]]

en·cy·clo·pe·di·a (ĕn sī′klə pē′dĭ ə), *n.* **1.** a work treating separately various topics from all branches of knowledge, usually in alphabetical arrangement. **2.** a work treating exhaustively one art or science, esp. in articles arranged alphabetically; a cyclopedia. **3.** (*cap.*) the French work edited by Diderot and D'Alembert.

end[2] (ĕnd), *v.t.* *Now Dial.* to put (wheat, hay, etc.) into a barn, stack, etc. [? var. of *inn* to lodge, der. INN]

end-, var. of **endo-,** before vowels, as in *endamoeba.*

en·dam·age (ĕn dăm′ĭj), *v.t.*, **-aged, -aging.** damage.

en·da·moe·ba (ĕn′də mē′bə), *n.* a protozoan, genus *Endamoeba*, one species of which causes dysentery and liver abscess. Also, **en′da·me′ba.** [f. END- + AMOEBA]

en·dan·ger (ĕn dān′jər), *v.t.* to expose to danger; imperil. —**en·dan′ger·ment,** *n.*

end-blown (ĕnd′blōn′), *adj.* (of a flute) having a mouthpiece at the end of the tube, so that the player's breath is directed into the instrument.

en·dear (ĕn dĭr′), *v.t.* **1.** to make dear, esteemed, or beloved: *he endeared himself to his mother.* **2.** *Obs.* to make costly. —**en·dear′ing·ly,** *adv.*

en·dear·ment (ĕn dĭr′mənt), *n.* **1.** act of endearing. **2.** state of being endeared. **3.** action or utterance manifesting affection; a caress or an affectionate term.

en·deav·or (ĕn dĕv′ər), *v.i.* **1.** to exert oneself to do or effect something; make an effort; strive. —*v.t.* **2.** to attempt; try: *he endeavors to keep things nice about his place.* —*n.* **3.** a strenuous effort; an attempt. Also, *Brit.*, **en·deav′our.** [ME *endeavor(en)*, der. EN-[1] + DEVOIR. Cf. F *en devoir* in duty] —**en·deav′or·er,** *n.* —**Syn. 1, 2.** struggle, labor, essay, undertake, seek, aim. See **try. 3.** exertion, struggle, essay. See **effort.**

en·dem·ic (ĕn dĕm′ĭk), *adj.* **1.** Also, **en·dem′i·cal.** peculiar to a particular people or locality, as a disease. —*n.* **2.** an endemic disease. [f. s. Gk. *éndēmos* belonging to a people + -IC] —**en·dem′i·cal·ly,** *adv.*

En·der·by Land (ĕn′dər bĭ), a part of the coast of Antarctica, in the central part of the **Enderby Quadrant** (the quadrant below Africa): discovered, 1831.

en·der·mic (ĕn dûr′mĭk), *adj.* acting through the skin, as a medicine. [f. EN-[2] + DERM(A) + -IC]

en dés·ha·bil·lé (äN dĕ zȧ bē yĕ′), *French.* in dishabille or undress.

En·di·cott (ĕn′dĭ kət, -kŏt′), *n.* **John,** 1588?–1665, colonial governor of Massachusetts, born in England. Also **En′de·cott.**

end·ing (ĕn′dĭng), *n.* **1.** a bringing or coming to an end; termination; close. **2.** the final or concluding part. **3.** death. **4.** *Gram.* an inflexional morpheme at the end of a word form, as *-s* in *cuts.* **5.** (in popular use) any final word part, as the *-ow* of *widow.* [ME; OE *endung*]

en·dive (ĕn′dīv, äN′dēv; *Fr.* äN dēv′), *n.* **1.** *U.S.* a plant, *Cichorium endivia*, of two main types, one with finely divided, much curled leaves and one with broad, fleshy leaves, both used for salads. **2.** *Brit.* chicory (defs. 1, 2). [ME, t. F, t. ML: m.s. *endivia*, t. MGk.: m. *endívi*, t. L: m. *intibus*, *intibum*]

vanced or radical character. Also, **en·cy/clo·pae/di·a.** [t. LL, t. pseudo-Gk. (occurring in mss. of Quintilian, Pliny, and Galen): m. *enkyklopaideía*, for *enkýklios paideía* general education, complete round or course of learning. See ENCYCLIC, CYCLOPEDIA]

en·cy·clo·pe·dic (ĕn sī/klə pē/dĭk), *adj.* pertaining to or of the nature of an encyclopedia; relating to all branches of knowledge. Also, **en·cy/clo·pae/dic, en·cy/clo·pe/di·cal.**

en·cy·clo·pe·dism (ĕn sī/klə pē/dĭz əm), *n.* **1.** encyclopedic learning. **2.** (*often cap.*) the doctrines and influence of the Encyclopedists. Also, **en·cy/clo·pae/dism.**

en·cy·clo·pe·dist (ĕn sī/klə pē/dĭst), *n.* **1.** a compiler of or contributor to an encyclopedia. **2.** (*often cap.*) one of the collaborators in the French Encyclopedia. Also, **en·cy/clo·pae/dist.**

en·cyst (ĕn sĭst/), *v.t.*, *v.i.* *Biol.* to enclose or become enclosed in a cyst. **—en·cyst/ment, en/cys·ta/tion,** *n.*

end[1] (ĕnd), *n.* **1.** an extremity of anything that is longer than it is broad: *the end of a street, rope, rod, etc.* **2.** an extreme or furthermost part of anything extended in space: *the ends of the earth.* **3.** anything that bounds an object at one of its extremities; a limit. **4.** act of coming to an end; termination. **5.** the concluding part. **6.** a purpose or aim: *to gain one's ends.* **7.** the object for which a thing exists: *the happiness of the people is the end of government.* **8.** issue or result. **9.** termination of existence; death. **10.** a cause of death, destruction, or ruin. **11.** a remnant or fragment: *odds and ends.* **12.** *Football, etc.* either of the players at the ends of the forward line. **13. at loose ends,** in disorder. **14. make both ends meet,** to keep within one's means. **—***v.t.* **15.** to bring to an end, or natural conclusion. **16.** to put an end to by force. **17.** to form the end of. **—***v.i.* **18.** to come to an end; terminate; cease: *he ended by settling down.* **19.** to issue or result: *extravagence ends in want.* [ME and OE *ende*, c. G *ende*. See AND] **—end/er,** *n.*
—Syn. 3. tip, bound, limit, terminus. **4.** END, CLOSE, CONCLUSION, FINISH, OUTCOME refer to the termination of something. END implies a natural termination, completion of an action or process, or attainment of purpose: *the end of a day, of a race, to some good end.* CLOSE implies a planned rounding off of something in process: *the close of a conference.* CONCLUSION suggests a decision or arrangement: *all evidence leads to this conclusion, the conclusion of peace terms.* FINISH emphasizes completion of something begun: *a fight to the finish.* OUTCOME suggests the issue of something which was in doubt: *the outcome of a game.* **5.** finale, peroration. **6.** See **aim. 8.** outcome, consequence. **9.** destruction, extermination, annihilation, ruin. **15.** conclude, finish, complete, terminate. **16.** close, stop, discontinue. **—Ant. 4.** beginning, start. **15.** begin.

clusion; boundless; infinite; interminable; incessant. **2.** made continuous, as by joining the two ends of a single length: *an endless chain or belt.* **—end/less·ly,** *adv.* **—end/less·ness,** *n.* **—Syn. 1.** limitless, illimitable, immeasurable, unending, unceasing, continuous, continual, perpetual, everlasting. See **eternal.**

end·long (ĕnd/lông/, -lŏng/), *adv.* *Archaic or Dial.* **1.** lengthwise. **2.** on end. [ME *endelong*, r. OE *andlang* ALONG]

end man, 1. a man at one end of a row or line. **2.** a man at either end of the line of performers of a minstrel troupe, who plays on the bones or tambourine and carries on humorous dialogue with the interlocutor.

end·most (ĕnd/mōst/), *adj.* furthest.

endo-, a word element meaning "internal," as in *endocardial.* Also, **end-.** [t. Gk., comb. form of *éndon* within]

en·do·blast (ĕn/dō blăst/), *n.* *Embryol.* the prospective endoderm; the blastemic cells which are to form the endoderm. **—en/do·blas/tic,** *adj.*

en·do·car·di·al (ĕn/dō kär/dĭ əl), *adj.* **1.** within the heart; intracardiac. **2.** pertaining to the endocardium.

en·do·car·di·tis (ĕn/dō kär dī/tĭs), *n.* *Pathol.* inflammation of the endocardium. [NL; f. ENDOCARD(IUM) + -ITIS] **—en·do·car·dit·ic** (ĕn/dō kär dĭt/ĭk), *adj.*

en·do·car·di·um (ĕn/dō kär/dĭ əm), *n.* *Anat.* the delicate serous membrane which lines the cavities of the heart and aids in forming the valves by duplication. [NL: f. *endo-* ENDO- + *-cardium* (comb. form repr. Gk. *kardía* heart)]

en·do·carp (ĕn/dō kärp/), *n.* *Bot.* the inner layer of a pericarp, as the stone of certain fruits.

Fruit of peach
A, Endocarp; B, Epicarp; C, Mesocarp; ABC, Pericarp

en·do·cen·tric construction (ĕn/dō sĕn/trĭk), a grammatical construction which contains as one of its immediate constituents a word or other form (called the *head*) which belongs to the same form class and may play the same grammatical role as the construction itself (opposed to *exocentric construction*). Example: *cold water* (having the noun *water* as head), or *good work* where both constituents as a unit function as the word *work* would alone.

en·do·crine (ĕn/dō krīn/, -krĭn), *n.* **1.** an endocrine gland or organ. **2.** an internal secretion. **—***adj.* **3.** of or pertaining to the endocrine glands or their secretions: *endocrine function.* [f. ENDO- + m.s. Gk. *krínein* separate] **—en·do·cri·nal** (ĕn/dō krī/nəl), **en·do·crin·ic** (ĕn/dō krĭn/ĭk), **en·doc·ri·nous** (ĕn dŏk/rə nəs), *adj.*

b., blend of, blended; c., cognate with; d., dialect, dialectal; der., derived from; f., formed from; g., going back to; m., modification of; r., replacing; s., stem of; t., taken from; ?, perhaps. See the full key on inside cover.

Glossary of Diction

66. Look up in the Glossary any expression which you are uncertain about. Be sure to read the following introduction before trying to use the Glossary.

The most extensive glossary of diction is a good modern dictionary. But dictionaries have to include so many words and phrases that they cannot devote much space to any one. This glossary lists a few expressions that bother standard English speakers and writers, with comments on the usage of these expressions.

When expressions are labeled nonstandard, dialect, standard, provincial, jargon, informal, formal, or slang, look up the discussion of the label in sections 50–56 (pages 295–303) or on pages 91–94. Nonstandard diction is out of place in college writing (except in dialogue to connote certain kinds of speakers); therefore you should immediately break the habit of using in writing any expression marked *nonstandard* in the Glossary. Breaking such a habit is not hard and it does not require special talent. Simply practice using the standard form — over and over and over — just as you would correct a fault in your golf swing or swimming stroke.

Functional varieties, such as colloquial, slang, and conversational, are harder to handle. Your dictionary can tell you that *crooked* (meaning dishonest) is colloquial, but the dictionary cannot tell you whether or not a colloquial expression is appropriate in a particular paper you are writing. A serious newspaper editorial on ethics in government might include the phrase *crooked politicians* if the diction of the editorial included other colloquial expressions such as *grafters*, *influence-peddling*, *racketeer*, *shenanigans*, and *insiders*. On the other hand, a letter to your college newspaper (where informal language is normal) on the honor system might be very dignified, using terms like *integrity*, *defraud*, and *probity;* here *dishonest* would be better than *crooked*. A colloquial expression in a formal discourse is like serving a cola drink in bottles at a formal dinner party. On the other hand, colloquial expressions are appropriate and effective when the situation calls for relaxed, unpretentious language. Neither this textbook nor any other can tell you when to use or not to use any particular expression; all the textbook can do is help you become aware of the complex implications and suggestions of certain words.

The Glossary is based on recent editions of reputable dictionaries, standard books on the English language, special studies of particular expressions published in books and articles, and careful observation of effective modern writing. The short bibliography of usage below will help you supplement the Glossary which follows it.

A Short Bibliography of Usage

The most convenient and condensed source of information on a question of usage is a good recent dictionary (see pp. 318–319). The sources listed below present more detailed discussions, and several of them are concerned with principles and methods of deciding questions of usage.

American Speech. New York: Columbia University Press, 1925– .

A quarterly journal containing articles, reviews, and several regular departments.

College English. Chicago: University of Chicago Press, 1939– .

The organ of the college section of the National Council of Teachers of English. Monthly October–May.

A regular department on usage, "Current English Forum," is found in *College English* and in the *English Journal.*

Curme, George O., *Syntax.* Boston: D. C. Heath and Company, 1931.

——, *Parts of Speech and Accidence.* Boston: D. C. Heath and Company, 1935.

Fries, C. C., *American English Grammar.* New York: Appleton-Century Co. (NCTE Monograph No. 10), 1940.

——, *The Teaching of the English Language.* New York: Thomas Nelson and Sons, 1927.

Hall, J. Lesslie, *English Usage.* Chicago: Scott, Foresman and Company, 1917.

Horwill, H. W., *A Dictionary of Modern American Usage.* Oxford: Clarendon Press, second edition, 1944.

Jespersen, Otto H., *A Modern English Grammar on Historical Principles.* New York: G. E. Stechert and Company, 1909–.

——, *Essentials of English Grammar.* New York: Henry Holt and Company, 1933.

Kenyon, John S., and Thomas A. Knott, *A Pronouncing Dictionary of American English.* Springfield: G. & C. Merriam Co., 1944. Addenda, 1949.

Krapp, George P., *The Knowledge of English.* New York: Henry Holt and Company, 1927.

Leonard, Sterling A., *Current English Usage.* Chicago: National Council of Teachers of English, 1932. (This book is out of print, but the grammatical portion of it is reprinted in Albert H. Marckwardt and Fred Walcott's *Facts about Current English Usage.* New York: D. Appleton-Century Company, 1939.)

Pooley, Robert C., *Teaching English Usage.* New York: D. Appleton Century Co. (NCTE Monograph No. 16), 1946.

——, *Grammar and Usage in Textbooks on English.* Madison, Wisconsin: University of Wisconsin, 1933.

Robertson, Stuart, *The Development of Modern English.* New York: Prentice-Hall, second edition, revised by F. G. Cassidy, 1953.

Summey, George, Jr., *American Punctuation.* New York: Ronald Press, 1949.

University of Chicago Press, *A Manual of Style.* Chicago: University of Chicago Press, tenth ed., 1949.

For more specific studies of particular words or constructions see the annual bibliography in *Publications of the Modern Language Association* and the quarterly bibliography in *American Speech.*

Glossary

A, An Use *a* before a consonant sound, *an* before a vowel sound. Examples: *an* atom, *a* novel, *an* hour, *a* union, *a* one-step, *a* wonder, *a* (or *an*) historical event (depending on whether the consonant *h* is pronounced).

Accept, except Confusing one for the other is an error in spelling. Look up the meanings of these words.

Ad An informal shortening of *advertisement.* Many clippings, such as *auto, exam, gym, doc, math, phone, photo, prof,* and *lab* are informal; others, such as *bus, mob, piano, taxi,* and *wig* are used in both formal and informal discourse. When doubtful, consult your dictionary.

Affect, effect Do not spell one when you mean the other. Look up the meanings of these words.

Aggravate Informal in the sense of "irritate" or "annoy." In formal English it means "make worse" or "make more severe."

Ain't *Ain't* never appears in standard written English.

All the farther, deeper, slower, etc. Nonstandard when used for *as far as, as deep as, as slow as*, etc., which are adverbial. Compare the standard usage: "As the hours passed, the disagreement grew all the deeper"; here the phrase is adjectival.

All ready, already These homophones are spelled differently. *Already* is provincially used with the past tense, as in "Did they leave already?" Prefer the present perfect tense: "Have they left already?"

All together, altogether These homophones are spelled differently. Look up their meanings.

Almost See **Most.**

Alright A simplified spelling of *all right*, objectionable to many users of standard English. Compare *all wrong*. To be safe, avoid *alright*.

Also Not a conjunction in standard English. Write "They ordered dessert and coffee" not "They ordered dessert, also coffee."

Alternative Formerly used when there were only two choices, now usual when there are several choices.

A.M., P.M., a.m., p.m. Use only after a specific time: 5:15 p.m. As synonyms for *morning* or *afternoon* these terms are examples of trite humor. Use either capitals or small letters, but be consistent.

Among Usually *among* implies the relation of a thing (or things) to a vague or collective group, as in *The Liberals quarreled among themselves, He lost the escaped convict among the freight cars in the yard, The novel was shelved among the biographies.* Do not write *a contract among three parties, a marker among the pages of the book*, where *between* is preferred. See **Between.**

Amount, number *Amount* applies to a mass: "a small amount of water"; *number* applies to countable objects: "a number of eggs."

And See **Good and, Try and.**

And etc. Here *and* is unnecessary; *etc.* means "and others."

Any In comparisons of two things of the same class, *any other* is standard: "Mt. Everest is higher than any other mountain" (not *any mountain*), but "Mt. Everest is higher than any volcano." In the latter sentence two different classes are compared.

Any more Normally used in negative constructions: "Latin is not required in this school any more." Provincially used in colloquial positive constructions: "History is required in this school any more."

Anyplace Colloquial; but disliked by many educated people.

Anything like Colloquial for *at all like, in any way like.*

Anywheres Now nonstandard.

As Now colloquial when used for *that* or *whether*. Write "I don't know that I will," not *as I will.*

As to Jargon for *about* or *of* in such sentences as "There is no doubt as to (prefer *about*) which train is faster," and "We are certain as to (prefer *of*) her reliability."

Asset The connotation of this word is that of business English; hence it is better replaced by *resource* or *source of strength* in a noncommercial context.

Auto See **Ad.**

Awful, awfully Trite as intensives meaning *very, very great.*

Awhile, a while Distinguish between *awhile* (an adverb) and *a while* (an article plus a noun). Compare "Please wait awhile" and "Please wait for a while."

Bad An adjective, not an adverb, in standard English. Write "The orchestra played badly (not *bad*) last night"; but write "I don't feel bad about it" (where *bad* is an adjective).

Balance Colloquial for *remainder,* but becoming more formal. Some people still object to the usage.

Beside Usually a preposition, as in "The city is beside a lake." *Besides* is usually an adverb, as in "The lake is shallow; besides, it is frozen all winter."

Better See **Had better.**

Between See **Among.** Usually *between* implies the specific relation of a thing (or things) to separate, specific things, as in *the opening between the columns, a number between ten and fifteen, the agreement between the partners, torn between three choices.*

Between you and I Nonstandard.

Bursted Now nonstandard; use *burst.*

Bust Humorous or informal. Note that *bust* cannot always be replaced by *burst,* as in *went busted* (bankrupt), *bust* (subdue) *a bronco, bust* (reduce in rank) *an officer, trust busting.*

But, but that, but what Informal in such sentences as "No one doubts but that (formal *that*) he will run again," and "Who questions but what (formal *that*) this action is necessary?"

Calculate Provincial in the meanings *plan, expect, think.*

Can, may In asking or granting permission, *can* is informal, as in "Can I go to the blackboard?" Literary: "May we use your name as a reference?" In the negative, *can't* is standard: "The building can't be used for such meetings."

Can but, cannot but, cannot help but, can't help but *Can but,* meaning *can only,* as in "We can but agree" is literary, as is *cannot but* in "They cannot but agree." *Cannot (can't) help but,* as in "The opposition party cannot help but agree" (meaning *cannot help agreeing*), is common in colloquial English and frequently occurs in writing, although some people dislike it.

Can't hardly Colloquial.

Case Frequently unnecessary, as in *This is true in the case of doctors* instead of *This is true of doctors.* Avoid except when needed.

Claim Now standard in the meanings *assert* and *maintain.*

Considerable Colloquial in America as a noun meaning *much* or *a good deal.*

Contact As a verb meaning *meet* or *get in touch with* this word is disliked by many people. Its other verbal uses are old and established.

Continual, continuous *Continual* means *regular,* as in "The continual dripping of the faucet annoyed Joseph." *Continuous* means *uninterrupted, constant,* as in "Continuous pressure is maintained by a spring."

Could of A misspelling of *could've,* a contraction of *could have.* In normal speech unstressed *have* and *of* are pronounced alike. Write *could have.*

Couple Colloquial in the sense of *a few, approximately two.*

Data This is the plural form of *datum,* but it is often used as a collective singular, as in "This data is trustworthy."

Date Colloquial meaning *appointment, make an appointment, have* *engagements with*, and *person with whom one has an engagement.*

Deal Colloquial or commercial jargon in the sense of *transaction.*

Definitely Faddishly over-used in recent years. Now trite as an intensive meaning *quite, certainly.*

Different from, than, to *Different from* is always safe; *different to* is more common in Britain than in America; *different than* is standard but some people dislike it. *Than* is useful when a clause follows, as in "It was different in color than he had expected." See Gladys D. Haase, "Than," *College English*, X (March, 1949), 345–347.

Done Nonstandard for *did;* colloquial for *have done, have finished.*

Don't Now nonstandard as a contraction of *does not* in writing.

Doubt Observe the idiomatic uses of this word. "I doubt that she will sing" means I think it improbable. "I do not doubt that she will sing" means I think it probable. "I doubt if she will sing" is less formal. See **But; But that.**

Dove One of the two past tense forms of *dive;* in formal writing *dived* seems to be more frequent.

Due to Because many people dislike *due to* as a preposition, as in "Due to the election, all the streets were crowded," prefer *because of* or *on account of*. Note that *owing to,* a similar phrase, is not disliked, and *due to* is normal in adjective phrases: "The quarrel was due to a misunderstanding."

Each other The expressions *each other* and *one another* are freely interchangeable.

Effect, affect Do not spell one when you mean the other. Look up the meanings of these words.

Either, neither These words are normally used with reference to one of two, not one of three or more. Thus write "Any (not *either*) one of the three doors can be locked." For agreement in number, see § 5b.

Enthuse Common in spoken English, but disliked by many people. Avoid in writing.

Equally as good A blend of *equally good* and *just as good.* Write "His arguments are equally good" or "His arguments are just as good."

Everyplace See **Anyplace.**

Every so often Colloquial. In writing prefer *ever so often* or *every now and then.*

Exam See **Ad.**

Expect Colloquial when it means *suspect, think, suppose.*

Extra Trite substitute for *very, unusually,* with a commercial connotation, as in "extra heavy cover" or "extra fine piano accompaniment." Prefer such synonyms as "unusually heavy cover" and "particularly fine piano accompaniment."

Farther, further Interchangeable in standard English, except that *farther* is less common in the sense of *more.* Write *further* (not *farther*) *information, explanation,* etc.

Feature When it means "give special prominence to" this word is colloquial or business jargon, as in "Today the store is featuring men's suits."

Fine Standard English as a term of approval, but over-used. Similar trite adjectives are *grand, lovely, nice, wonderful,* which may be appropriate in conversation but can be replaced by more specific modifiers in serious writing. As an adverb meaning *well, fine* is colloquial.

First rate Colloquial when used to mean *extremely good, very well.*

Fix Colloquial when it means *condition, repair, arrange, improve, get ready, take revenge on.*

Folks Colloquial for *relatives, family.*

Funny Colloquial for *strange, remarkable, queer.*

Gent Nonstandard shortening of *gentleman.*

Get The use of function words such as *get, do, let, be,* and *have* in phrases is a striking characteristic of modern English of all types. Some examples with *get* are as follows:

Standard: *get ready, get off, get along, get out.*
Slang: *get me?, get going, get wise to, get it in the leg.*
Colloquial: *it gets me, I get you, get by with, get caught.*

Although *get* is a very useful word it is easily over-used.

Good Although once used adverbially, in standard English *good* is now used only as an adjective. Avoid such usages as *She cooks good.*

Good and Colloquial as in *good and strong, good and hot.*

Got, gotten In informal standard English *have got* meaning both *possess* and *must* is usual; in very formal English *have* and *must* are preferred. Both *got* and *gotten* are standard participial forms of *get*, except that *gotten* is not used in the sense of *possess*. Examples: "Relations between the two countries have got (or *gotten*) better," but "We've got (not *gotten*) a ton of coal downstairs."

Grand See **Fine.**

Granted The common expression is *taken for granted*, not *taken for granite*.

Guess Colloquial in America for *believe, suppose, think*.

Gym See **Ad.**

Had have, had of, hadn't of Nonstandard. Use *had* alone.

Had ought, hadn't ought, didn't ought Now nonstandard.

Had better, had rather Interchangeable with *would rather, would better*.

Hardly *When* (not *than*) is idiomatic after *hardly*, as in "It was hardly time to leave when (not *than*) Alice called." *Can't hardly* is colloquial.

Has got, have got See **Got.**

Healthful, healthy Usually interchangeable; see *ACD, NCD, NWD*.

Heap, heaps Colloquial in the sense of *a great deal*.

Himself See § 13d.

Human As a noun meaning a *human being*, this word is common in colloquial English, rare in formal writing.

If *If* and *whether* are interchangeable in standard English clauses indicating doubt or uncertainty: "The clerk was not sure whether (or *if*) our package was ready." In formal English *whether* is more common when a choice is emphasized: "It is not certain whether *juke* or *jook* is the older spelling."

In, into Compare "The baby fell in his play-pen" and "The baby fell into his play-pen." *Into* is preferred when motion or change is emphasized.

In back of Informal for *behind*, modeled on *in front of*.

In regards to Nonstandard for *in regard to* or *as regards*.

Inside of Colloquial. In writing, *inside* is preferred.

Intents and purposes A standard expression (not *intensive purposes*).

Irregardless Nonstandard or humorous.

It's, its The genitive of *it* is not spelled with an apostrophe; compare *his, hers, theirs.* The contraction of *it* and *is,* as in "It's my book," has the apostrophe.

-ize A standard English suffix which makes such verbs as *apologize, penalize,* and *sterilize,* but which is frequently used to make unnecessary verbs like *finalize, moistureize,* and *renovize* (which do not improve on *terminate, moisten,* and *renovate*). Awkward verbs in *-ize* are characteristic of gobbledygook.

Kind, sort Colloquial with a plural verb or modifier, as in "These kind of people are hard to deal with." Formal usage prefers the singular: "This kind of person," "That sort of writer."

Kind of, sort of Colloquial when used adverbially. In writing prefer *rather* or *somewhat.*

Lady Affected where *woman* would be the normal word, as in "The women (not *ladies*) employed as cooks were not members of a union."

Lay See **Lie.**

Learn Now nonstandard or archaic in the sense *to teach.*

Leave Nonstandard in the meaning *permit.* "The officer refused to let (not *leave*) me go home.

Liable In formal writing *liable* normally suggests danger or risk of something undesired; in informal English it means *apt* or *likely.*

Lie Intransitive verb, as in "I will lie down." The past tense is *lay:* "He lay there all afternoon," and the past participle is *lain:* "He has lain there a long time." In nonstandard English this verb is confused with the transitive verb *lay,* which must have an object, as in this standard English sentence: "Lay it on the table where I laid mine."

Like In written English *as* or *as if* is preferred to *like* to introduce a clause. Colloquial: "No one else could arouse the English like Churchill did." Formal: *as* Churchill did.

Like for Although the *for* is unnecessary in such a sentence as "We would like for you to inspect the house," it is frequent in informal English and is by no means nonstandard.

Line of Usually wordy or trite. Prefer "A poll *like* (not *along the line of*) Dr. Gallup's."

Loan Standard American English as a verb, although many people prefer *lend.* See *ACD* and *NCD.*

Locate Colloquial in the meaning *to settle.*

Lot, lots of Colloquial in the sense of *many, much.*

Lovely See **Fine.**

Mad In the meaning *angry* this word is now colloquial.

Math See **Ad.**

May See **Can.**

Mean Colloquial in America in the sense of *bad-tempered, malicious.*

Might of A misspelling of *might've,* the contracted form of *might have.* In normal speech unstressed *have* and *of* are identical. Write *might have.*

Mighty Colloquial when it means *very.*

Most Compare the following usages:

Informal: Agnes likes most all my friends.
Formal: The dean approves almost all the suggestions.

Muchly Nonstandard or humorous.

Myself, himself, herself, yourself, etc. See § 13d.

Neither See **Either.**

Nice See **Fine.**

No account Colloquial shortening of *of no account,* "worthless."

No place See **Anyplace.**

Nothing like Informal for *not in any way like.*

Nowhere near Informal for *not nearly.*

Nowheres Nonstandard for *nowhere.*

Of See **Could of, Might of.**

Off of The *of* is superfluous in such expressions as "He stepped off of the porch." *Off* alone is sufficient.

Only Commonly placed in an illogical position, as in the sentence *We only want to reserve one cottage,* but since the meaning is clear such a sentence is not faulty. When misunderstanding is possible, place *only* close to the word it modifies.

Out loud Informal. *Aloud* is the formal synonym.

Outside of Standard except in the sense "except, besides"; in this sense it is colloquial.

Over with Colloquial for *completed, finished.*

Pair In informal usage the plural after a number may be *pair,* as in *three pair of scissors.* In more formal English it is *pairs.*

Per Expressions like *per day, per yard, per person* are standard

English, but *a day, a yard,* etc. are more natural. *Per diem, per capita, per cent* are usual. In technical expressions like *miles per hour, revolutions per minute, per* is also usual.

Per cent, percentage After numerals *per cent* is usual; after other expressions, *percentage* is most common. "Twenty per cent voted *no;* a larger percentage did not vote." No period is needed after *per cent,* since it is not an abbreviation, and it may be spelled as one word or two.

Person The standard word for an individual human being; *party* is legal jargon.

Phone See **Ad.**

Plan on Some people prefer *plan to;* both are standard English.

Plenty In formal writing usually a noun, sometimes a predicate adjective. As an adverb or attributive adjective it is colloquial, as in *There were plenty chairs, The room is plenty large.*

Principal, principle *Principal* is an adjective meaning highest in rank, authority, importance, etc., and a noun meaning either *chief* (teacher, actor, participant, etc.) or capital sum of money. *Principle* is a noun meaning fundamental rule or truth. They are identical in speech; so be sure to write the one you mean.

Prof See **Ad.**

Proposition Commercial or colloquial synonym for *proposal, matter.*

Quite In informal English it frequently means *very* or *rather;* in formal writing it means *wholly, completely.* Do not confuse with *quiet.*

Racket Meaning "loud noise," *racket* is standard English; meaning "dishonest business," it is informal; meaning "occupation," it is slang.

Raise *Rear* is more formal in the meaning *bring up,* but *raise* is common in standard American English.

Rarely ever The *ever* is unnecessary here. *Rarely if ever* is a standard expression.

Real A colloquial substitute for *very. Really* is more formal.

Reason is because See § 14.

Refer back The *back* is unnecessary except when the phrase means *refer again.*

Reverend In standard English used only before the full name, initials, or such titles as *Mr.* and *Dr.*, not before the surname alone: *Reverend Humphrey Olds, Reverend H. P. Olds, Reverend Mr. Olds.* Provincial: *Reverend MacArthur, the Reverend MacArthur, Rev. MacArthur.*

Right In American English right may mean *straight*, as in *She went right to the library.* As a substitute for *very* or *somewhat*, as in *It's right warm today*, it is colloquial.

Said As an adjective only in legal jargon.

Same As a pronoun only in legal jargon.

Scarcely Normally followed by *when*, not *than*. "The deer had scarcely come into view when (not *than*) he shot."

Seldom ever The *ever* is unnecessary here.

Set, sit *Set* is usually transitive, *sit* intransitive. *I set the clock; I sit on the steps.* But note that *the sun sets.*

Shall, will See § 9.

Shape Colloquial for *condition.* Compare "The best boxer's in good shape" and "The buildings are reported to be in good condition."

Show up Informal for *appear, arrive, expose.*

So (1) *So* is overused as a connective between clauses.

(2) *So* as a substitute for *very* is overused, especially in advertising jargon.

Examples: *I am so tired. Gypso is so economical.*

Some Colloquial for *somewhat, rather*, as in *She is playing some better this season.* Compare *The pianist's performance is somewhat better this season* (formal).

Someplace Nonstandard for *somewhere.*

Someway Colloquial for *somehow.*

Somewheres Provincial for *somewhere.*

Sort See **Kind.**

Sort of See **Kind of.**

Statue, stature, statute. Distinguish between these words.

Stop Colloquial for *stay.* Compare the conversational "I am stopping at Uncle Joe's" with the more formal "She is staying at a hotel."

Such (1) When *such* is followed by a relative clause, the preferred relative is *as* (not *who, which,* or *that*). "I shall follow such rules *as* I think are best." (2) In result clauses *such* should be followed by *that*, not by *so that:* "That afternoon *such* a dark cloud gathered *that* we had to postpone our trip." (3) Colloquial in "It was such a lovely afternoon," "He is such a nuisance." *Such* means "to the degree" and in formal writing is followed by a clause defining the degree. Use *no such*, not *no such a:* "There is no such thing."

Superior than Unidiomatic for *superior to:* "The workmen were really superior to their master" (not *than their master*). Do not confuse *superior to* and *better than.*

Sure Colloquial for *surely, certainly, indeed, yes,* as in: "He sure is an eloquent speaker." "Are you going?" "Sure."

Sure and See **Try and.**

Suspicion The use of the noun *suspicion* for the verb *suspect* is an American provincialism.

Swell Trite colloquial synonym for "good."

Take Used in many colloquial expressions. "Take off" ("to parody," or "a parody"), "take stock in," "take on too much work" are colloquialisms. "Take in" (a show, the town, etc.) is colloquial or slang. "Take on" in the sense "act violently" and "take sick" are colloquial or provincial.

Take and Often redundant: "He knocked the ball over the fence," not "He took and knocked the ball over the fence." This construction is conversational or nonstandard. See **Try and, Good and.**

Tasty Colloquial or provincial for *agreeable, attractive, of good taste, savory.*

Terrible, terribly; terrific, terrifically Trite colloquial synonyms of *very, extremely.*

Than Often misused for *when.* See **Hardly, Scarcely.**

That, this When used as adverbs, as in *that far, this high, that frightened, this* and *that* are colloquial or provincial substitutes for *very, so, as far as that,* etc.

That there, this here Expressions like "that there man," and "this here can opener" are nonstandard.

These kind (sort), those kind (sort) See **Kind.**

This here See **That there.**

Through Informal in the sense "finished." See **Done.**

Till A synonym for *until,* not an abbreviation.

Too Informal for "very" in negative constructions such as *not too successful, not too happy.*

Try and In expressions like "Let's try and catch the bus" the *and* is a colloquial substitute for *to*. Some people object to it.

-type In informal English *-type* is compounded with other words to make adjectives which modify nouns; examples are *new-type refrigerator* (which isn't necessarily a new refrigerator) and *motorcycle-type seat* (which may be designed for bicycles). In many such expressions *type* is unnecessary and wordy, as it certainly is in *portable-type heater, house-type trailer, floor-type wax,* and *dark-type hair.* In formal English *new type of refrigerator* is preferred.

Unique Trite colloquial substitute for *odd, rare, unusual.*

Until After *hardly* and *scarcely* the standard idiom is *when,* not *until* or *till.* Prefer *that* in expressions like "It was so noisy that (not *until*) the rooms had to be soundproofed."

Up The adverb *up* after a verb often forms with it a verb-adverb combination having the meaning of a single verb: *rise up* (for arise), *wake up* (awake). Very often *up* adds the idea of completeness, finality, or intensity to the idea expressed by the simple verb: *eat up* as contrasted to *eat, burn up, break up, pile up, double up, run up, settle up,* all of which are acceptable.

But omit *up* unless it really adds something to the meaning of the preceding verb. In colloquial usage *up* is often used redundantly: *end up, divide up, open up, rest up, write up, finish up, fold up* (*a paper*). *Up* is colloquial in "What is he up to?" "It is up to him," "He is up against it," and "He is hard up." "Beat her up" is colloquial. "He beat up on her" is slang.

Used to Normally pronounced *usta,* but correctly spelled *used to.*

Used to could, would Nonstandard for *used to be able to,* or simply *used to.*

Very The use of *very* to modify a past participle is unidiomatic in standard English. Write "Her singing was very much admired" (not *very admired*), "That was a very widely appreciated action" (not *very appreciated*). Past participles which are regularly used as adjectives, however, are commonly modified by *very:* "He is very tired," "She is a very excited girl." If you are not sure whether a particular past participle is regularly used as an adjective, it is wise to put another adverb after *very*.

Wait on In standard English one waits *on* (serves) a customer, but waits *for* (awaits) someone or something that is coming. *Wait on* for *await* is an American regionalism.

Want In standard English *want* does not take a that-clause as its object. Write "We want this meeting to be successful," not "We want that the meeting should be successful."

Want for Provincial for *want* in the sense of *desire*. In standard "He did not want for friends" the verb means *lack*.

Want in (off, out, etc.) Used instead of *want to get in* (*off*, *out*, etc.) in some dialects, especially in the Midland section of the United States.

Way Colloquial or provincial as a shortening of *away*, as in "It was way back in 1910."

Ways Colloquial for *way* or *distance* as in *a long ways off*.

We Affected for *I* unless the writer actually represents a group.

What See **But that, but what.**

When See § 14 for *when* in definitions.

Where Colloquial for *that* in constructions like "I read in the *News* where (write *that*) the general apologized to the corporal." In expressions like "Where is the station at?" omit the *at*.

Which, who, what, that See § 13.

While See **Conjunctions,** § 12.

Who, whom See § 7.

Whose Frequently used to refer to neuter antecedents to avoid an awkward *of which* construction, e.g. "Omit the poems whose authors are unknown" is preferable to "Omit the poems the authors of which are unknown." In some contexts the choice can be avoided; for example, "Omit the anonymous poems."

Will, shall See § 9f.

Without Nonstandard for *unless* in a sentence like "The payment cannot be refunded without (prefer *unless*) the slip is presented."

Would of A misspelling of *would've*, contraction of *would have*.

Writer Affected when used to avoid plain *I*.

Yet Provincial when used with a simple past tense, as in "Did you do it yet?" (Prefer *Have you done it yet?*)

You all, Y'all Southern colloquialism for plural *you* (two or more).

Nonstandard in the South when the reference is clearly to one person.

You was Nonstandard (formerly usual) for *you were*. English is inconsistent in using a plural form here in the singular, and in some dialects the inconsistency is resisted by the use of *you was*. However, *you was* is so strongly disapproved by so many educated people, that you should always write *you were*.

For information on expressions not listed in this glossary, consult a good recent dictionary.

UNITY

For maximum effectiveness, a sentence must be unified. It must hold the reader's attention on one main communication, without distraction and without diffusion. Although a good sentence may contain many meaningful elements, they must be combined coherently, with minor parts in subordinate constructions and the major predication in an unmistakably prominent position.

Sentence Unity

67. Avoid sentences containing unrelated elements and improperly related elements.

Children speak in simple, highly unified sentences such as *I'm hungry, The dog barked,* and *It's cold.* As we become more mature, our sentences become more complex, more loaded with details, and more accurate in making fine distinctions. At the same time we run the risk of including too much in a single sentence, and the risk of including unrelated elements. Sentences which combine unrelated matter and improperly related matter are inefficient, just as a person who tries to do too many things at once is inefficient. However, there is no ironclad rule of thumb for recognizing sentence unity. For instance, consider this sentence:

On the table lay an old Bible, which was bound in leather.

Here two predications are made, but both have the same subject, and the second is related to the first, adding a descriptive detail. Compare this faulty sentence:

Many major political issues arose during President Roosevelt's administration, and he was Assistant Secretary of the Navy during World War I.

The two clauses have something in common, references to President Roosevelt, but there is no relationship between the two statements. Common elements do not necessarily make for unity. Neither of the statements tells the reader the cause, result, time, manner, place, or purpose of the other, and they do not make up a unified communication.

Although the following sentence makes three statements, it is unified by repetition of the subject *we* and the pivotal phrase *machine-made;* the three clauses add up to a single communication:

> We sleep on machine-made products; we eat machine-made food; sometimes we breathe machine-made air.

Obviously one thing is being said, illustrated by three specific examples. Sometimes unity is violated by putting in two sentences elements that form a single whole, elements that should be put together in one sentence:

> Roman civilization barely reached the Celts. It left but few traces among them.

These two statements should have been written as one sentence:

> Roman civilization barely reached the Celts and left but few traces among them.

Although violations of unity are sometimes a matter of what is said, they are more often a matter of how it is said. See §§ 68–74 for examples.

EXERCISE

Rewrite any of the following selections which violate unity.

1. The main problem considered at the meeting was the national emergency, and the Council elected new officers.
2. The purpose of the seminar is to give citizens an opportunity to discuss current issues. Visiting experts provide information and guidance.
3. The program is now carried by fourteen state radio stations, and the director writes the scripts.
4. When the governor was sworn in, a boyhood dream came true. He is a farmer and business man from the southern mountain section.

5. Labor Commissioner Ford uses a five-passenger sedan. This car is owned by the state.
6. Department store sales in 1950 were above 1949, and stores in the cities did better than in small towns, but all the stores reported more business in 1950 than in 1949.
7. Tax collections increased greatly during the year, but the county needs a new jail and there is not enough money in the treasury to build one, so the commissioners want to float a bond issue, which many citizens oppose.
8. Colonel Rand is building a new home. It is on Cat Lane. The architect is Sarah Roze. It will have seven rooms and two baths. The style is modernistic. Concrete, aluminum, and glass are the principal building materials.
9. I am enjoying my vacation and the weather is very, very hot.
10. Benson was injured in the accident; he lives in Galveston.

Coördination

68. Avoid excessive, illogical, inaccurate, and misleading coördination.

When you coördinate two or more elements, first make sure that they are of equal logical importance; then express them in the same grammatical construction. Do not fail to use or to repeat the sign of coördination. Choose the coördinating conjunction which reveals the precise relationship between the parts of the sentence it connects. See §§ 86 and 88.

68a. Avoid excessive and illogical coördination.

Avoid joining by a coördinating conjunction or conjunctive adverb parts of a sentence that do not make statements of equal importance and that do not have the same grammatical form.

Excessive He was ten years younger than his brother, and he was still a college student when the war began, but when he returned to his native state, from which he had been absent for five years, he found himself thrown at once into one of the most exciting political campaigns that took place during the century. (The obvious remedy for such a straggling compound sentence is to place all subordinate ideas in subordinate grammatical form or to divide the straggling compound sentence into shorter, well-unified sentences. Whenever possible, *reduce predication* — that is, use a subordinate clause instead of a main clause, a phrase instead of a clause, a word instead of a phrase. A good rule for the beginner is to cultivate the habit of beginning his sentences with a subordinating conjunction, a participle, or a phrase.)

See Reduction of Predication in § 16.

Faulty He had no thought of deliberately deceiving his friend in this manner and cause him all this trouble. (Although the ideas of deceiving and causing are of equal importance, they are not put into the same grammatical construction. It is careless to use different grammatical constructions for ideas of the same importance. Use parallel grammatical construction for parallel ideas. For a fuller discussion of parallelism, see §§ 86 and 88.)

He took down the dusty old volume and which had not been opened for many years. (Omit *and*, the sign of coördination, and the less important idea will be grammatically subordinated to the first.)

68b. Avoid inaccurate coördination.

When you have good reason to use a coördinate construction, make the coördination plain to the reader. Choose the coördinating conjunction which reveals the precise relationship between the parts of the sentence it connects. Do not fail to use or to repeat the sign of coördination.

Inaccurate John often played the piano, while his brother wrote poetry. (*But* or *whereas* is the more accurate conjunction here.)

These rules of poetic justice were closely followed by the dramatists of the period, and today they are ignored completely. (The proper coördinating conjunction here is *but*, not *and*.)

The San Francisco conference was one which we had expected to hold without the Soviets and the Indians had indicated they would attend. (The conjunction *and* makes the first and third clauses coördinate and momentarily makes *Soviets* and *Indians* coördinate. By inserting *which* after *and* we make the second and third clauses coördinate and make the meaning unmistakable.

He told us how he slowly climbed the mountain as the sun rose and tightened the pack on his back from time to time to make sure that the jolting would not disturb the rare specimens which he had very painfully collected as he tramped over the stony ground and mounted on cardboard. (Repeat the signs of parallelism, *how* plus *he* before *tightened*, and *which* plus *he had* before *mounted*. The omission of these signs of parallelism exasperates the reader by implying that the sun "rose and tightened the pack on his back" and that "he had tramped over the stony ground and mounted on cardboard.")

EXERCISE

Revise any of the following sentences that have faulty or undesirable coördination.

1. S. L. Thomas, the air-conditioning engineer, and who received his B.S. degree in 1940, has been engaged to air-condition the university library.
2. Miss Ray is only a farmer's daughter and she has become the star of a prize-winning play on Broadway.
3. Refrigerators without frozen-food compartments are hard to sell; and we have several in stock, and we should have a sale immediately.
4. He is a man deserving our pity and that should be given a job.
5. The surf was rough and we enjoyed the swim and the fishing was poor so the people who preferred fishing didn't enjoy the trip as much as the swimming group.
6. Saroyan is best known as a short story writer and he has now written a popular song.
7. The team needs a left halfback, but none of the freshman backs has ever played left halfback.
8. François Villon was a poor student, fond of pleasure, and stole when hungry.
9. Edgar Allan Poe was also a poor student, fond of pleasure, but there is no record of his having to steal.
10. Major Seelie is stationed in Kansas and he is assigned to the headquarters of a new division.

Subordination

69. Reserve the main clause for emphatic and important elements only. Use dependent clauses, phrases, and other subordinate constructions for the less emphatic and less important parts of the sentence.

Whenever possible, *reduce predication* — that is, use a subordinate clause instead of a main clause, a phrase instead of a clause, a word instead of a phrase. The skillful writer composes his sentences so that they abound in subordination. By this means he gives emphasis and clearness to his main thought and unity and compactness to his sentences.

69a. Avoid illogical, or upside-down, subordination.

Compare these two sentences:

When the power went off the radio wouldn't operate.

The power went off when the radio wouldn't operate.

In the first sentence the important (emphatic) statement is *the radio wouldn't operate;* the time and probably the cause of its failure is *the power went off*. The second sentence makes *the power went off* the important communication; the clause *the radio wouldn't operate* tells the time (and, by implication, the cause). Both sentences are grammatically correct, but the first is much more likely to be a true statement; it is not likely that the failure of a radio would cause the power to go off. The second sentence is an example of upside-down subordination.

Sometimes the choice of the clause to subordinate is not a matter of logic or fact but a matter of the writer's purpose. Compare these two sentences:

When the treads were worn off, the tire was discarded.

The treads were worn off when the tire was discarded.

Both sentences are efficient; a preference for one or the other depends strictly on what the writer wishes to emphasize. If the important fact is *treads were worn off*, the first is upside-down; if the important fact is *tire was discarded*, the second is upside-down. Let your meaning be your guide.

Since speakers do not normally bother to plan and revise sentences in spoken English, upside-down subordination is common in conversation, where context and gesture correct lapses in logic. In writing, particularly serious and formal writing, the writer is expected to indicate the important parts of his sentences by putting them in emphatic constructions.

69b. Avoid overlapping subordination.

A sentence containing a series of overlapping constructions, that is, a series in which each construction depends upon the preceding, is likely to be awkward and annoying. Such a sentence is sometimes called the "house-that-Jack-built" sentence. A series of overlapping *which, who, that, for, of, so that, but,* or possessive constructions can become especially inept.

Weak He was quite different from the other men in the crew, who soon found that he was a youth who had never been on a ship.

Improved He was quite different from the other men in the crew, who soon found that he was a youth with no previous experience aboard ship. (The second *who*-clause has been reduced to a phrase.

Weak My uncle's chauffeur's dog died.

Right The dog owned by my uncle's chauffeur died.

EXERCISE

Correct any faulty subordination in the sentences below.

1. The author he selected was Hemingway, who has just written a new novel which has been panned by most critics, who think he should have done a better job.
2. Atkins had just left the barber shop when he saw the explosion that destroyed six blocks of downtown buildings.
3. Some alumni magazines are very respectable journals, while ours is a trashy collection of local items about publicity-seeking alumni.
4. The two brothers had never worked for the same firm and they were both plumbing salesmen.
5. A man who is afraid cannot lead people who are angry in a situation which is as critical as this one is.
6. The taxi driver took off his hat, loudly demanding to know what the

woman intended when she held out her hand and shouting that he would call a policeman.

7. When the drowning child had just been pulled up on the beach, I reached the scene.
8. While I prefer fiction by realistic novelists of our own age, my brother always reads detective stories.
9. We are indebted to O. J. Humble, who is manager of the local power company office, for calling to our attention the danger of dead limbs which are allowed to remain in trees along Main Street.
10. While Rome burned, Nero fiddled.

Choppy Sentences

70. Do not use a series of short, jerky sentences except for special effects.

Aside from being monotonous, choppy sentences can give undue emphasis to unimportant ideas. Except in short passages where you have a clear-cut reason for doing otherwise, reserve main clauses for principal thoughts, and use subordinate constructions for subordinate thoughts.

Lacking Emphasis and Unity He sped through the passages. He went with a very swift step. I could scarcely keep up with him. He went straight to the door of John's room. He did not wait for an invitation to enter. He opened it immediately.

More Unified and Emphatic He sped through the passages with so swift a step that I could scarcely keep up with him, straight to the door of John's room, which he immediately opened without waiting for an invitation to enter.

See §§ 67, 68, and 69.

EXERCISE

Wherever possible, combine the choppy sentences below into single complex or compound-complex sentences. If unity demands more than one sentence, use as few main clauses in each sentence as possible. Subordinate all unimportant ideas by putting them into subordinate constructions that are clear and smooth.

1. Some dialect expressions are widespread. One is *reckon* for *think.* Others are restricted to a small area. An example is *pightle*, meaning *barnyard.* It is used only in rural Long Island.
2. Some dialect expressions are common in particular occupations. Cotton farming is an example. To a cotton farmer *chop cotton* means to weed and thin the cotton stalks. This phrase would rarely be used outside the cotton states. Thus it can be called a dialect or occupational jargon term.
3. There are dialect terms that are older than standard terms. *Learn*, meaning "teach," is one. Standard words are sometimes older than dialect words. *Hazy* is older than *smurry.* Therefore we can't say that dialect is either older or younger than standard English. It can be either.
4. Some Appalachian dialect is close to Shakespearean English. But some of it is strictly American and new. Some standard American is like Shakespearean English, and some is quite new. It is silly to say that Kentucky mountaineers speak "pure Shakespearean English." They speak pure Kentucky mountaineer English.
5. Novelists use dialect for atmosphere. They don't always get it right. Some of them copy other novelists. They don't listen to actual dialect speakers. That is why they make a lot of mistakes.

Incomplete Thought

71. Do not leave gaps in the expression of your thought. Complete what you begin. Do not force your reader to fill in gaps caused by your own loose thinking.

In passing from one subject to another, whether within the same sentence or in different sentences, indicate the transition as clearly as possible. See § 89 for a full discussion of transition.

Logically Incomplete The piles of corn were often left in the field several days, and we usually killed the field mice.

Complete The piles of corn were often left in the field several days, and when we loaded them into the wagon, we usually killed the field mice that we found in them.

Logically Incomplete Russia gained control of Czechoslovakia, which was formed from World War II.

Complete Russia gained control of Czechoslovakia, which had been formed by agreements made during World War II.

So, *such*, and *too* are often left dangling. In formal writing, these words usually require an accompanying *that*-clause or its equivalent to indicate clearly the degree, quality, or proportion implied in *so*, *such*, or *too*. The use of these words as loose equivalents of the intensive adverbs *very*, *indeed*, *exceedingly*, and *greatly*, is common only in informal English. See Too in § 66.

Informal His sculpture is too abstract.
Formal His sculpture is too abstract to be intelligible.
Standard His sculpture is very abstract.

EXERCISES

A. Fill any gaps in the following sentences.

1. The bureau looked many years for a tin deposit in this area, and the chamber of commerce hopes it will bring a big industry.
2. Johnson was hurrying to meet the cashier before the bank closed, but he had not changed his watch to daylight saving time.
3. The child was a pitiful example of unbalanced diet.
4. The loyalty board cleared Jasper, and he has been in the state prison at Jonesville six years.
5. The heating system was only a year old and we almost froze during the strike.

B. Rewrite any of the following sentences (which would be appropriate in magazine or newspaper advertising) in order to make them appropriate to more formal writing.

1. Vitaplus is such a tasteless tonic.
2. El Rollo is so easy on the throat and lungs.
3. Hart Brothers always sell for less.
4. Plush & Co. has moved to Dellar Street, so prices are lower.
5. Better bargains are yours at Lloyd's.

Incomplete Construction

72. Do not leave any elements of a sentence grammatically incomplete. Do not start with one construction and shift to another before completing the first.

For mixed constructions, see § 94.

Incomplete With these combinations put together in an excellent manner is the reason that this story is the best. (*Is* has no subject.)

Complete Since these combinations are put together in an excellent manner, this story is the best.

Transition not Marked One cannot pick up a newspaper without seeing a partial fulfillment of someone's ambition. The ambitions of women are very different from those of men. (What idea in the writer's mind served as a link between the vaguely related thoughts of the two sentences? See §§ 89 and 90.)

EXERCISES

A. Complete the incomplete constructions in the sentences below:

1. The old man having lived in Mexico made him able to read Spanish.
2. There was a sort of lever turned on the air stream.
3. These moral problems are but a few of which occur in our lives.
4. Anyone who would vote for that perjurer I would consider that he was lower than a baby-snatcher.
5. On account of the late hour was why the lights were off.

B. Directions given under Exercise A.

1. Because of Larry's silly infatuation for the new girl across the street is the reason that he refused to play tennis with me this afternoon.
2. We eat breakfast at nine, but father at seven.
3. Studying history requires a thorough reading of the text, parallel reading, and book reports.
4. If everyone were candid, this world would be very different from the world we are familiar.
5. Statistics prove that in the states in which this barbarous punishment has been abolished are safer and society better protected than in the others.

Incomplete or Illogical Comparisons

73. Be sure that all comparisons are clear and logical.

One type of comparison, called the absolute comparative, does not require completion, may even be impossible to complete: *the lower classes, higher education, the younger generation.* Some incomplete comparisons are standard, especially in spoken English, when the comparison is with something previously mentioned, something to be mentioned later, or something which the reader or listener readily supplies: *It's warmer today, He is feeling better, Professor Winchell looks older since his accident.* Advertising writers commonly use incomplete comparisons, possibly to avoid unsupported superlatives (which might be illegal): *Brown's sells for less; Better shoes at Hite Brothers; Gentler, better tasting cigarettes.*

In formal writing complete all comparatives (except absolute comparatives) so that the reader will not have to supply missing elements. Make all comparisons logical and consistent. Some common violations of this principle are as follows:

a. The omission of than *or* as *in a double comparison.*

Incomplete	I am as tall, if not taller, than my brother.
Right but Awkward	I am as tall as, if not taller than, my brother.
Better	I am as tall as my brother, if not taller.

b. The omission of the standard of comparison.

Vague We have learned to appreciate the greater maneuverability of the planes. (Greater than what?)

Clear We have learned to appreciate the greater maneuverability of the newer planes as compared to the older.

Vague He has some moderately long descriptions which can be grasped much more easily.

Clear He has some moderately long descriptions which can be grasped much more easily than shorter descriptions by other authors.

c. The omission of one term of the comparison.

Incomplete The labor commissioner antagonized her more than the union representative.

Complete The labor commissioner antagonized her more than he antagonized the union representative.

Complete The labor commissioner antagonized her more than the union representative did.

Note that a conversational remark like *I see her more than James* is an incomplete comparison, but preceding remarks usually prevent any misunderstanding.

d. The comparison of things which are not consistent or capable of comparison.

Illogical My profession is better than a dentist.

Logical My profession is better than dentistry.

Illogical Stevenson did not often imitate other authors, even though his style might seem like Lamb or some other essayist.

Logical Stevenson did not often imitate other authors, even though his style might seem like that of Lamb or some other essayist.

e. The inexact use of than any other, than any, of any, of all, all else, of all other. *Be sure not to confuse an individual and a class.*

Illogical Mayor Dominick is said to be the richest of any man in town.

Logical Mayor Dominick is said to be the richest man in town.

Illogical I like *Hamlet* best of all Shakespeare's other plays.

Logical I like *Hamlet* best of all Shakespeare's plays. (After a superlative like *most, best,* etc., do not use *other.*)

f. The use of a singular noun after an of-*phrase following a superlative.*

Illogical She is the best of any woman novelist now living.

Logical She is the best of all women novelists now living.

More Concise She is the best living woman novelist.

g. The use of the comparative to refer to more than two or of the superlative to refer to fewer than three (in formal English).

Formal He is the taller of the two brothers.
He is the tallest of the three brothers.

EXERCISES

A. Revise the incomplete and illogical comparisons in the following sentences:

1. Joyce thinks Kantor plays the harp better than anybody.
2. Life on Egdon Heath was different from all places.
3. Those tulips are as pretty, if not more so, as her zinnias.
4. Joan was as big, if not bigger, than any baby in the block.
5. She thinks we get much better meat than the supermarket.

B. Directions given under Exercise A.

1. The scenery in Yellowstone Park, in my opinion, is the prettier than all the national parks.
2. This case book has a number of useful cases which can be applied easier when the law clerk is in a hurry.
3. Our committee is more indebted to him than the senator.
4. He is the handsomer of the quartet.
5. This candidate can type the fastest of nearly any typist examined by the personnel office.

Miscellaneous Omissions

74. Do not omit words essential to your sentences.

The following are miscellaneous types of annoying omissions. Other types are discussed in the three preceding sections.

a. The omission of part of a verb phrase requiring a different verb form from that used in the accompanying verb phrase.

Faulty I always have and always will *take* an interest in painting.
Better I have always *taken* and always will *take* an interest in painting.
Faulty He has stayed and will for many months.
Better He has stayed and will stay for many months.

b. The use of is, was, *etc., both as a copula and as part of a verb phrase.*

Faulty The new country club is very pretty and praised by everybody.
Better The new country club *is* very pretty and *is praised* by everybody.

NOTE. One verb form should never be forced to perform two syntactical functions.

c. The failure to repeat the verb when the subject of a following clause demands a different verb form.

Faulty About the time they were almost worn out and one of them contemplating suicide, a ship appeared in the distance. (The singular subject *one* cannot agree with *were*, which appears in the first clause.)

Better About the time they were almost worn out and one of them *was* contemplating suicide, a ship appeared in the distance.

d. The omission of or the failure to repeat an article, pronoun, preposition, or subordinating conjunction necessary to full and accurate expression.

This fault is especially common with parallel sentence elements. (See §§ 86 and 88.) What effect would the omission of the italicized words have upon the meaning of the following sentences?

I asked for the secretary and *the* treasurer.

Last night my barn and *my* garage burned down.

He carried a red and *a* black flag.

He was praised by those who knew him best, and particularly *by* his brothers.

I showed *that* my brother was unable to come.

This habit shows *that* the familiar lines were already becoming impressed upon his memory.

In formal writing and in all cases where ambiguity would result, do not omit *that* after such verbs as *say, think, suppose, hope, see, show, feel, fear,* and *wish.* The omission of *that* often causes the subject of the *that*-clause to be mistaken for the object of *show, saw,* or some other main verb. Study the last two examples above and see §§ 72, 73, and 97. A clause following the nouns *opinion, view, thought, statement, idea,* etc., usually begins with *that* to prevent momentary misreading.

e. The omission of a preposition necessary to grammatical completeness.

Faulty He showed a striking aptitude and a remarkable power in this kind of work.

Correct but Awkward He showed a striking aptitude *for,* and a remarkable power *in,* this kind of work.

Better He showed a striking aptitude for this kind of work and a remarkable power in it.

EXERCISES

A. Supply any words necessary to complete the following sentences.

1. This is a program for which the staffs of the two bureaus have been and continue to be trained.
2. A night game was played in Detroit and cancelled because of rain in Boston.
3. In spite of his conservatism, he is a candidate likely to have appeal in labor circles, and this newspaper believes he does.
4. After an extended search in the garbage dump, the police discovered the old lady after all had not lost her diamond.
5. The guards had been alerted and took extra precautions with him.

B. Directions given under Exercise A.

1. I am puzzled by your reply and coming to see you tomorrow.
2. The manager thought he remembered the night watchman on duty had spoken to him at the stage door.
3. The Vice President and President of the Senate are the same man.
4. These tomatoes never have and never will bring top prices.
5. The club is in need of a houseboy and yard man.

EMPHASIS

We often need to give emphasis to certain parts of a sentence. A good general rule is to put important words in important positions; or, in a paragraph, to place the important sentence so that it commands attention. Emphasis is secured by means of suspense, climax, balance, repetition, proper subordination, separation, and variety.

Suspense — The Periodic Sentence

75. Use suspense as a means of securing emphasis.

Emphasis may be given to an important element by keeping the secret of the sentence from the reader until he reaches the last word. Compare the following sentences:

It is the great prerogative of innocence to dread no eye, to suspect no tongue.

To dread no eye, to suspect no tongue is the great prerogative of innocence.

The second sentence is the more emphatic because we are held in suspense until we reach the last word. Such a sentence is called periodic (see p. 28). Note the effectiveness of the following:

1. Battered by the winter gales, her crew half-mad from overwork and lack of sleep, her stores completely exhausted, the old ship slowly moved up to her anchorage.
2. Coming over the brow of the hill where the valley opened out below, I saw far down a long slope the tall chimney of my new home.

EXERCISES

A. Improve the following sentences by putting the important elements at the beginning or at the end. Notice how many of the revised sentences are periodic.

1. The surrounding area will be able to furnish enough employees for the plant, it is said.
2. The new industry will employ about 800 men, according to present estimates.
3. This campaign can be completed in a month, if we get the coöperation of local business men, and if our staff works hard.
4. Greene was determined not to give up, however, even in the face of increasing difficulties.
5. He wrote his wife that the boat was unsuitable, since it had sleeping quarters for only three people.

B. Directions given under Exercise A.

1. The younger partners were afraid, but the old man insisted that the company expand, on the other hand.
2. He mailed the crucial letter on Tuesday, after sitting up all Monday night composing his answer.
3. The editor was instructed to buy the manuscript, although the company had never published any poetry and O'Neal was unknown.
4. I find it very easy for social life to interfere whenever I sit down to study my daily assignments.
5. If this income tax bill is passed many citizens will leave the state, we believe.
6. Competent students will not work on the college newspaper if the faculty imposes a censorship plan, according to rumor.

Climax

76. Arrange parallel elements in climactic order for emphasis.

In a sentence containing parallel members of differing values, a progress from those of lesser value to those of greater is most emphatic. Compare the relative importance of the parallel members in the following sentences:

Unemphatic Professor Holliday's business experience includes two years as a shipping clerk, five years as president of a bank, and three years as manager of a retail store.

Emphatic Professor Holliday's business experience includes two years as a shipping clerk, three years as manager of a retail store, and five years as president of a bank.

Unemphatic The orator drew a grim picture of the party, torn by internal strife, unsettled in policy, and vague in ideas.

Emphatic The orator drew a grim picture of the party, vague in its ideas, unsettled in its policy, and torn by internal strife.

EXERCISES

A. Revise the sentences below in order to improve the climactic order.

1. It was the fate of the correspondents left in the overrun country to suffer imprisonment, public insults, and censorship.
2. People came to see the alleged "miracle" in thousands, hundreds, and dozens.
3. The opposition miscounted the ballots, lied about our candidate, and bribed people not to vote.
4. It was frightening to see how the movement spread from state to county to city overnight.
5. My best friend and roommate borrows my suits, my shirts, and even my socks.

B. Directions given under Exercise A.

1. In an instant there spread over his face a look of terror, uneasiness, and fright.
2. *The Good Earth* is a novel which very vividly explains man's dependence on the earth and what it produces not only for his life but also for his prosperity.
3. The whole plot deals with war and men in the army — their food, their wounds, their death, their morale, and their jokes.
4. Hidden under the swan's beautiful exterior, composed of handsome, flowing lines and graceful motion, lies a savage, treacherous nature combining the insidious wiles of a snake, the ferocity of a wildcat, and the tenacity of a bulldog.
5. If they fail to carry out all the orders and laws of their government, and to give every sign of doing so enthusiastically, they will either be killed or sent to a prison camp.

Balance

77. Use the balanced sentence to emphasize similarity or contrast.

A sentence is balanced when one part corresponds to another in construction and phrasing; balance is the extension of parallelism throughout two or more constructions or sentences. See §§ 86 and 88.

Our senses perceive no extreme. Too much sound deafens us; too much light dazzles us; too great distance or proximity hinders our view. (Similarity of ideas reflected in the use of similar constructions. For the semicolon as a mark of balance see § 19b.)

It is as easy to deceive oneself without perceiving it as it is difficult to deceive others without their perceiving it. (Contrast emphasized by the use of balance.)

Everyone complains of his memory; no one complains of his judgment. (Contrast.)

We always love those who admire us, but we do not always love those whom we admire. (Contrast.)

He [man] wants to be great, and he sees himself small. He wants to be happy, and he sees himself miserable. He wants to be perfect, and he sees himself full of imperfections. (Here balance is skillfully used both in the series and in the separate sentences.)

EXERCISE

Improve the balance of the selections below.

1. The average movie bores me. The plot is usually outlandish. There are few believable characters. The conversation sounds very unreal. The women especially have no facial expressions except dumb beauty.
2. History tells us who and when. It is the business of sociology to tell us what. The where is learned from geography.
3. Why is it that city people think the country is the place for a vacation and the city attracts country people at the same time?
4. To err is human but forgiving is a divine trait.
5. Old-fashioned grammarians tried to say what the English language should be; modern grammarians examine actual usage and describe it for us.

Repetition for Emphasis

78. Repeat important words for emphasis.

Quite frequently a word or an expression should be repeated for rhetorical effectiveness. Do not repeat unimportant words merely because you are too lazy to find appropriate synonyms.

See § 83 for Faulty Repetition and § 97 for Repetition for Clearness.

Note the effect of repetition in the sentences below.

He will find one English book and one only where, as in the *Iliad* itself, perfect plainness of speech is allied with perfect nobleness; and that book is the Bible.

I saw him climbing the fence with his knife between his teeth; that knife I determined to have.

Street after street, and all the folks asleep — street after street, all lighted up as if for a procession and all empty as a church — till at last I got into that state of mind when a man listens and listens and begins to long for the sight of a policeman.

See §§ 77 and 86 for emphasis through the repetition of the same grammatical structure.

EXERCISES

A. Find five examples of repetition in current magazines or newspapers; explain why each is effective.

B. Write ten forceful sentences such as might occur in a newspaper editorial on some controversial issue, using repetition in each.

C. Find all the repetitions of words (other than connectives and articles) in the following sentences. Revise those sentences in which the repetition is ineffective.

1. The fictional treatments of these cruelties are as various as are the cruelties themselves.
2. The council requested that requests for excuses for absence be referred to the dean of men's office.
3. Although he had taught public speaking, the speaker said that he was not qualified to speak on sermons.

4. Judge Chambers called the opposing attorneys into his chambers in the courthouse for a conference.
5. The current spate of short-story anthologies and collections, he finds, gives ample evidence that there is a hopeless confusion of standards in the short story.
6. It is a retreat from scholarship to scholasticism, a retreat to a method as sterile as the wooden criticism of the eighteenth century.
7. We must resist witch hunts, resist tricky loyalty oaths, resist all reactionary attacks on traditional American freedom of thought.
8. The first week was a nightmare — I rushed from rush party to rush party, scarcely having time to change dresses.
9. But you don't find feelings in written words unless there were feelings in the man who used them.
10. And so I think that all university men ought to rouse themselves now and understand what is the object of a university.

Subordination for Emphasis

79. Subordinate the less important parts of your sentences.

Subordination is a most valuable means of securing emphasis in the sentence, for by this device a writer can indicate the relative importance of his ideas and reveal the precise shades of emphasis he desires. The brevity and compactness resulting from the skillful use of subordination also add much to the force of the sentence. The main idea should be in the main clause and all other ideas subordinate constructions. These subordinate ideas may be in the form of dependent clauses, phrases, or single words. Note the difference in directness and emphasis in the contrasted sentences below.

Unemphatic It was against orders and it was dangerous to light the head lamp, but we had to do it.

Emphatic Although it was dangerous and against orders, we had to light the head lamp.

Unemphatic We lit the lamp, and I moved to the front seat, and I held my sombrero over the light and muffled most of it, but I liberated a concentrated stream of silver, and this played on the road ahead.

Emphatic We lit the lamp, and, moving to the front seat, I muffled most of the light by holding my sombrero over the lamp, but I liberated a concentrated stream of silver that played on the road ahead.

Unemphatic We came to the end of the street, and we struggled for several minutes, for we wanted to get through the crowd which had gathered to see the fight; and at last we succeeded in forcing our way through.

Emphatic When we came to the end of the street, we struggled for several minutes in the effort to get through the crowd which had gathered to see the fight; and at last we succeeded in forcing our way through.

Emphatic and Concise After several minutes of struggle at the end of the street with the crowd that had gathered to see the fight, we finally forced our way through.

EXERCISE

Make the following selection more emphatic by subordinating the less important elements. (See Reduction of Predication in § 16.) Instructors may wish to make two assignments of this exercise.

One course has taught me much about language. I took this course last fall as an elective. We learned new classifications of sentences: reports, directives, definitions, judgments, and phatic noises. We didn't use declarative, subjunctive, imperative, and interrogative classifications.

It was very revealing to apply these new classifications. For example we collected reports. Some were declarative sentences, for example "Oil floats on water," "Reno is west of Los Angeles," and "New editions of dictionaries list new words." Other reports were in the form of questions. For example a boy said, "Do you think I'm blind?" meaning *I see it.* Another said, "Isn't it time to go to class?" meaning *It's time to go to class.* The construction was interrogative; the intent was to report.

We found directives very interesting. A few were imperative sentences like "Keep off the grass" and "Keep to the right." Others were questions. "Will you open the door?" "Will you let me by?" "May I see it now?" Some were single words on signs. For example EXIT, CURVE, LADIES, CASHIER, and DANGER. Directives can be declarative sentences. "Johnson is a fascist" is a directive to regard him permanently as a fascist. "Jones is a Republican" directs the listener to treat him as an unchanged Republican. We learned a useful point. Directives occur in various forms.

Judgments and definitions are alike in one feature. They can't be either true or false. A judgment indicates one person's attitude. "Ravel's *Bolero* is great music" is a judgment. It is true for some people, and it is false for some people. Judgments really tell about the speaker, not about the thing judged. Definitions likewise can't be either true or false. "A deer is a ruminant mammal" is a definition. This tells how the speaker uses the word *deer*. At a later date he may use it differently. Meanings of words change. In the Middle Ages *deer* meant *wild animal*.

Phatic noises amused our class. They are things people say to be sociable. "Good morning" and "How are you?" and "I had such a good time" and "How's your Aunt Matilda?" and "Nice day, isn't it?" are phatic expressions usually. They aren't insincere, just sociable.

Separation for Emphasis

80. Emphasize an important element by making it a sentence by itself.

The future was barred to my progress. For consolation and encouragement I turned to the past.

Here the greatest possible emphasis is given to each unit, since each is a separate sentence. Whether to express the ideas in separate sentences or to combine them in one depends upon the logical relationship between the ideas and the degree of emphasis the writer wishes to secure for each. The simple sentences above may also be combined into a compound or a complex sentence:

The future was barred to my progress, and I turned for consolation and encouragement to the past. (The writer, Hazlitt, here presents the two ideas as of equal importance.)

Since the future was barred to my progress, I turned to the past for consolation and encouragement. (In this sentence one idea is singled out for special emphasis, and the other is stated as a subordinate clause.)

The form of sentence which is best in a given case will depend upon the thought and the purpose. The following quotation from Stewart Edward White's *The Mountains* shows how relative degrees of emphasis may be secured by the choice of the appropriate form of sentence:

The very breath of our bodies seemed driven back, so that as we faced the elements, we breathed in gasps, with difficulty. Then we dropped down into our blankets. We lay in a little backwash of the racing winds, still as a night in June. Over us roared the battle. We felt like sharp-shooters in the trenches, as though, were we to raise our heads, at that instant we should enter a zone of danger. So we lay quietly on our backs and stared at the heavens.

Some modern prose writers use a series of short sentences to gain a staccato effect. If you use this style, do not let it become a mannerism. (See § 70.) The paragraph below illustrates the effective use of separate sentences for the different ideas.

It is day in the big city. What noise and bustle! People run madly across the streets. Taxicabs spin around the corners. Smoke pours forth from the factory stacks. Elevated trains shake the earth with rumblings. Subways under the earth shoot to all corners of the city. An occasional airliner roars overhead. Policemen's whistles direct automobiles, busses, taxicabs, people — all frantic to rush in different directions at the same time.

EXERCISES

A. From a book or an article in a current magazine copy five sentences that were deliberately made short for emphasis. (Clue: look for sentences beginning with a connective such as *however*, *for*, *and*, or *but*.)

B. Rewrite in two sentences any of the sentences below which could be made more emphatic by separation.

1. Jenkins owned property on the Alabama river and opposed building a flood-control dam with public funds, but when a flood ruined his home and destroyed his cattle, he regretted opposing the dam.
2. Mrs. Jenkins, who had favored the flood control project, said that he would live to regret his opposition, and he did.
3. Floods have been prevented on the Tennessee by the TVA dams, and floods on the lower Ohio have been reduced in severity.
4. The sinking of the *Lusitania* was a terrible catastrophe, but I don't think it was justification for a nation to go to war.
5. Fires, explosions, and floods are brought on by something that men do or have done, and so they can be prevented.
6. Although the city fire inspectors have been exonerated of any blame

for the hotel fire, they admitted that they had not been insistent about some regulations, and they should be removed from office.

7. Dr. Grace is quite competent; he has had previous administrative experience, he is popular with students, faculty, and alumni, and he is demonstrably able to raise money.
8. The college abolished intercollegiate football a dozen years ago, but it has no trouble attracting excellent students and a world-famous faculty.
9. Millvale needs a new hospital, for although the present hospital is good it is too small, and although Millvale people can go to the county hospital it is in Exeter, sixty miles away.
10. If professional baseball could survive the scandal of 1919, basketball can survive the attacks of critics, and I think it will.

Variety in Sentence Structure

81. Vary the structure of your sentences.

Unless you are deliberately repeating a grammatical construction to gain parallelism, balance, effective repetition, or some other rhetorical effect, vary the structure of your sentences by occasionally departing from the usual word order (subject, verb, complement). Practice putting less important ideas (modifiers, for example) at the beginning or, better still, in the middle of your sentences, and reserve the end of the sentence for the most important ideas. Use periodic or balanced sentences as well as loose sentences, complex as well as simple or compound, short as well as long sentences, questions and exclamations as well as statements. Practice variety in subordination by avoiding the too frequent use of the participial construction or of *after*, *when*, *where*, *as*, and *while* as subordinating conjunctions. Do not overwork *and*, *but*, *for*, *also*, *then*, *next*, and *so* as connectives, or *this*, *these*, *it*, *that*, and *those* as reference words. Do not begin a series of sentences with *there is*, *there are*, or *it is*.

EXERCISES

A. Rewrite each of the following selections to add variety.

1. Georgia is a South Atlantic state. It is the largest state east of the

Mississippi. It is bounded by Florida, Alabama, Tennessee, North Carolina, and South Carolina. It was one of the original thirteen states. Its capital is Atlanta.

2. Coming out of the night club, he walked rapidly west. Bending his head against the cold wind, he hurried toward the girl's apartment. Reaching into his overcoat pocket, he fondled the stubby automatic nervously. Pausing at the door to glance up and down the street, he wondered whether he had been seen.

3. The characters in *From Here to Eternity* are dumb, but I suppose they are realistic. The language is frequently dirty, but it is probably what they would use. The plot is well organized, but I didn't read it for the story.

4. There was trouble in Iran over the oil nationalization program. There was trouble in Korea, where North Koreans and Chinese were fighting U.N. troops. Indo-China was a danger spot. There were other places like Eastern Germany and Italy which could have become battlefields any day.

5. Father likes the news programs and panel discussions. Mother and Sister like the dramatic shows and old movies. I want to see the sports events and a few musical programs. Nobody at our house watches television comics.

B. Examine the sentence structure in the following passage and determine how Thackeray has gained variety.

They talk of murders being pretty certainly found out. Psha! I have heard an authority awfully competent vow and declare that scores and hundreds of murders are committed, and nobody is the wiser. That terrible man mentioned one or two ways of committing murder, which he maintained were quite common, and were scarcely ever found out. A man, for instance, comes home to his wife, and . . . but I pause — I know that this Magazine has a very large circulation. Hundreds and hundreds of thousands — why not say a million of people at once? — well, say a million read it. And amongst these countless readers, I might be teaching some monster how to make away with his wife without being found out, some fiend of a woman how to destroy her dear husband. I will *not* then tell this easy and simple way of murder, as communicated to me by a most respectable party in the confidence of private intercourse. Suppose some gentle reader were to try this most simple and easy receipt — it seems to be almost infallible — and come to grief in consequence, and be found out and hanged? Should I ever pardon myself for having been the means of doing injury to a single one of our esteemed subscribers? The prescription whereof I speak — that is to say, whereof I *don't* speak — shall be buried in this bosom. No, I am a humane man. I am not one of your Bluebeards to go and say to my wife, "My dear! I am going away for a few days to Brighton. Here are all the keys of the house. You may open every door and closet, except the one at the end of the oak-room opposite the fireplace, with the little bronze Shakespeare on the mantelpiece (or what not)." I don't say this to a woman — unless, to be sure, I want to get rid of her — because, after such a caution, I know she'll peep into the closet. I say nothing about the closet at all, keep the key in my pocket, and a being whom I love, but who, as I know, has many weaknesses, out of harm's way. (*From* "On Being Found Out")

Smooth and Emphatic Word Order

82. Arrange the words in your sentences in a smooth, natural, logical, and emphatic order.

Word order is smooth and natural when it conforms to the normal patterns which we learn when we learn to talk: subject-verb-complement, adjective-noun, adverbs close to the words they modify, and related words close together.

For the sake of emphasis, of course, one may at times wish to depart from the natural order, use suspense, or write a periodic sentence; but these devices are helpful only when they result in greater force. (For misplaced modifiers, see § 91.)

Awkward, Unnatural Order A girl, if she sunburns easily, should take an umbrella to the beach.

Smoother and More Natural If she sunburns easily, a girl should take an umbrella to the beach.

A girl who sunburns easily should take an umbrella to the beach.

Awkward, Unnatural Order Wholly sympathetic, however, is the reader with Maurice, who shot the spy.

Smoother and More Natural The reader is, however, wholly sympathetic with Maurice, who shot the spy.

82a. Do not use the participial construction at the end of a sentence very frequently.

Avoid especially the overuse of phrases that begin with "thus causing" or "thereby causing." See § 92.

Unemphatic Concrete and specific words have been chosen, thus causing the reader's senses to be appealed to directly. (The subordinate idea in this sentence is improperly placed in the most emphatic position in the sentence.)

Emphatic The choice of concrete and specific words results in a direct appeal to the reader's senses.

Unemphatic He had returned from a walk through the various manufacturing plants of his company, dining about thirty minutes later with several other officials. (Unemphatic because the main idea is subordinated. The sentence may be improved by changing *dining* to *dined* and thus giving equal importance and the same grammatical form to the two ideas: *returned* and *dined*. Or, if additional emphasis is desired on the second idea, subordinate the first idea: "Having returned," or "After he had returned.")

NOTE. Many good sentences end with a participial construction. If the word modified by the participle is immediately clear and if the idea expressed is not too important to be placed in this subordinate grammatical form, the use of such a construction enables the writer to reduce predication and save words. Contrast the following emphatic sentences with the unemphatic ones above:

Annoyed by these frequent demands upon his time, he finally called his friend, begging him to come to his aid.

The Liverpool-bound liner *Borgen* rammed and sank the freighter *Polk City* ten miles from New York, sending her to the bottom in twenty minutes. (Some grammarians call such a participle a "coördinating participle" used to replace one of the main verbs. *Sending* here is virtually equivalent to "and sent.")

82b. Do not begin or end a sentence with weak, unimportant words.

The beginning and the end of the sentence are the most conspicuous positions. Minor and unimportant words should, therefore, be placed in the middle of the sentence, and the important words reserved for the beginning and the end — the most important for the end. End with words that deserve distinction. Notice how emphasis is gained by placing the important elements in conspicuous positions:

Unemphatic I think his whole theory is absurd, however.
His whole theory, however, is absurd, I think.

Emphatic I think, however, that his whole theory is absurd. (The important word is placed in the most emphatic position.)

Parenthetical expressions like "I think" and transitional words or sentence modifiers such as *however, therefore, thus, indeed, certainly, too, then,* and *also* are often best tucked into the middle of the sentence so that the beginning and the end may be reserved for the more important words and ideas.

82c. Avoid suspended prepositions and other constructions which cause too many pauses in the sentence.

Awkward He had no respect for, or love of, his employer. (Awkward separation of preposition and object, and unnatural pause after the prepositions.)

Smoother He had no respect for his employer nor love of him.
He neither respected nor loved his employer.

Choppy and Jerky He, too, being, as it were, an accomplice to the crime, murder, had, as was natural under the circumstances, little to say.

Smoother Since he was also an accomplice to the murder, he naturally had little to say.

See also § 95 and § 74e.

82d. Avoid the suspended *as*-clause.

Awkward This new boat is as fast as, if not faster than an outboard.

Smoother This new boat is as fast as an outboard, if not faster.

In a double comparison to be completed by both *as* and *than*, complete the first comparison before beginning the second. See §§ 73 and 95.

82e. Avoid the unnecessary use of impersonal constructions: *there is, there are, it is.*

Weak There were five of us who took part in the concert.
There had been a curious look pass over his face when I informed him that I had not come at all that night.

Such roundabout constructions are wordy and unemphatic. A direct, straightforward statement is more concise and therefore more emphatic.

Stronger Five of us took part in the concert.
A curious look passed over his face.

Remember, however, that it is frequently necessary, especially in formal English, to use impersonal constructions.

EXERCISES

A. Revise the following sentences to make them smoother and more emphatic.

1. This foreign aid bill will send goods to and ask no repayment from some nations which were fascist sympathizers.
2. Incidentally, the word *the* is an adverb in some sentences.
3. Some mountaineer expressions used in the United States are archaic in standard English, resulting in the superstition that mountaineers talk Old English.
4. There are five deans on the campus who it is believed will retire next year.
5. The general's political beliefs were little better known, if as well known, than King Tut's.

B. Directions given under Exercise A.

1. The Point Four program, which was a worthwhile undertaking to me, although disliked by many people in my home state, and which was supported in the East, had been neglected by the newspapers, I think.
2. I don't believe that we can establish an honor system here until students are willing to report violators though.
3. It was very clear that the President would not agree to sending an ambassador to Spain at that time.
4. As soon as possible, nineteen quarts of the extinguisher will be rushed to the fire zone.
5. If Secretary Acheson, knowing what he did, tried, in the face of congressional opposition, to work out a peaceful settlement, he should have been given credit for delaying the war.

Faulty Repetition

83. Avoid useless and awkward repetition.

Repetition may be undesirable unless an element is repeated either for emphasis or for clearness. Careless or awkward repetition may be corrected (1) by the use of synonyms, (2) by the use of pronouns or other reference words, or (3) by recasting and condensing the sentence.

Faulty When he was asked to back up his friend in public, George had to back down from his earlier position. (Find a synonym for either *back up* or *back down.*)

83a. Avoid the monotonous repetition of the same word or phrase especially if the word is used in two different senses.

Faulty He believed that people would believe his story about the accident.

Better He believed that people would accept his story about the accident.

Faulty Since I have reported on this book since seeing you, I shall now deal with the part of the book dealing with the battle of Waterloo.

Better Because I have reported on this book since seeing you, I shall now deal with that part of it which describes the battle of Waterloo.

83b. Avoid the careless repetition of the conjunction that.

Faulty He said *that* if there were no more heavy rains, *that* we should be able to take the trip. (Omit the second *that.*)

83c. Avoid the distracting repetition of similar sounds.

Faulty She stood quite quietly.

See § 63.

83d. Avoid a monotonous series of sentences similar in length or structure.

See §§ 70 and 81.

EXERCISES

A. Some of the repetition in the following sentences is desirable for clearness or emphasis. Eliminate the undesirable repetition.

1. When the traffic policeman left me he turned to the left on Elm.
2. These goods are as good as anything a chain store sells.
3. Teresa warned him, but her warning came too late.
4. They must meet the lower meat prices or lose customers.
5. He thought of sheep, nothing but sheep, but still he lay awake.

B. Directions given under Exercise A.

1. Public housing, public welfare, public waterworks, public schools — the old county has gone to the dogs!
2. Later we went to a late show at the neighborhood movie.
3. Whoever thinks that whoever heads this committee will have an easy job is mistaken.
4. Please ask the hall supervisors to announce this announcement tomorrow morning.
5. The gravel-voiced coach crunched across the gravel walk.

C. Some of the following sentences would be improved by substituting a pronoun for a word which is repeated. Indicate which sentences you would change, and what pronoun you would use.

1. Although diesel locomotives are replacing steam engines on the Southern, diesels are not used by the Birmingham and Atlantic.
2. The doctor advised him to give up steak, but he hasn't been able to afford a steak for the past year.
3. Several airlines use the DC–4; the DC–4 is a plane that was developed during World War II.
4. No commercial airline uses the helicopter, but the helicopter is used by several post offices to move air mail from the roof of the post office to the airport.
5. My favorite philosopher is Arthur Schopenhauer, although I do not agree with everything Schopenhauer says about women.
6. The most impressive new singer at the Metropolitan was Ljuba Welitch, and opera lovers are certain to hear Miss Welitch in many roles in the future.
7. Greendale is floating a bond issue to build a stadium — a stadium, when there isn't a public library in the whole county.
8. There was a big public reception for General MacArthur; General MacArthur's wife once lived here many years ago.

9. Many automobiles should be banned from the streets by law, especially those automobiles with defective brakes.
10. There is a revival of interest in handmade pottery, and many amateurs are now producing pottery wherever suitable clay is found.

Passive Voice

84. Use the passive voice when the agent is unknown or unimportant, or when the receiver of the action is more important than the agent.

Examples Five hundred men were wounded in that battle.
The whole Democratic ticket was elected by a landslide majority.
The chair got wet when he left it outdoors.

The use of the passive voice may detract from the interest and emphasis of a sentence.

Unemphatic A most delightful day was spent by all.
Better All (*or* Everyone) spent a most delightful day.
Unemphatic I was thanked by both of them with a smile.
Better Both of them thanked me with a smile.
Awkward This book is announced to be published next month. (The double passive is especially awkward.)
Better The publishers announce that the book will appear next month.

84a. Avoid shifting from active to passive or from passive to active within the same sentence or short passage.

Faulty The long-expected letter was then received, which he read with great pleasure.
Better He then received the long-expected letter, which he read with great pleasure.

See also § 98a.

EXERCISE

Rewrite the following sentences to make them more emphatic.

1. Morale is improved and work is more efficient when there is a systematic wage system in effect.

2. A good time is being had by all at the beach cottage.
3. Taste is cheapened, time is wasted, good authors are neglected, and education is made a farce by this newfangled system.
4. Parents are warned by us that children without driver's licenses are subject to heavy fines.
5. *King Lear* was not selected by me for the college drama club's spring play.

Absolute Phrases

85. Although the absolute phrase is often a convenient means of subordinating, the writer should observe the cautions below.

85a. An absolute phrase is usually awkward when it contains a perfect participle or a personal pronoun.

Awkward and stilted *The motor having been repaired,* we set out on our journey.

Better When the motor had been repaired, we set out on our journey. Having repaired the motor, we set out on our journey.

Awkward *We seeing* him in daily life, it is probable that we should see nothing in him but what is commonplace.

Better If we should see him in daily life, we should probably see nothing in him but what is commonplace.

Awkward John suddenly became ill. *He being alone,* Cecil remained with him until the doctor came.

Better John suddenly became ill. Since he was alone, Cecil remained with him until the doctor came.

See Absolute in § 16 for the definition and further examples.

85b. An absolute phrase at the end of the sentence usually detracts from the emphasis.

The most emphatic position in the sentence should not be occupied by a weak grammatical construction.

Unemphatic The author constantly uses suspense, the reader being kept on the alert from the beginning of the story to the end.

Emphatic The author's constant use of suspense keeps the reader on the alert from the beginning of the story to the end.

See also § 82. For the punctuation of absolute phrases, see § 17g.

GENERAL EXERCISES IN EMPHASIS

A. Phrase each of the following sets of rough notes into an emphatic sentence.

1. Corporal Connor had fine war record. Wounded four times. In six major battles. Won eight medals.
2. Cox has good ideas but cannot speak well in public. Elton, a fine speaker, has no good ideas.
3. Burrows is good teacher. Lectures are carefully prepared. Is well informed. Interested in students.
4. Rita Towne is generous with talent. Sings in choir. In glee club. At women's club meetings.
5. He has bad leg. Injured in high school. Should never play football. Fine athlete.

B. Revise each of the following sentences to make it more emphatic.

1. John misspells words in his letters, his class reports, and his notes, I have heard.
2. The book is old, it is bound in paper, and it is, with no pages missing, in good condition.
3. The President was given a huge ovation by the people in Portland.
4. This is an outrage, if he means what he says.
5. The candidate is, although he will not admit it, in favor of a medical insurance plan, which, in view of our condition, we cannot afford, I think.
6. The prospects for increased business in Greenville are good, I am told, although I have not been there recently.
7. The debate coach thought Albert could bring the argument to a tremendous climax and thought he should keep his hands out of his pockets.
8. The position, in the modern world, of America has changed since World War II, I believe.
9. "Now, come on," she kept repeating.
10. In the novel, several scenes in which prisoners are tortured are included.

CLEARNESS

Writing clearly is a matter of the writer's (1) selecting and ordering his words and sentences to communicate accurately, and (2) keeping the reader's attention focussed on the meaning and not distracted by violations of conventions of sentence structure. If the reader is puzzled by a sentence, or if he is diverted from the meaning by the wording, the writing is not clear. In casual conversation vague, general, and elliptical sentences are common because they accurately communicate the vague, general, and elliptical thinking that is common in such conversation. In serious writing the writer is expected to revise and tidy up his sentences if he has anything important to communicate; he is expected to write what he means so that the reader can follow his train of thought without tripping over words or unexpected constructions.

Parallelism

86. Sentence elements that are coördinate should wherever possible be parallel in structure.

Note that parallelism is a special type of coördination. An infinitive should be paired with an infinitive, a gerund with a gerund, a phrase with a phrase, a clause with a clause, etc. (See §§ 68, 87, 88.) Observe the parallel subordinate clauses below:

But one transparent blue morning, when a stillness almost preternatural spread over the sea, however unattended with any stagnant calm; when the long burnished sun-glade on the waters seemed a golden finger laid across them, enjoining some secrecy; when the slippered waves whispered together as they softly ran on; in this profound hush of the visible sphere a strange spectre was seen by Daggoo from the mainmast-head. (MELVILLE, *Moby Dick*, chap. LIX.)

Mixed He was told to report to the field and that he would find his uniform in the Locker Building.

Parallel He was told to report to the field and to call at the Locker Building for his uniform.

Mixed I thought of walking down Flint Street and deliver my letter to the editor in person. (*Deliver* should be changed to the gerund *delivering* so as to make it agree in form with *walking*, with which it is logically coördinate.)

The play is serious, noble, and appeals to each generation alike. (Items in such a series as this — *a*, *b*, and *c* — should be the same parts of speech. The parallelism above is faulty because the last member of the series is not an adjective. Either change the verb to an adjective: "The play is serious, noble, and appealing" — or write two clauses or sentences: "The play is serious and noble. It appeals to each generation alike.")

Faulty He had no sense of time, of responsibility, and of the latter defect I had no idea until he began working for me.

Improved He had no sense of time or of responsibility. I had, however, no idea of the latter defect until he began working for me.

86a. Avoid incongruous or misleading parallelism. Use the same structure only for elements which are of equal value.

Faulty Each one must furnish his own supply of paper and bring white paper. (The second part is not of equal importance with the first and should not have the same grammatical form.)

Improved Each one must furnish his own white paper.

Faulty He was interested in history, economics, science, and inventors. (The last word is incongruous with the others.)

Improved He was interested in history, economics, science, and inventions.

NOTE. In formal writing *so*, *then*, and *also* are not generally used to connect coördinate elements.

Faulty We took the necessary fishing tackle, also several guns.

Improved We took the necessary fishing tackle and also several guns.

Faulty He walked up the front steps then rang the bell.

Improved He walked up the front steps and then rang the bell.

He walked up the front steps, then rang the bell. (Here the comma marks the ellipsis of *and*.)

EXERCISE

Revise the following sentences to correct the faulty, incongruous, or misleading parallelism.

1. To read the first few chapters attentively and then skipping rapidly through the remainder of the book is unfair to the author.
2. The chamber of commerce asked the planning board to defer a decision on zoning Elm Heights and for immediate action on the express highway project.
3. He insisted on having a good boat, good fishing tackle, and that we find an experienced guide.
4. The *American Scholar* is a quarterly magazine containing serious articles and published by the Phi Beta Kappa society.
5. Jazz records, collecting ludicrous misprints, and old automobile license plates are Professor Wilkes' hobbies.
6. The old edition was noted for its clear definitions and being conservative on pronunciations.
7. This college is widely famed for its beautiful campus, beautiful co-eds, and encourages social activities.
8. Writing is both easy for him and provides him with an extra income.
9. Although she is bored by other girls and boys interest her, she doesn't go to many parties.
10. Eight o'clock classes are unpopular and graduate students teach most of them, since professors refuse to work at that early hour.

"And Which," "And Who"

87. Use an "*and which*" or "*and who*" clause only after a preceding "*which*" or "*who (whom)*" clause. The same principle applies to "*and that*," "*but which*," and similar constructions.

And, but, or, and other coördinating conjunctions connect only sentence elements of the same grammatical form and the same importance. Remember that parallelism is a special form of coördination. See § 68.

Illogical The house, large and roomy, *and which* was built many years ago, belonged to my grandfather.

Improved The house, *which* was large and roomy, *and which* was built many years ago, belonged to my grandfather.
The large and roomy house, which was built many years ago, belonged to my grandfather. (Here the omission of *and* leaves only one subordinate *which* clause.)

EXERCISE

Revise the following sentences:

1. The general is a man I would hate to see in public office and whom we need in the defense department.
2. This assignment should be completed in two weeks and which must be turned in not later than December 1.
3. Eliot's *The Cocktail Party* is long and garrulous and which the critics disagree on will be staged here this spring.
4. Doctor Wertz, an able and popular surgeon, and who married the leading banker's daughter, was the villain.
5. In spite of its prolixity, the play has some attractive parts but which are all short and unimportant.

Correlatives

88. Use correlatives (*both . . . and, either . . . or,* etc.) only before grammatically coördinate sentence-elements.

Since correlatives connect sentence elements of equal value — parallel, or coördinate, elements — the words following the correlatives should be of the same grammatical construction: two substantives, two verbs, two modifiers. The most common correlatives are *both . . . and, either . . . or, neither . . . nor, not only . . . but also, as . . . as,* and *whether . . . or*. For parallelism, see § 86.

Faulty Mr. Small both talked longer and more rapidly than I had expected.

Better Mr. Small talked both longer and more rapidly than I had expected.

Faulty Either you will report on time or be penalized for your absence.

Better You will either report on time or be penalized for your absence.

Faulty This nation not only has achieved great success in science but also in the arts.

Better This nation has achieved great success not only in science but also in the arts.

EXERCISE

Correct any misplaced correlatives which you find in the following sentences.

1. Neither can the student understand the dialect nor follow the plot.
2. The artist both represented the shapes of the worshippers and the colors in the old cathedral square.
3. Not only does this tax burden the salaried people but also men and women living on pensions and annuities.
4. After all, he liked neither to sing nor to act in musicals.
5. Either to drive over twenty-five miles an hour or parking more than an hour in a restricted zone will risk a fine.

Transition

Our own thought processes are so familiar to us that we are likely to forget the difficulties which our readers may have in following what we have written. Even if the sentences are arranged in a perfectly logical order, signs of transition from one step to another are usually needed as guides to our readers.

89. Make your transitions clear. Pass from one element to the next in such a way that there can be no doubt about what you mean.

Repeat a key word or phrase. Choose the exact connective or employ a formal mark of transition (*secondly, on the other hand, next,* etc.) or a pronoun or other reference word. Obviously, a useful aid to smooth transition is a competent knowledge of connectives and care in selecting the exact one which is needed. Note the easy movement of the following paragraph:

The steps drew swiftly nearer, and swelled out suddenly louder as they turned the corner of the street. The lawyer, looking forth from the entry, *could soon see* what manner of man he had to deal with. *He* was small and very plainly dressed, and the *look* of *him* even *at that distance,* went somehow strongly against the watcher's inclination. *But he* made straight for the door, crossing the roadway to save time; *and as he came,* he drew a key from his pocket like one approaching home. (STEVENSON, *Dr. Jekyll and Mr. Hyde.*)

We should study three kinds of transition: the transitional *word,* the transitional *phrase,* and the transitional *sentence.* Examples are *however, on the other hand, to consider another phase of the question, as I said, in short, it needs only to be mentioned, turning now to the other side, Let us continue, My last point can be handled very briefly.*

Inexact Transition The brush and trees became so thick until we were compelled to let the horses guide themselves. (Change *until* to *that.*)
I stepped up on the porch just at that time, so I could hear what he was saying to his wife. (Change *so* to *so that.*)
It was as a sculptor that he won his reputation, *and* those early drawings of East Side types are still worthy of notice. (The thought obviously calls for *but* instead of *and.*)

Transition Unmarked The doctor recommended Pisa, a recognized resort for invalids. Elizabeth's brothers and sisters were concerned about her. Their father refused to give his permission. (The reader cannot pass easily from one sentence to another.)

Clear The doctor recommended Pisa, a recognized resort for invalids. Although Elizabeth's brothers and sisters wanted her to go, her father *so resented the plan* that he refused to give his permission.

For transition within sentences, see § 71; for transition between paragraphs, see § 37e and p. 67.

EXERCISES

A. List all the transitional words and phrases in the selections on page 55.

B. Copy a paragraph from a current magazine and underline all the transitional expressions in it. Classify and list the various types of transition used.

C. Write an explanation three or four paragraphs long of why you think some individual would make a good mayor (or senator, or governor, or dean of men, etc.), using as few transitional words as you can; then rewrite your explanation including smooth transitions.

D. Repeat Exercise C, this time narrating an incident. Compare the transitional expressions used in explanation with those used in narration.

Sequence

90. Arrange the parts of a sentence and a series of sentences according to a planned sequence.

Finish one thought before you begin another, and begin the second where you leave off the first. The following sentences violate the principle of logical sequence of ideas. See § 71.

Faulty The most serious problem was malaria. All swamps in the camp area were either drained or sprayed. Mosquitoes were breeding in the swampy lowlands and infesting the barracks.

Better The most serious problem was malaria. Mosquitoes were breeding in the swampy lowlands and infesting the barracks. All swamps in the camp area were either drained or sprayed.

Faulty Men speak of international law but there is no international government. Law has to be enforced. To enforce law requires a government.

Better Law requires enforcement, and enforcement requires government. There is no international government, hence no international law.

Faulty President Truman won the election in 1948, surprising the "experts," after making an extensive "whistle stop" campaign across the country.

Better After making an extensive "whistle stop" campaign across the country, President Truman surprised the "experts" and won the election in 1948.

EXERCISE

Revise the following sentences to improve the logical sequence of sentences and internal parts of sentences. Supply transitional expressions where they are needed.

1. I attended grade school in Blytheville and graduated from the University of Arkansas in 1949. Instead of going to public high school, I went to Castle Heights Military Academy.
2. Theodore acted in the title role, directed the production, and even wrote the play.
3. She hired a schoolboy to mow the grass, wax the floors, rake the lawn, and wash the windows.
4. Operation of the brakes should be checked carefully after the overhauling is completed. The master cylinder should be refilled with fluid and the valves examined. The brake shoes on the wheels should be examined for wear and replaced when they are slick.
5. The first thing I do before going to the beach is get the portable radio ready. Sometimes I take along some recent magazines. Almost as important as the radio is the camera.
6. Mechanics 105 is a required course. Every student must take analytic geometry before he can take calculus. The calculus is a prerequisite to Mechanics 105.
7. They looked a long time for a house because an apartment down town wouldn't provide her space for a rose garden and since he didn't want to live in a suburb and have to ride a train to and from work, so a house with a yard in the city was what they needed.
8. Mr. Hawley is a possible candidate. He is not particularly popular in labor circles. Mr. Walker is favored by labor leaders, but he makes a very poor speech. The labor vote here is not well organized. Hawley might be the party nominee.

Position of Modifiers

91. Indicate clearly the relation between modifiers and the words they modify.

In English, word order is of great importance in showing clearly the relation between words in the sentence. Every modifier, therefore, should be so placed that the reader may immediately connect it with the word it modifies.

Clear He stumbled almost at the water's edge. *Or,* He almost stumbled at the water's edge. (The position of *almost* is determined by the meaning.)

91a. Do not place a modifier in such a position that it may be taken to modify either the preceding or the following part of the sentence.

Not Clear Though his style is easy and rhythmical in its structure and correctness it is not really so good as Scott's.

Clear Though his style is easy and rhythmical, it is really not so good in structure and correctness as Scott's.

Not Clear He said that if we did not pay, within a week, in spite of all our protests, he would present the note at his bank.

Clear He said that if we did not pay within a week, he would, in spite of all our protests, present the note at his bank.

Take care to place the adverbs *only, just, merely, ever, almost,* and *even* so that their reference may be immediately clear.

Ambiguous Any person who will read a good book, even the most humble, will find something of himself in that book.

Clear Any person, even the most humble, who will read a good book will find something of himself in that book.

91b. Place a relative or other clause so that its relation to the antecedent is unmistakable.

Not Clear He rode silently down the road leading over the hill, which had been recently paved.

Clear He rode silently over the hill, down the road which had been recently paved.

Remember that in speech we make the reference of an adverb clear by stress; thus in the sentence *We only wanted to see Stanton,* either *see* or *Stanton* will be stressed, and *only* can occur before *wanted.* But in writing we have no conventional stress mark; hence the position of modifiers is much more important in writing than in speech.

Not Clear In this essay Stevenson discusses both everyday things of life and things that we have not seen in a way as simple as one friend talking to another.

Clear In this essay Stevenson discusses, in a way as simple as one friend talking to another, both the everyday things of life and things which we have not seen.

See also the exercises under § 82.

91c. Place every modifier so that related words will come close together.

Not Clear The man who was driving was thrown when the horse stumbled and his arm was broken.

Clear When the horse stumbled, the man who was driving was thrown and his arm was broken.

Misleading Mrs. Thomas went to North Dakota after her husband entered prison to live with relatives.

Clear After her husband entered prison, Mrs. Thomas went to North Dakota to live with relatives.

See also §§ 68, 86, 90, and 95.

EXERCISES

A. Insert *almost, just,* or *only* in each of the following sentences so that it clearly modifies the italicized word. Assume that all the sentences are in formal English.

1. Veterans are allowed *one* exception under this regulation.
2. We want *to protect* the interests of the absent stockholders.
3. This letter *persuades* us that you do not intend to pay the bill.
4. That information was *exactly* what the auditor needed.
5. If this refers to *Jackson*, one statement is incorrect.

B. Insert the phrase *with great speed* in each of the following sentences so that it unmistakably modifies an appropriate word.

1. The national guard company arrived and set up a barricade.
2. He talked so that the meeting would be over before midnight.
3. They pondered the problem, hoping that the diver would come.
4. Someone who writes shorthand is needed when she starts testifying.
5. Swimming doggedly, the life-guard finally reached the spot where the motor launch had turned around.

Dangling Modifiers

92. Avoid dangling modifiers: modifiers which cannot be connected immediately and unmistakably with the words to which they refer.

Occasionally a dangling modifier makes a sentence ridiculous, e.g., "Reaching the age of six, my family moved to Spokane." More commonly (as in the examples below) a dangling modifier simply violates a convention of formal written English and may momentarily distract the reader. A dangling element usually occurs when the writer shifts his construction in mid-sentence, forgetting to provide a subject for the modifier to modify.

92a. Avoid dangling participles, gerunds, and infinitives.

Dangling participle:

Faulty	The details are properly selected and well combined by the author, thus giving a better effect than he could by mere enumeration.
Unemphatic	The author chooses properly and combines skillfully the details in this story, thus giving a better effect than he could attain by mere enumeration. (See § 82a.)
Better	By properly selecting and skillfully combining the details in this story, the author gives a better effect than he could attain by mere enumeration.

Dangling gerund:

Faulty	On approaching the island, a high cliff can be seen.
Better	As one approaches the island, he can see a high cliff. On approaching the island, one can see a high cliff.

Dangling infinitive:

Faulty	To receive maximum benefits, the accident must take place on the company's premises or property.
Better	To receive maximum benefits, the insured must experience the accident on the company's premises or property.

92b. In general, do not begin a sentence with a verbal in *-ing* unless the verbal clearly refers to the subject of the following (governing) clause; and do not end a sentence with a participle unless the participle clearly refers to some word in the preceding clause.

A sentence containing a dangling verbal may be corrected either by (1) expanding the verbal phrase into a full subordinate clause, or by (2) recasting the sentence so as to make the verbal agree with the subject of the governing clause. Both of these methods of correction are illustrated in § 92a. (See also § 82a.)

92c. Avoid dangling elliptical clauses and phrases.

An elliptical clause is one from which the subject or predicate — or both — is omitted. Such a clause "dangles" when the omitted subject or predicate is not the same as the subject or predicate of the main clause. To correct this error, expand the elliptical clause by supplying the omitted subject or predicate, or make the subject of both clauses the same. The same principle applies to elliptical phrases.

Dangling elliptical clause:

Faulty When on the top of the ridge, the distant mountains could easily be seen.

Better When on the top of the ridge, I could easily see the distant mountains. (Do not be afraid to begin a clause or a sentence with *I*.)

Dangling phrase:

Faulty In early childhood my grandfather took me to many circuses.

Better In early childhood I was often taken to circuses by my grandfather.

In early childhood I often went to circuses with my grandfather. (This sentence is preferable to the preceding because it avoids the unemphatic passive construction.)

92d. Distinguish between a participle and a preposition or prepositional phrase.

Such words and phrases as *according to*, *assuming*, *granting*, *owing to*, *relating to*, *rejecting*, *excepting*, *regarding*, *considering*, *concerning*, *speaking of*, etc., are prepositions or are so often used as prepositions as not to constitute dangling modifiers. See **Due to** in § 66.

Standard Speaking of names, his uncle's is one of the most peculiar I have ever heard.

EXERCISE

Revise any objectionable constructions in the following sentences, paying attention to the degree of formality of each sentence.

1. Considering these objections, do you still want the bill passed?
2. The dean's umbrella always gets blown inside out when rushing to an early class on a windy day.
3. Trying to find a telephone to summon help, my eye fell on your lighted windows.
4. Granting these extenuating circumstances, the Honor Court still finds the student guilty and recommends suspension.
5. Settling down to a long period of negotiating, the labor contract was first reconsidered in the light of wage controls.
6. To help the reader who looks for particular items, an index should be prepared by the author.
7. Assuming that this law will be declared unconstitutional, no segregation is likely to remain in effect in the university.
8. On seeing her in a bathing suit, my memory was jogged and I remembered meeting her at the beach two summers earlier.
9. Finally painted, the house was ready for the new pastor.
10. Coming through a crack in the floor, my nose detected smoke that smelled like burning rubber and chicken feathers.

Reference of Pronouns

93. Make the reference of all pronouns immediately clear to the reader.

The reference word should be placed so that no intervening word may wrongly be taken as the antecedent, or the antecedent should be repeated, or the sentence entirely recast for the sake of clearness.

93a. Avoid ambiguous reference.

Do not use a pronoun which may refer to any one of two or more antecedents. Often the result is a short circuit between the pronoun and the wrong antecedent.

Vague John told his father that he would be nominated soon.

Undesirable John told his father that he (John) would be nominated soon. (Such an explanatory parenthesis is usually a confession of inability to write a clear sentence.)

Better John told his father that he expected to be nominated soon. John said to his father, "I expect to be nominated soon." (Since this kind of obscurity is especially common in indirect discourse, the use of direct discourse affords a simple remedy.)

Vague But suddenly he caught sight of something half hidden by the end of the crumpled parchment deed *which* was not old.

Clear But suddenly he caught sight of something which was not old, something half hidden by the end of the crumpled parchment deed.

Vague Nobody could tell whether this was the Italian *who* had not been there.

Clear Through Correct Position Nobody who had not been there could tell whether this was the Italian.

93b. In all cases where obscurity would result, avoid general reference.

Sometimes the use of *that, which,* or *it* to refer to the whole idea of a preceding clause instead of to a specific noun in the clause causes obscurity.

Obscure While Elizabeth was trying to write he talked incessantly about the likelihood of a flood, and it disturbed her.

Correct an error of this sort either by revising the sentence in such a way as to omit the pronoun or by giving the pronoun a definite antecedent. When the pronoun refers to the whole idea of the preceding clause, this general idea may be expressed by a noun like *fact, matter, process, practice, circumstance* accompanied by *this, that,* or *which.* Better still, get rid of the pronoun by changing the construction.

Clear While Elizabeth was trying to write he talked incessantly about the likelihood of a flood, and his talking disturbed her.

Clear While Elizabeth was trying to write he disturbed her by talking incessantly about the likelihood of a flood.

Since the general reference of a pronoun to a clause or sentence does not often result in actual obscurity, this use of pronouns in informal English is quite common, as in the following examples:

Acceptable While I was writing he talked incessantly. *This* distracted my attention.

The "third termites" want to remain where they are, to burrow deeper. This is understandable.

In formal English, however, it is conventional for a pronoun to refer clearly to a definite substantive as an antecedent, not to a clause or a sentence.

Informal High-carbon steel is very hard, which makes it suitable for knives and tools.

Formal High-carbon steel is very hard; this fact makes it suitable for knives and tools.

93c. Avoid vague or weak reference.

Do not use a pronoun to refer to a word which has not been expressed but must be inferred from the context.

Vague July 14 is a national holiday in *France*. *They* always celebrate this day very elaborately.

Formal July 14 is a national holiday in *France*. The *French* always celebrate this day very elaborately.

Vague His father is a banker. *This* is the profession I intend to enter.

Formal His father is a banker. Banking is the profession I intend to enter.
His father is engaged in banking, a profession I intend to enter.
His father is a banker, as I intend to be.

93d. In formal English avoid remote reference.

Do not use a pronoun to refer to a noun which is in a subordinate or parenthetical construction. Place the antecedent of the pronoun in an emphatic position in the sentence or repeat the antecedent.

Vague Limmason is the hero of "The Man Who Was," which is one of Kipling's best stories. *He* knew intimately the life of India.

Clear Kipling knew intimately the life of India.

93e. Avoid the use of *such, same,* or *said* instead of *it, this, that, the preceding, the above-mentioned,* etc., except in legal documents.

Jargon I received your letter and noted contents of *same* very carefully. The book had been lost two weeks. Then when *said* book was returned, *same* was found to be badly mutilated.

93f. Avoid an inconsistency or shift in number or gender between pronoun and antecedent in formal English.

Colloquial The choir *was* to raise five hundred dollars for *their* pipe organ. (*Choir* is first regarded as a singular, the subject of *was*, but it is next regarded as a plural. In formal writing use *its* or *the* for *their* or keep *their* and change *was* to *were*.)

See also §§ 6, 13a, and 98e.

EXERCISES

A. Correct any faulty reference of pronouns in the following sentences. Note that sentences 2, 6, and 8 are obviously conversational.

1. The chairman of the board of trustees wrote a letter dismissing the president, which he later claimed was based on a misunderstanding of the situation.
2. Our crowd liked President Hylton, but that didn't mean anything to the economic royalists who wanted to get rid of him.
3. Red China had ignored every offer to meet them halfway.
4. Apples are grown by many farmers in this county, but they do not grade and pack them properly for the city market.
5. Every person whose driver's license has expired must arrange for their driving test before applying for a new one.
6. Upton Sinclair has written some very effective propaganda novels, but that doesn't qualify him for a Pulitzer prize.
7. The indictment charged that "said John Doe did wilfully conspire with said Sarah Roe to commit an unlawful act and same was committed in this county on December 14, 1900."
8. It says in the paper that Brooklyn shellacked the Senators.
9. The smaller room is soundproof, which will make it more desirable for the recording studio.
10. The members of the council were puzzled by its new assignment.

B. Directions given under Exercise A. Assume that the sentences are in formal English.

1. Although Keats used many of the same poetic forms that Shelley did, he excelled in writing odes.

2. This committee is now in position to give their attention to the petition submitted by the bar association.
3. It is always interesting to watch the shrimp fleet come in. They will sometimes sell small quantities to people who happen to be at the dock.
4. The fog horn blows at intervals of ten seconds during a heavy fog and warns boats coming into the basin of the Red Dog reef, which makes it hard for summer cottagers to sleep.
5. My roommate was delighted with many details of Lilliputian life; it is a fictitious country described by Swift in *Gulliver's Travels*.
6. Charlene was very proud of her hair and complexion; it was a fiery red with not a sign of gray.
7. Mencken wrote for a newspaper for many years, although he became nationally known as a magazine editor, which probably accounted for his clear, forceful style.
8. The students in the group who are not interested in Elizabethan music which has a choice should go to the lecture instead.
9. Beverages are not legal in this county which contain more than 3.2 percent of alcohol.
10. Children should not be allowed to ride the university's horses unless their parents give written permission and the unruly ones have red warning ribbons on their tails.

Mixed Constructions

94. Do not confuse different syntactical constructions.

Do not begin a sentence with one construction and end with another. Note the following types and examples of the blending or confusion of two different constructions:

Mixed idioms:

Faulty *Despite of* this fact, he will agree to our proposal. (*Despite* and *in spite of* are confused.)

Faulty I used to could. (A nonstandard confusion of "I once could" and "I used to be able to.")

Blending types of phrases:

Faulty He has no room in which to work in. (*Room in which to work* and *room to work in* are here blended.)

Confusing the tenses of direct and indirect discourse:

Faulty I advised him to come as soon as he *can*. (Here the tense of the direct "Come as soon as you can" is improperly retained in the indirect discourse.)

Confusing the word order of direct and indirect questions:

Faulty He asked me was I going. (The inverted order of the direct question "Are you going?" is provincially used in the indirect question.)

Shifting a construction to turn an adverbial phrase or clause into a noun clause (a subject or a predicate nominative):

Faulty On account of my being late was the reason he scolded me. (Here the adverbial phrase "on account of my being late" demands "he scolded me" to complete it; instead, it is colloquially used as the subject of the copula *was*.)

Faulty The reason he scolded me was on account of my being late. (After *was* substitute "my lateness" or "that I was late.")

Beginning a sentence with one construction and switching to a different one before completing the first:

Faulty I enjoy the ornamentation of a style, which, although it is hard to understand, its lineaments are perfectly artistic. (*Which* is left without a predicate.)

See §§ 14, 71, 72, 73, and 87.

EXERCISE

Revise the following sentences to remove the mixed or confused constructions.

1. We might could find a replacement in our Chicago store.
2. On account for that honest if misguided remark he got in trouble.
3. The ambassador asked could he remain in Chile another month.
4. The reason why the treaty must be rejected is because it does not require the volunteer army to disband.
5. He said that I was to leave as soon as I can get a reservation.
6. He understood that the zone was to be extended was why he put up the service station outside the commercial limit.

7. The reason I got such a good grade was on account of the extra time I spent on my term paper.
8. The fact that the air force reserve quota was completed the minister's son enlisted in the marine corps.
9. Although the ore mine is ten miles away, however the coal and limestone are very near the furnace.
10. Doctors give many reasons which I cannot decide whether they apply to this situation or not.

Split Constructions

95. Avoid "split" constructions.

Grammatically related words usually belong close together. Aimless separation of closely related words is likely to cause obscurity or awkwardness. See §§ 82, 91.

95a. Avoid the split infinitive unless emphasis, smoothness, or clearness demands it.

The split infinitive (e.g. *to finally learn*) is an old and useful English construction. In the sentence *It angered him to gradually lose the use of his arm,* the adverb is wisely placed between *to* and *lose* so that it clearly modifies *lose* and does not occupy an emphatic position. Of course *It angered him to lose the use of his arm gradually* is the best order if his anger is caused by the gradualness of the loss. Compare *He taught her to accurately take notes,* in which the infinitive is unnecessarily split and *accurately* loses its proper emphasis. The order *He taught her to take notes accurately* emphasizes his teaching of accuracy and avoids separating related words. Whether to use or avoid a split infinitive is a matter of style rather than a question of correctness. Since many people object to splitting an infinitive, the student should use the construction only when it improves his sentences in smoothness, emphasis, or clearness.

Justified The directors asked the city council to eventually buy the hospital which they owned. (Putting *eventually* after *council* would violate clearness; putting it after *buy* would violate smoothness by separating related words.)

Justified The historian's intention was to carefully translate the documents into English. (Putting *carefully* after *was* would be awkwardly elegant; putting it after *translate* would make a split construction more distracting than the split infinitive.)

Distracting The rangers are trained to at all times watch for forest fires. (The inserted element is long, and it needlessly interrupts the infinitive.)

Revised The rangers are trained to watch at all times for forest fires. (This emphasizes *forest fires.*)

The rangers are trained to watch for forest fires at all times. (This emphasizes *at all times.*)

95b. Avoid the aimless separation of such closely related sentence elements as subject and verb, subject and predicate complement, verb and object, preposition and object, reference word and antecedent.

Awkward He, being suddenly called home, was unable to take part in the work. (Subject and verb needlessly separated; the strong emphasis on *he* is not intended.)

Better Being suddenly called home, he was unable to take part in the work.

Awkward She saw, at one sharp glance, the open box on the table. (Verb and object needlessly separated.)

Better At one sharp glance she saw the open box on the table.

Awkward He got revenge by beginning to accuse the enemies in turn who persecuted him. (Separation of the *who*-clause and its antecedent.)

Better He got revenge by beginning to accuse in turn the enemies who had persecuted him.

Awkward Lake Summit is one of the prettiest, if not the prettiest, lake I ever saw.

Better Lake Summit is one of the prettiest lakes I ever saw, if not the prettiest.

NOTE. It is perfectly correct to end a sentence with a preposition.

95c. Avoid the needless separation of the parts of a verb phrase.

Awkward There on the corner rose the great building which Maxwell *had* late in the spring *turned* over to the company. (*Had* and *turned* should not be separated without good reason.)

95d. Avoid the needless separation of coördinate (parallel) sentence-elements.

See §§ 82, 86, 90, 91.

Awkward When we had found a shelter, we dressed for the night, when we had re-spread our bedding. (The *when*-clauses are coordinate modifiers of the main clause and should be placed together.)

We put our arms around each other's shoulders as I got to my feet, and helped each other down the slope. (Place the coordinate parts of a compound predicate together.)

EXERCISE

Revise any of the following sentences which contain objectionable split constructions.

1. Theses of this kind are not, until they have been rewritten to eliminate the academic jargon, ready to be published.
2. University art galleries should, in spite of the preferences of the art faculty, show paintings by followers of many different theories and schools.
3. The bandmaster offered to by himself entirely rearrange the musical score.
4. The student-government president wanted to firmly support the faculty committee on athletics and physical education in their insistence on lowered admission charges.
5. They were asked to positively repudiate and denounce the suggestion that a third party be organized in the South.
6. Desmond Shannon, unaware that the murderer sat waiting for him in the unlighted room, walked rapidly down the hall toward the door.
7. The split infinitive is a construction at all times to be carefully used.
8. The displaced people wished for, but could hardly expect, kind treatment at the police station.
9. A full scale war is something the administration did not wish or ask for.
10. The radio program was at that crucial instant interrupted for a news flash on a local baseball game.

Mixed or Inappropriate Figures

96. Remember that a figure of speech is used instead of a literal expression to improve communication, to make something clearer or more striking or more emphatic.

To write that a bathing suit fits "like the skin on a peach" is effective, since any reader can be trusted to understand the figure, and it is more striking than "fits tight." But to write that a newspaper editor is "a modern Laocoön" is not likely to be effective for a very large audience. More people would be mystified than enlightened by the figure. However, readers need not have had experience with the subject of the figure to understand it. Such tropes as *a graveyard at night, the clang of a jail door, voices of angels,* and *delirious with joy* are more often imagined than experienced. Figures of comparison are particularly subject to exaggeration beyond remembered reality, but when something is said to be as *hot as the hinges of Hell,* as *seductive as a siren,* or as *deafening as the trump of doom,* one need not have felt the hinges or heard the sirens or the last trumpet to understand the intensity intended by the writer. Use figures of speech, but select figures that are familiar to the reader or that can be imaginatively grasped.

Examples The machine is simply a big ball-point fountain pen, with which traffic engineers mark the center lines on highways. (The writer assumes that the reader is familiar with ball-point fountain pens and will understand the highway marker better because of the metaphor.)

The poem is dignified and solemn, with many archaic words, like the diction of the Bible. (The writer assumes that the reader will understand immediately what he means by "archaic words" from the simile "like the diction of the Bible.")

96a. Do not use confused, unsustained, or inappropriate figures of speech.

Faulty The funeral procession wound through the streets at dusk like black cats marching on a fence and casting sheep's eyes at the dog-faced fireplugs.

The succession of animals practically destroys any clear meaning. The sentence could stop after "fence." Most confused figures come from an infatuation with words and too little attention to sense.

96b. Avoid mixed figures.

Mixed This fascist is a bull in a china shop, coiled like a serpent in the forest waiting to gobble up the trusting Little Red Riding Hood youth of our fair city.

96c. Keep figures sustained.

Do not shift between figurative and literal in a sentence or short passage when logic suggests continuing with one mode of expression.

England became Queen of the Sea when she defeated the Armada, and since that time England has had the largest navy in the world. (The figure in the first part of the sentence should be sustained throughout the sentence or not introduced at all.)

The icy breath of Winter had chilled all hearts, and drivers hastened to put on their chains.

96d. Avoid inappropriate, forced, or far-fetched figures.

Plain literalness of statement is always preferable to any figurative statement that gives the impression of self-conscious elaborateness, insincerity, or artificiality.

Can it be said that our colleges and universities are drifting from the solid literature and manly sports and actually promoting physical debasement and mental decay? Are the clabber-brained professors and teachers diluting the veins of the students with the whey of debauchery? We are inclined to believe that this "festivity" must have been a humdinger. (Note the forced figures, the shift from literal statement to figurative, and the lack of harmony in the tone of different parts of this passage.)

96e. Avoid trite figures of speech.

For examples see § 60.

EXERCISE

In the following sentences revise the figures which you decide are ineffective.

1. The minister glowered at the congregation like a hen admonishing her brood of chickens.
2. There was a look of terror in the waiter's eyes which he wiped off and swallowed with relief when the fire truck arrived.
3. Frank is a happy-go-lucky rolling stone that gathers roses and lives but for the pleasures of today.
4. The soft moonlight played on her face like a flashlight on a doorknob.
5. Democracy will sweep across the world like a tremendous prairie fire borne on a tidal wave, making hungry, hopeless people better off in many a foreign country.
6. Zimmerman came tearing down the left sideline like a freight engine on a steep grade and danced elusively through the enemy defense to score the first touchdown of the game.
7. Bradley stood firm, looking as assured and cool as the inside of a new deep freeze.
8. No mere politician can blow away the clouds of uncertainty that begloom the nation and clog our feet on the road of destiny.
9. On the steady rock of the Constitution we stand, confident that the shifting sands of politics cannot move us.
10. This storm of criticism must be met with an umbrella of truth.

Repetition for Clearness

97. When necessary for clearness, do not hesitate to repeat such sentence elements as articles, possessive pronouns, prepositions, the sign of the infinitive, verbs (especially auxiliary verbs), subordinating conjunctions, and connectives between parallel sentence-elements.

See §§ 74, 78, and 83.

Notice the obscurity that results from failure to repeat words necessary for clearness:

My friend and ∧ brother went with me. (Possessive pronoun to be inserted at the caret.)

You should ask what laws cover the case and ∧ carefully study the evidence. (Auxiliary verb *should* to be repeated.)

The story deals with the trials of a young couple who live beyond their means in order to keep up appearances and ∧ thereby invite disaster. (Relative pronoun *who* to be repeated in parallel clauses. See § 86.)

These people try to cast a glamour of romance over the world and ∧ soften its stern realities. (*To* should be repeated.)

I cut six logs; then laid them in a row. (The subject should be repeated or *and* inserted when two or more verbs are joined by *then, also, still, therefore,* etc.)

EXERCISE

In the following sentences supply the words that should be repeated for clearness.

1. The sheriff advised us to bandage the watchman's head and arm ourselves before moving any more valuable stock that night.
2. The planter was accompanied by his wife and barber.
3. These people have wormed their way into the students' confidence; also have bought several businesses near the campus.
4. It was rumored that Jones had gone to Chicago and Nashville had once been his home.
5. This is a poor story because the characters are unmotivated and unexplained incidents are narrated several times.
6. After the hero had abandoned his mother and his sister had given up trying to find him, the remorseful girl continued to look for him.

Point of View

98. Choose one point of view and keep it unless there is good reason for changing to another.

98a. Avoid aimlessly shifting the subject, voice, or mood in a sentence.

Faulty He came back to college in the fall, and all his energies were exerted toward making a scholar of himself. (Shift of subject and voice.)

Improved He came back to college in the fall and exerted all his energies toward making a scholar of himself.

Faulty We went through a cotton mill, where it interested us very much to watch the operatives. (Shift in subject and from a personal to an impersonal construction.)

Improved We went through a cotton mill, where we became very much interested in watching the operatives.

Faulty If anybody wants a good laugh, just read one of Irvin Cobb's stories. (Shift in mood and person.)

Improved If anybody wants a good laugh, he should read one of Irvin Cobb's stories.

98b. Avoid aimlessly shifting the tense from the present to the past or from the past to the present in narration.

Undesirable The flames were mounting higher and higher, and we began to wonder whether they would reach the window where she stood. A fireman runs up with a shout, but she did not hear him, and just stood there. She stands for a long time, as if dazed, and then was hidden by the smoke.

Improved The flames were mounting higher and higher, and we began to wonder whether they would reach the window where she stood. A fireman ran up with a shout, but she did not hear him, and just stood there. She stood for a long time, as if dazed, and then was hidden by the smoke. (Or the verbs could all be put in the present tense if, for example, this were describing a play or a novel.)

98c. Avoid aimlessly shifting from a formal to a colloquial style in the same passage.

Undesirable This piece of research will make demands upon your scholarship as well as upon your ingenuity; it is up to you to work to the limit. (See § 55.)

Improved This piece of research will make demands upon your scholarship as well as upon your ingenuity; you are expected to do your best.

98d. Avoid shifting from indirect to direct discourse.

Faulty He asked me *would I come*. (The word order of direct discourse is here incorrectly retained in the indirect discourse. See § 94.)

Improved He asked me whether I would come.

98e. Avoid shifting the number, person, or class of pronouns, or the number of collective nouns.

Faulty If *one* determines to avoid all misspellings, *you* (*they*) can learn to spell correctly.

Improved If *one* determines to avoid all misspellings, *he* can learn to spell correctly.

If *you* determine to avoid all misspellings, *you* can learn to spell correctly.

Faulty Take pains with spelling and one can avoid all misspellings.

Improved Take pains with spelling and you can avoid all misspellings.

Faulty We examined the trees that had been cut down and which were to be used for the walls of the cabin. (Needless shift from *that* to *which*.)

Improved We examined the trees that had been cut down and that were to be used for the walls of the cabin.

Faulty The jury was requested to put their decisions in writing. (Here the collective noun *jury* is first regarded as a singular subject of *was* and is then regarded as a plural, to which *their* refers. Keep a consistent point of view throughout the sentence.)

Improved The jury was requested to put its decisions in writing.

The jurors were requested to put their decisions in writing. (Note the plural *jurors* instead of the collective *jury*.)

EXERCISE

Correct the undesirable shifts in the following sentences.

1. If one attempts to understand all the price and wage regulations you would find it a full-time job.
2. There are some simplified manuals that are easy to read and which contain the most important regulations.
3. Breakfast was eaten, camp was broken, and we were ready to leave by sunrise.
4. The committee is meeting in the church office, and they are scheduled for an all-day meeting.
5. She wondered was it a stolen car.
6. This desecration of the library is intolerable; the drunks will have to get out fast.
7. This newspaper does not condone appeasement; we must punish the aggressors and make known our intentions to keep the peace; but this newspaper knows that *appeasement* is a smear word.
8. If one cannot locate the reference books immediately, call the reference librarian to your assistance.

9. The *Times* is opposed to the investigation, but it is supported by the *Evening Post*.
10. We then moved downstream, wading whenever we can, and fished with no luck at all until late afternoon.

Logical Thinking

99. Avoid loose and illogical thinking; make sense, not nonsense.

Double talk written by a professional gag writer and uttered by a radio or television comedian is normally recognized as harmless nonsense, designed to amuse an audience. But nonsense can be written by people who are trying to be serious, who are trying to explain or report or persuade. It may appear in formal sentences which are complete, unified, and grammatically correct. For example, the following sentence contains no fault in diction, syntax, punctuation, or completeness: *Since geriatrics is the science of old age and its diseases, all people who retire because of age should be required to take a course in geriatrics to be eligible for retirement benefits.* However, despite its formal correctness and adequate diction, the statement is simply nonsense, for there is no logical connection between eligibility for old age benefits and knowledge of the science of old age. Another example is *The inner unity of the essential American spirit abhors the class legislation typified by the individual income tax.* Fuzzy thinking here produces nonsense phrased in a dignified sentence. What actually is communicated? What evidence could be presented? What is meant by *inner unity?* By *essential?* By *spirit?* By *abhors?* By *typified?* Where would the reader go to verify the statement? What tests could he apply to it? Plain nonsense can usually be recognized by the student who examines statements closely, analyzing them and asking questions designed to make clear the meaning.

Many lapses and faults in logic fall into easily recognizable and identifiable types: non sequiturs, weak generalizations, biased opinions, and circular reasoning. Such illogical thinking may be due to poor training in thinking, hasty jumping to conclusions before examining sufficient evidence, or prejudice (which ignores or distorts evidence).

Study and analyze the following common types of illogical reasoning. There is some overlapping of types, because any one fallacy frequently involves others.

Begging the question:

The uneconomic and wasteful farm subsidy program should be abolished; then everybody in the country would be better off because our tax money would not be dumped down a million rural rat holes. (The writer assumes, but does not demonstrate, that the subsidy program is wasteful; his conclusion is nothing but a restatement of his assumption.)

Unwarranted conclusion:

City slums are thick with foreign-born immigrants; they simply do not have the ability to become solid, prosperous American citizens. (The writer jumps to the conclusion that foreign-born people cannot become prosperous because there are many unprosperous immigrants.)

Hasty generalization:

Marshburg, Lowndesville, and Center, all of which were coached the last three years by State alumni, have had poor basketball teams; State just doesn't turn out competent coaches. (The conclusion about all coaches graduated from a school is based on records of three men in three years.)

Biased opinion:

Miss Rodehever, who has lived all her life in Illinois and has taught students from many parts of the country, is convinced that the best accent in America is that of the Middle West. (Being a Middle Westerner, the teacher is possibly more loyal to her own speech than objective about the other American types.)

Misuse of statistics:

Brick masons got a dollar an hour before World War I; now they get $2.25 an hour. Their demand for a wage raise is nonsense. (This argument assumes that a dollar has a fixed value; it ignores the decreased buying power of money in an inflationary period.)

False assumption:

That man never got nearer to a war than the draft board that rejected him; of course he couldn't write a novel about life in an army post. (The unstated false assumption is that a person must be a member of the army to write about soldiers.)

EXERCISE

Which of the following passages contain illogical thinking? What faults do they contain? Remember that you are concerned with the reasoning, not with whether you agree or disagree with the conclusions.

1. Although many comic books do emphasize violence and bloodshed, children know the characters are not real; hence it is unlikely that comic books harm children.
2. Since civil service jobs are permanent (provided the jobholders stay in good health and behave) and guarantee pensions after retirement, bureaucrats are people with no initiative; they are content to stay in a rut all their lives.
3. Modern dictionaries record all sorts of erroneous meanings. Any mistake that becomes widespread is put in dictionaries now as a true meaning. For this reason, I think lexicography is a lost art.
4. James Anders disagrees with his union president on price controls. Alice Struble objects to the political views of the policy committee of her union. It is clear that union leadership does not represent the rank and file membership.
5. Since Franklin's "Honesty is the best policy" is a cynical appeal to expediency, it is a highly immoral statement.
6. Cats are as intelligent as dogs. They won't come when you call them unless they are hungry. Thus cats are independent, with minds of their own.
7. The word *transpire* came from Latin *trans* (across) and *spirare* (breathe), so it cannot really mean *happen* or *occur*.
8. White races believe they are superior to yellow people. Since the leading scientists of the world are white and they believe the yellow races are inferior, it is clear that the white races are better stock than the yellow.
9. The prefix *in-* means "not," as in *incompetent, insane, inaccurate,* and such words. Therefore *inflammable* cannot properly mean "capable of being set on fire."
10. Of course there is no noise when an iceberg cracks in the Bering sea with no man or animal near enough to hear it. A sound is a sensation

produced on an eardrum, and if there is no eardrum present, there can be no sound.

11. It is ridiculous to oppose the United Nations because we would surrender part of our sovereignty to foreigners. When the United States was formed, the people in Georgia surrendered part of their sovereignty to people in New Jersey and in other states who were "foreigners" at that time. Georgia didn't disappear.
12. Communists try to level out the population. Anyone who wants to use federal money to equalize education and improve the schools in the backward states is a communist.

Letter Writing

Business Letters

100. Learn the conventional forms for the various parts of a letter.

There are certain forms and conventions, within which there are some variations, for writing letters. It is very important to include (a) the date, (b) the name and address of the addressee, and (c) the name and address of the writer; this information is put in standardized forms which permit little or no originality.

In addition to the body of the letter, there are five parts, as follows: (1) heading, (2) inside address, (3) salutation, or greeting, (4) complimentary close, and (5) signature. Either block or indented layout may be used, and either open or close punctuation is acceptable (but be sure to follow one style consistently in any letter). Two marks of punctuation are invariable: colon after the salutation, and comma after the complimentary close. Any variation in these marks will be regarded as eccentric or old-fashioned.

100a. Heading. Unless your paper is a printed letterhead, write the full address of the writer and the date of the letter.

The heading is usually put in the upper right hand corner, and may be either block or indented, with open or close punctuation:

block, open punctuation	*indented, close punctuation*
39 Farwell Street	39 Farwell Street,
Columbus 17, Mass.	Columbus 17, Mass.,
July 31, 1952	July 31, 1952.

Notice that even in open punctuation a comma is required within the date, and a period must be put after every abbreviation. It is permissible to put the date alone at the top of the letter and put the sender's address below the signature so that the name and address form one convenient unit.

The best usage requires that you heed the following suggestions. Do not omit such words as *Street, Road, Avenue.* Rarely use any abbreviations for these words. Avoid the use of # or *No.* before the numeral. In writing dates, do not use the forms 3/25/1952 or 3/25/52, and do not follow the number with *st, nd, rd, d,* or *th.*

100b. Inside address. Place the address of the person written to several lines below the heading and at the left-hand margin. It should be identical with the address on the envelope.

The inside address notifies the person opening the letter who is to receive it, and identifies the carbon copy for the sender. In modern usage the block form with open punctuation is preferred:

Mr. James Montgomery
17 Richelieu Street
Springfield 9, Mass.

Miss Olga Stein, President
Antique Publishing Company
Tuscaloosa, Alabama

An official title may be placed on the same line with the name (after, never before the name) or on the second line, depending on the length of the title.

Dr. L. D. Stevens, Dean of Men
Southeastern University
Atlanta, Georgia

Professor G. L. Champion
Chairman of the Board of Trustees
Southeastern Scholarship Foundation
Richmond, Indiana

In the inside address, follow the same form you used in the heading. The inside address is occasionally placed at the very end of the letter, below the signature and flush with the left-hand margin of the page.

The first line of the inside address should be flush with the left-hand margin of the body of the letter. Some title should always precede the name of the person addressed. In the case of individuals, use *Mr., Dr., Professor* (never *Prof.*); in the case of firms or organized bodies use *Messrs.* for a group composed of men, *Mmes.* (*Mesdames*) for a group composed of women. *The Honorable* is used for a person holding an important government position; e.g., a senator, a member of the cabinet, or a governor. See also § 33a for permissible abbreviations.

100c. Salutation. Place the salutation (greeting) two or three spaces below the inside address flush with the left margin.

The following forms are conventional:

Dear Sir:	(Standard)
Dear Mr. Broun:	(More personal)
My dear Sir:	(Very formal)
My dear Mrs. Broun:	(Formal)
Gentlemen:	(Standard)
Mesdames:	(Standard)

When the word *dear* appears in the salutation, it is always capitalized except when *My* precedes it. For special forms of greetings to persons in official and ecclesiastical positions, see *Webster's New International Dictionary*, Second Edition, pp. 3012–14, or the *American College Dictionary*, p. xxxiii.

If a letter addressed to a firm or an organization should be called to the attention of a particular individual, the word *attention*, followed by that person's name, may be put on the same line with the salutation or between the inside address and the salutation. This line may be underlined to emphasize it.

In the two letters which follow, note that in the first, written by a private individual, the complete heading is typed, whereas in the second the heading (except for the date) appears as a printed letterhead. Note also that since the first letter is addressed to the company the salutation *Gentlemen* is used, but that the writer also wishes to reach a particular member of the firm with whom he has previously corresponded, and so above the salutation includes the line, "*Attention* of *Mr. Lawrence Kelvin.*" In both letters, the name of the writer is typed at the end for clearness, and ample space is left for the written signature between the complimentary close and the typed name. In both letters, also, the titles of books are underlined.

HEADING (*typed*)

1306 Queen City Avenue
Kansas City, Kansas
September 13, 1952

INSIDE ADDRESS

Kelvin Book Co.
10 Nassau Street
New Orleans, Louisiana

Attention of Mr. Lawrence Kelvin

SALUTATION

Gentlemen:

BODY

On August 30 I ordered from you one copy of J.D. Wilson's Guide to New Orleans, third edition, 1947, and one copy of Louisiana Menus, 1950.

You sent the Wilson book that I ordered, but instead of Louisiana Menus, 1950, you sent Louisiana Men of 1950. Your invoice listed properly the books I ordered.

I am returning the book sent by mistake, and will appreciate your mailing immediately one copy of Louisiana Menus, 1950.

COMPLIMENTARY CLOSE

Sincerely yours,

SIGNATURE

James Hutton
James Hutton

HEADING (PRINTED)

KELVIN BOOK CO.
10 Nassau Street
New Orleans, Louisiana

DATE (TYPED)

15 September 1952

INSIDE ADDRESS

Mr. James Hutton
1306 Queen City Avenue
Kansas City, Kansas

SALUTATION

Dear Mr. Hutton:

BODY

Thank you for your letter of September 13, informing us that you received the wrong book in our shipment of September 3.

We are mailing you today by book post one copy of Louisiana Menus, 1950, the book you had ordered.

We are sorry this mistake occurred, and hope that you have not been seriously inconvenienced.

COMPLIMENTARY CLOSE

Very truly yours,
KELVIN BOOK CO.

SIGNATURE

Lawrence Kelvin

Lawrence Kelvin
Manager

100d. Body of the letter. Make the body of your letter conform to the rules of good usage.

A letter is a form of composition; punctuation, grammar and spelling, paragraphing, clearness and emphasis have to be considered just as in any other kind of writing. Those who have mastered the principles of writing will find very little difficulty in composing a good letter, whether it be the formal business type or the informal personal kind.

Arrange the parts of your letter according to a plan. Suppose, for example, you are applying for a position. The first paragraph should state the purpose of the letter; following paragraphs, your personal data (age, sex, health, and other pertinent facts); education (schools, degrees, pertinent courses); experience (emphasizing any past experience which would prepare you for the position you are seeking); references (giving names and business addresses); and finally, should offer to fill out an application form or call for an interview. An order letter should list the goods ordered (specifying quantities, items, sizes, colors, styles, etc.) and state how payment is to be made and how the goods should be shipped (parcel post, railway express, truck, freight, air), and should give your exact shipping address. A letter of complaint should identify the goods or services at fault, state the complaint, and state the adjustment expected.

Avoid stereotyped expressions such as *contents noted, yours in hand, enclosed please find,* and *your favor of the 30th.* The diction of business English is plain standard English, employing only such technical terms as are needed, such as *draft, account receivable, FOB,* and *invoice.*

Be *clear, concise,* and *courteous.*

The body of the letter should begin two spaces below the greeting. Paragraphs may be indented or left flush with the left margin: if the indented form has been used in the heading and the inside address, it is preferable to indent the paragraphs of the body of the letter; if the block form has been used in the heading and inside address, it is permissible not to indent the paragraphs. Allow five spaces for the indention in a typed letter; in longhand allow about an inch.

It is preferable to single-space typed letters and to double-space between paragraphs. Right and left margins should be as nearly equal as possible from the edges of the page. There is no reason to avoid the use of *I*; to do so results in the awkward passive construction: "Your letter of January 27 has been received." Prefer: "I have received. . . ."

100e. Complimentary close. Use an approved form for the complimentary close, the phrase by which one brings the letter to an end.

The following are the customary forms:

Yours truly,
Yours very truly,
Yours respectfully,
Very truly yours,

The complimentary close should begin in or near the middle of the page about two spaces below the last line of the body of the letter. The first word should be capitalized, and the whole phrase is always followed by a comma. As a rule, do not use *Yours sincerely* or *Cordially yours* in business letters, except when you are writing to a person whom you know well. The nature of the complimentary close naturally depends upon the tone of the greeting and the body of the letter. The phrase *Yours respectfully* should be reserved for those in high office, or for a correspondent much older than the writer.

Avoid such phrases as *Yours for good business, Yours for efficiency, Beg to remain,* or *Thanking you in advance* (or other participial phrases).

100f. Signature. Always write your signature legibly.

If the name of the writer does not appear on the letterhead, it may be typewritten beneath the signature. The signature is not followed by a mark of punctuation.

Do not use a professional or honorary title or a degree with the signature. An unmarried woman may, however, put *Miss* in parentheses before her name for clear identification. A married woman may sign her name in either of two ways. Suppose Ruth Collins has married George Webster. She may then sign her own name, Ruth Collins Webster, preceded by *Mrs.* in parentheses, or she may sign her own name and under it write in parentheses her married name, Mrs. George Webster. The signature Ruth Webster or Ruth Collins Webster does not indicate how she should be addressed.

100g. The outside address (address on the envelope) should follow one of the models given below.

The form should normally be the same as that of the heading and the inside address.

```
James Hutton,
   1306 Queen City Avenue,
      Kansas City, Kansas.

                         Kelvin Book Co.,
                            10 Nassau Street,
                               New Orleans, Louisiana.
```

```
J. L. Morrow
84 Seens Street
New Orleans, Louisiana

                              Mr. Karl Johnson
                              31 Filmore Street
                              Los Angeles, California
```

100h. Use good stationery.

Paper and envelopes should always be of good quality and should match in color. Business letters are usually typewritten on paper about 8½ by 11 inches in size. Use one side of the sheet only. Be careful to avoid wrinkles, smears, and noticeable erasures.

Personal Letters and Notes

100i. Learn the proper form for personal letters and notes.

The personal letter is the most common form of written expression. In this type there is, of course, less formality than in the business letter. It is worth while to read the published letters of some well-known person in order to see how pleasant such communications may become.

Interest, charm, and general tone are all-important in the personal letter and note. There is, of course, no formula for these qualities, since they depend to a great extent upon the writer's personality and the degree of intimacy between the correspondents. Reading and practice will achieve much in this branch of writing, as in all others.

The form of the personal letter is the same as that for business or professional correspondence — with these exceptions:

The inside address may be omitted. Or, if used, it may be placed at the lower left after the body of the letter. This practice is more common in the personal letter than in the more formal business letter.

After the greeting, the comma is preferred to the more formal colon. The following forms are usual:

Dear Hildegarde,	(intimate)
Dear Mrs. Winters,	(friendly)
Dear Judge Winters,	(formal)
Dear Winters,	(informal)
My dear Miss Temple,	(most formal)

The complimentary close is adapted to the tone of the letter and the degree of intimacy between the correspondents. The following are usual forms:

Sincerely yours,
Very sincerely,
Cordially yours,
Yours affectionately,
Very cordially yours,
Very sincerely yours,

Formal Social Notes

100j. Learn the conventional form for formal social notes.

The following are examples of formal social notes. They are invariably written in the third person. No abbreviations are used, except *Mr.*, *Mrs.*, and *Dr.* Dates and hours are written in full. The heading is dropped to the lower left. No inside address is used.

Mrs. Blenkinson requests the pleasure of Dr. Bodwin's company at dinner on Friday evening, May the seventh, at seven o'clock.

10 Manson Avenue, [Mrs. Blenkinson's address]
April the thirtieth.

Dr. Bodwin accepts with pleasure the kind invitation of Mrs. Blenkinson to dinner on Friday evening, May the seventh, at seven o'clock.

17 Dale Street, [Dr. Bodwin's address]
May the first.

Dr. Bodwin regrets that he is unable to accept the kind invitation of Mrs. Blenkinson to dinner on Friday evening, May the seventh, at seven o'clock.

17 Dale Street,
May the first.

EXERCISES

A. Write a letter to a mail order company ordering a pair of shoes, two shirts (or dresses), and a raincoat. Be sure to specify colors, sizes, and styles, and state how payment is being made.

B. Write a letter to a mail order company ordering several articles of sports equipment, giving necessary details.

C. Write a letter to a railroad passenger agent asking for a special pullman car for a college glee club trip. Include details on places and dates of performances and number of people in the party.

D. Assume that you forgot an invitation to have dinner with a minister who had been a college roommate of your father's. Write him a note of apology.

E. Write to a former high-school friend whom you haven't seen in several years answering an inquiry about how you like the college you are attending.

Précis Writing

◇◇

101. Learn the principles of précis writing.

Précis writing is a form of composition which possesses great practical value. The term *précis* was taken from French and means literally a "cut-down statement." The précis must contain the essence of a longer selection, and it must be *concise, accurate,* and *well expressed.*

The précis originated in connection with diplomatic correspondence, where strict accuracy and careful expression are necessary. If the secretary of a diplomat has to prepare a body of correspondence for ready reference, it is not enough to "summarize" the letters. He must make a précis of each letter in the group under consideration and thus produce an exact statement of the heart of the matter, phrased in clear and readable form. If the final record is to be a truthful presentation of what has been written, the most careful consideration and the most precise transcript are necessary to secure the desired result.

The method may be used in dealing with any kind of material of which we wish to present an accurate impression. The insistent demand for accuracy calls for thoughtful reading; the necessity for clearness enforces straightforward expression. Thus the writer of a précis must think carefully, and must compose clearly and concisely. He must avoid hasty conclusions and mental short cuts; he must resist the tendency toward wordiness, repetition, or loose style.

The following simple rules should be followed in making a précis:

101a. Select the pith of the material.

To be sure that you omit no essential thoughts of the author, read the material until you have thoroughly mastered it, being sure to identify the topic sentence of each paragraph.

101b. In a précis, reproduce the relative emphasis the author gives to his thoughts.

101c. Follow the plan of your original.

Remember that you are not to rearrange thoughts or facts, but to reproduce them faithfully in a highly condensed form.

101d. Use your own words.

The language of the original will probably be unsuitable for your purposes. Your aim must be to state the heart of the passage in words of your own choosing.

101e. Write good English.

A précis must be a model of clear sentence work. There must be no weak or disconnected phrasing and no gaps in the thought.

101f. Note the following general comments.

LENGTH. As a general rule, a précis is about one third as long as the original. In practice it is often possible to reduce the length still further. The main point is to see that nothing vital is left out. Usually the nature of the original will control the length.

TIME. As in all writing, practice will give increased speed. The student should be warned, however, against mere facility in getting ideas down on paper. Accuracy is far more important than speed, and accuracy is attainable only through close attention. Be accurate, therefore, and let the matter of time take care of itself.

MATERIAL. The principles of précis writing apply alike to a single paragraph and to a longer unit, such as an essay or a poem. Since your aim is to reproduce the essence of the material, you must master its content so that nothing vital is omitted.

PRACTICAL VALUE. In certain fields the précis is an actual necessity; in all fields it has great practical value. As a form of composition it is highly instructive. It tends to increase the vocabulary; it develops clearness of thought; it enforces firmness of style. There can be nothing loose or sloppy about a good précis.

And though it cannot reproduce stylistic beauty, it must be clear, orderly, and readable.

In note taking and in general reading, the making of précis can be very useful to the student. The demand for clear expression and accurate interpretation — a demand which is absolutely invariable — will ensure the development of the best possible medium for reporting and preserving the essential meaning of the original.

ORIGINAL

There is another and weightier reason for a cautious approach to the question of finding a proper designation for what is obviously a war but cannot officially be called one. The President's advisers in both the White House and the State Department believe that if the most important job of the government today is to mobilize with the speed and efficiency necessary to meet our present commitment, the second most important job is, in all probability, to avoid giving the world, and in particular the Soviet Union, the impression that we consider a general war inevitable. It is believed that to announce total mobilization now — and a declaration of a national emergency would be tantamount to doing so — would have either of two consequences, both of them bad. One, perhaps the less likely of the two, is that total mobilization, accompanied by a determination not to fight Russia unless we were directly provoked by her, would be welcomed by Stalin as a further drain on our strength and wealth. If Stalin thought that by jabbing through the Iron Curtain here and there he could keep us totally mobilized for the next fifteen or twenty years, he might well consider that a safe and highly expedient way of wearing us down. The more likely consequence of total mobilization, however, and the one more widely feared here, is that it would, in the jargon of modern diplomacy, "freeze the course of events" and make total war inevitable. The feeling is that the most likely Russian reaction to the spectacle of total mobilization in this country would be to assume that we had abandoned our intention to limit the scale and area of hostilities and had decided to bring about a general war ourselves. In that case, Russia, sensibly enough, would proceed to get the jump on us by seizing strategic bases and, no doubt, by pouring her own troops into Korea.[1]

[1] Richard Rovere, in *The New Yorker*, August 5, 1950, p. 45. Reprinted by permission. Copyright 1950 The New Yorker Magazine, Inc.

PRÉCIS A

Although they believe that we should mobilize sufficiently to meet our present commitment in Korea, the President's advisers think that we should not announce total mobilization, for two reasons. First, total preparation without actual warfare would wear us down, accomplishing Stalin's purpose for him. Second, total mobilization is more likely to make war inevitable by inciting the Russians to keep ahead of us.

PRÉCIS B

Agreeing that we should increase our mobilization, the President's advisers believe that we should avoid total mobilization (1) because it could accomplish Stalin's purpose by weakening us, and (2) because total mobilization could incite the Russians to compete with us and eventually bring on war.

EXERCISES

A. Write a précis of the second paragraph on page 53.

B. Write a précis of the second paragraph on page 55.

C. Write a précis of a theme you have written.

D. Write a précis of a passage assigned by your instructor.

E. Write a précis of an article in an encyclopedia.

FH59

INDEX

A, *An*, 334
Abbreviations, 220–21, *exercise*, 221; in addresses, 418; capitalization of, 220; in dates, 212, 418; in connected writing, 220; by ditto marks, 221; in footnotes, 262; periods after, 190; of titles with proper names, 220, 418
Absolute, defined, 152
Absolute phrase, 383–84; punctuation of, 173
Abstract noun, *see* Noun, 159
Accept, *except*, 334
ACD, see *American College Dictionary*, 318
Acknowledgment of borrowed material, 259
Ad, 334
Address, inside, 418–19; outside, 424
Adjective, 134–36, *exercises*, 136; clause, 145–46; comparison of, 154; with copula, 135; defined, 152; distinguished from adverb, 134; as noun, 135; noun as, 135; uses of comparative and superlative, 136, 361
Adjective clause, defined, 152; uses, 145–46, *exercises*, 146
Adverb, 134–36, *exercises*, 136; clause, 144–46; comparison of, 154; defined, 153; conjunctive, 138; distinguished from adjective, 134; as subordinating conjunction, 138
Adverbial clause, defined, 153; uses, 144–46, *exercises*, 146
Affect, *effect*, 334
Aggravate, 335
Agreement, grammatical, defined, 153
Agreement of pronoun and antecedent, 115–16, *exercises*, 116; collective nouns, 115; inconsistency in gender and number, 115, 400; indefinite antecedents, 115
Agreement of verb and subject, 108–13, *exercises*, 113; collective nouns, 111; compound subject, 110; after *here*, *there*, *it*, 111–12; phrasal subject indicating quantity, 113; plural subject with singular meaning, 112; relative pronoun with plural antecedent, 112; singular subject with *or*, *nor*, *but*, 110–11; singular subject with a parenthetical element, 110; singular subject with a plural modifier, 109
Aiken, Janet R., quoted, 51
Ain't, 335
All ready, 335
All right, see *Alright*, 335
All the farther, *deeper*, *slower*, 335
All together, *altogether*, 335
Allen, Frederic L., quoted, 52
Almost, position of, 393; see also *Most*, 342
Already, *all ready*, 335
Alright, *all right*, 335
Also, as a conjunction, 335
Alternative, 335
Altogether, see *All together*, 335
Alumna, *-ae*, *-i*, *-us*, 283
A. M., *P. M.*, 218, 220, 235
Ambiguous reference, 397–98
American College Dictionary (*ACD*), 318; specimen page, 330–31
Among, 335
Amount, *number*, 335
An, see *A*, 334
Analogy, 54
And, see *Good and*, 339, *Try and*, 346
And etc., 335
And which, *and who* clause, 387–88, *exercise*, 388

Anglicized plurals, 282
Antecedent, agreement with pronoun, 115–16; defined, 153; reference to, 397–400
Any, 109, 335–36; in comparisons, 361; see also *Anybody*
Anybody, agreement of pronoun with, 115; agreement of verb with, 109
Any more, 336
Anyone, see *Anybody*
Anyplace, 336
Anything like, 336
Anywheres, 336
Apostrophe, 196–98, *exercises*, 198; to form genitive case, 196–97; to form plurals, 197; to mark omissions, 197; position of, 198
Appositive, case of, 117; commas to set off, 173; defined, 153
Appositive phrase as a sentence, 101
Appropriateness, of fragment, 102–03; of diction, 332–33
Apt, see *Liable*, 341
Archaic words, 295
Article, defined, 153; marking common nouns, 216; omission of, 363
As, case after, 118; as a conjunction, 139; omission of, 360; punctuation of, 174; for *that* or *whether*, 336
As if, 139
As to, for *about*, 336
As-clause, suspended, 378
Asset, 336
Assumption, false, 413
At, see *Where*, 347
Auto, see *Ad*, 334
Auxiliary, defined, 153; modal, 122–23; omission of, 362; repetition of for clearness, 408; uses, 124–28; *see also* Function word, 156
Awful, *awfully*, 336
Awhile, *a while*, 336

Babbitt, Irving, quoted, 54
Bad, 336
Badly, 312, 336
Balance, 28–29, 368, *exercise*, 32, 368; defined, 368; uses of, 28, 368
Balance, 336
Be, as subjunctive form, 123
Beatty, Richmond C., quoted, 71
Begging the question, 413
Beginning and ending of themes, 84–85, *exercises*, 85; of sentences, 374, 377
Believe, parenthetical, 119
Beside, *besides*, 336
Better, see *Had better*, 340
Between, 336
Between you and I, 117–18, 336
Biased opinion, 413
Bibliographical forms, 250–52, 271; material, 238–45
Bibliography of usage, 333–34
Bit, as participle, 129
Body of letter, 422
Books, reference, 238–42
Borned, 129
Borrowed material, 259
Both . . . and, see Correlative conjunctions, 388
Brackets, 199–200, *exercise*, 200; to enclose interpolations, 200, 251
Bursted, 129, 336
Business letters, 417–24, *exercises*, 426; forms, 417–24; models, 420–21
Bust, *busted*, *busting*, 337
But, 101, 110, 137; comma before, 168; as coördinating conjunction, 137; in double negatives, 147; singular subjects joined by, 110; as preposition, 163
But that, *but what*, 337

Calculate, 337
Can, *may*, 337
Can but, *cannot but*, *cannot help but*, 147, 337
Cancelling and deleting, 200
Cannot help but, 147, 337
Can't hardly, 337; see also *Hardly*, 340
Capitalization, 214–19, *exercises*, 219; of abbreviations, 220; of first word of sentence, 214–15; of lines of poetry, 215; of proper adjectives, 216; of proper names, 215–17; in resolutions, 218; of titles, 217–18
Card catalogue, 246–47; author card, 246–47; title card, 247; use of, 246
Caret, for insertions, 222
Case, 337
Case, 117–21, *exercises*, 121; of appositives, 117; after *as*, 118; common,

117, 153; defined, 117, 153–54; in elliptical clauses, 118; genitive (possessive), 119; of noun governing gerund, 120; objective, 117–18, 119; of parenthetical expressions, 119; periphrastic genitive, 120; possessive, *see* Genitive; of pronoun complement, 118; of pronoun modifying a gerund, 120; of pronoun after a preposition, 117; subjective, 117; after *than*, 118; of *who*, 119; of *whose* with a neuter antecedent, 121, 347
Catalogue, card, 246–47
Chase, Stuart, quoted, 59
Choosing a subject, 49–50; 75–77; 248–49
Choppy sentences, 356, *exercise*, 356
Claim, 337
Clause, adjective, 144–46; adverbial, 144–46, 168–71, 402; confusion of, 144–46, *exercises*, 146; coördinate, 104–06, 168, 351–53, *exercise*, 353; defined, 97, 154; dependent, 7–14, 95–99, 123, 137, 179; elliptical, 118, 396; independent, 95–99, 104–06, 137–38; introductory adverbial, 168–69; kinds of, 144–45, 154; nonrestrictive, 169–71; noun, 144–46, 402; parallel, 385–88; punctuation of, 168–71, 179, 185–86, *exercises*, 179–84, 187, 188; relative, 169–71, 393; restrictive, 169–71; subordinate, 7–14, 132, 354–55, *exercise*, 355, 370–72
Clearness, 385–415; "and which," "and who," 387–88, *exercise*, 388; correlatives, 388–89, *exercise*, 389; dangling modifiers, 394–96, *exercise*, 396; mixed constructions, 401–02, *exercise*, 402; mixed figures, 406–07, *exercise*, 407; parallelism, 385–87, *exercise*, 387; point of view, 409–11, *exercise*, 411; position of modifiers, 392–94, *exercises*, 394; reference of pronouns, 397–400, *exercises*, 400; repetition for, 408–09, *exercise*, 409; sequence, 391, *exercise*, 391; split constructions, 403–05, *exercise*, 405
Climax, 24–31, 366, *exercises*, 31, 367
Close, of letter, 423
Coherence, 232–33, *exercises*, 233
Collective noun, *see* Noun, 159; pronoun agreement with, 115; verb agreement with, 111
Colloquial English, 93–94, 301, 322
Colon, 188–89, *exercise*, 189; for anticipation, 188; between independent clauses, 188; in salutation of letter, 189, 419; to separate chapter from verse, items in dates, minutes from hours and seconds, 189, place of publication from publisher, 189, 250, titles from subtitles, 189
Columbia Dictionary of Modern European Literature, quoted, 61
Comma, 168–79, *exercises* 179–84; after complimentary close, 423; to emphasize a contrast, 172; in footnotes, 262; to prevent misreading, 176; and quotation marks, 205; to separate adjectives in series, 176; to separate coördinates in series, 174–75; to separate independent clauses, 104–06, 168; to separate items in series, 174–75; to set off absolute phrases, 173; to set off appositives, 173–74; to set off dates, 174; to set off direct quotations, 205; to set off geographical expressions, 174; to set off interjections, 174; to set off introductory adverbial modifiers, 168–69; to set off inserted elements, 171; to set off nonrestrictive modifiers, 166–71; to set off *replied*, *said*, etc., 177; to set off sentence modifiers, 172; to set off vocatives, 174
Comma fault (splice), 104–06, *exercises*, 106
Comma, unnecessary, 177–79
Common noun, *see* Noun, 159; distinguished from proper noun, 215–16
Comparative, absolute, 360; and superlative, uses of, 136, 361
Comparison, defined, 154; incomplete, 360–61, *exercises*, 361
Complected, 297
Complement, case of, 118; defined, 154; predicate, 162
Complete comparisons, 360–61, *exercises*, 361
Complete sentence, 95–99; *see also* Period fault, 100

Complex sentence, defined, 154; structure of, 7–14; for variety, 39, 374
Composition, 224–71; arranging material, 258–59; bibliography, 250–52; choosing subject, 224–26; gathering material, 237–58; model pages, 265–71; outlining, 226–29; paragraph, 229–33, *exercises*, 233; reading for information, 253–54; research paper, 259–71; using library for material, 237–47; taking notes, 254–59; *see also* 72–86
Compound-complex sentence, defined, 154
Compound personal pronouns, 142
Compound predicate, defined, 155; illustrated, 8
Compound sentence, defined, 8, 154
Compound words, hyphenated, 214, 284–85; plurals of, 283; spelling, 284–85; *exercises*, 285; written solid, 285; written as two words, 285
Concrete noun, 160; words, 309
Confusion of similar words, in spelling, 274–75, *exercises*, 275
Conjugation, defined, 155; illustrated, 125–26
Conjunctions, 137–39, *exercises*, 139; and conjunctive adverbs, 138; coordinating, 137; correlative, 388; defined, 155; *directly*, 138; *for*, 137; *like*, 139; *immediately*, *on account of*, *so*, 138; subordinating, 137; *yet*, 138
Conjunctive adverbs, defined, 155; distinguished from adverbs, 138; punctuation of, 105, 185
Connectives, 13–14, 389, *exercises*, 14; *see also* Conjunctions, Prepositions
Connotation, 304–05, *exercises*, 305
Considerable, 337
Consonant, final, doubling, 278–79, *exercises*, 279
Consonants, hyphen between, 213
Construction, defined, 155; incomplete, 359, *exercise*, 359; mixed, 401–02, *exercise*, 402; overlapping, 355; split, 403–05, *exercise*, 405; *see also* Periphrastic, 161
Contact, 337
Continual, *continuous*, 337
Contractions, agreement with subject, 112; apostrophe with, 197; use of, 93–94, 220–21
Conversational sentences, 5–6, 102
Coördinate clauses, punctuation of, 104–06, 168, 185
Coördinate, defined, 155
Coördinating conjunctions, comma before, 168, 179; *for*, *so*, *yet*, as, 137; use of, 105, 137
Coördination, 17–20, 351–53, *exercises*, 20, 353; excessive, 351; inaccurate, 352
Copula, adjective after, 134; case after, 118; defined, 155; in two functions, 362
Copulative verb, *see* Copula, 155
Correct diction, defined, 298–99, *exercises*, 299
Corrections in manuscript, 222
Correlative conjunctions, 388–89, *exercise*, 389
Could of, 337
Couldn't scarcely, 147, 297
Couple, 337

Dangling modifiers, 394–96, *exercise*, 396
Dash, 194–95, *exercise*, 195; at beginning of line, 223; to emphasize a parenthesis, 195; to heighten suspense, 194; to indicate interruption, 194; misuse, 195; other punctuation marks with, 195
Data, 337
Date, 337–38
Deal, 338
Declension, defined, 155; illustrated, 117
Definitely, 338
Demonstrative pronouns, 140–41; used as articles, 141
Denotation, 304–05, *exercises*, 305
Departure from normal word order, effective, 25, 374; faulty, 376–79, *exercises*, 379
Dependent clause, defined, 95, 98; written as a sentence, 101
Development of paragraph, 50–63, *exercises*, 63; by analogy, 54; by causes and effects, 52; by a combination of methods, 56; by com-

parison and contrast, 53; by definition, 55; by examples and instances, 51; by logical divisions, 52
Dialect, 295–96
Dialogue, 204–06, *exercises*, 206; punctuation of, 205–06; quoting consecutive paragraphs, 204; separate paragraphs for each change of speaker, 204; separation of quotations from introductory words, 177, 205; *see also* Quotation marks, 192–93
Diction, 293–348, *exercises*, 305; archaic words, 295; bibliography, 333–34; colloquial, 94, 301; connotation, 304–05, *exercises*, 305; correctness, 298–99, *exercises*, 299; denotation, 304–05, *exercises*, 305; dialect, 295; effectiveness, 293–94; emphatic, 309–10, *exercises*, 310; enlarging vocabulary, 317–18, *exercises*, 318; euphony, 36, 316, *exercise*, 316; exactness, 307, *exercises*, 307; fine writing, 312, *exercise*, 312; functional varieties, 91–94, 300–01, *exercise*, 301; glossary, 332–48; idiom, 296–97, *exercises*, 297; improprieties, 299–300; improvement, 293–94; labels, 91–94; national use, 295–96, *exercises*, 296; nonstandard, 299, *exercises*, 299; obsolete words, 295; provincial, 93; slang, 302–03, *exercises*, 303; standard usage, 295; technical words, 94, 295; triteness, 310–11, *exercises*, 311; wordiness, 313–15, *exercise*, 315; using dictionary, 318–23, *exercises*, 323
Dictionaries, desk, 318–19; historical, 241; unabridged, 319
Dictionary, use of, 318–23, *exercises*, 323; arrangement of contents, 319; compounding, 319; correctness in pronunciations, 321; etymology, 322; finding words, 319; labels, 322; order of meanings, 321–22; pronunciation, 320–21; pronunciation key words, 321; proper names, 322–23; spelling, 319; syllabication, 319; specimen pages, 328–31
Didn't ought, see *Hadn't ought*, 340
Different from, than, to, 338
Digraph, 213
Direct address, *see* Vocative, 166; punctuation of, 174
Direct discourse, defined, 155; quotation marks enclosing, 202; shifting to indirect, 410; tense in, 402
Direct object, *see* Object, 160
Direct quotations, in notes, 255–57; punctuation of, 177, 204–06
Directly, as subordinating conjunction, 138
Directness, in writing, 34–37, *exercises*, 37
Ditto marks, 221
Doesn't, 112; see also *Don't*, 338
Done, 338
Don't, 112, 338
Double negative, 147–48, *exercises*, 148
Doubling final consonant, 278–79, *exercises*, 279
Doubt, 338
Dove, 129, 338
Dropping final *-e*, 279–80; *-y*, 280–81
Drownded, 129
Due to, 338

E, final, dropping, 279–80, *exercises*, 280
Each, pronoun agreement with, 115; verb agreement with, 109–10
Each other, one another, 338
Eastman, Max, quoted, 55
Economy, in words, 35–36, *exercises*, 37
Editorial *we*, see *We*, 347
Effect, affect, 338
Effectiveness, 293–415
Ei and *ie*, 277–78, *exercises*, 278
Either, neither, 338; agreement of pronoun with, 115; agreement of verb with, 109–10
Either . . . or, see Correlatives, 388
Ellipsis, defined, 155
Elliptical clause or phrase, dangling, 396
Emphasis, 24–31, 366–84, *exercises*, 31, 384; active voice, 382, *exercise*, 383; balance, 28, 368, *exercise*, 368; climax, 24, 366–67, *exercises*, 367; italics, 24, 209; repetition, 29, 369, *exercises*, 369; separation, 372–73, *exercises*, 373; subordination, 370–72, *exercise*, 371; suspense, 27, 365,

exercises, 365; variety, 374, *exercise*, 374; word order, 25, 376–79, *exercises*, 379
Emphatic diction, 309, *exercises*, 310
Emphatic elements, punctuation of, 172, 186, 188
English grammar, defined, 89
English plurals, irregular, 281–83
Enlarging vocabulary, 293, 317–18, *exercises*, 318
Enthuse, 338
Equally as good, 338
Essential modifier, *see* Restrictive modifier, 169–71
Etc., comma before, in series, 176; see also *And etc.*, 335
Etymological kinship, 276–77, *exercises*, 277
Etymology, meaning and use of, in dictionaries, 322
Euphony, 36, 316, *exercise*, 316
Even, position of, 393
Ever, position of, 393
Every, 110
Every so often, 339
Everybody, agreement of pronoun with, 115; agreement of verb with, 109
Everyone, see *Everybody*
Everyplace, see *Anyplace*, 336
Exact diction, 307, *exercises*, 307
Exam, see *Ad*, 334
Except, see *Accept*, 334; as subordinating conjunction, 138
Excessive coördination, 311
Exclamation point, position of, 192; uses of, 191
Expect, 339
Expletive, defined, 156; number of verb after, 111–12
Extra, 339

False assumption, 413
False parallelism, 20
Farther, *further*, 339
Faulty parallelism, 18–20
Faulty repetition, 380, *exercises*, 380
-fe, *-ff*, *-f*, plurals of nouns ending in, 282, *exercises*, 283
Feature, 339
Figures, numerical, plurals of, 197; separated by comma, 212
Figures of speech, mixed or inappropriate, 406–07, *exercise*, 407; uses of, 406
Final consonant, doubling, 278–79, *exercises*, 279
Final *-e*, dropping, 279–80, *exercises*, 280
Final *-y*, dropping, 280–81, *exercises*, 281
Fine, 339
Fine writing, 41, 312, *exercise*, 312
Finite verb, defined, 156
First rate, 339
Fix, 339
Flat adverbs, 134
Folks, 339
For example, phrase beginning with, as a sentence, 101
Foreign languages, plurals of nouns borrowed from, 282–83
Form, case, 117; and function, *see* Noun, 159, Parts of speech, 161; letter, 411–26; research paper, 259–71; tense, 124–26
Formal English, defined, 92, 94, 301
Fortune, quoted, 60
Fragment, sentence, 95, 100–03, *exercises*, 103
Function, defined, 156; *see also* Noun, 159, Parts of speech, 160
Function word, defined, 156
Functional varieties, 90, 92–94, 300–01, 332–33, *exercise*, 301
Funny, 339
Further, see *Farther*, 339
Fused sentence, 107–08, *exercises*, 108
Future tense, time, 125, 127–28

Gender, defined, 156; pronoun agreement in, 115–16
General reference of pronouns, 398–99
Generalization, hasty, 413
Genitive (possessive) case, defined, 156; formation of, 119, 197; uses, 120–21
Genitive case of pronoun, as adjective, 140
Gent, 339
Gerund, case of noun or pronoun before, 120; dangling, 395; defined, 156; use, 96

Get, 129, 339
Glossary of diction, 332–48
Good, 339
Good and, 339
Got, gotten, 129, 339–40
Govern, defined, 156
Grammar, defined, 89–91; in dictionaries, 322; rules of, 95–147, *exercises*, 148
Grammatical subject, agreement of verb with, 109; of complement with, 118–19; defined, 153
Grammatical terms, 152–66
Grand, see *Fine*, 339
Granite, taken for, see *Granted*, 340
Greeting (salutation), of letter, 419
Guess, 340
Guides, bibliographical, 243–45
Gym, see *Ad*, 334

Had better, had rather, 340
Had have, had of, hadn't of, 340
Had ought, hadn't ought, didn't ought, 340
Hardly, in double negatives, 147; with *than, when*, 340
Harte, Bret, quoted, 231
Has got, have got, see *Got*, 339–40
Hasty generalization, 413
He, after *is, was, were*, etc., 118; as antecedent of *one*, 142
Heading, of letter, 417, 426
Healthful, healthy, 340
Heap, heaps, 340
Help but, as double negative, 147; see also *Can but*, 337
Her, after *is, was, were*, etc., 118
Here, introductory, number of verb after, 112
Herself, 142
Hersey, John, quoted, 62
Him, after *is, was, were*, etc., 118; as antecedent of *one*, 142
Himself, 140, 142
Hindus, Maurice, quoted, 30
His, as antecedent of *one*, 142
Historical present, 126–27, 410
Homophone, defined, 157; spelling, 274–75
Hopkins, William S., quoted, 55
Human, as noun, 340
Huxley, Aldous, quoted, 53
Huxley, Thomas H., quoted, 232
Hyphen, 284–85, *exercises*, 285; between syllables, 213–14; in compound numbers, 284; in compound words, 284–85

I, after *is, was, were*, etc., 118; capitalization of, 218
Idiom, defined, 296–97; list, 297; mixed, 401; *exercises*, 297
If, for *whether*, 340
Illogical comparisons, *see* Incomplete comparisons, 360–61
Illogical coördination, 351; subordination, 354
Illogical thinking, *see* Logical thinking, 412–14
Immediately, as subordinating conjunction, 138
Impersonal constructions, unnecessary use of, 378–79
Improprieties, 299–300
In, into, 340
In back of, 340
In regards to, 340
Inaccurate coördination, 352; words, *see* Exact diction, 307
Inappropriate diction, 301; figures, *see* Mixed figures, 406
Incomplete comparisons, 360–61, *exercise*, 361; comparison of incomparable things, 361; inexact use of *than any* (*other*), *of any, of all* (*else, other*), 361; omission of *as*, 360; omission of one term, 360; omission of standard, 360; omission of *than*, 360; use of comparative to refer to more than two or superlative to refer to fewer than three, 136, 361; use of a singular noun after an *of*-phrase following the superlative, 361
Incomplete construction, 359, *exercises*, 359
Incomplete thought, 357–58, *exercises*, 358
Indefinite pronouns, agreement of pronouns in number with, 115; agreement of verbs with, 109–10; *you* and *they* as, 142
Indenting, inserted quotations, 204, 261, 263; paragraphs, 229

Independent clause, *see* Clause
Independent element, defined, 157; punctuation of, 168–75
Indexes, periodical, 244–45
Indirect discourse, *see* Direct discourse, 155
Infinitive, as dangling modifier, 395; defined, 157; forms, 125; split, 403–04; tense of, 133
Infinitive phrase, used as a sentence, 101
Inflection, defined, 157
Informal English, 93, 94, 301
Inserted element, punctuation of, 171
Inside of, 340
Intensive pronoun, 140
Intensive purposes, see *Intents and purposes*, 340
Interjection, defined, 157; punctuation of, 174, 191
Interrogative pronoun, 140
Intransitive, defined, 157; illustrated, 6–7
Irregardless, 340
Irregular plurals, 281–83, *exercises*, 283
Irregular verbs, 129–30
Is, was, were, case of pronoun after, 118–19; followed by an adjective, not an adverb, 134–35; used in more than one function, 362
It, case after introductory, 111; with general antecedent, 398; without antecedent, 141; number of verb following, 112
Italics, 208–10, *exercises*, 210; for contrast, 210, for emphasis, 24, 209; in footnotes and bibliographies, 250, 262, 269–71; for foreign words and abbreviations, 208; in titles, 203, 209; underlining to indicate, 208
It's, its, 119, 197, 340–41
It's me, 118
-ize, verb-forming suffix, 341

Jacobson, Dr. Max, quoted, 60
Johnson, Wendell, quoted, 52
Just, position of, 393

Key, V. O., quoted, 68
Kind, sort, 115, 341
Kind of, sort of, 341

Lady, 341
Laid, lain, lied, see *lie*, 129
Language and writing, difference between, 4–5
Lay, principal parts, 129; see also *Lie*, 341
Learn, meaning *teach*, 341
Leave, meaning *permit*, 341
Legibility, 221
Length, of paragraph, 229–30; of précis, 430
Letters of the alphabet, plurals of, 197
Letter writing, 411–27, *exercises*, 426; address, 418; body, 422; business, 417–24; complimentary close, 423, 425; contents, 422; formal social notes, 426; greeting (salutation), 419, 425; heading, 417–18; inside address, 418; models, 420–21; outside address, 424; personal, 425; salutation (greeting), 419, 425; signature, 423–24; social notes, 426; stationery, 424; titles in, 418
Letterhead, 417
Liable, 341
Library, use of, 237–47; bibliographical guides, 243–44; card catalogue, 246–47; newspaper indexes, 245; reference books, 238–42; reference room, 238
Lie, principal parts, 129; usage, 341
Like, as a conjunction, 139, 341
Like for, 341
Likely, see *Liable*, 341
Limiting adjective, defined, 158; use to recognize common nouns, 216
Lincoln, Abraham, quoted, 20
Line of, 341
Linking verb, *see* Copula, 155
Literary titles, capitalization of, 218; in italics, 209; in quotation marks, 203
Loan, 341
Locate, 342
Logan, Andy, quoted, 69
Logical comparisons, 360–61
Logical thinking, 412–14, *exercise*, 414; begging the question, 413; biased opinion, 413; false assumption, 413;

hasty generalization, 413; misuse of statistics, 413; unwarranted conclusion, 413
Lot, lots of, 342
Lovely, see *Fine*, 339
Lowes, John L., quoted, 70–71

Mad, meaning *angry*, 342
Main clause, *see* Independent clause, 157; *see also* 97–98
Major sentence, 5–6, 102
Manuscript form, general, 221–23; corrections, 222; erasures, 222; indentation, 222; paging, 222; punctuation marks at beginning of line, 223; research papers, 259–71; spacing in, 222, 223; titles, 222–23
Material, arrangement of, in research papers, 258–59; collection of, 250–58; for précis, 430
Math, see *Ad*, 334
May, see *Can*, 337
Me, after *between*, 117; after *is, was, were*, etc., 118
Mean, 342
Mechanics, 208–23; abbreviations, 220–21, *exercise*, 221; capitals, 214–19, *exercises*, 219; italics, 208–10, *exercises*, 210; manuscript form, 221–23; numbers, 211, *exercise*, 212; syllabication, 213–14, *exercises*, 214
Melville, Herman, quoted, 385
Merely, position of, 393
Might of, 342
Mighty, 342
Mill, J. Bentham [pseud.], quoted, 51
Minor sentence, 5, 95, 100, 102
Miscellaneous omissions, 362–63, *exercises*, 364; *see also* Omissions
Misplaced modifiers, 35, 392–94
Misspelling, reasons for, 272; remedies for, 272–87
Misuse of statistics, 413
Mixed constructions, 401–02, *exercise*, 402
Mixed figures, 406–07, *exercise*, 407
Modal auxiliary, defined, 158; uses, 122–23
Mode, *see* Mood
Modification, defined, 158
Modifier, defined, 158
Modifiers, dangling, 394–96, *exercise*, 396; elliptical clauses and phrases, 396; restrictive, 169–71; verbals, 395
Modifiers, position of, 392–94, *exercises*, 394; keeping related words together, 394; making relationships clear, 392; relative clause and antecedent, 393; "squinting," 393
Mood, defined, 158–59; polite imperative in question form, 159, 192; subjunctive, 122–24
Most, 342
Muchly, 342
Myself, 140, 142

Namely, phrase beginning with as a sentence, 101
Names, capitalization of, 215–19; in italics, 209; proper, 215–19; in quotation marks, 203
National use, 295–96, *exercises*, 296
Natural word order, 376
NCD, see *Webster's New Collegiate Dictionary*, 318; specimen page, 328–29
Negative, double, 147–48, *exercises*, 148
Neither, agreement of pronoun with, 115; agreement of verb with, 109–10; as correlative, 388; use of, see *Either*, 338
Nice, see *Fine*, 339
No account, 342
Nobody, agreement of pronoun with, 115; agreement of verb with, 109
No place, see *Anyplace*, 336
Nock, Albert J., quoted, 56
Nominative absolute, *see* Absolute, 152
None, agreement of pronoun with, 115; agreement of verb with, 109
Nonessential modifier, *see* Nonrestrictive modifiers
Nonrestrictive modifiers, marked by *who* and *which*, 143; punctuation of, 169–71; tests to distinguish from restrictive, 170
Nonsense, 412
Nonstandard English, 91, 94, 295; *see also* Correct diction, 298–99
Note cards, 255–57

Note taking, 254–57
Nothing like, 342
Noun, as adjective, 135; cases of, 117; classes of, 159–60; defined, 159; gender of, 156; genitive of, 119, 120; inflection of, 117, 159; preceding gerund, 120; plural of, 281–83; plural in *of*-phrase following a superlative, 362; *see also* Abstract, Common, Concrete, and Proper nouns
Noun clause, 144–46; *see also* Substantive clause, 165
Nowhere near, 342
Nowheres, 342
Number, see *Amount*, 335
Number, 108–16; defined, 160
Numbers, representation of, 211–12, *exercise*, 212; abbreviation in, 212; at beginning of sentence, 212; commas with groups of three, 212; hyphen in compound, 212; page, 222, 263; spelled out, 211–12; written in figures, 211–12
NWD, see *Webster's New World Dictionary*, 319

O, oh, 218
-o, plurals of nouns ending in, 282, *exercises*, 283
Object, defined, 160; forms for, 117
Objective complement, defined, *see* Object, 160
Obscurity, 398, 408; *see also* Clearness
Obsolete words, 295
Of, see *Could of*, 337, *Might of*, 342, *Off of*, 342
Of any, all, all else, all other, inexact use of, 361
Off of, 342
Omission, of *as* in comparisons, 360; apostrophe from some names, 198; auxiliary verbs, 363; comma before words in series, 175; conjunction *that* from noun clause, 145; essential words, 363; inside address from personal letters, 425; letters or figures, indicated by apostrophe, 197; of elements, marked by periods, 191; necessary preposition, 363; period after some abbreviations, 190; part of a verb phrase, 362; question mark after a "polite imperative," 192; standard of comparison, 360; term of a comparison, 360; *than* in a comparison, 360
On account of, as a subordinating conjunction, 138
One another, see *Each other*, 338
Only, in double negatives, 147; position of, 342, 393
Order, in paragraph, 57–63, *exercises*, 63; in theme, 77–80, *exercises*, 80; of words, 376–79, *exercises*, 379
Out loud, 342
Outline, mechanics of, 226–29; preparation of, 77–80, *exercises*, 80; types of, 226; value of, 226
Outside of, 342
Over with, 342
Overlapping subordination, 355

Page numbering, 222, 263
Pair, 342
Paradigms of English verbs, 125–26
Paragraph, 43–71, 229–37, *exercises*, 67, 233–37; coherence, 232; development of, 50–56, *exercises*, 56; order in, 57–63, *exercises*, 63; substance, 46–49, *exercises*, 49; topic sentence, 43–44, *exercises*, 44; 231, *exercise*, 234; transition, 64–67, *exercise*, 67; 232–33; unity, 230–31, *exercises*, 233
Parallel sentence elements, in climactic order for emphasis, 366; separated, 405
Parallelism, 17–20, 385–87, *exercises*, 20, 387; for clearness, 385; defined, 18; false and faulty, 20
Parataxis, 106
Parentheses, 199–200, *exercise*, 200; in bibliographical forms, 251, 271; to enclose figures, 199; to enclose inserted matter, 199; in enumerations, 199; misused, 200
Parenthetical element, defined, 160; position of, 378; punctuation of, 171–77
Parse, defined, 160
Participial construction, at end of sentence, 376–77; case of noun or pronoun before, 121; punctuated as a sentence, 101

Participle, in absolute phrase, 383; as dangling modifier, 395; defined, 160; distinguished from gerund, 121; forms of, 125; tense of, 133
Parts of speech defined, 161; *see also* Adjective, 152, Adverb, 153, Conjunction, 155, Interjection, 157, Noun, 159, Preposition, 163, Pronoun, 163, Verb, 166
Party, see *Person*, 343
Passive voice, 382, *exercise*, 382; *see also* Voice, 166
Past perfect, 125, 127, 161
Past tense, 124–26, 161
Per, 342–43
Per cent, percentage, 343
Period, after abbreviations, 190; at end of sentence, 190; to indicate ellipsis (omission), 191; with other marks of punctuation, 190–91
Period fault, 100–03, *exercises*, 103
Periodic sentence, 25–28, 365, *exercises*, 31–32, 365
Periodical indexes, 244–45
Periphrastic forms, defined, 161; idiomatic use of, 120; illustrated, 117, 124–26
Person, 343
Person, agreement in, 109; defined, 161
Personal letters, 425–26, *exercises*, 426; notes, formal, 426
Personal pronoun, 139–40, 142; agreement with antecedent, 115–16; case of, 117–20; *you, they*, as indefinites, 142
Phenomena, phenomenon, 283
Phone, see *Ad*, 334
Phrase, absolute, 383–84; appositive as sentence, 101; defined, 161–62; elliptical as dangling modifier, 396; infinitive as sentence, 101; in mixed constructions, 401, 402; nonrestrictive, 169–71; participial as sentence, 101; prepositional, 396; punctuation of, 168–73; restrictive, 169–71; transitional, 390
Pivotal words, defined, 26; position, 27
Place names, in dictionaries, 322
Plan on, 343
Plenty, 343
Plural, form and meaning of, 108; pronouns and antecedents, 115; verbs and subjects, 108–13
Plurals, spelling of, 197, 281–83, *exercises*, 283
Point of view, 409–11, *exercise*, 411; shifts, from indirect to direct discourse, 410; in number, person, or class of pronoun, 410; in style, 410; in subject, voice, or mood of verb, 409; in tense, 410
Polite imperative, 159, 192; *see also* Mood, 158
Position of modifiers, 392–94, *exercises*, 394
Possessive case, *see* Genitive
Précis writing, 428–32, *exercises*, 432
Predicate, defined, 162
Predicate adjective, *see* Predicate complement
Predicate complement, case of, 118; defined, 162
Predicate nominative, *see* Predicate complement
Predicate objective, *see* Object, 160
Predicate verb, *see* Predicate, 162
Predication, 4–7; defined, 163; reduction of, 164
Predicative verb, *see* Finite verb, 156
Preposition, case after, 117; defined, 163; *due to* as a, 338; at end of sentence, 404; faulty omission of, 363; idiomatic use of, 296–97; *like* as a, 139; necessary for clearness, completeness, 363; object of, 117; suspended, 378
Prepositional phrase, 396; see also *Due to*, 338
Present perfect, 125, 127
Present tense, 124–26; historical, 126–27, 410
Present writer, see *Writer*, 347
Principal clause, *see* Independent clause *s.v.* Clause
Principal parts of verb, defined, 163; listed, 125, 129–30; of strong verbs, 128–30
Principal, principle, 343
Prof, see *Ad*, 334
Progressive tense constructions, defined, 163; past, 126; present, 126
Prolixity, 314

Pronominal adjective, 140
Pronoun, 139–43, 397–400, *exercises,* 143, 400; agreement with antecedent, 115–16, 140–41, *exercises* 116, 143; agreement with verb, 109–12, *exercises,* 113; case of, 117–21, *exercises,* 121; classes of, 139–40; defined, 139; genitive case of, with apostrophe, 197; *it* as a, 141–42; omission of, 363; reference of, 141, 397–400, 410, *exercises,* 400; uses of, 141–43, *exercises,* 143
Pronunciation, in dictionaries, 320–21, *exercises,* 323; of homophones, 157, 274–75; and spelling, 273–74, *exercises,* 274; of *used to,* 346
Proper names, *see* Proper noun
Proper noun, capitalization of, 215–18, *exercises,* 219; defined, 215–16; in dictionaries, 322–23, *exercise,* 324; plurals of, 216, 282; without apostrophe, 198
Proportion, in theme, 82–83, *exercises,* 83
Proposition, 343
Provincial English, 93, 295–96
Punctuation, 167–206, *exercises,* 206; of abbreviations, 190; absolute phrases, 173; addresses, 174, 417–18; adjectives in series, 176, 179; adverbial modifiers, 168–69, 178; appositives, 173–74, 178, 189, 194; bibliographical items, 189, 250; breaks in thought, 194; chapter and verse numbers, 189; complimentary close of letter, 423; compound question, 192–93; contrasted elements, 172–73; coördinate clauses, 168–69, 185; dates, 174; direct questions, 186, 192; direct quotations, 177, 205; ellipses, 191; emphatic elements, 172, 185, 188, 194, 195; end of sentence, 190, 191, 192; exclamations, 191; figures, 199, 212; footnote items, 262; fragmentary sentences, 190; hours and minutes, 189; independent clauses, 168–69, 185, 188; indirect questions, 190; indirect quotations, 178; initials following a name, 174; inserted elements, 171, 200; interjections, 174, 191; interpolations, 200; interrupted sentences, 194; introductory modifiers, 168–69; items in series, 174–76; misleading constructions, 176, 186; *namely, that is,* etc., 173–74; nonrestrictive modifiers, 169–71; parenthetical elements, 195, 199; restrictive modifiers, 169–73, 178; *said, replied,* etc., 177, 186; salutation of letters, 186, 189, 419, 425; sentence modifiers, 172–73; series, 174–76, 178; titles and subtitles, 174, 189; vocatives, 174
Punctuation marks, 168–207; brackets, 199–200; colon, 188–89; comma, 168–79; dash, 194–95; exclamation point, 191–92; parentheses, 199–200; period, 190–91; question mark, 192–93; semicolon, 185–87; unnecessary commas, 177–79; *see also* Apostrophe, Capitals, Italics, Quotation marks, Dialogue and quoted matter

Question mark, 192–93, *exercise,* 193; inside or outside quotation marks. 205
Quite, 343
Quotation, direct, in notes, 255–57; punctuation of, 202, 205–06
Quotation marks, 201–04, *exercises,* 206, 210; to define words, 203; to enclose direct quotations, 202; to enclose quotations within quotations, 203; to enclose titles, 203; to mark special words, 201; with other punctuation marks, 205–06; to translate words, 203; unnecessary, 203–04
Quoted matter, punctuation of, 204–06, *exercises,* 206; single spaced and indented, 204, 261, 263; verse, 223
Quoted sentence as dependent clause, 145

Racket, 343
Raise, 343
Rarely ever, 343
Rather, see *Had better,* 340
Real, 343
Rear, see *Raise,* 343
Reason is because, 146

Reciprocal pronouns, 140
Reduction of predication, defined, 164, *exercise*, 371
Refer back, 343
Reference books, 238–45; bibliographical, 243–45; biographical, historical, and literary, 240–41; dictionaries, 241, 318–19; encyclopedias, 239; miscellaneous, 242
Reference of pronouns, 141, 397–400, 410, *exercises*, 400; ambiguous, 397–98; general, 398–99; inconsistency in, 400; *it*, without antecedent, 141; obscure, 398–99; remote, 399; *said*, *same*, *such*, as pronouns, 399; shifting, 410; *that*, *this*, *these*, *those*, without antecedent, 141; weak, 399
Referent, defined, 164
Related words, defined, 164; position of, 376, 394
Relative clause, position of, 393; punctuation of, 169–70
Relative pronoun, 140; number of verb with, 112–13; as subordinating conjunction, 138
Repetition, for clearness, 408–09, *exercise*, 409; for emphasis, 29–31, 369, *exercises*, 369; faulty, 380, *exercises*, 380; *see also* Miscellaneous omissions, 362
Representation of numbers, 211–12, *exercise*, 212
Research paper, 248–71; arranging material, 258–59; bibliography, 250; choosing subject, 248–49; footnotes, 261–62; gathering material, 250–58; manuscript form, 259–71; model pages, 265–71; style and mechanics, 259–71; taking notes, 254–58
Resolved, in formal resolutions, capitalized, 218; italicized, 209
Restrictive modifier, 169–71; introduced by *that*, 143
Retained object, *see* Intransitive, 157
Reverend, *the Reverend*, 297, 343–44
Right, 344
Roosevelt, Theodore, quoted, 27
Rosenfeld, John, quoted, 53
Rovere, Richard, quoted, 431
Run-on sentence, *see* Fused sentence, 107
Rung, 129

-*s* or -*es*, plurals in, 281, *exercises*, 283
Said, as adjective, 344, 399; parenthetical, 119; punctuation of, 177
Same, as pronoun, 344, 399
Scarcely, in double negative, 147; with *than*, 344
Seen, 130
Seldom ever, 344
Semicolon, 185–87, *exercise*, 187; clearness, 185–86; conjunctive adverbs, 138; emphasis, 185–86; independent clauses, 185; misuse, 186–87
Sentence, balanced, 28–29; choppy, 356; clear, 385–415; complete, 4–8; complex, 7–14, 154; compound, 8, 154, 168, 185; emphatic, 24–31, 365–84; fused, 107–08; incomplete, 95–99, 357–63; periodic, 25–28, 365; simple, 8, 165; topic, 43–44, 231; transitional, 67, 390; unified, 349–55; varied in structure, 39–41, 374
Sentence, defined, 95–99; and thinking, 3–41
Sentence element, defined, 164
Sentence fragment, 101–03
Sentence modifier, defined, 164; punctuation of, 172
Sequence, of sentence elements, 391, *exercise*, 391; of tenses, 132–33, *exercises*, 133
Set, *sit*, 344
Shall, as auxiliary, 127–28
Shape, 344
She, after *is*, *was*, *were*, etc., 118
Sherwood, Robert E., quoted, 71
Shifts, aimless, indirect to direct discourse, 410; number, 410; style, 410; verb forms, 409–10
Show up, 344
Shrunk, 130
Signature of letter, 423–24
Simple predicate, defined, 162
Simple sentence, defined, 165
Simple subject, defined, 165
Single quotation marks, 203
Sit, see *Set*, 344
Slang, 302–03, *exercises*, 303
Slidden, 130
Smooth word order, 376–79

So, dangling, 358; as coördinating conjunction, 137, 138; usage, 344
Social notes, formal, 426
Some, 344
Somebody, agreement of pronoun with, 115; agreement of verb with, 109
Somebody's else, 312
Someone, agreement of verb with, 109
Someplace, 344
Someway, 344
Somewheres, 344
Sort, agreement of pronoun with, 315; with plural verb or modifier, see *Kind*, 341
Sort of, see *Kind of*, 341
Sound and form of words, confusion of, 274–75, *exercises*, 275
Speech, parts of, defined, 161; *see also* Adjective, 152, Adverb, 153, Conjunction, 155, Interjection, 157, Noun, 159, Preposition, 163, Pronoun, 163, Verb, 166
Spelling, 272–92; compound words, 284–85, *exercises*, 285; *ei* and *ie*, 277–78, *exercises*, 278; etymological kinship, 276–77, *exercises*, 277; doubling final consonant, 278–79, *exercises*, 279; dropping final *-e*, 279–80, *exercises*, 280; dropping final *-y*, 280–81, *exercises*, 281; list, 286–92; plurals, 281–83, *exercises*, 283; pronunciation and, 273–74, *exercises*, 274; recording errors, 287; similar forms, 274–75, *exercises*, 275
Splice, comma, 130
Split constructions, 403–05, *exercise*, 405; coördinate elements, 405; infinitive, 403–04; parts of verb phrase, 404; sentence elements, 404
Split infinitive, 403–04
Sprung, 130
-st, plural of nouns ending in, 222
Statue, stature, statute, 344
Steinbeck, John, quoted, 102
Stevenson, Robert L., quoted, 232, 390
Stop, 344
Strong verb, defined, 165; list of forms, 129–30
Style, 93, 259
Subject and verb, agreement of, 108–13, *exercises*, 113
Subject, choosing a, 49–50, 75–77, 248–49
Subject, defined, 165
Subjective complement, *see* Predicate complement, 162
Subjunctive mood, 122–24, *exercises*, 124; forms, 123–24; functions, 123–24; *see also* Mood, 156–57
Subordinate clause, 7–14, 132, 354–55
Subordinating conjunction, 13–14; adverb as, 138; position and use of, 137
Subordination, defined, 7–14, *exercises*, 14; for emphasis, 370–71, *exercise*, 371; for unity, 354–55, *exercise*, 355
Substance, in paragraphs, 46–49, *exercises*, 49; in themes, 73–75, *exercises*, 75
Substantive, defined, 165
Substantive clause, defined, 165
Such, 344–45, 399
Summarizing paragraph, 67
Sung, 130
Sunk, 130
Superior than, 345
Superlative, defined, *see* Comparison, 154; uses of, 136, 361
Sure, 345
Sure and, see *Try and*, 346
Suspended expression, punctuation of, 172
Suspense, for emphasis, 27–28, 365, *exercises*, 365
Suspicion, 345
Swell, 345
Swum, 130
Syllabication, 213–14, *exercises*, 214
Syntax, defined, 165

Take, 345; *see also* Verb-adverb combinations, 166
Take and, 345
Take for granite, see *Granted*, 340
Tangled constructions, 34; *see also* Mixed constructions, 401
Tasty, 345
Technical words, 94, 295
Tense, 124–33, *exercises*, 130, 133; emphatic, 126; forms, 125–26; future, 125, 127–28; future perfect, 125; historical present, 126; past, 125;

past perfect, 125, 127; present, 125, 126, 132; present perfect, 125, 127; progressive, 126; sequence of, 132–33, *exercises*, 133; timeless present, 124, 132; uses of, 124, 126–28; of verbals, 125, 133
Terrible, terribly, 345
Terrific, terrifically, see *Terrible, terribly*, 345
Thackeray, William M., quoted, 375
Than, case after, 118; in comparisons, 360; for *when*, 345; with *inferior*, 297
Than any (*other*), in comparisons, 361
That, as adverb, 345; careless repetition of, 380; necessary use of, 145, 363; omission of, 145, 363; reference to either persons or things, 142; in restrictive clauses, 143; vague use of, 141
That is, phrase beginning with, as a sentence, 101; punctuation of, 173
That there, this here, 345
Them, after *is, was, were*, etc., 118
Themes, 72–86; beginning and ending of, 84–85, *exercises*, 85; order in, 77–80, *exercises*, 80; proportion in, 82–83, *exercises*, 83; substance, 73–75, *exercises*, 75
There, introductory, number of verb following, 112; unemphatic constructions with, 378
Thereby causing, overuse of phrases beginning with, 377
These, vague use of, 141
These kind, sort, see *Kind*, 341
They, after *is, was, were*, etc., 118
Thinking, logical, 412–14, *exercise*, 414; relation to language and writing, 3–4
This, vague use of, 141; with *kind, sort*, see *Kind*, 341
This here, see *That there*, 345
Those, vague use of, 141
Those kind, sort, see *Kind*, 341
Thought, incomplete, 357, *exercises*, 357
Through, for *finished*, 345
Thus causing, overuse of phrases beginning with, 377
Till, 345
Time element, in précis writing, 430
Timeless present tense, 124
Timeless truths, tense of, 132
Titles, abbreviation of, 220; capitalization of, 217; in letter addresses, 418
Titles, literary, capitalization of, 218; italics for, 209; plural in form with singular verb, 111; quotation marks for, 203
Too, 346, 358
Topics for themes, *see* Choosing a subject
Topic sentence, 43–44, 231; *exercises*, 44, 234
Transition, 64–67, 389–90, *exercises*, 67, 389
Transitional paragraph, 67; phrase, 65, 390; sentence, 67, 390; word, 65, 232, 289–90
Transitive, *see* Intransitive, 157
Triteness, 40–41, 310–11, *exercises*, 311; figures, 407
Try and, 346
-type, 346

Unique, 346
Unity, defined, 349–50; in paragraphs, 43–44, 231; in sentences, 349–63
Unnecessary commas, 177–79
Unnecessary words, 35–36, 313–15, 380, *exercises*, 315, 380
Unpleasant sound, 36, 316, *exercise*, 316
Until, 346
Unwarranted conclusion, 413
Up, 346; *see also* Verb-adverb combinations, 166
Us, after *is, was, were*, etc., 118
Usage, bibliography of, 333; glossary of, 332–48; national, 295; standard, 295
Used to, 346
Used to could, would, 346
Using dictionary, 318–27

Vague language, 307; reference of pronouns, 141, 399
Value of précis, 429
Variety, 39–41, 374, *exercises*, 41, 374; in diction, 40–41; in sentence structure, 39, 374
Verb, agreement with subject, 108–13,

exercises, 113; conjugation of, 124–26; defined, 166; principal parts of irregular, 129–30; *see also* Mood, 158–59, Person, 161, Predicate, 162, Number, 160; Tense, 124–30, Voice, 166
Verb-adverb combination, 166; see also *Take*, 345, and *Up*, 346
Verb phrase, defined, 166
Verbal, as dangling modifier, 395; defined, 166; distinguished from verb, 96; modifying a noun, as a sentence, 101
Verbosity, 314
Very, 346; see also *Too*, 346
Vocabulary, enlarging, 293, 317–18, *exercises*, 318; *see also* Using a dictionary, 318–27
Vocative, defined, 166; punctuation of, 174
Voice, defined, 166; passive, 382; shifting, 382

Wait on, 347
Want, 347
Want for, 347
Want in (*off*, *out*), 347
Warburg, James P., quoted, 61
Way, 347
Ways, 347
We, 347; after *is*, *was*, *were*, etc., 118
Weak verb, defined, 166; conjugation of, 125–26
Webster's New Collegiate Dictionary (*NCD*), 319; specimen page, 330–31
West, Rebecca, quoted, 62
What, see *But what*, 337
When, in definitions, 145–46
Where, for *that*, 347; in definitions, 145–46
Whereas, capitalized in formal resolutions, 218
Which, usage, 142–43
White, Marsh W., quoted, 54
White, Stewart E., quoted, 372
Whiteside, Thomas, quoted, 66
Who, usage, 118–19, 142–43
Who, *whom*, 118, 119
Whoever, *whomever*, 119
Whose, for *of which*, 121, 347
Will, as auxiliary, 127–28
Wilson, Woodrow, quoted, 26
Without, 347
Wolfe, Thomas, quoted, 70
Word order, confused, 402; in mixed constructions, 402; of modifiers, 392–94; natural, defined, 376; participial phrase at end of sentence, 376–77; smooth and emphatic, 376–79; suspended preposition, 378; variety in, 374; weak word at end of sentence, 377; *see also* Split constructions, 403–05
Wordiness, 313–15, *exercise*, 315
Words, *see* Diction, Spelling, Vocabulary, Word order
Would better, see *Had rather*, 340
Would of, 347
Would rather, see *Had rather*, 340
Writer, 347
Writing, fine, 41, 312, *exercise*, 312

Y, final, dropping, 280–81
-y, plurals of nouns ending in, 282, *exercises*, 282
Yet, as coördinating conjunction, 137, 138; with past tense, 347
You all, *Y'all*, 347–48
You was, 348